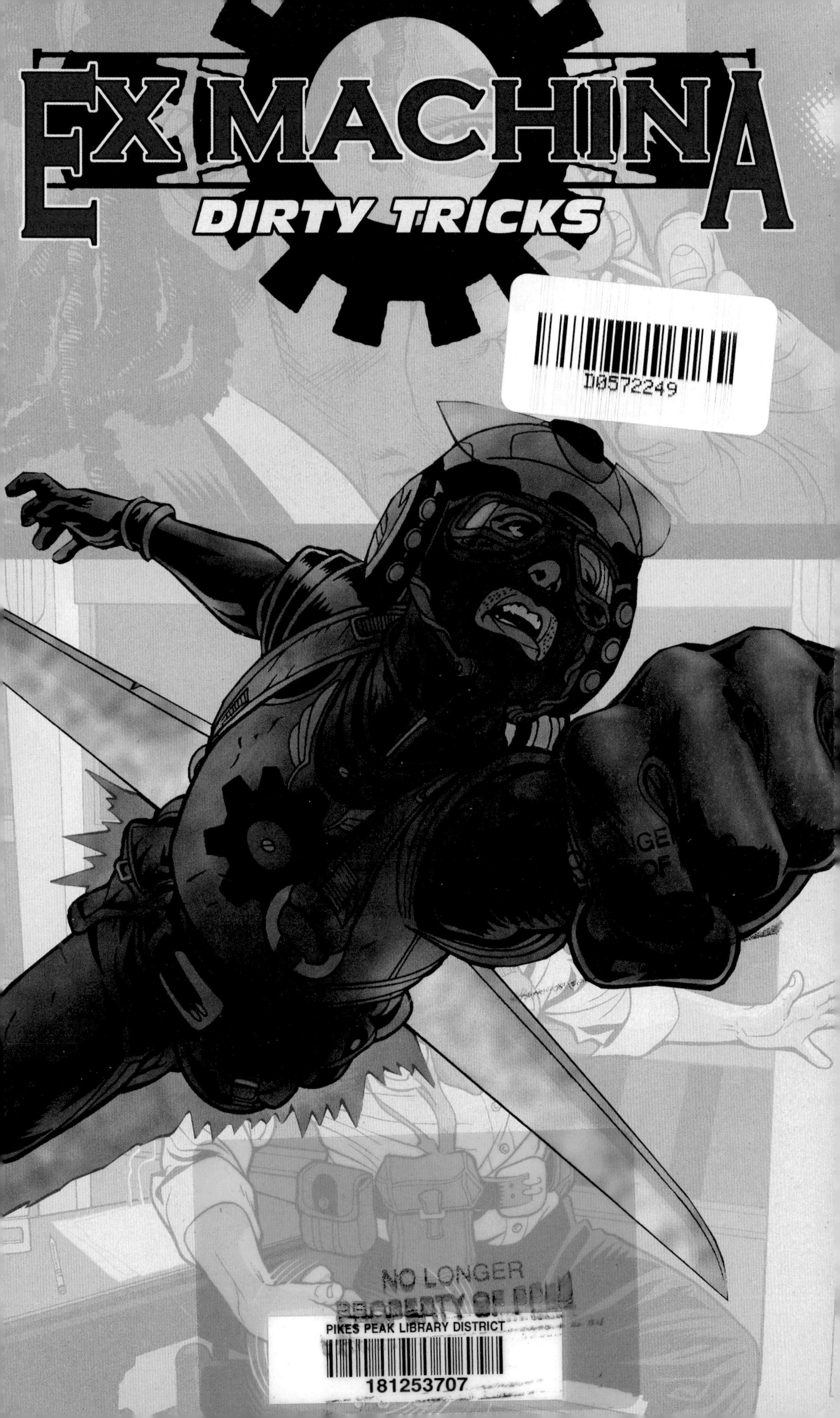
EX MACHINA
DIRTY TRICKS

CREDITS

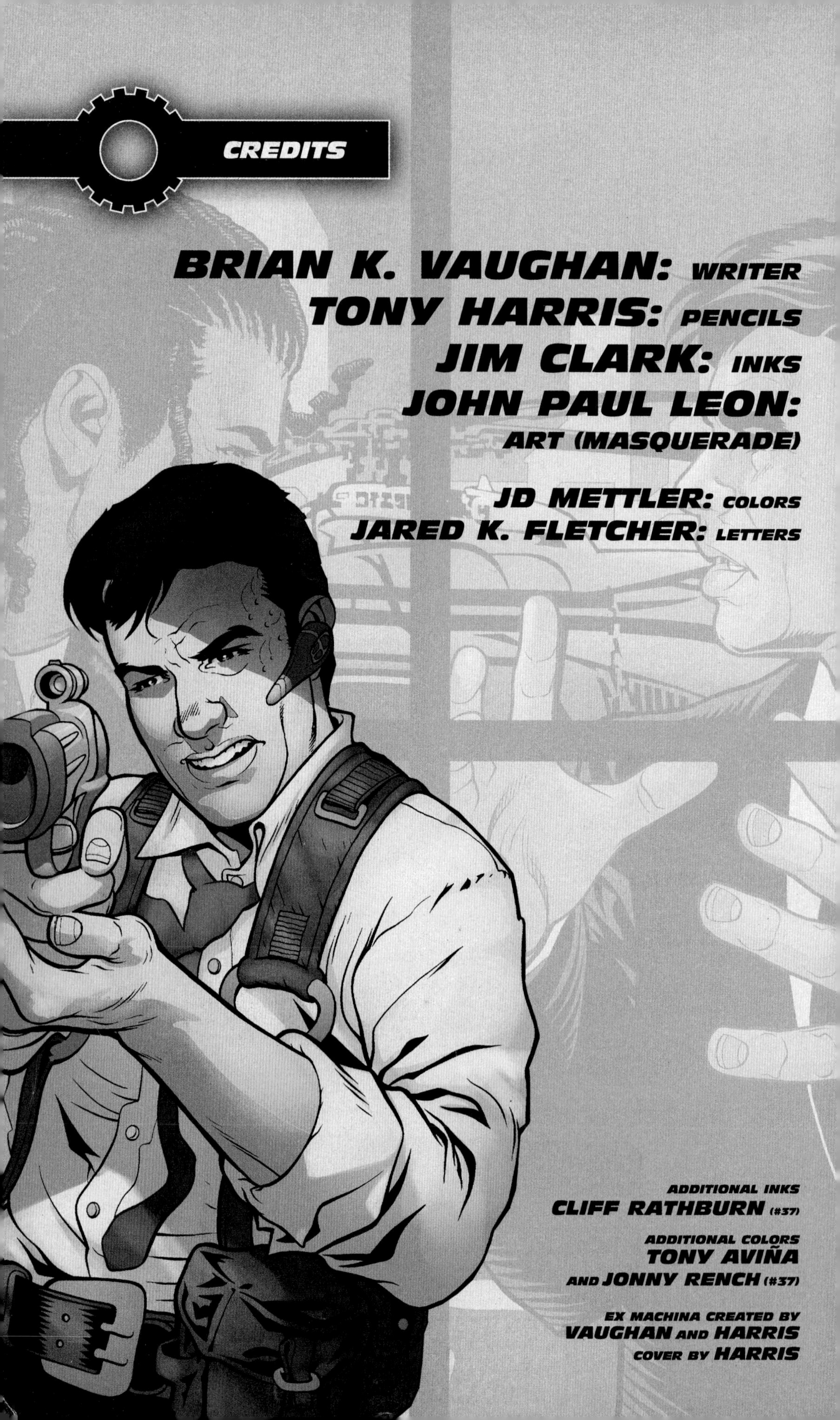

BRIAN K. VAUGHAN: WRITER
TONY HARRIS: PENCILS
JIM CLARK: INKS
JOHN PAUL LEON: ART (MASQUERADE)

JD METTLER: COLORS
JARED K. FLETCHER: LETTERS

ADDITIONAL INKS
CLIFF RATHBURN (#37)

ADDITIONAL COLORS
TONY AVIÑA
AND **JONNY RENCH** (#37)

EX MACHINA CREATED BY
VAUGHAN AND **HARRIS**
COVER BY **HARRIS**

LEGAL

Jim Lee — Editorial Director
Hank Kanalz — VP – General Manager
Ben Abernathy — Editor – Original Series
Kristy Quinn — Editor
Ed Roeder — Art Director

DC COMICS
Paul Levitz — President & Publisher
Richard Bruning — SVP – Creative Director
Patrick Caldon — EVP – Finance & Operations
Amy Genkins — SVP – Business & Legal Affairs
Gregory Noveck — SVP – Creative Affairs
Steve Rotterdam — SVP – Sales & Marketing
Cheryl Rubin — SVP – Brand Management

SUSTAINABLE FORESTRY INITIATIVE
Certified Fiber Sourcing
www.sfiprogram.org

PWC-SFICOC-260

EX MACHINA: DIRTY TRICKS. Published by WildStorm Productions,
an imprint of DC Comics. 888 Prospect St. #240, La Jolla, CA
92037. Cover and compilation Copyright © 2010 Brian K. Vaughan
and Tony Harris. All Rights Reserved. EX MACHINA is ™ Brian K.
Vaughan and Tony Harris. Originally published in single magazine
form as EX MACHINA #35-39 © 2008, 2009 and EX MACHINA
SPECIAL #3 © 2007 Brian K. Vaughan and Tony Harris.

DC Comics, a Warner Bros. Entertainment Company.

ISBN: 978-1-4012-2519-3

Chapter 1

The Race

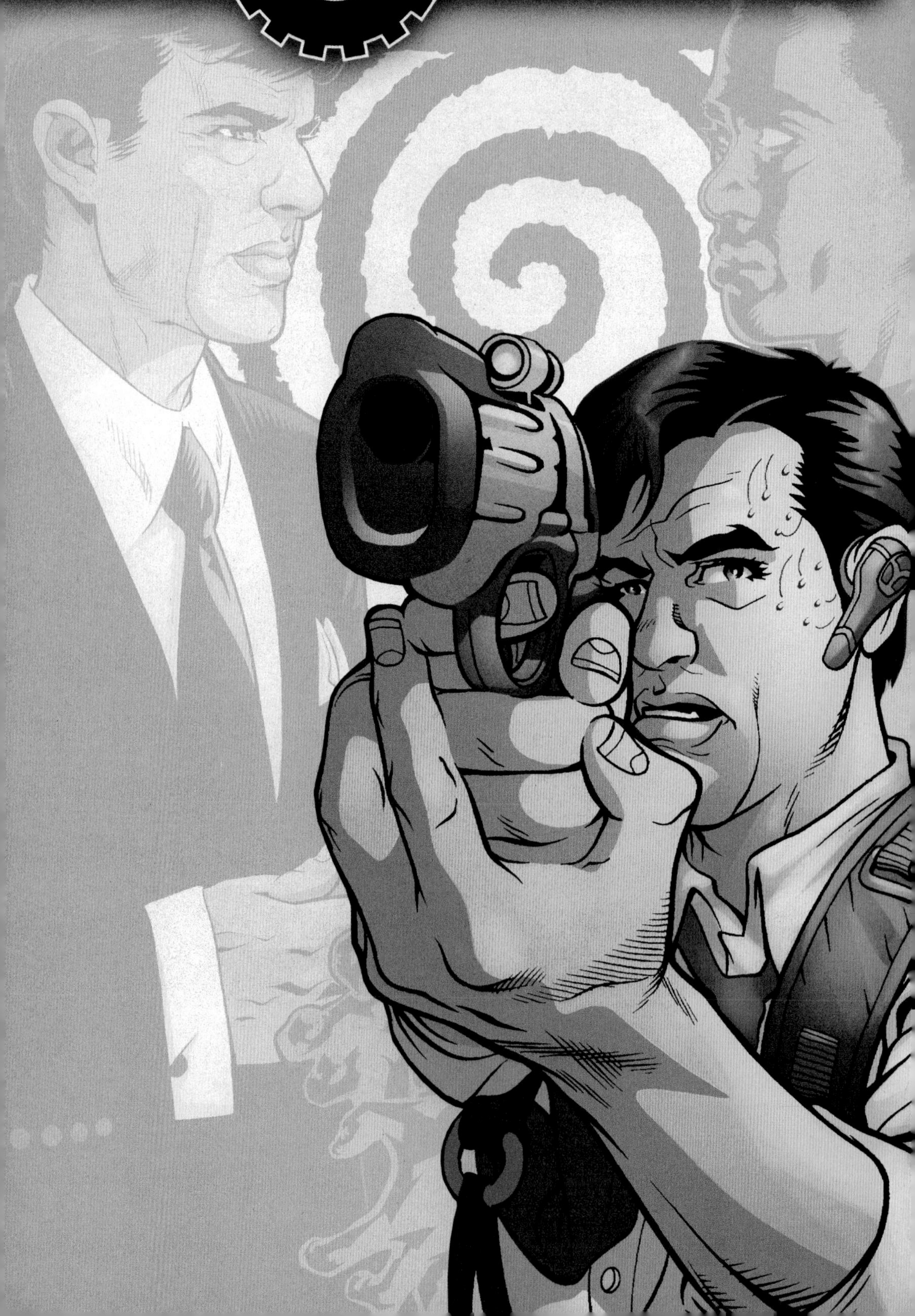

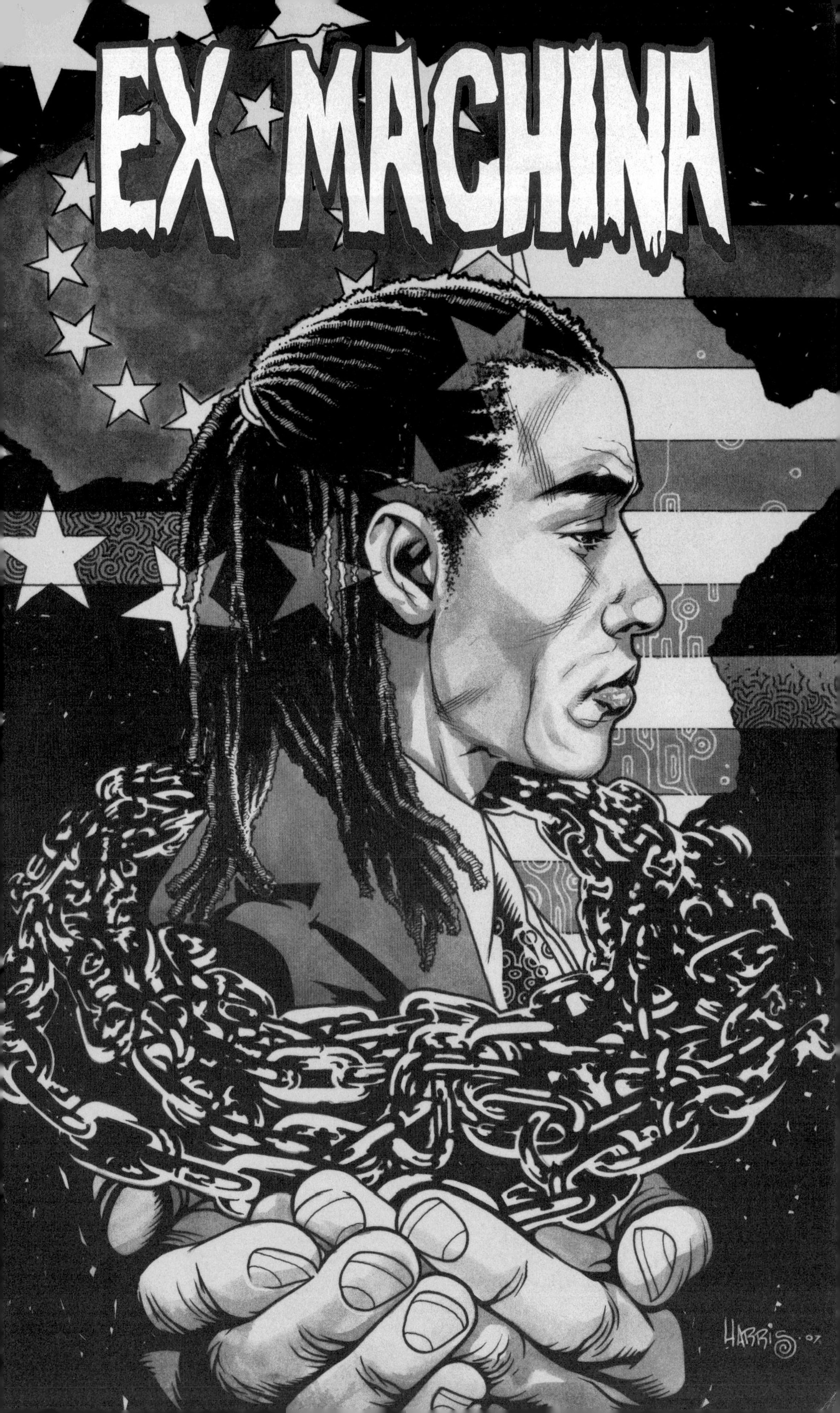
EX MACHINA
HARRIS '07

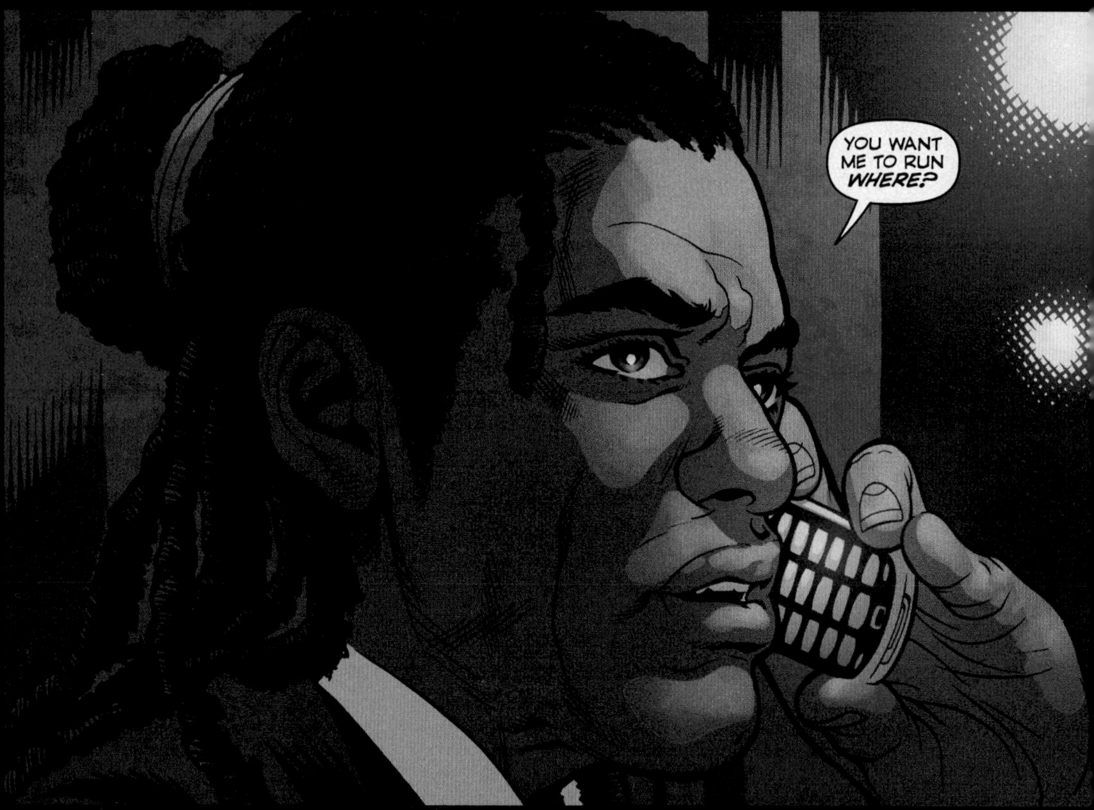
YOU WANT ME TO RUN *WHERE?*

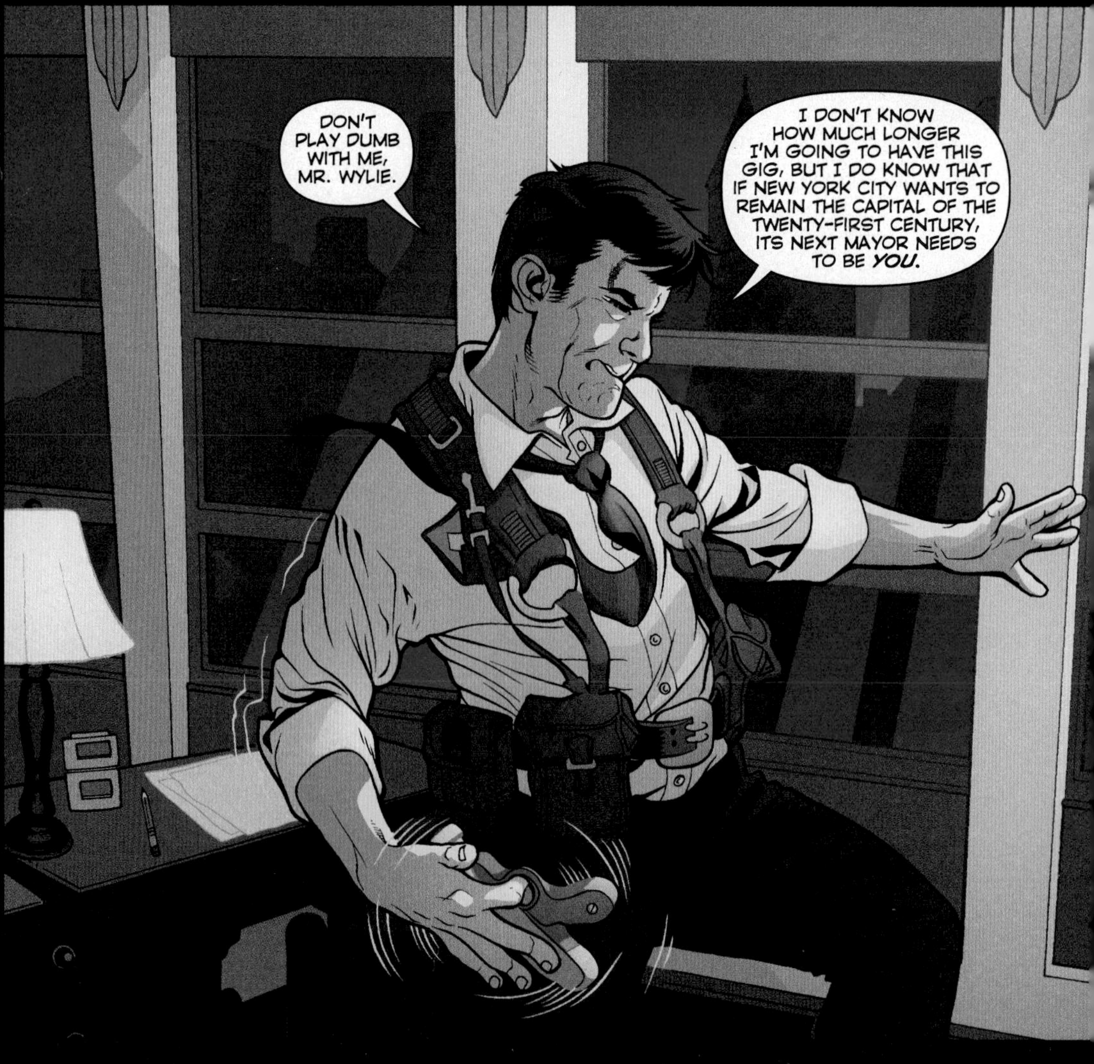
DON'T PLAY DUMB WITH ME, MR. WYLIE.
I DON'T KNOW HOW MUCH LONGER I'M GOING TO HAVE THIS GIG, BUT I DO KNOW THAT IF NEW YORK CITY WANTS TO REMAIN THE CAPITAL OF THE TWENTY-FIRST CENTURY, ITS NEXT MAYOR NEEDS TO BE *YOU*.

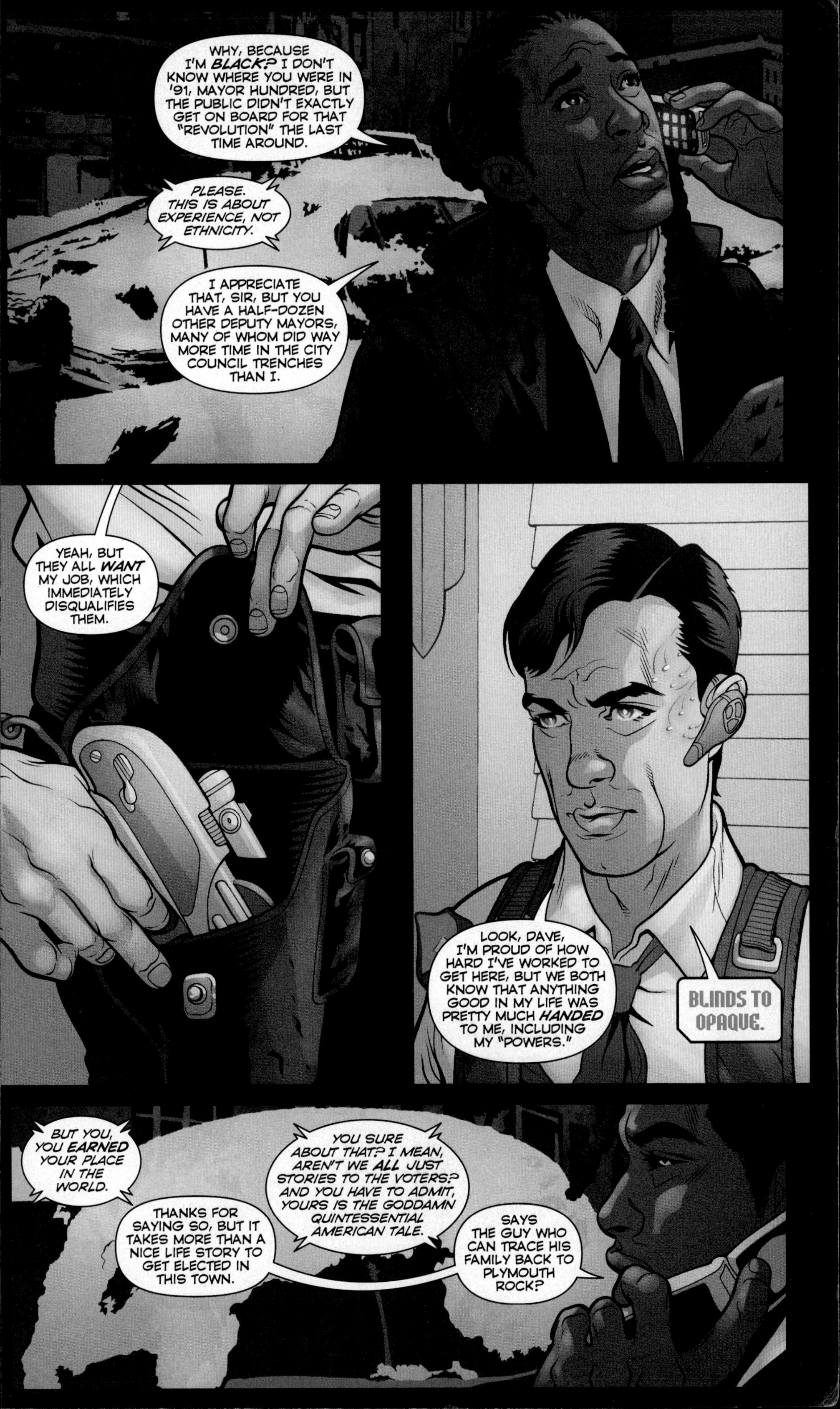
WHY, BECAUSE I'M ***BLACK?*** I DON'T KNOW WHERE YOU WERE IN '91, MAYOR HUNDRED, BUT THE PUBLIC DIDN'T EXACTLY GET ON BOARD FOR THAT "REVOLUTION" THE LAST TIME AROUND.
PLEASE. THIS IS ABOUT EXPERIENCE, NOT ETHNICITY.
I APPRECIATE THAT, SIR, BUT YOU HAVE A HALF-DOZEN OTHER DEPUTY MAYORS, MANY OF WHOM DID WAY MORE TIME IN THE CITY COUNCIL TRENCHES THAN I.
YEAH, BUT THEY ALL ***WANT*** MY JOB, WHICH IMMEDIATELY DISQUALIFIES THEM.
LOOK, DAVE, I'M PROUD OF HOW HARD I'VE WORKED TO GET HERE, BUT WE BOTH KNOW THAT ANYTHING GOOD IN MY LIFE WAS PRETTY MUCH ***HANDED*** TO ME, INCLUDING MY "POWERS."
BLINDS TO OPAQUE.
*BUT YOU, YOU **EARNED** YOUR PLACE IN THE WORLD.*
THANKS FOR SAYING SO, BUT IT TAKES MORE THAN A NICE LIFE STORY TO GET ELECTED IN THIS TOWN.
*YOU SURE ABOUT THAT? I MEAN, AREN'T WE **ALL** JUST STORIES TO THE VOTERS? AND YOU HAVE TO ADMIT, YOURS IS THE GODDAMN QUINTESSENTIAL AMERICAN TALE.*
SAYS THE GUY WHO CAN TRACE HIS FAMILY BACK TO PLYMOUTH ROCK?

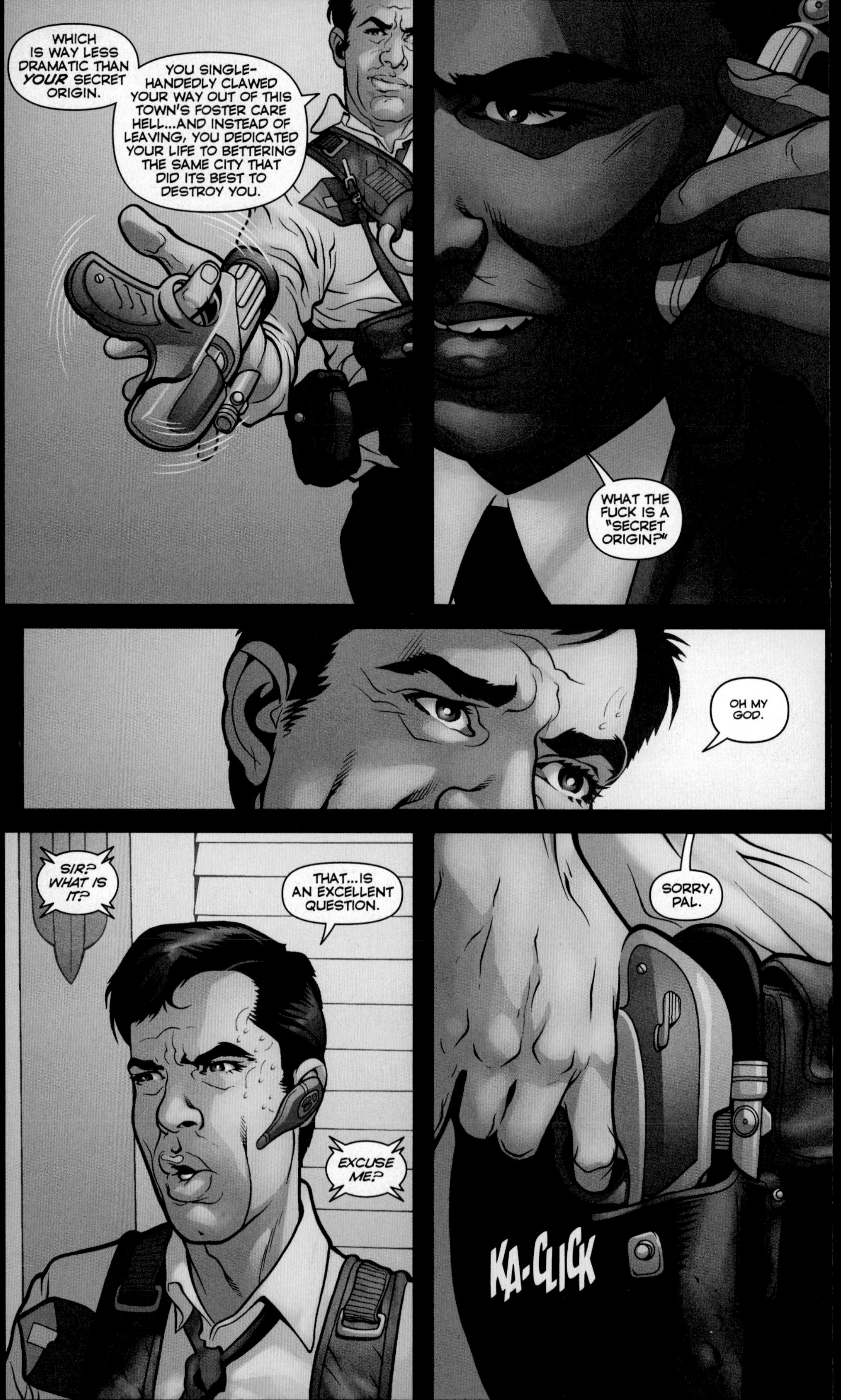
WHICH IS WAY LESS DRAMATIC THAN *YOUR* SECRET ORIGIN.
YOU SINGLE-HANDEDLY CLAWED YOUR WAY OUT OF THIS TOWN'S FOSTER CARE HELL...AND INSTEAD OF LEAVING, YOU DEDICATED YOUR LIFE TO BETTERING THE SAME CITY THAT DID ITS BEST TO DESTROY YOU.
WHAT THE FUCK IS A "SECRET ORIGIN?"
OH MY GOD.
SIR? WHAT IS IT?
THAT...IS AN EXCELLENT QUESTION.
EXCUSE ME?
SORRY, PAL.
KA-CLICK

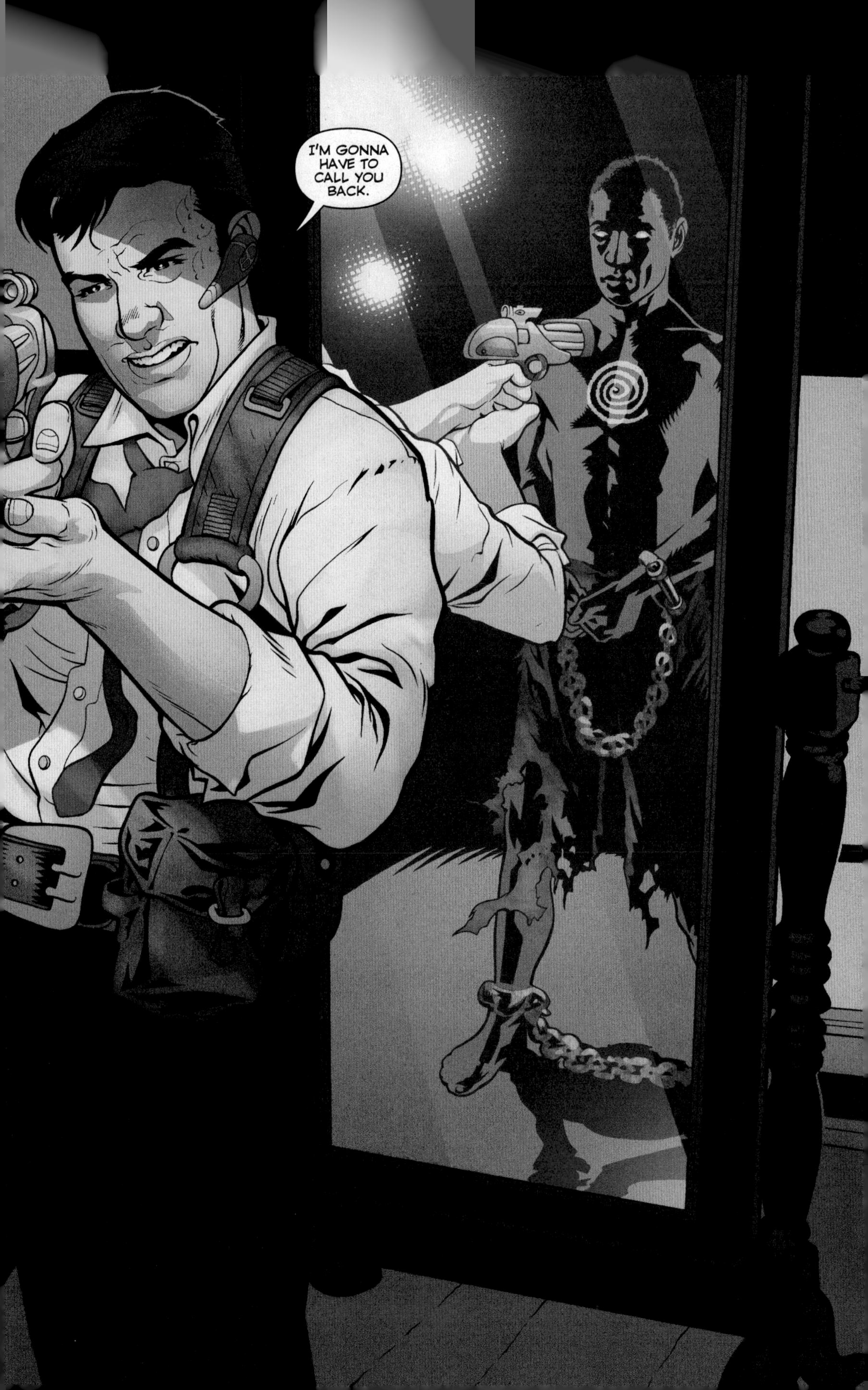
I'M GONNA HAVE TO CALL YOU BACK.

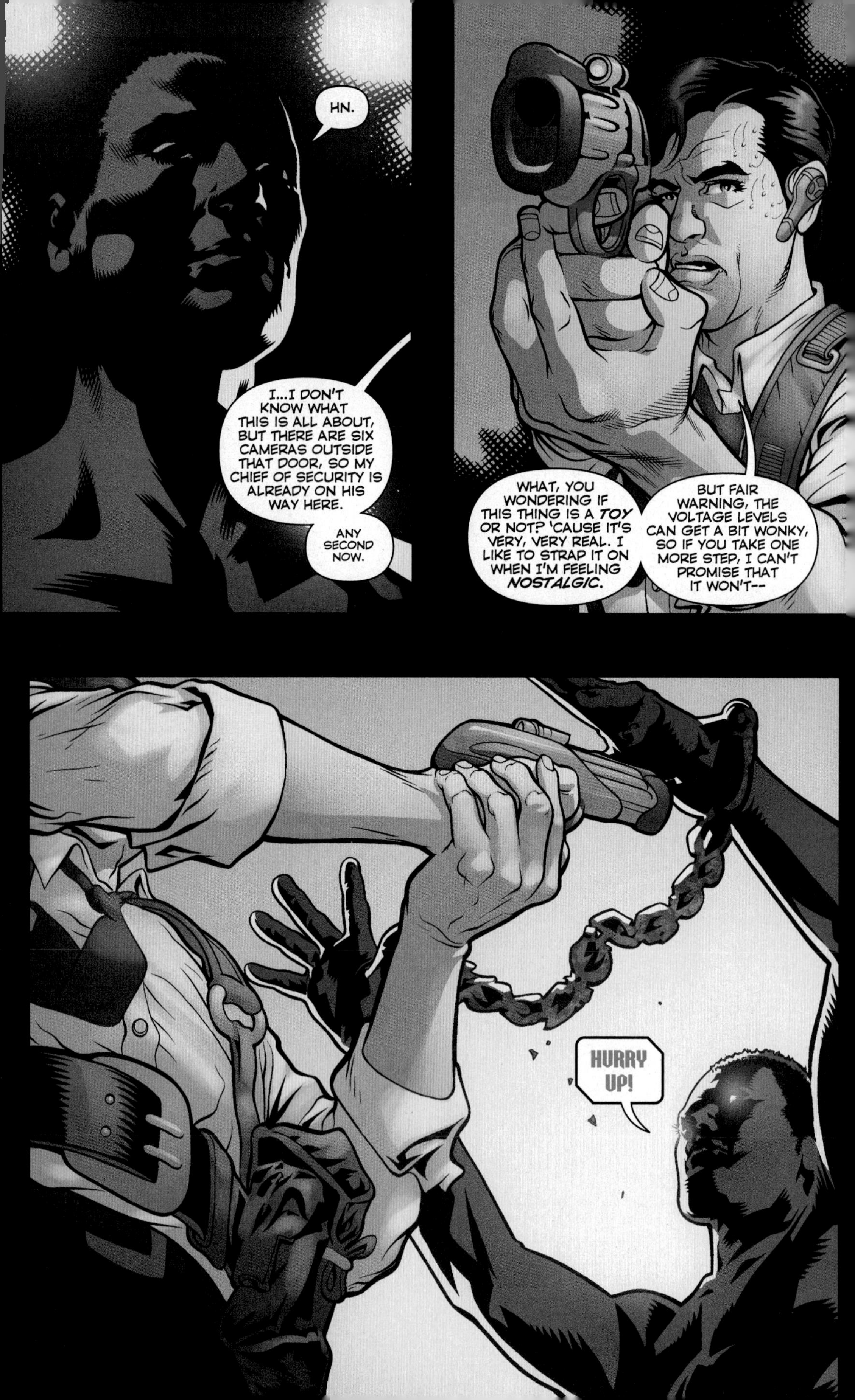
HN.
I...I DON'T KNOW WHAT THIS IS ALL ABOUT, BUT THERE ARE SIX CAMERAS OUTSIDE THAT DOOR, SO MY CHIEF OF SECURITY IS ALREADY ON HIS WAY HERE.
ANY SECOND NOW.
WHAT, YOU WONDERING IF THIS THING IS A TOY OR NOT? 'CAUSE IT'S VERY, VERY REAL. I LIKE TO STRAP IT ON WHEN I'M FEELING NOSTALGIC.
BUT FAIR WARNING, THE VOLTAGE LEVELS CAN GET A BIT WONKY, SO IF YOU TAKE ONE MORE STEP, I CAN'T PROMISE THAT IT WON'T--
HURRY UP!

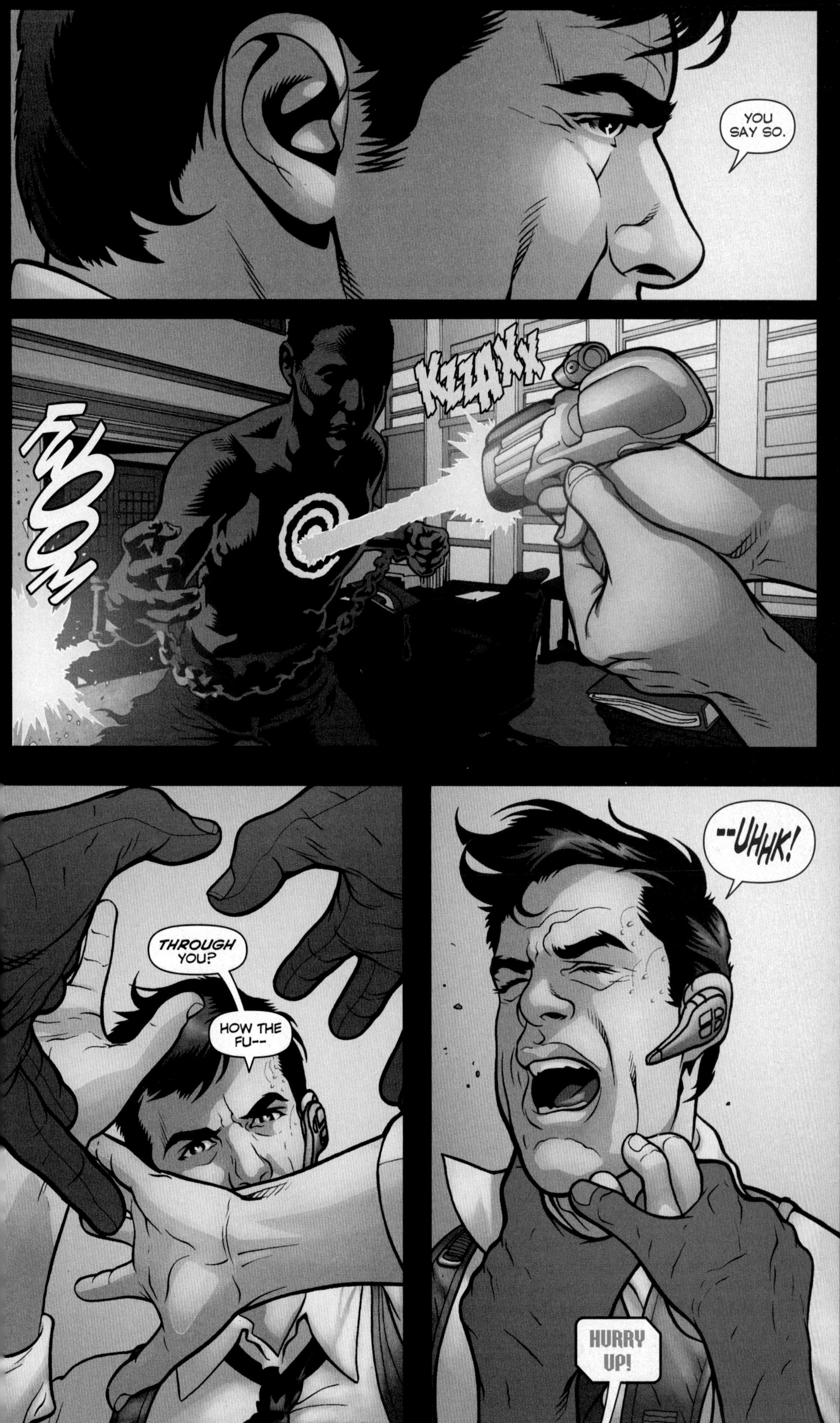
YOU SAY SO.
KZZAXX
FWOOM
THROUGH YOU?
HOW THE FU--
--UHHK!
HURRY UP!

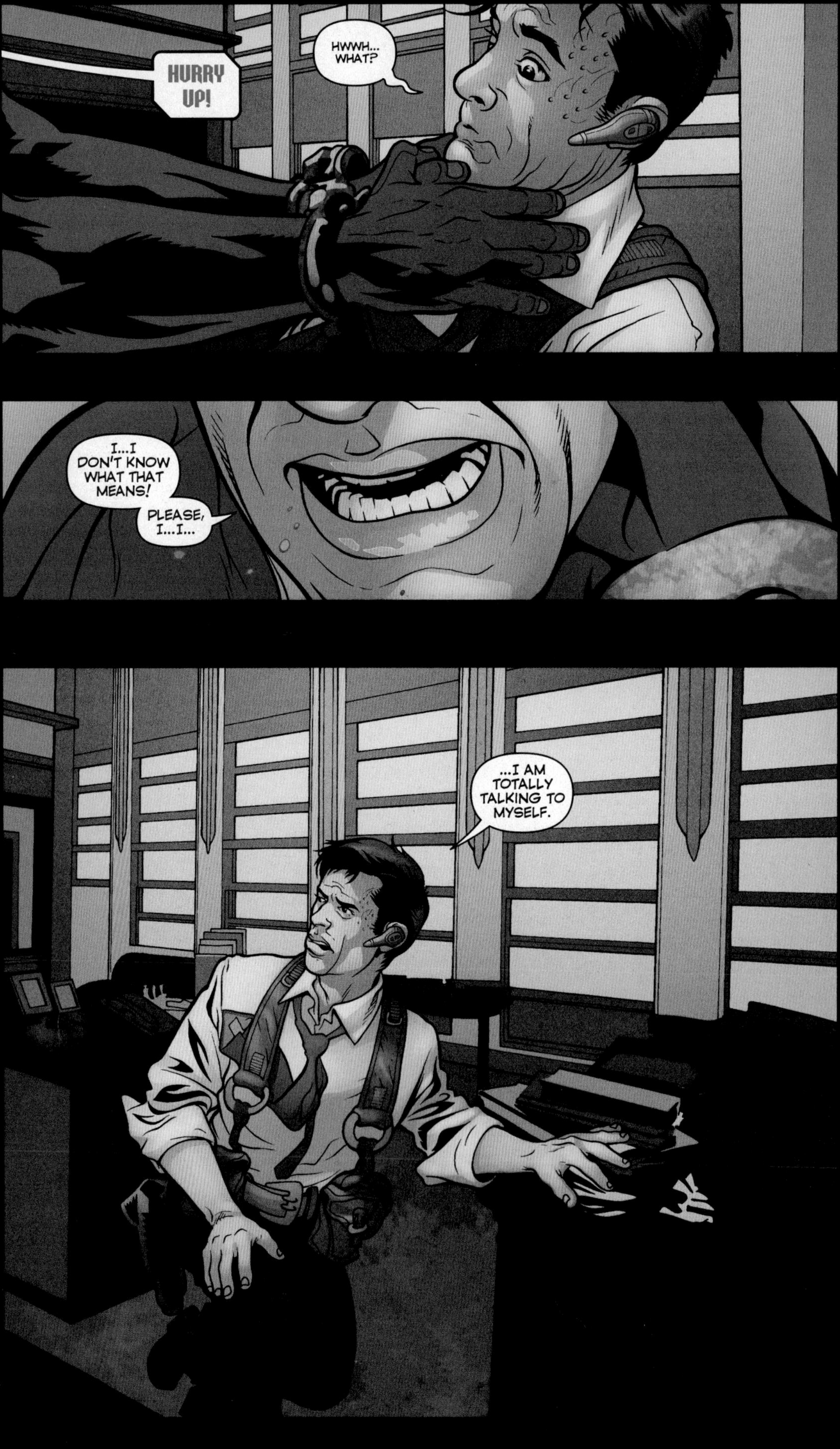
HURRY UP!
HWWH... WHAT?
I...I DON'T KNOW WHAT THAT MEANS!
PLEASE, I...I...
...I AM TOTALLY TALKING TO MYSELF.

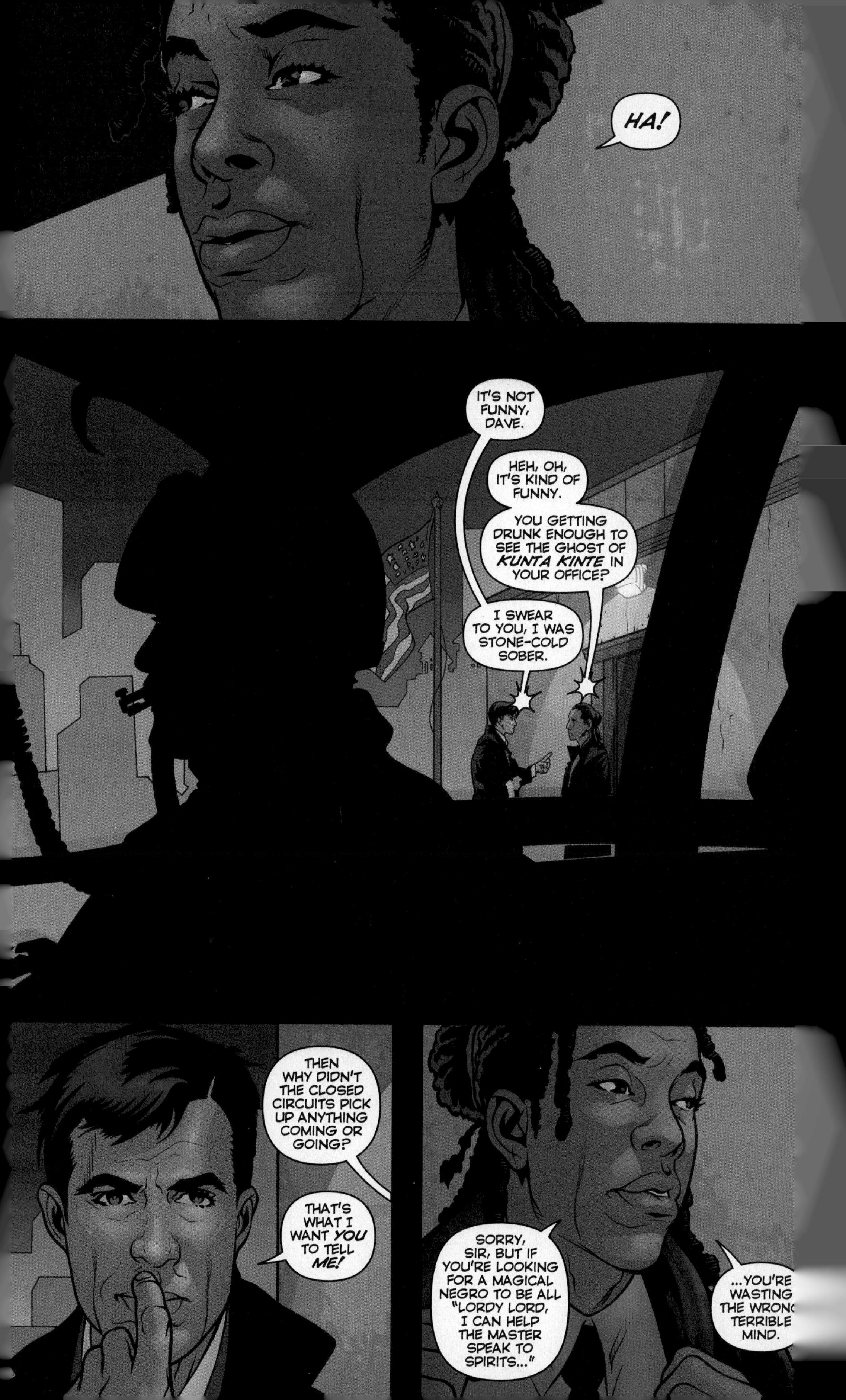
HA!
IT'S NOT FUNNY, DAVE.
HEH, OH, IT'S KIND OF FUNNY.
YOU GETTING DRUNK ENOUGH TO SEE THE GHOST OF KUNTA KINTE IN YOUR OFFICE?
I SWEAR TO YOU, I WAS STONE-COLD SOBER.
THEN WHY DIDN'T THE CLOSED CIRCUITS PICK UP ANYTHING COMING OR GOING?
THAT'S WHAT I WANT YOU TO TELL ME!
SORRY, SIR, BUT IF YOU'RE LOOKING FOR A MAGICAL NEGRO TO BE ALL "LORDY LORD, I CAN HELP THE MASTER SPEAK TO SPIRITS..."
...YOU'RE WASTING THE WRONG TERRIBLE MIND.

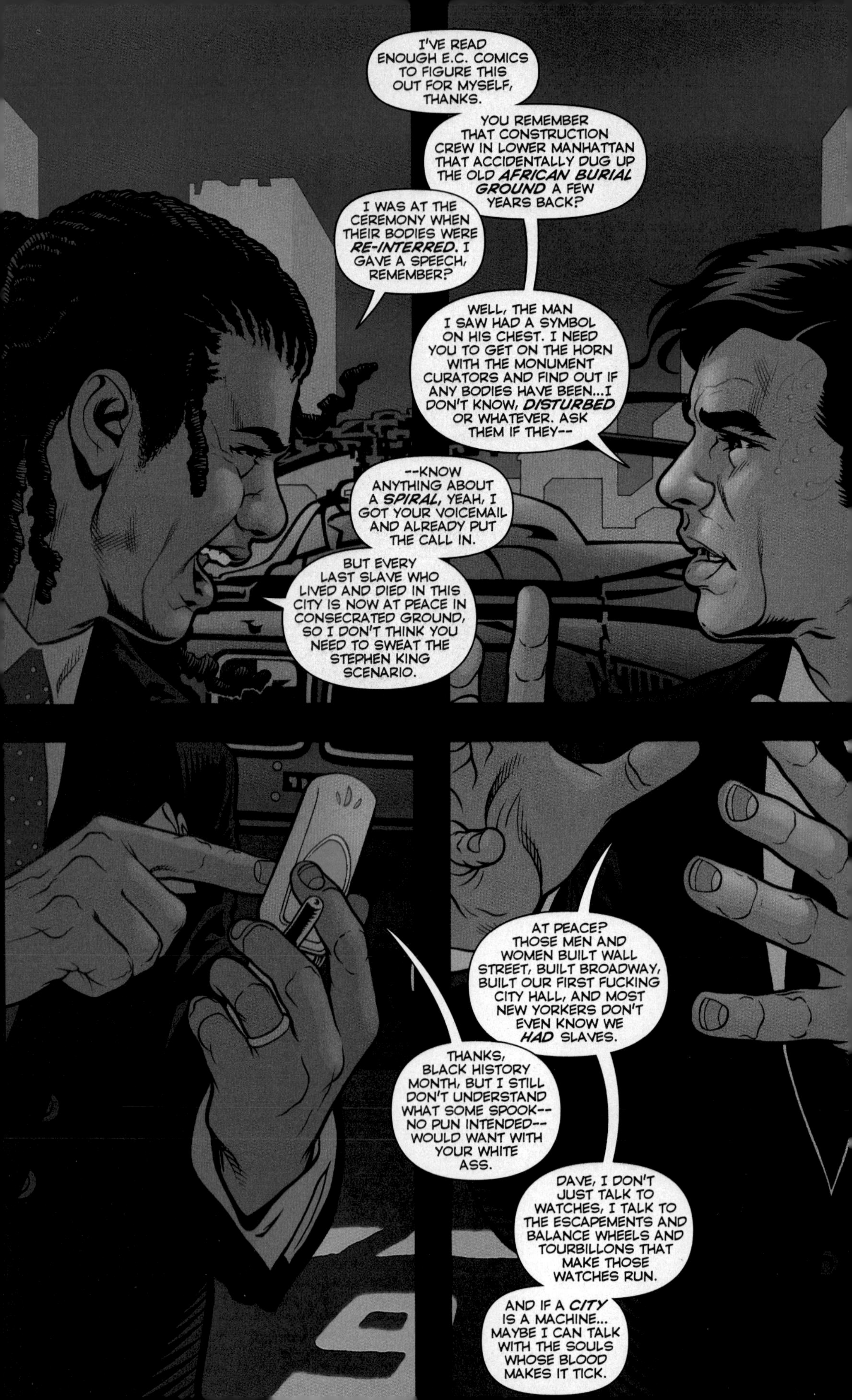
I'VE READ ENOUGH E.C. COMICS TO FIGURE THIS OUT FOR MYSELF, THANKS.
YOU REMEMBER THAT CONSTRUCTION CREW IN LOWER MANHATTAN THAT ACCIDENTALLY DUG UP THE OLD AFRICAN BURIAL GROUND A FEW YEARS BACK?
I WAS AT THE CEREMONY WHEN THEIR BODIES WERE RE-INTERRED. I GAVE A SPEECH, REMEMBER?
WELL, THE MAN I SAW HAD A SYMBOL ON HIS CHEST. I NEED YOU TO GET ON THE HORN WITH THE MONUMENT CURATORS AND FIND OUT IF ANY BODIES HAVE BEEN...I DON'T KNOW, DISTURBED OR WHATEVER. ASK THEM IF THEY--
--KNOW ANYTHING ABOUT A SPIRAL, YEAH, I GOT YOUR VOICEMAIL AND ALREADY PUT THE CALL IN.
BUT EVERY LAST SLAVE WHO LIVED AND DIED IN THIS CITY IS NOW AT PEACE IN CONSECRATED GROUND, SO I DON'T THINK YOU NEED TO SWEAT THE STEPHEN KING SCENARIO.
AT PEACE? THOSE MEN AND WOMEN BUILT WALL STREET, BUILT BROADWAY, BUILT OUR FIRST FUCKING CITY HALL, AND MOST NEW YORKERS DON'T EVEN KNOW WE HAD SLAVES.
THANKS, BLACK HISTORY MONTH, BUT I STILL DON'T UNDERSTAND WHAT SOME SPOOK--NO PUN INTENDED--WOULD WANT WITH YOUR WHITE ASS.
DAVE, I DON'T JUST TALK TO WATCHES, I TALK TO THE ESCAPEMENTS AND BALANCE WHEELS AND TOURBILLONS THAT MAKE THOSE WATCHES RUN.
AND IF A CITY IS A MACHINE... MAYBE I CAN TALK WITH THE SOULS WHOSE BLOOD MAKES IT TICK.

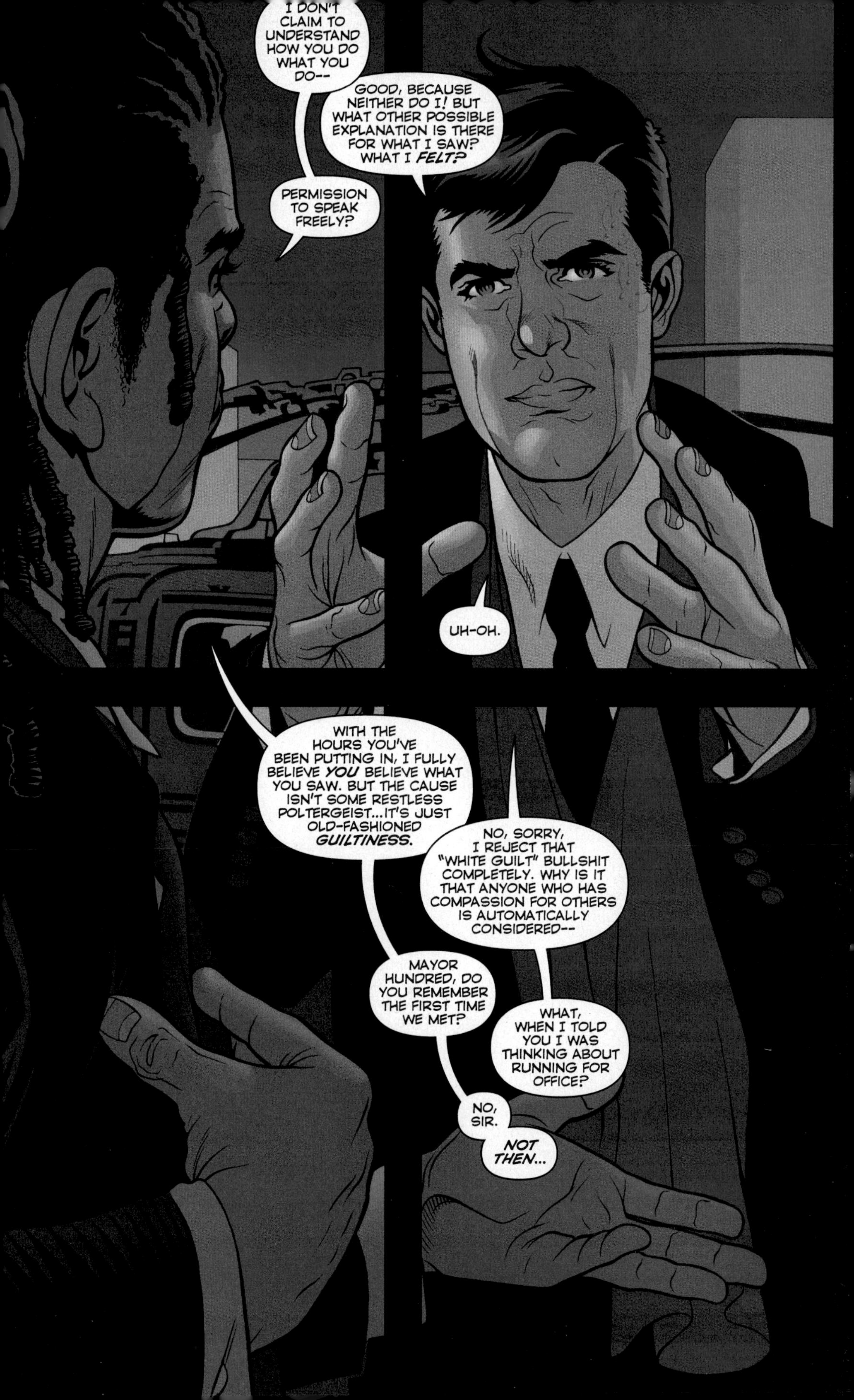
I DON'T CLAIM TO UNDERSTAND HOW YOU DO WHAT YOU DO--
GOOD, BECAUSE NEITHER DO I! BUT WHAT OTHER POSSIBLE EXPLANATION IS THERE FOR WHAT I SAW? WHAT I FELT?
PERMISSION TO SPEAK FREELY?
UH-OH.
WITH THE HOURS YOU'VE BEEN PUTTING IN, I FULLY BELIEVE YOU BELIEVE WHAT YOU SAW. BUT THE CAUSE ISN'T SOME RESTLESS POLTERGEIST...IT'S JUST OLD-FASHIONED GUILTINESS.
NO, SORRY, I REJECT THAT "WHITE GUILT" BULLSHIT COMPLETELY. WHY IS IT THAT ANYONE WHO HAS COMPASSION FOR OTHERS IS AUTOMATICALLY CONSIDERED--
MAYOR HUNDRED, DO YOU REMEMBER THE FIRST TIME WE MET?
WHAT, WHEN I TOLD YOU I WAS THINKING ABOUT RUNNING FOR OFFICE?
NO, SIR.
NOT THEN...

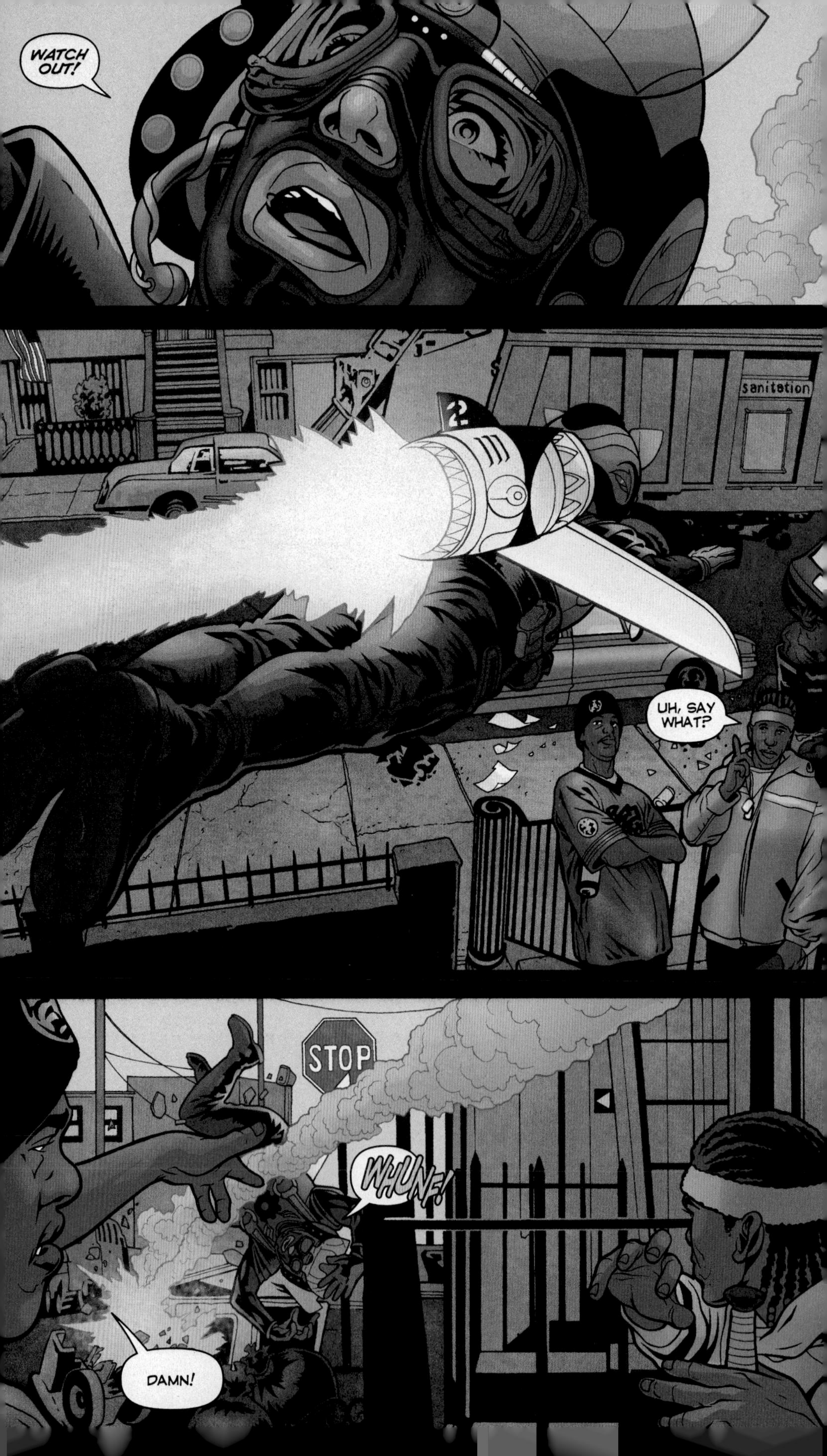
WATCH OUT!
sanitation
UH, SAY WHAT?
STOP
WHUNF!
DAMN!

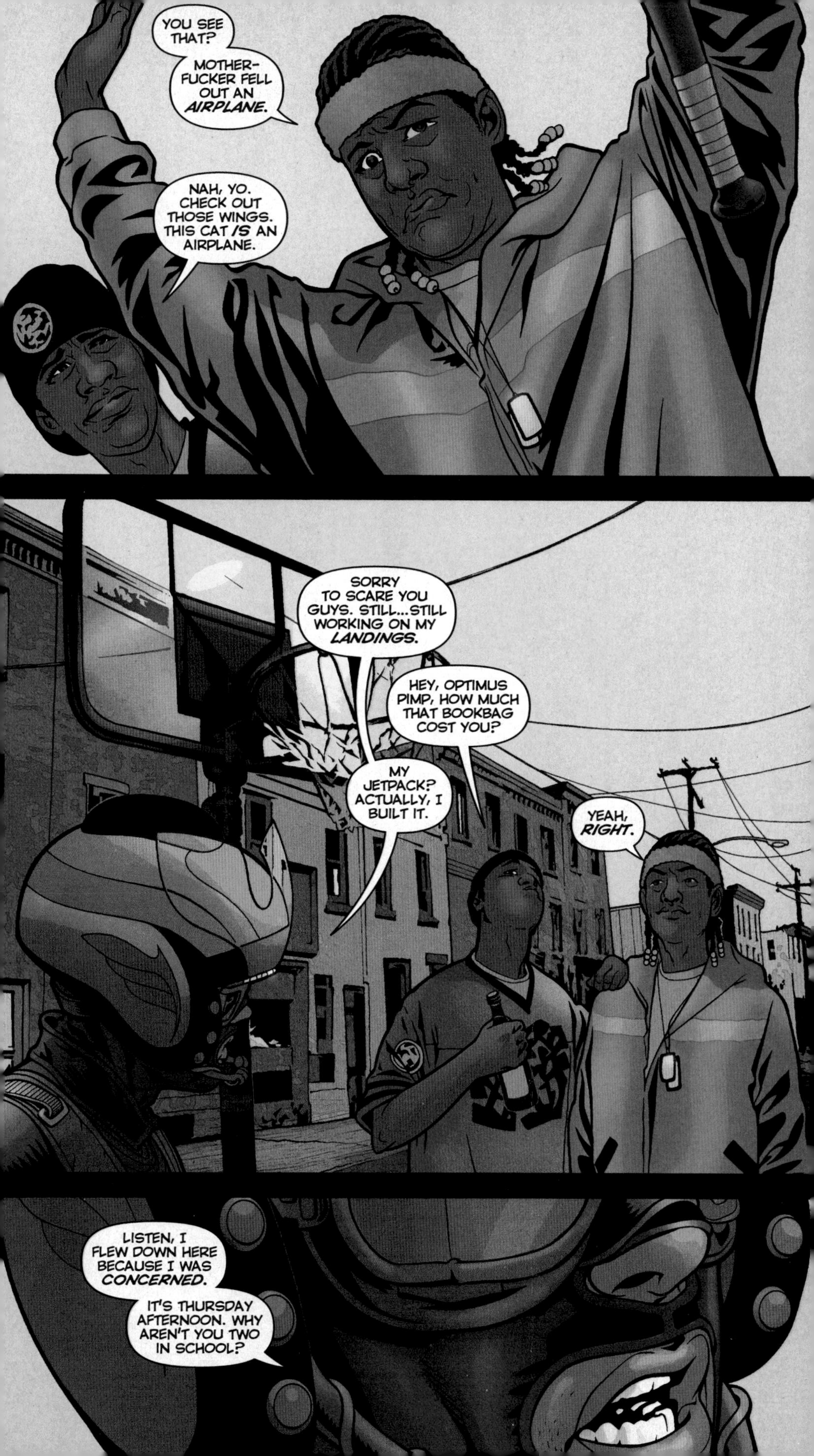
YOU SEE THAT?
MOTHER-FUCKER FELL OUT AN AIRPLANE.
NAH, YO. CHECK OUT THOSE WINGS. THIS CAT IS AN AIRPLANE.
SORRY TO SCARE YOU GUYS. STILL...STILL WORKING ON MY LANDINGS.
HEY, OPTIMUS PIMP, HOW MUCH THAT BOOKBAG COST YOU?
MY JETPACK? ACTUALLY, I BUILT IT.
YEAH, RIGHT.
LISTEN, I FLEW DOWN HERE BECAUSE I WAS CONCERNED.
IT'S THURSDAY AFTERNOON. WHY AREN'T YOU TWO IN SCHOOL?

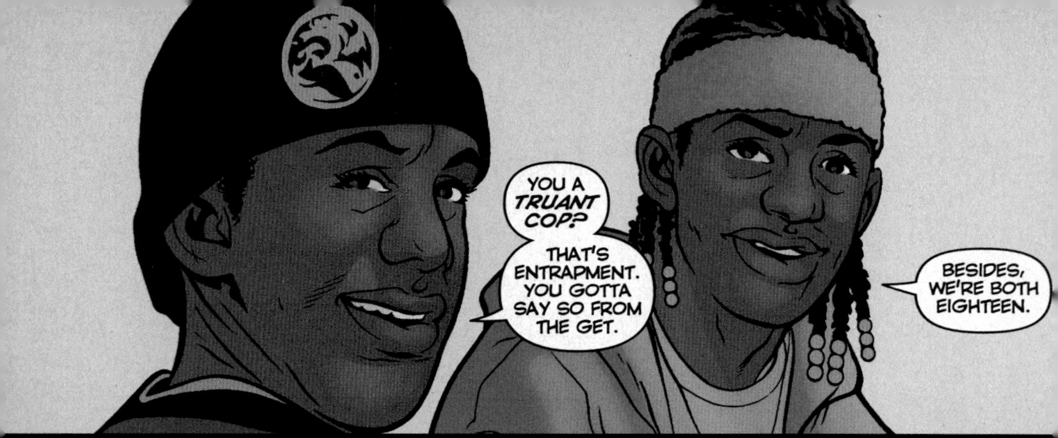
YOU A TRUANT COP?
THAT'S ENTRAPMENT. YOU GOTTA SAY SO FROM THE GET.
BESIDES, WE'RE BOTH EIGHTEEN.

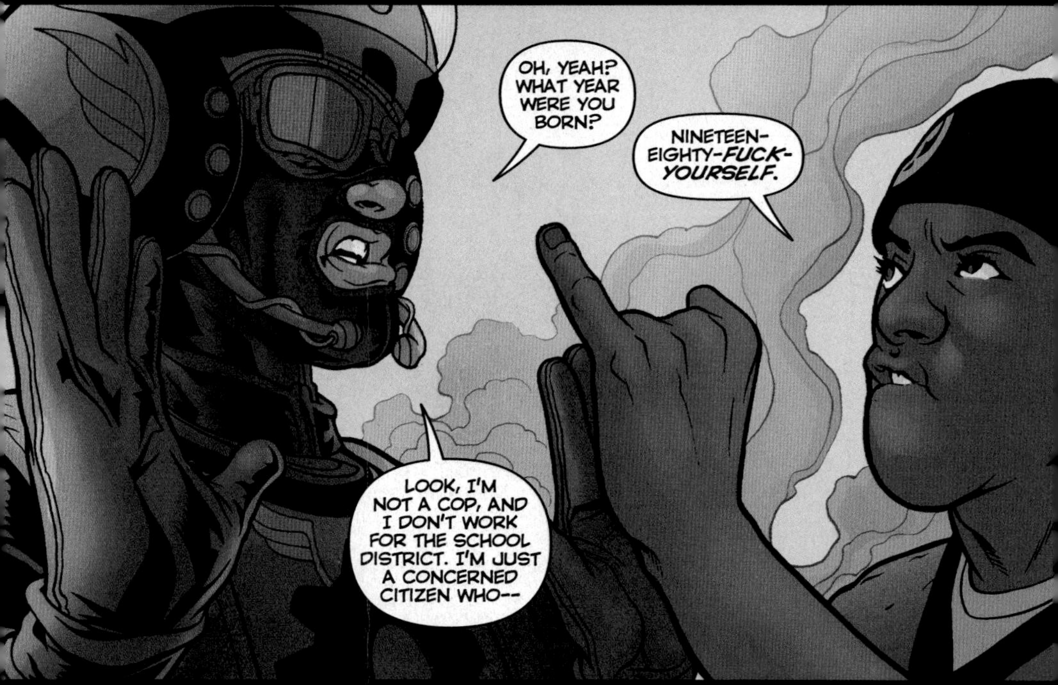
OH, YEAH? WHAT YEAR WERE YOU BORN?
NINETEEN-EIGHTY-FUCK-YOURSELF.
LOOK, I'M NOT A COP, AND I DON'T WORK FOR THE SCHOOL DISTRICT. I'M JUST A CONCERNED CITIZEN WHO--

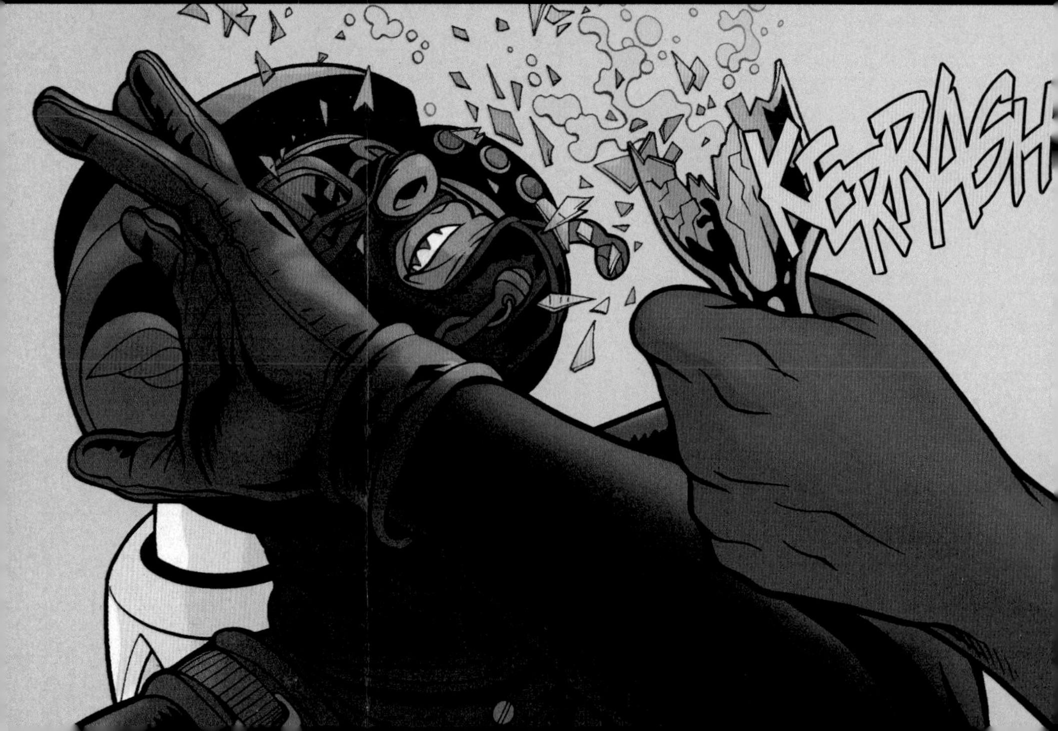
KERASH

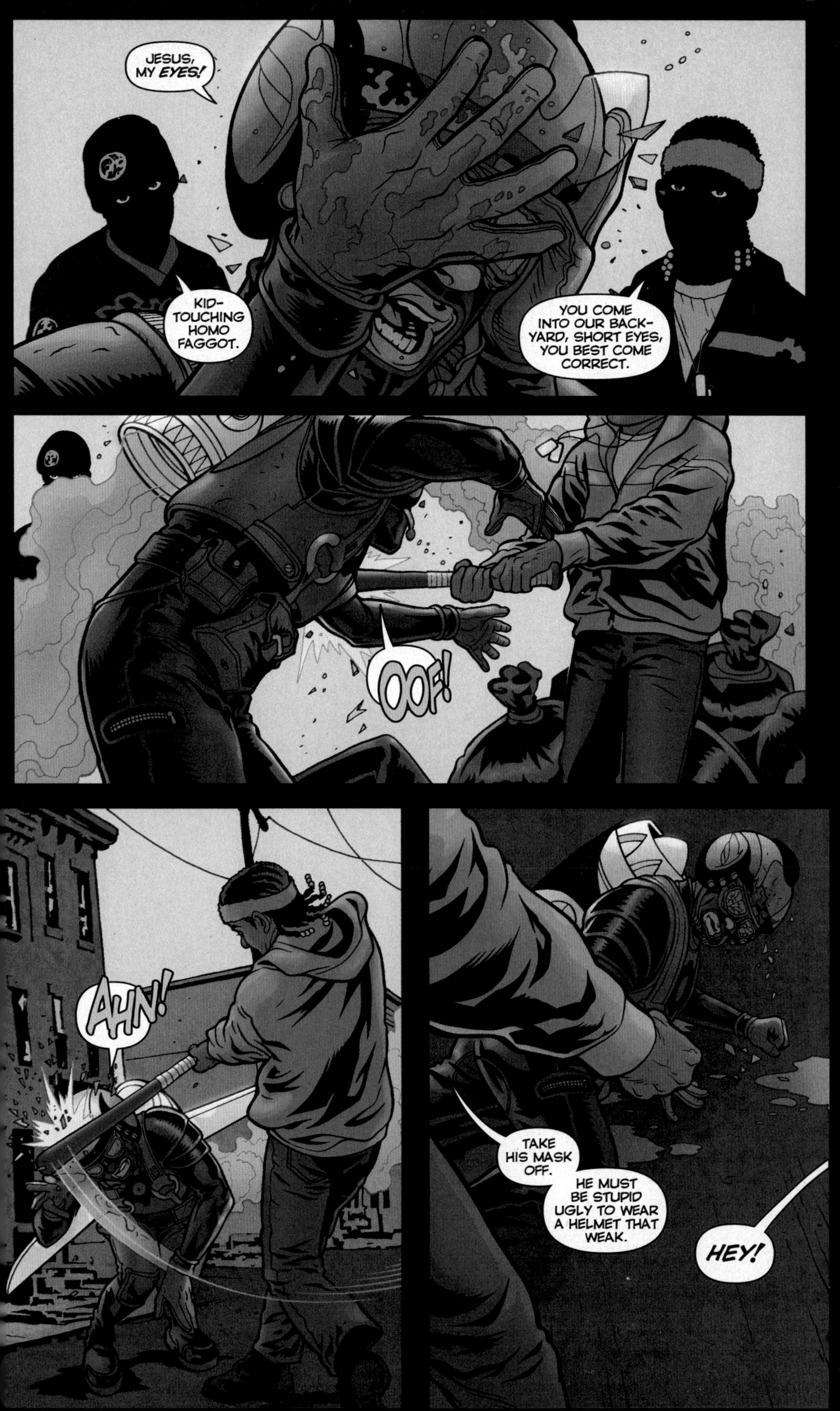
JESUS, MY EYES!
KID-TOUCHING HOMO FAGGOT.
YOU COME INTO OUR BACK-YARD, SHORT EYES, YOU BEST COME CORRECT.
OOF!
AHN!
TAKE HIS MASK OFF.
HE MUST BE STUPID UGLY TO WEAR A HELMET THAT WEAK.
HEY!

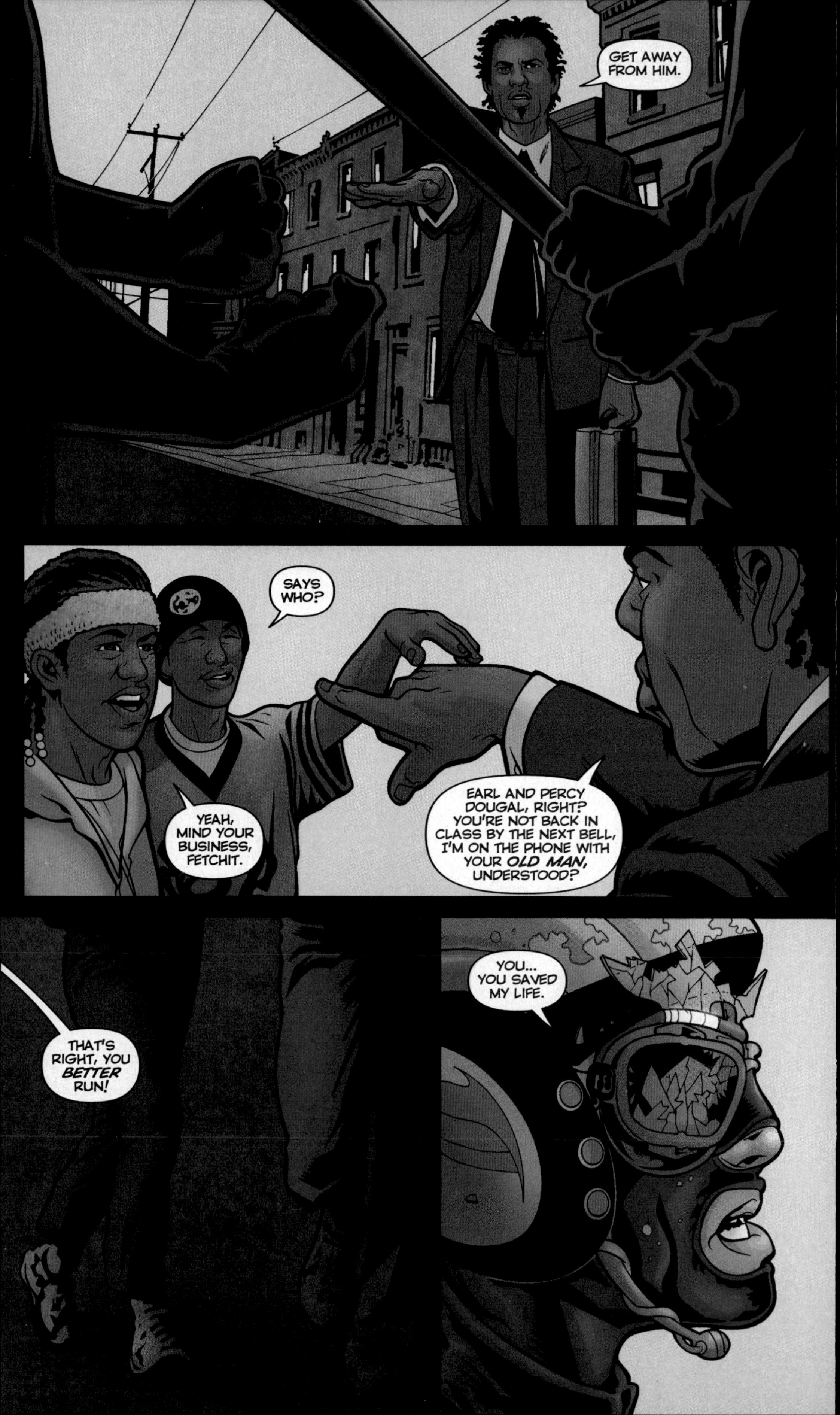
GET AWAY FROM HIM.
SAYS WHO?
YEAH, MIND YOUR BUSINESS, FETCHIT.
EARL AND PERCY DOUGAL, RIGHT? YOU'RE NOT BACK IN CLASS BY THE NEXT BELL, I'M ON THE PHONE WITH YOUR *OLD MAN,* UNDERSTOOD?
THAT'S RIGHT, YOU *BETTER* RUN!
YOU... YOU SAVED MY LIFE.

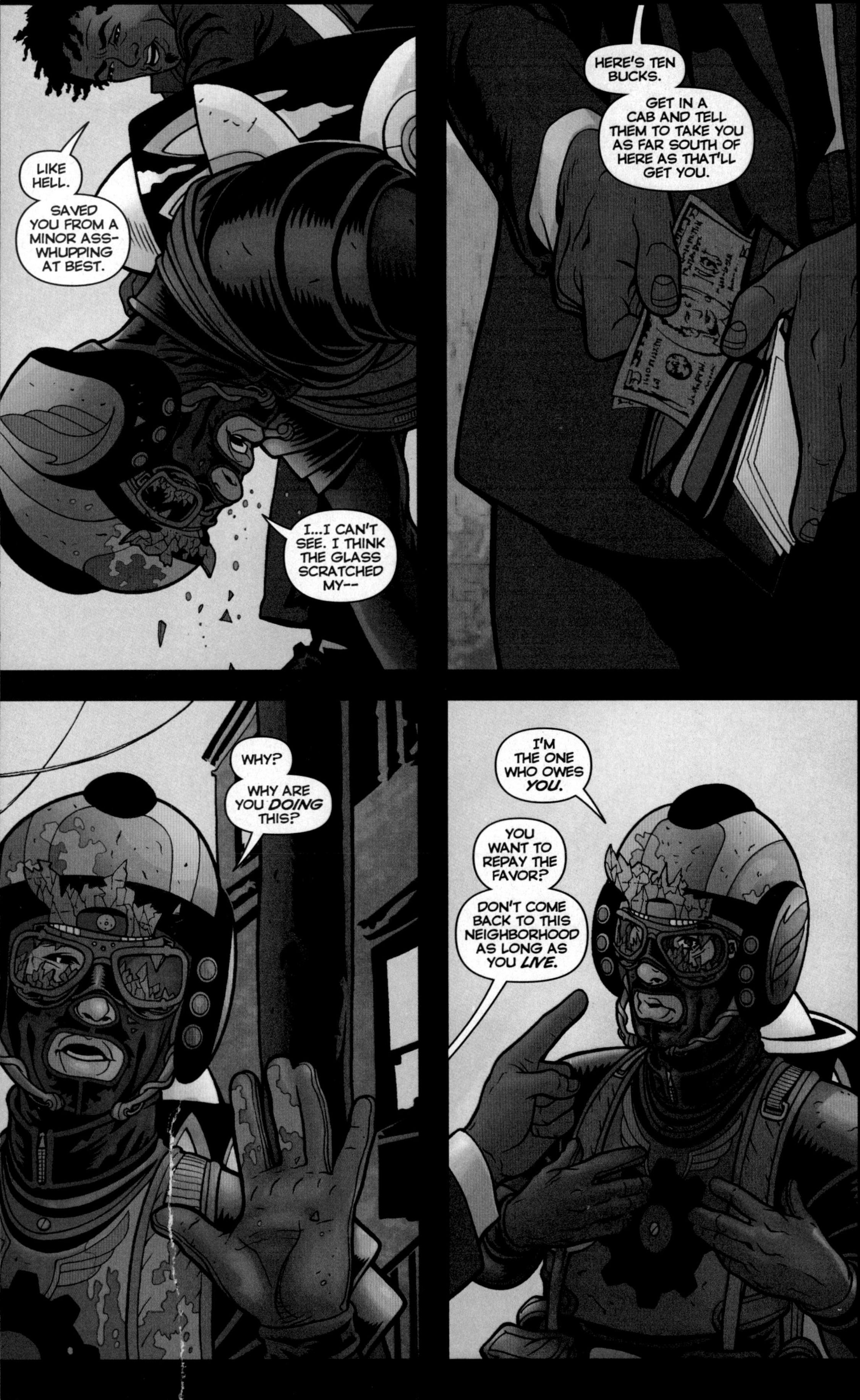
LIKE HELL.
SAVED YOU FROM A MINOR ASS-WHUPPING AT BEST.
I...I CAN'T SEE. I THINK THE GLASS SCRATCHED MY--
HERE'S TEN BUCKS.
GET IN A CAB AND TELL THEM TO TAKE YOU AS FAR SOUTH OF HERE AS THAT'LL GET YOU.
WHY?
WHY ARE YOU *DOING* THIS?
I'M THE ONE WHO OWES *YOU*.
YOU WANT TO REPAY THE FAVOR?
DON'T COME BACK TO THIS NEIGHBORHOOD AS LONG AS YOU *LIVE*.

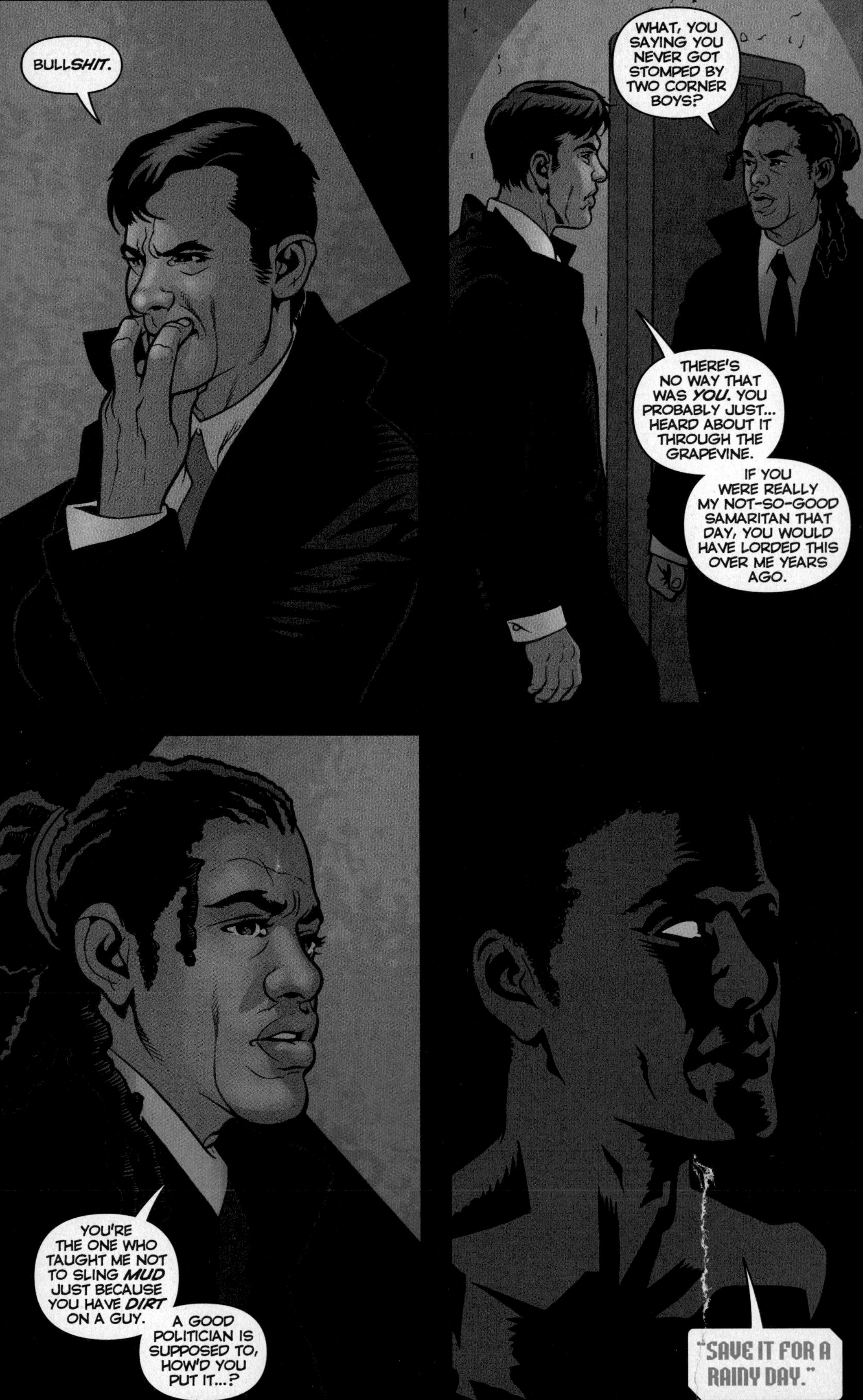
BULLSHIT.
WHAT, YOU SAYING YOU NEVER GOT STOMPED BY TWO CORNER BOYS?
THERE'S NO WAY THAT WAS YOU. YOU PROBABLY JUST... HEARD ABOUT IT THROUGH THE GRAPEVINE.
IF YOU WERE REALLY MY NOT-SO-GOOD SAMARITAN THAT DAY, YOU WOULD HAVE LORDED THIS OVER ME YEARS AGO.
YOU'RE THE ONE WHO TAUGHT ME NOT TO SLING MUD JUST BECAUSE YOU HAVE DIRT ON A GUY.
A GOOD POLITICIAN IS SUPPOSED TO, HOW'D YOU PUT IT...?
"SAVE IT FOR A RAINY DAY."

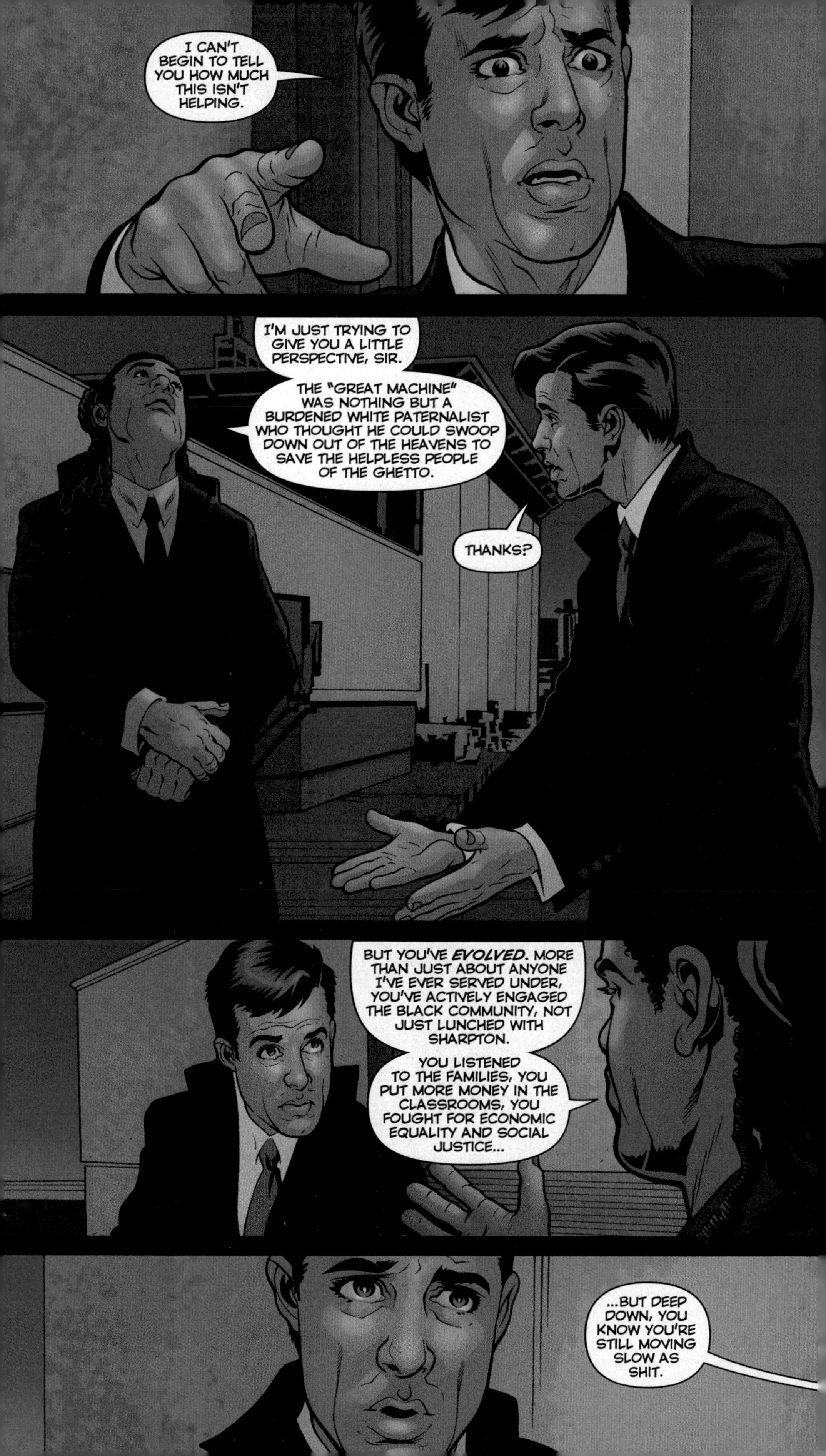
I CAN'T BEGIN TO TELL YOU HOW MUCH THIS ISN'T HELPING.
I'M JUST TRYING TO GIVE YOU A LITTLE PERSPECTIVE, SIR.
THE "GREAT MACHINE" WAS NOTHING BUT A BURDENED WHITE PATERNALIST WHO THOUGHT HE COULD SWOOP DOWN OUT OF THE HEAVENS TO SAVE THE HELPLESS PEOPLE OF THE GHETTO.
THANKS?
BUT YOU'VE EVOLVED. MORE THAN JUST ABOUT ANYONE I'VE EVER SERVED UNDER, YOU'VE ACTIVELY ENGAGED THE BLACK COMMUNITY, NOT JUST LUNCHED WITH SHARPTON.
YOU LISTENED TO THE FAMILIES, YOU PUT MORE MONEY IN THE CLASSROOMS, YOU FOUGHT FOR ECONOMIC EQUALITY AND SOCIAL JUSTICE...
...BUT DEEP DOWN, YOU KNOW YOU'RE STILL MOVING SLOW AS SHIT.

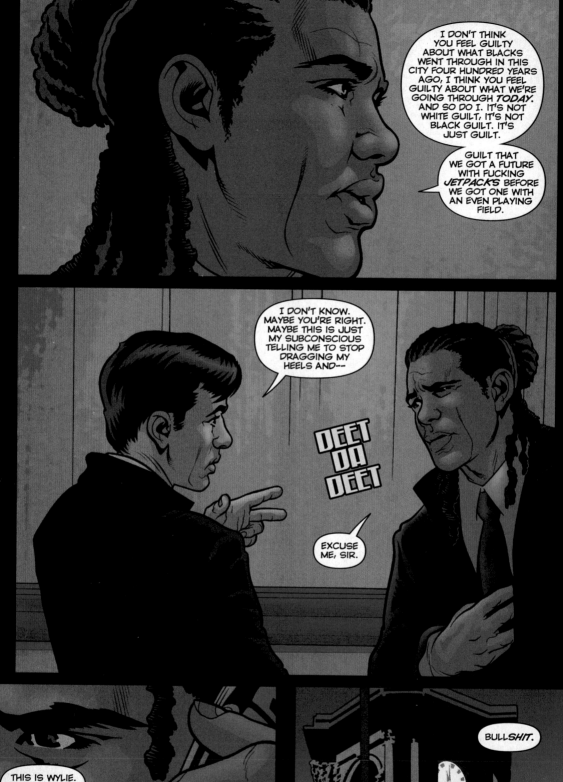

I DON'T THINK YOU FEEL GUILTY ABOUT WHAT BLACKS WENT THROUGH IN THIS CITY FOUR HUNDRED YEARS AGO, I THINK YOU FEEL GUILTY ABOUT WHAT WE'RE GOING THROUGH *TODAY.* AND SO DO I. IT'S NOT WHITE GUILT, IT'S NOT BLACK GUILT. IT'S JUST GUILT.

GUILT THAT WE GOT A FUTURE WITH FUCKING *JETPACKS* BEFORE WE GOT ONE WITH AN EVEN PLAYING FIELD.

I DON'T KNOW. MAYBE YOU'RE RIGHT. MAYBE THIS IS JUST MY SUBCONSCIOUS TELLING ME TO STOP DRAGGING MY HEELS AND--

DEET DA DEET

EXCUSE ME, SIR.

THIS IS WYLIE. UH-HUH. RIGHT, YEAH, WE...

WHAT DO YOU MEAN, THERE MAY HAVE BEEN A MISTAKE?

BULL*SHIT.*

GOD, I HATE WHEN YOU'RE RIGHT.

WHEN THOSE WORKERS FIRST STUMBLED ON THIS OLD GRAVESITE, THEY APPARENTLY FOUND ONE CASKET CARVED WITH A "STRANGE SYMBOL."

I DON'T KNOW WHAT'S SO STRANGE ABOUT A DAMN *SPIRAL*, BUT SINCE NO OTHER SLAVES HAD MARKINGS LIKE THAT ON THEIR PINE BOXES, THE ANTHRO-POLOGISTS FIGURED THE CORPSE INSIDE WAS JUST ANOTHER DEAD EUROPEAN.

AND THEN *YOU* CALLED.

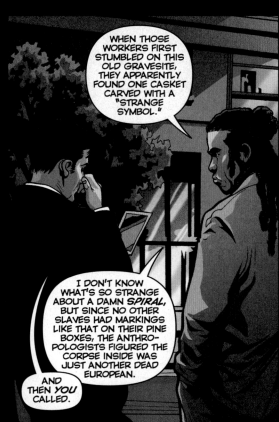

THE BRAIN TRUST AT HOWARD U. REEXAMINED THOSE REMAINS AND NOTICED THAT THE SKULL'S UPPER INCISORS HAD BEEN *FILED*, A MUTILATION SPECIFIC TO AFRICAN SLAVES.

SIR, IF YOU HADN'T TOLD ANYONE WHAT YOU SAW, THIS MAN NEVER WOULD HAVE BEEN GIVEN A PROPER RESTING SPOT...NEXT TO HIS BROTHERS AND SISTERS WHERE HE BELONGS.

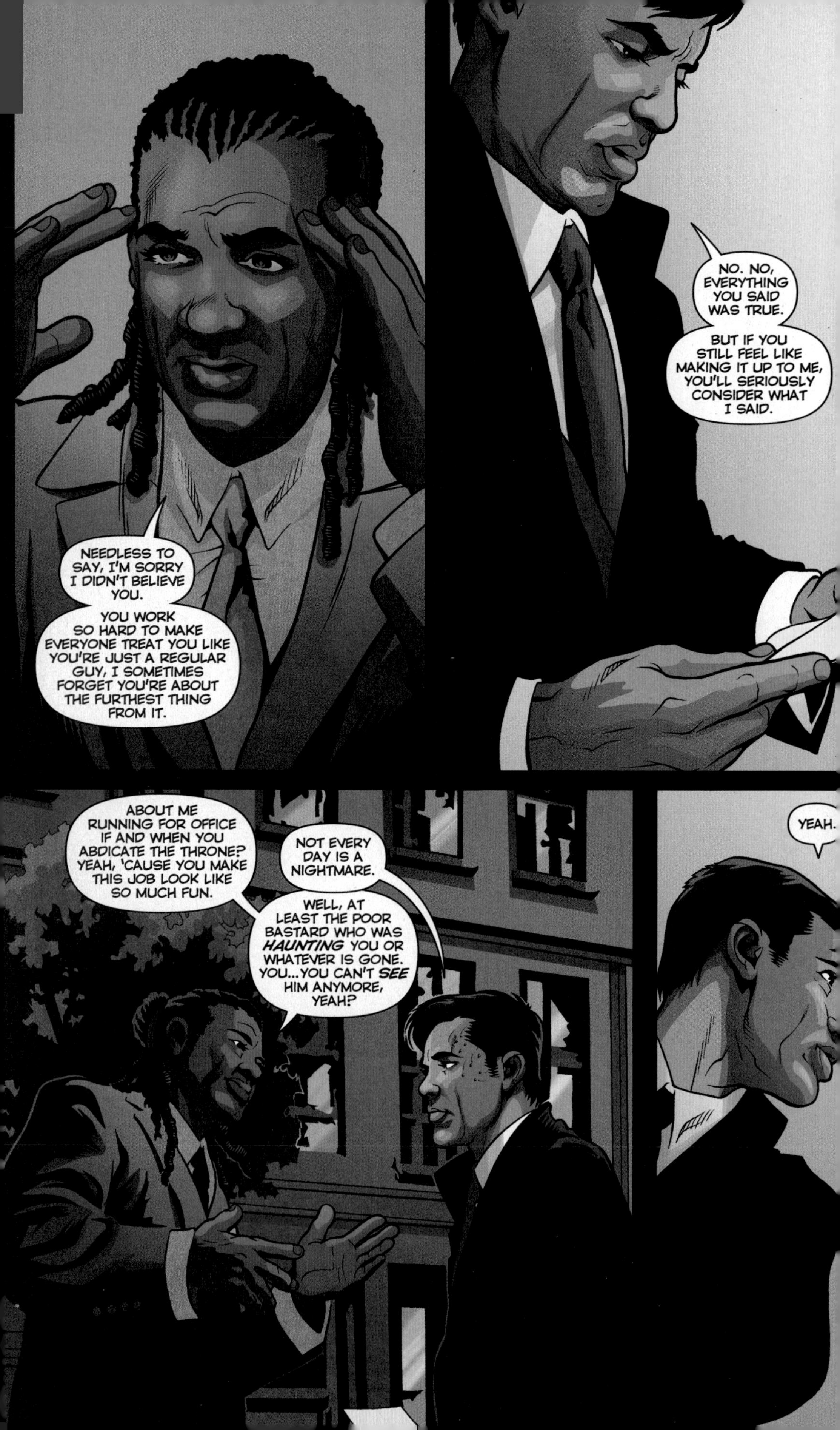
NEEDLESS TO SAY, I'M SORRY I DIDN'T BELIEVE YOU.
YOU WORK SO HARD TO MAKE EVERYONE TREAT YOU LIKE YOU'RE JUST A REGULAR GUY, I SOMETIMES FORGET YOU'RE ABOUT THE FURTHEST THING FROM IT.
NO. NO, EVERYTHING YOU SAID WAS TRUE.
BUT IF YOU STILL FEEL LIKE MAKING IT UP TO ME, YOU'LL SERIOUSLY CONSIDER WHAT I SAID.
ABOUT ME RUNNING FOR OFFICE IF AND WHEN YOU ABDICATE THE THRONE? YEAH, 'CAUSE YOU MAKE THIS JOB LOOK LIKE SO MUCH FUN.
NOT EVERY DAY IS A NIGHTMARE.
WELL, AT LEAST THE POOR BASTARD WHO WAS *HAUNTING* YOU OR WHATEVER IS GONE. YOU...YOU CAN'T *SEE* HIM ANYMORE, YEAH?
YEAH.

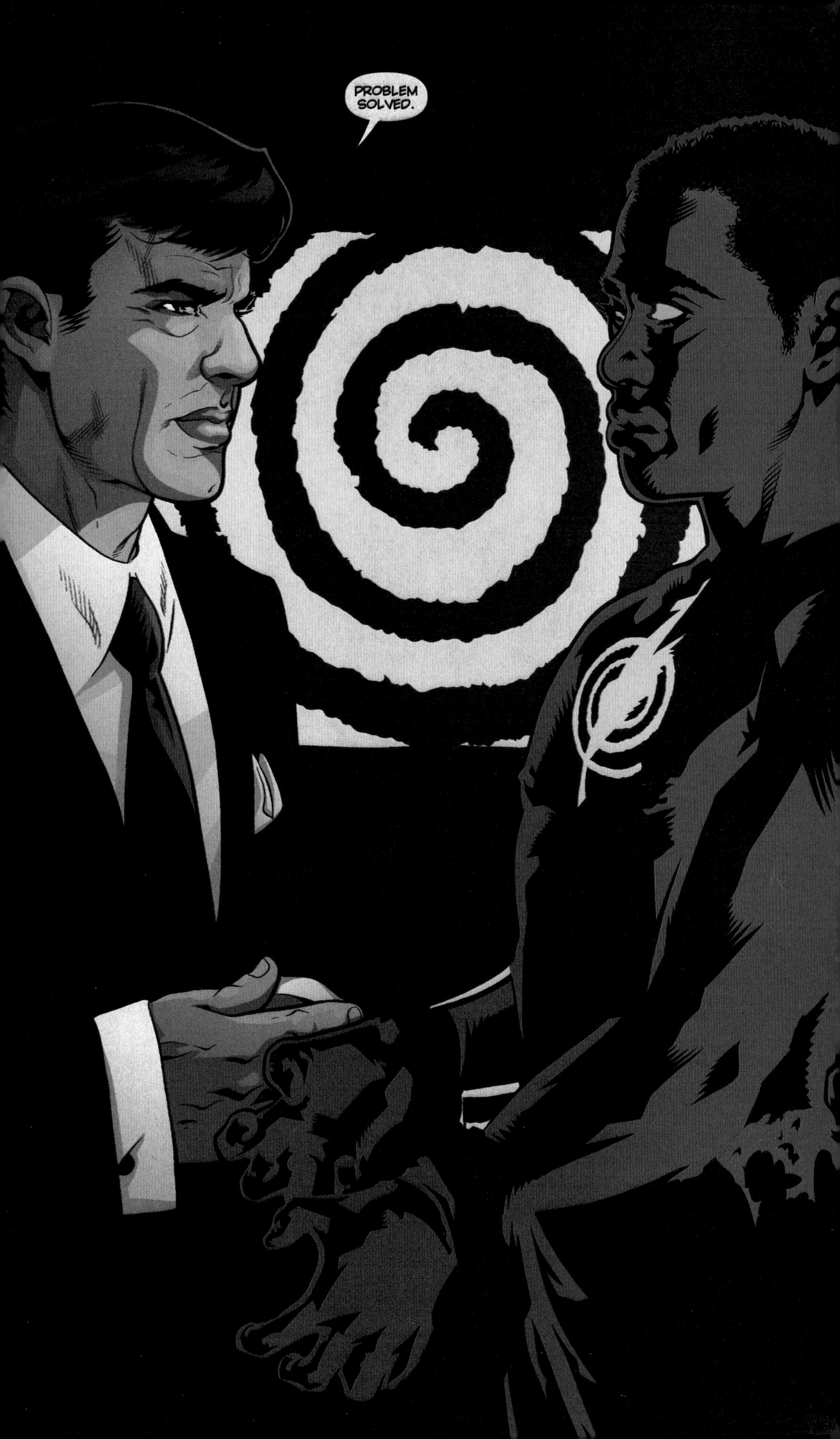
PROBLEM SOLVED.

Chapter 2
Dirty Tricks
part 1

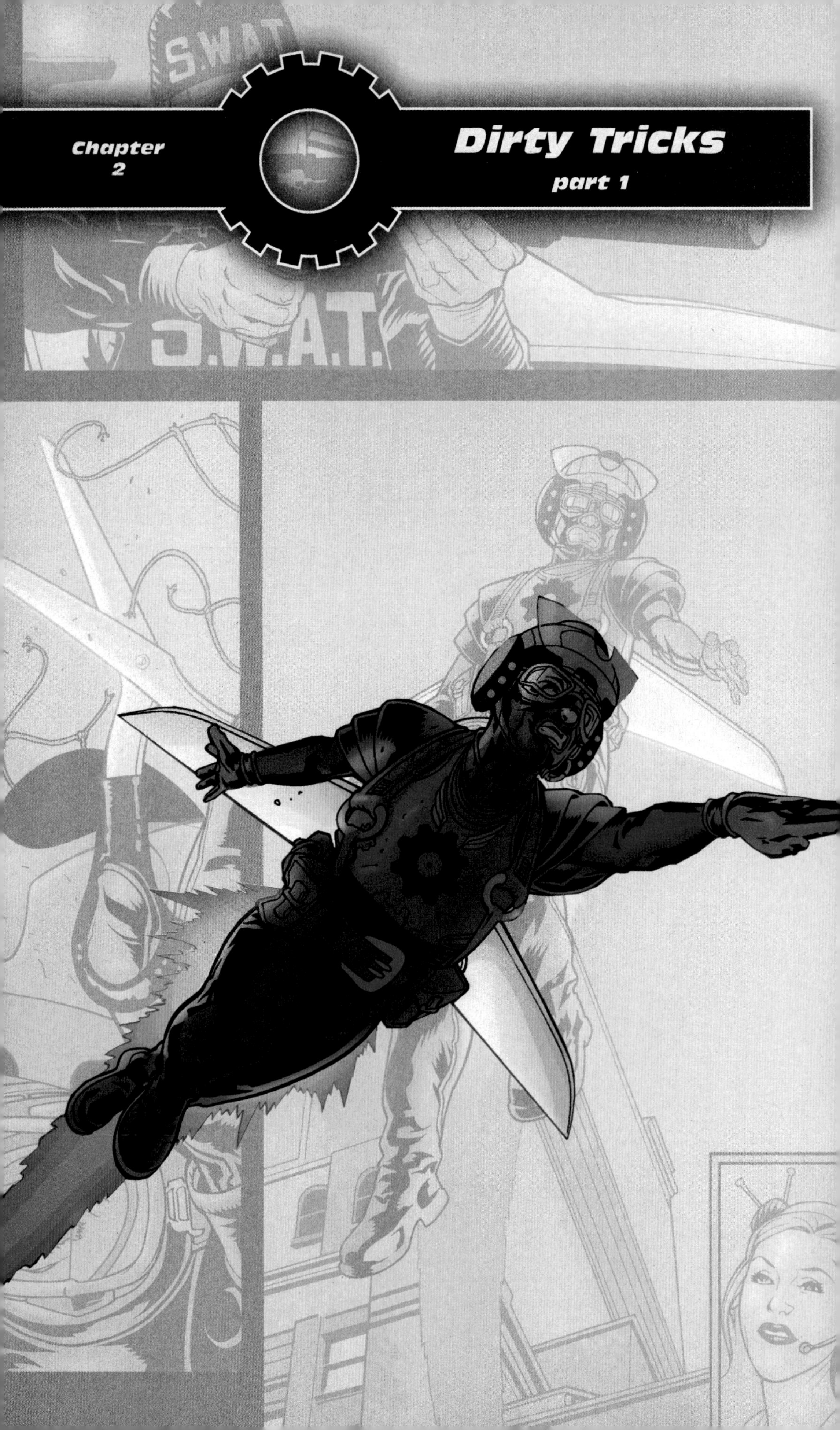
S.W.A.T.
S.W.A.T.

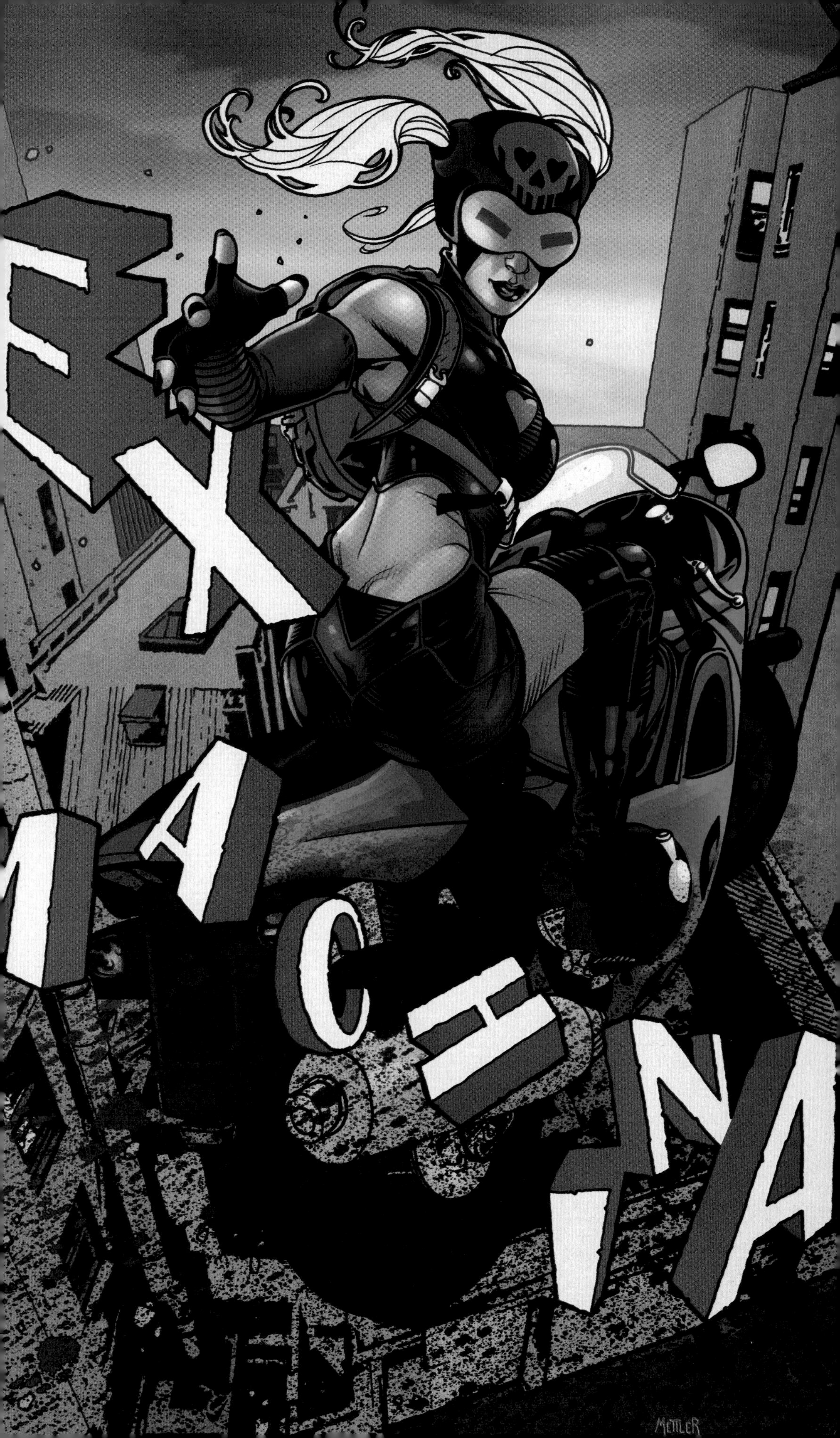
EX MACHINA
METTLER

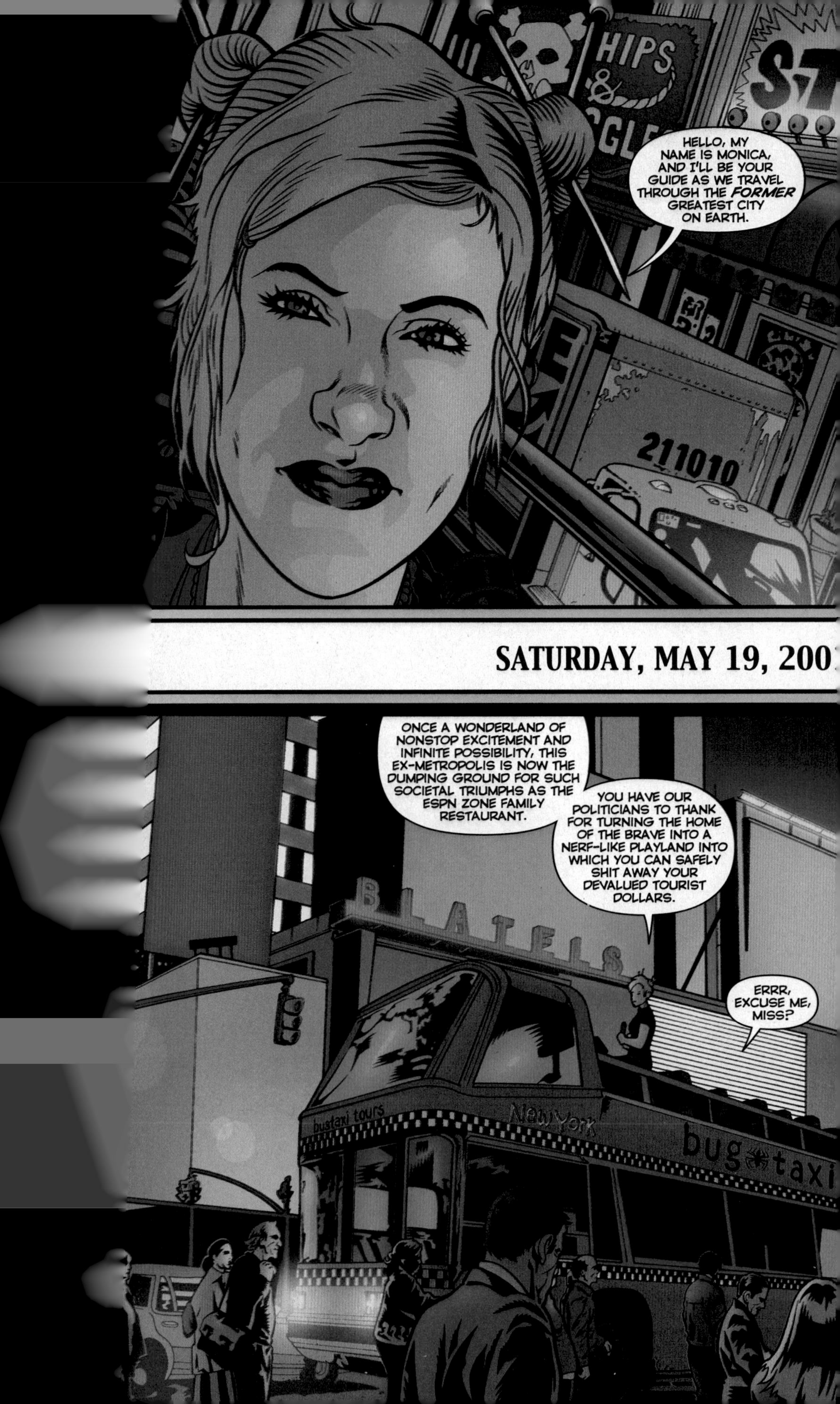
HELLO, MY NAME IS MONICA, AND I'LL BE YOUR GUIDE AS WE TRAVEL THROUGH THE *FORMER* GREATEST CITY ON EARTH.
SATURDAY, MAY 19, 200
ONCE A WONDERLAND OF NONSTOP EXCITEMENT AND INFINITE POSSIBILITY, THIS EX-METROPOLIS IS NOW THE DUMPING GROUND FOR SUCH SOCIETAL TRIUMPHS AS THE ESPN ZONE FAMILY RESTAURANT.
YOU HAVE OUR POLITICIANS TO THANK FOR TURNING THE HOME OF THE BRAVE INTO A NERF-LIKE PLAYLAND INTO WHICH YOU CAN SAFELY SHIT AWAY YOUR DEVALUED TOURIST DOLLARS.
ERRR, EXCUSE ME, MISS?
bustaxi tours
New York

WE SEE SOUP NAZI, YES?
WE COME ALL WAY FROM LISBON TO TASTE HIM.
HEH, DELIGHTFUL.
WHAT'S PORTUGUESE FOR "I QUIT?"
HEY!
YOU! CAN I BORROW YOUR CELL PHONE?
THE MOTOROLA IN YOUR LEFT POCKET?
20
New York
bug ta

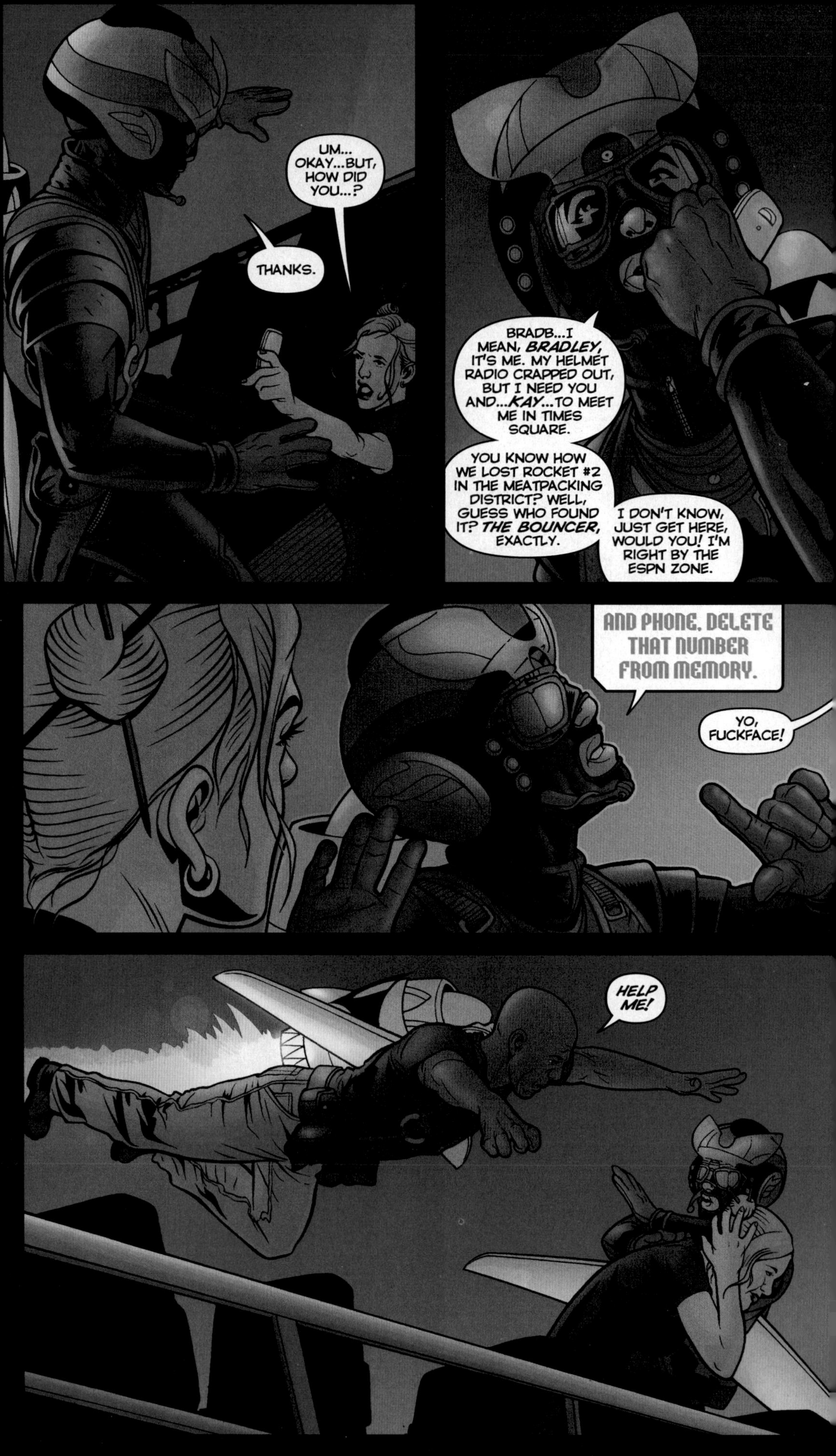
UM... OKAY...BUT, HOW DID YOU...?
THANKS.
BRADB...I MEAN, *BRADLEY*, IT'S ME. MY HELMET RADIO CRAPPED OUT, BUT I NEED YOU AND...*KAY*...TO MEET ME IN TIMES SQUARE.
YOU KNOW HOW WE LOST ROCKET #2 IN THE MEATPACKING DISTRICT? WELL, GUESS WHO FOUND IT? *THE BOUNCER*, EXACTLY.
I DON'T KNOW, JUST GET HERE, WOULD YOU! I'M RIGHT BY THE ESPN ZONE.
AND PHONE, DELETE THAT NUMBER FROM MEMORY.
YO, FUCKFACE!
HELP ME!

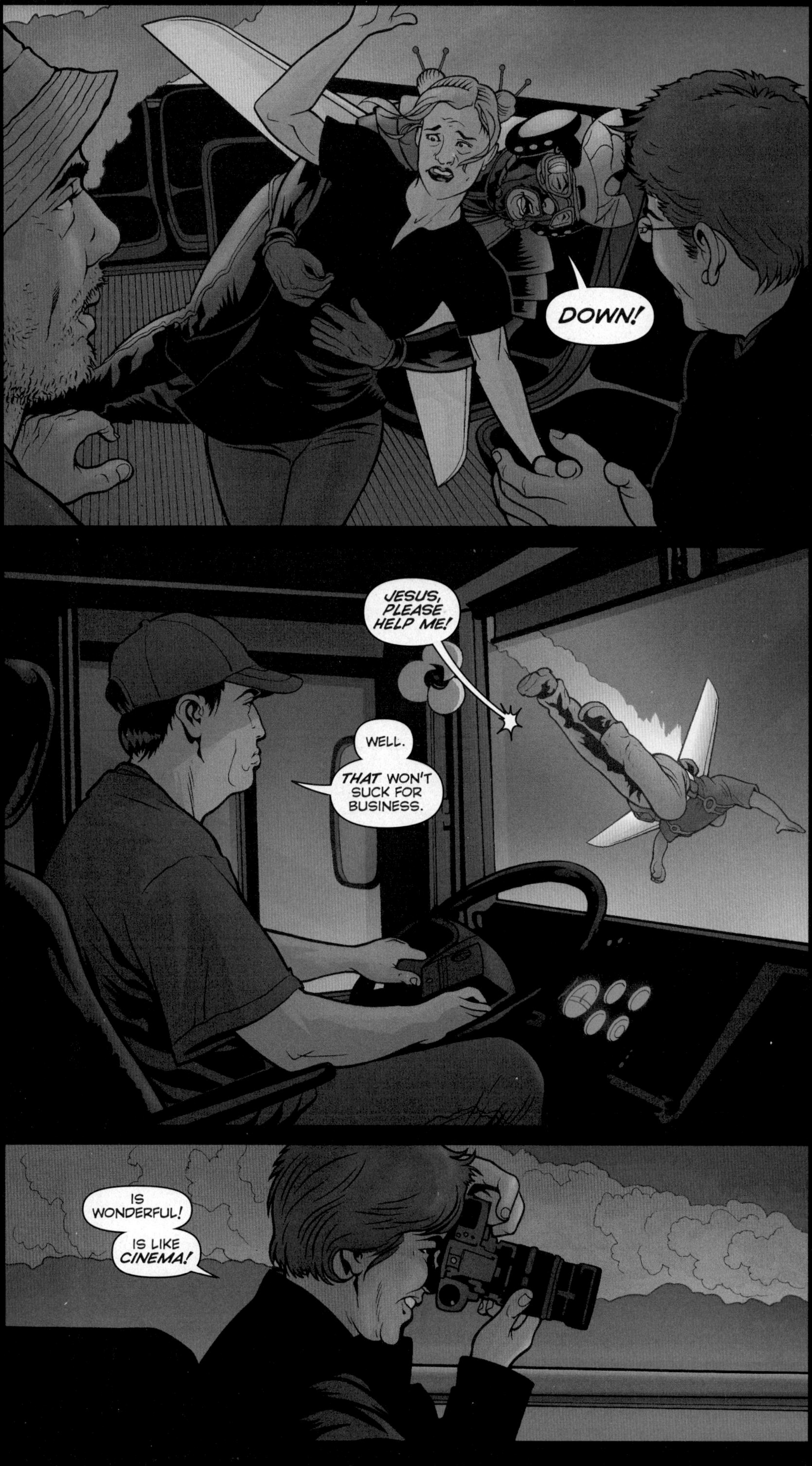
DOWN!
JESUS, PLEASE HELP ME!
WELL.
THAT WON'T SUCK FOR BUSINESS.
IS WONDERFUL!
IS LIKE CINEMA!

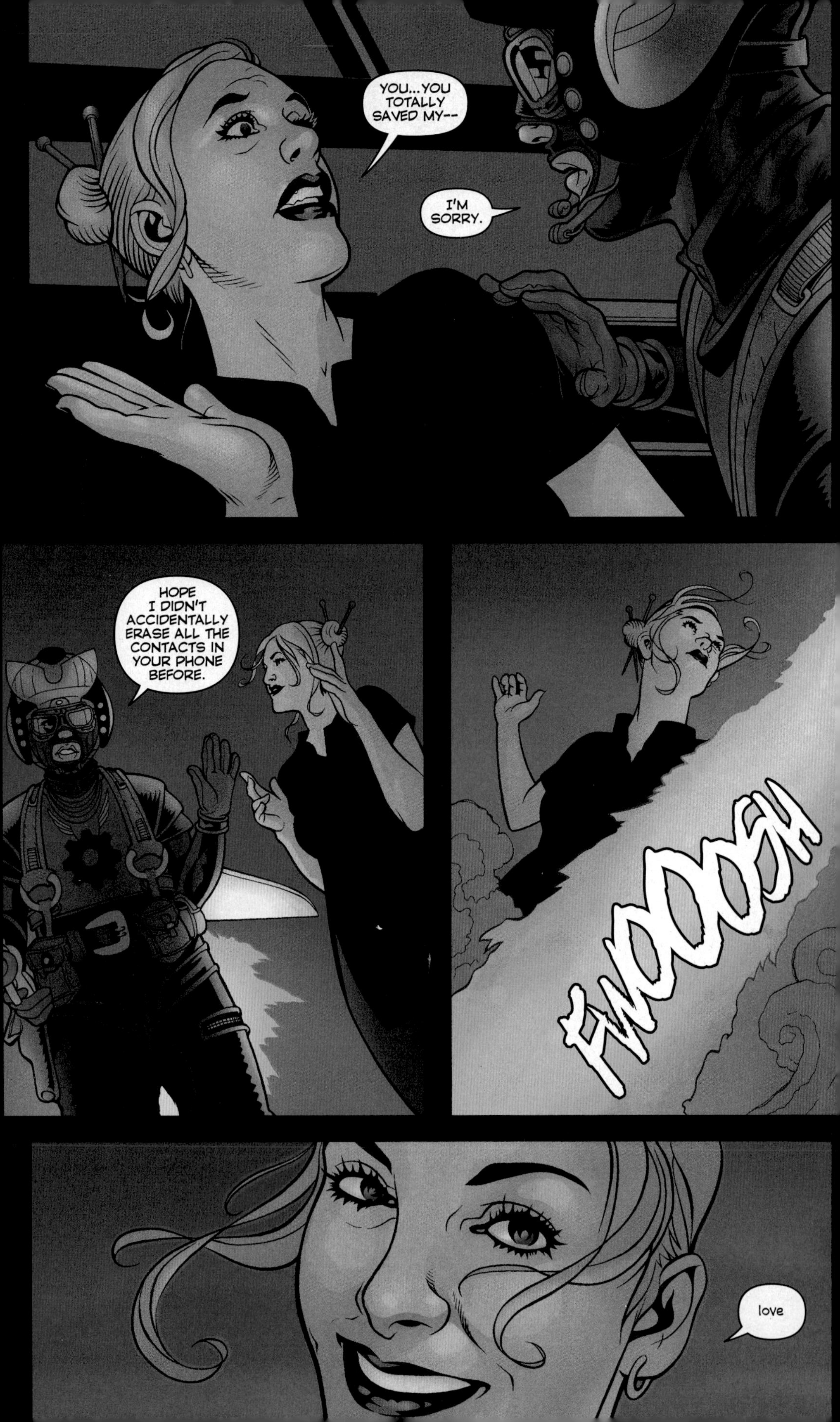
YOU...YOU TOTALLY SAVED MY--
I'M SORRY.
HOPE I DIDN'T ACCIDENTALLY ERASE ALL THE CONTACTS IN YOUR PHONE BEFORE.
FWOOOOSH
love

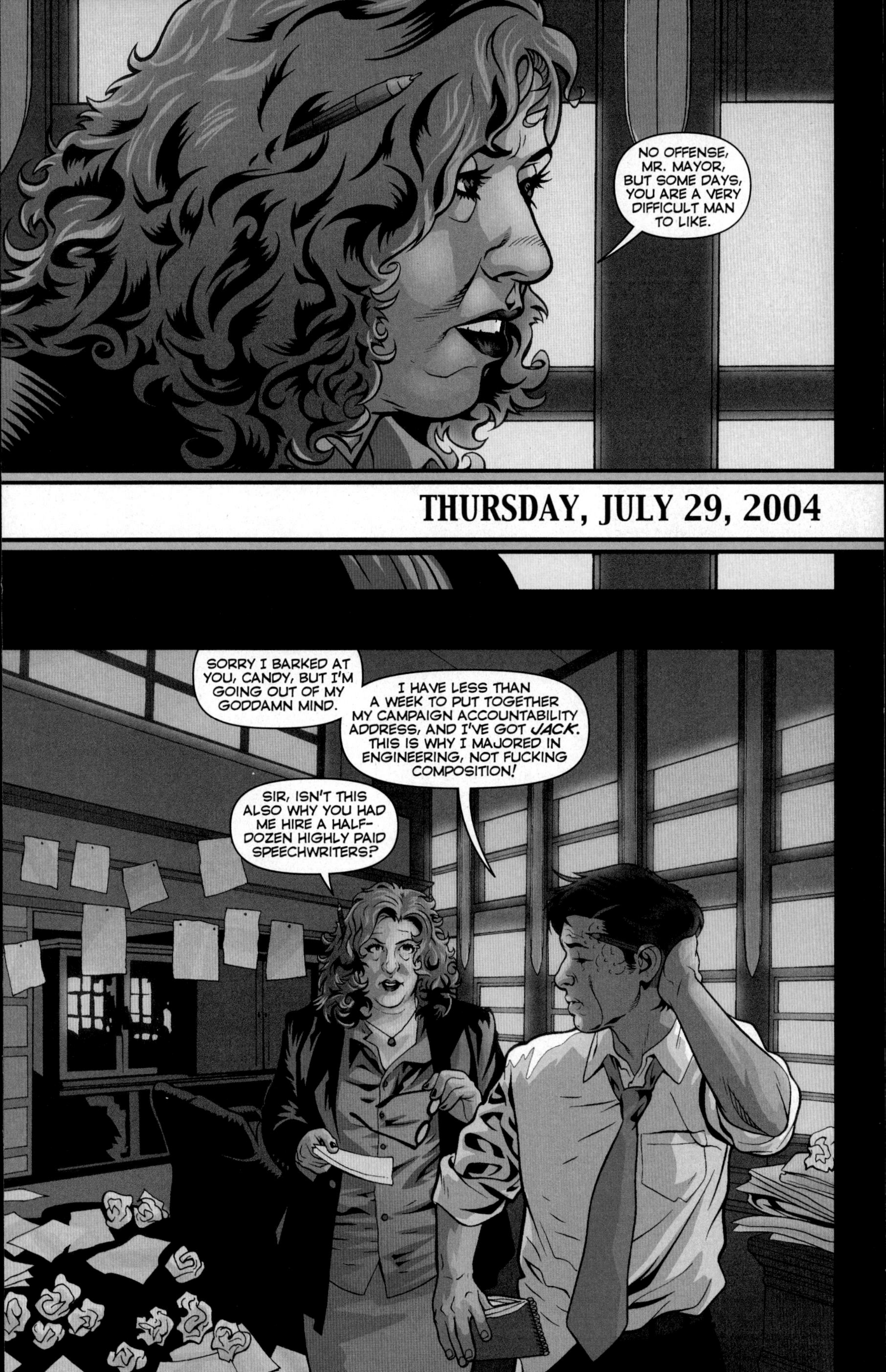
NO OFFENSE, MR. MAYOR, BUT SOME DAYS, YOU ARE A VERY DIFFICULT MAN TO LIKE.
THURSDAY, JULY 29, 2004
SORRY I BARKED AT YOU, CANDY, BUT I'M GOING OUT OF MY GODDAMN MIND.
I HAVE LESS THAN A WEEK TO PUT TOGETHER MY CAMPAIGN ACCOUNTABILITY ADDRESS, AND I'VE GOT JACK. THIS IS WHY I MAJORED IN ENGINEERING, NOT FUCKING COMPOSITION!
SIR, ISN'T THIS ALSO WHY YOU HAD ME HIRE A HALF-DOZEN HIGHLY PAID SPEECHWRITERS?

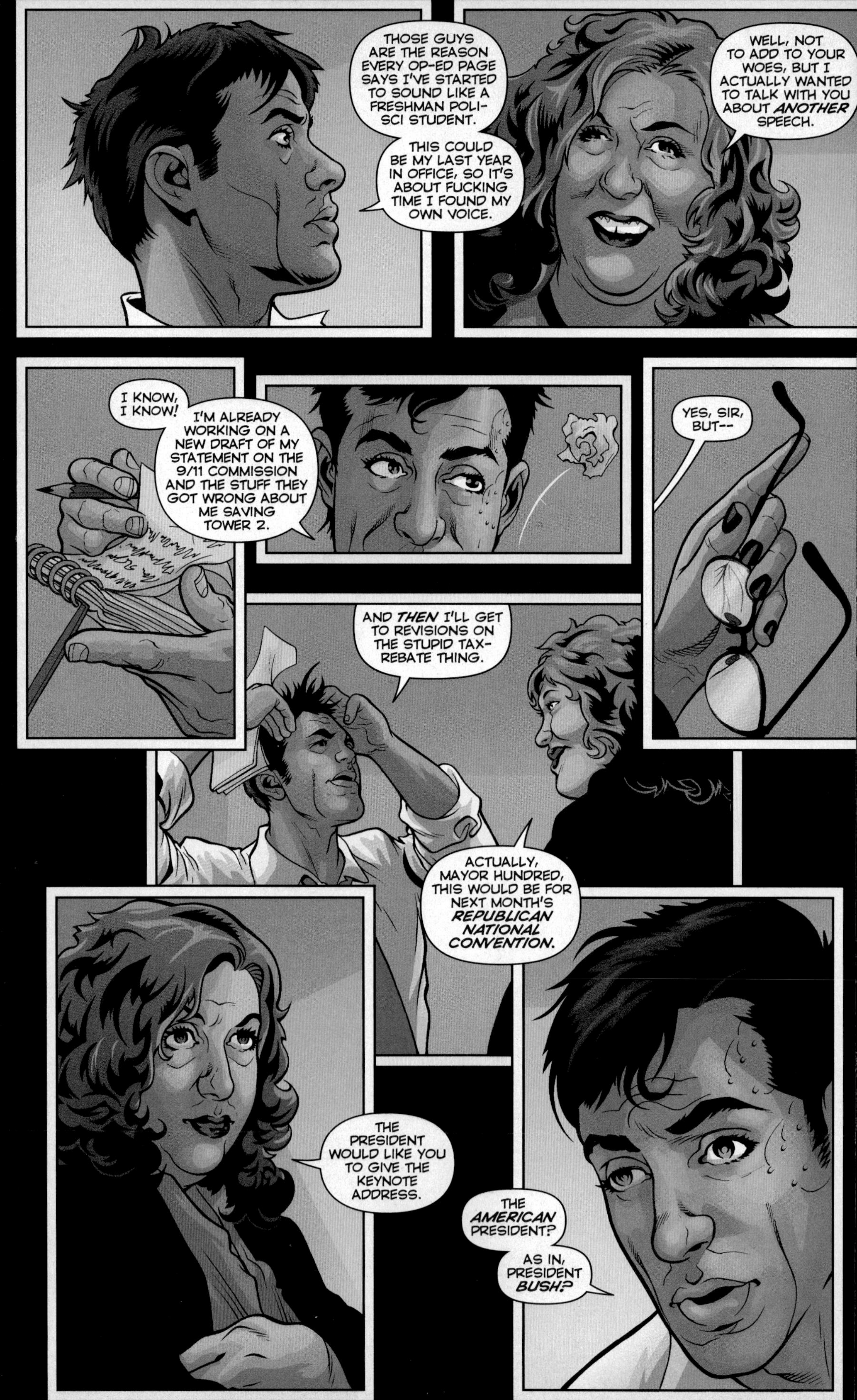
THOSE GUYS ARE THE REASON EVERY OP-ED PAGE SAYS I'VE STARTED TO SOUND LIKE A FRESHMAN POLI-SCI STUDENT.
THIS COULD BE MY LAST YEAR IN OFFICE, SO IT'S ABOUT FUCKING TIME I FOUND MY OWN VOICE.
WELL, NOT TO ADD TO YOUR WOES, BUT I ACTUALLY WANTED TO TALK WITH YOU ABOUT *ANOTHER* SPEECH.
I KNOW, I KNOW!
I'M ALREADY WORKING ON A NEW DRAFT OF MY STATEMENT ON THE 9/11 COMMISSION AND THE STUFF THEY GOT WRONG ABOUT ME SAVING TOWER 2.
YES, SIR, BUT--
AND *THEN* I'LL GET TO REVISIONS ON THE STUPID TAX-REBATE THING.
ACTUALLY, MAYOR HUNDRED, THIS WOULD BE FOR NEXT MONTH'S ***REPUBLICAN NATIONAL CONVENTION.***
THE PRESIDENT WOULD LIKE YOU TO GIVE THE KEYNOTE ADDRESS.
THE *AMERICAN* PRESIDENT?
AS IN, PRESIDENT *BUSH?*

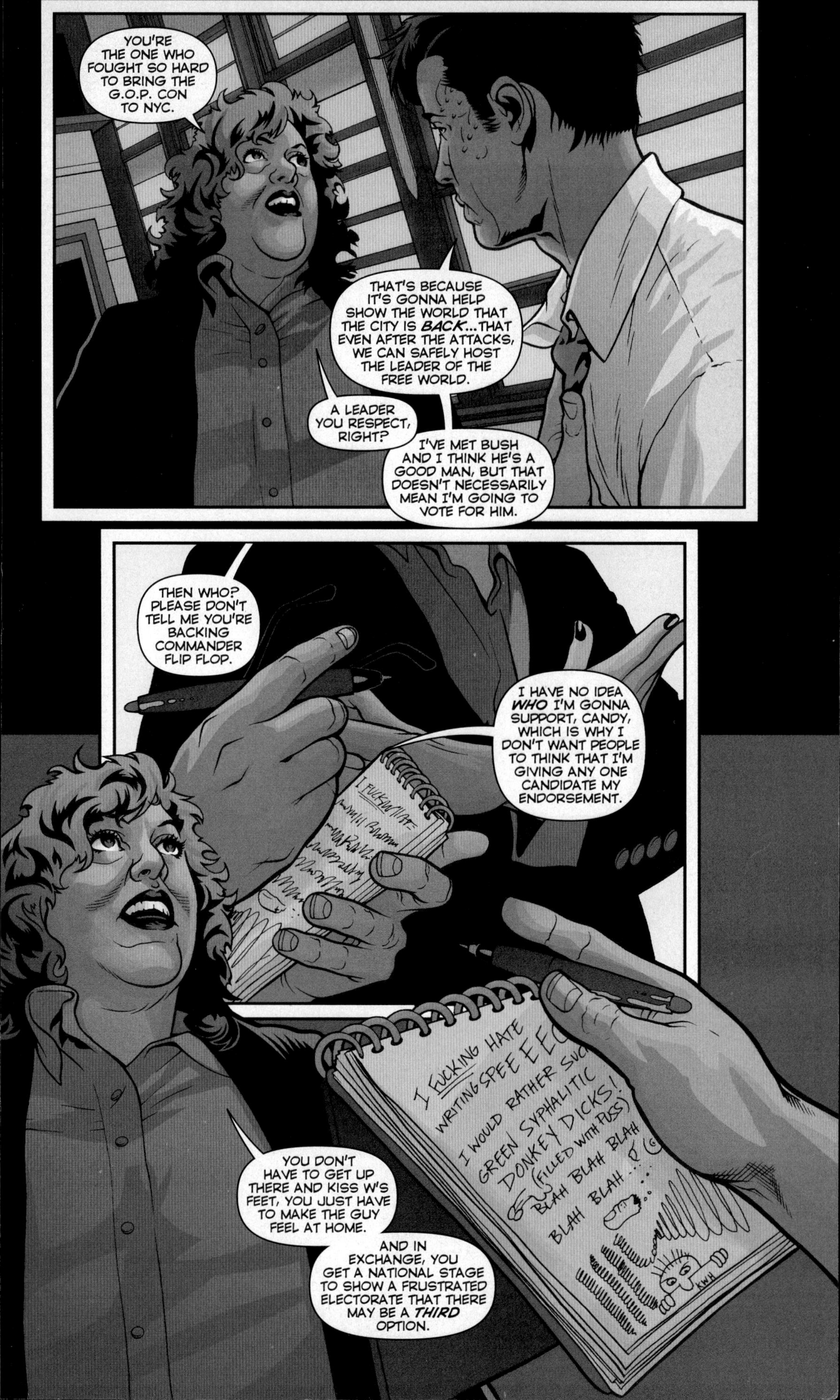
YOU'RE THE ONE WHO FOUGHT SO HARD TO BRING THE G.O.P. CON TO NYC.
THAT'S BECAUSE IT'S GONNA HELP SHOW THE WORLD THAT THE CITY IS *BACK*...THAT EVEN AFTER THE ATTACKS, WE CAN SAFELY HOST THE LEADER OF THE FREE WORLD.
A LEADER YOU RESPECT, RIGHT?
I'VE MET BUSH AND I THINK HE'S A GOOD MAN, BUT THAT DOESN'T NECESSARILY MEAN I'M GOING TO VOTE FOR HIM.
THEN WHO? PLEASE DON'T TELL ME YOU'RE BACKING COMMANDER FLIP FLOP.
I HAVE NO IDEA ***WHO*** I'M GONNA SUPPORT, CANDY, WHICH IS WHY I DON'T WANT PEOPLE TO THINK THAT I'M GIVING ANY ONE CANDIDATE MY ENDORSEMENT.
I FUCKING HATE
GREEN SYPHALITIC
DONKEY DICKS!
(FILLED WITH PUSS)
BLAH BLAH BLAH
BLAH BLAH...
BLAH BLAH
YOU DON'T HAVE TO GET UP THERE AND KISS W'S FEET, YOU JUST HAVE TO MAKE THE GUY FEEL AT HOME.
AND IN EXCHANGE, YOU GET A NATIONAL STAGE TO SHOW A FRUSTRATED ELECTORATE THAT THERE MAY BE A *THIRD* OPTION.

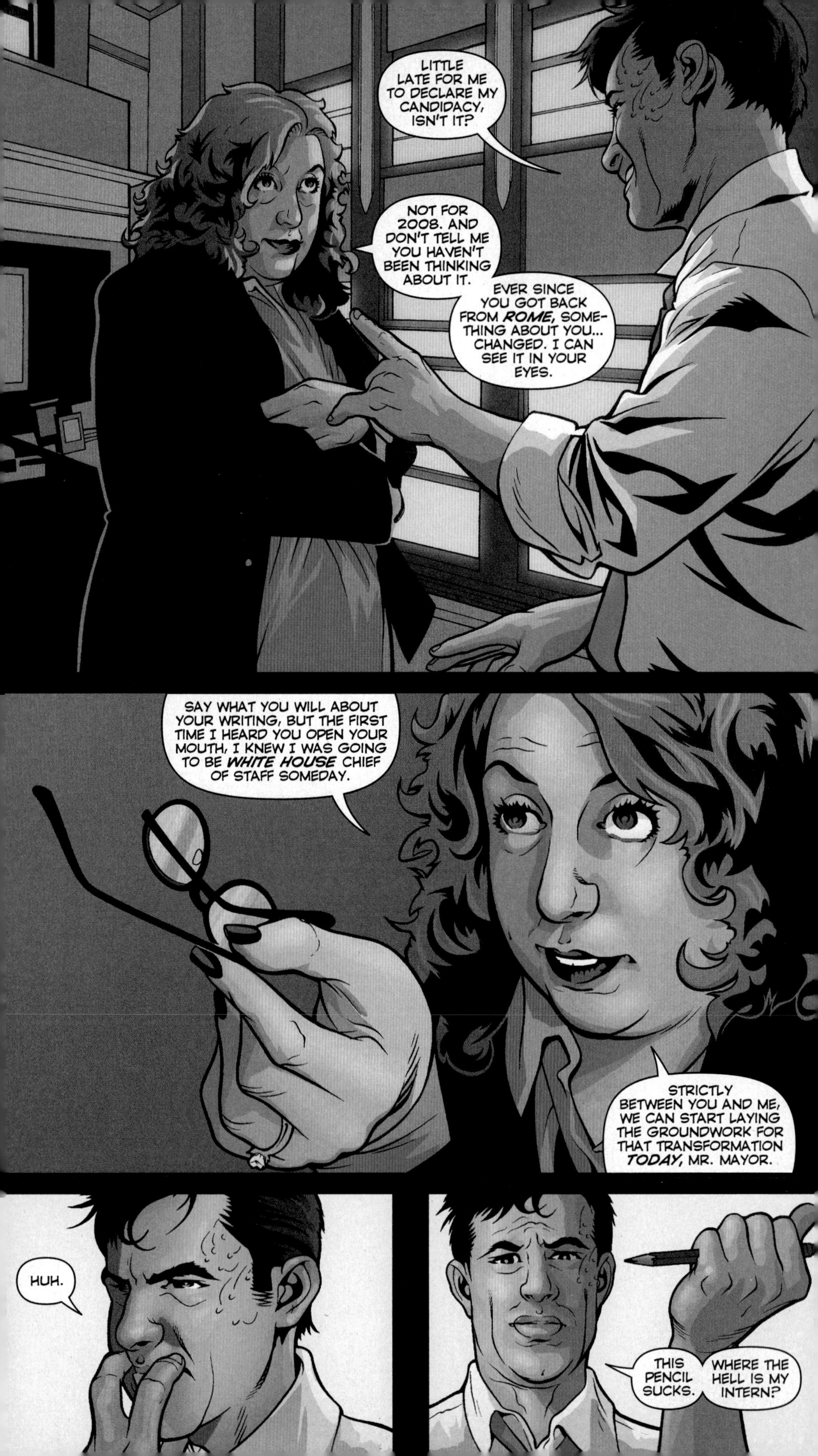
LITTLE LATE FOR ME TO DECLARE MY CANDIDACY, ISN'T IT?
NOT FOR 2008. AND DON'T TELL ME YOU HAVEN'T BEEN THINKING ABOUT IT.
EVER SINCE YOU GOT BACK FROM ROME, SOMETHING ABOUT YOU... CHANGED. I CAN SEE IT IN YOUR EYES.
SAY WHAT YOU WILL ABOUT YOUR WRITING, BUT THE FIRST TIME I HEARD YOU OPEN YOUR MOUTH, I KNEW I WAS GOING TO BE WHITE HOUSE CHIEF OF STAFF SOMEDAY.
STRICTLY BETWEEN YOU AND ME, WE CAN START LAYING THE GROUNDWORK FOR THAT TRANSFORMATION TODAY, MR. MAYOR.
HUH.
THIS PENCIL SUCKS.
WHERE THE HELL IS MY INTERN?

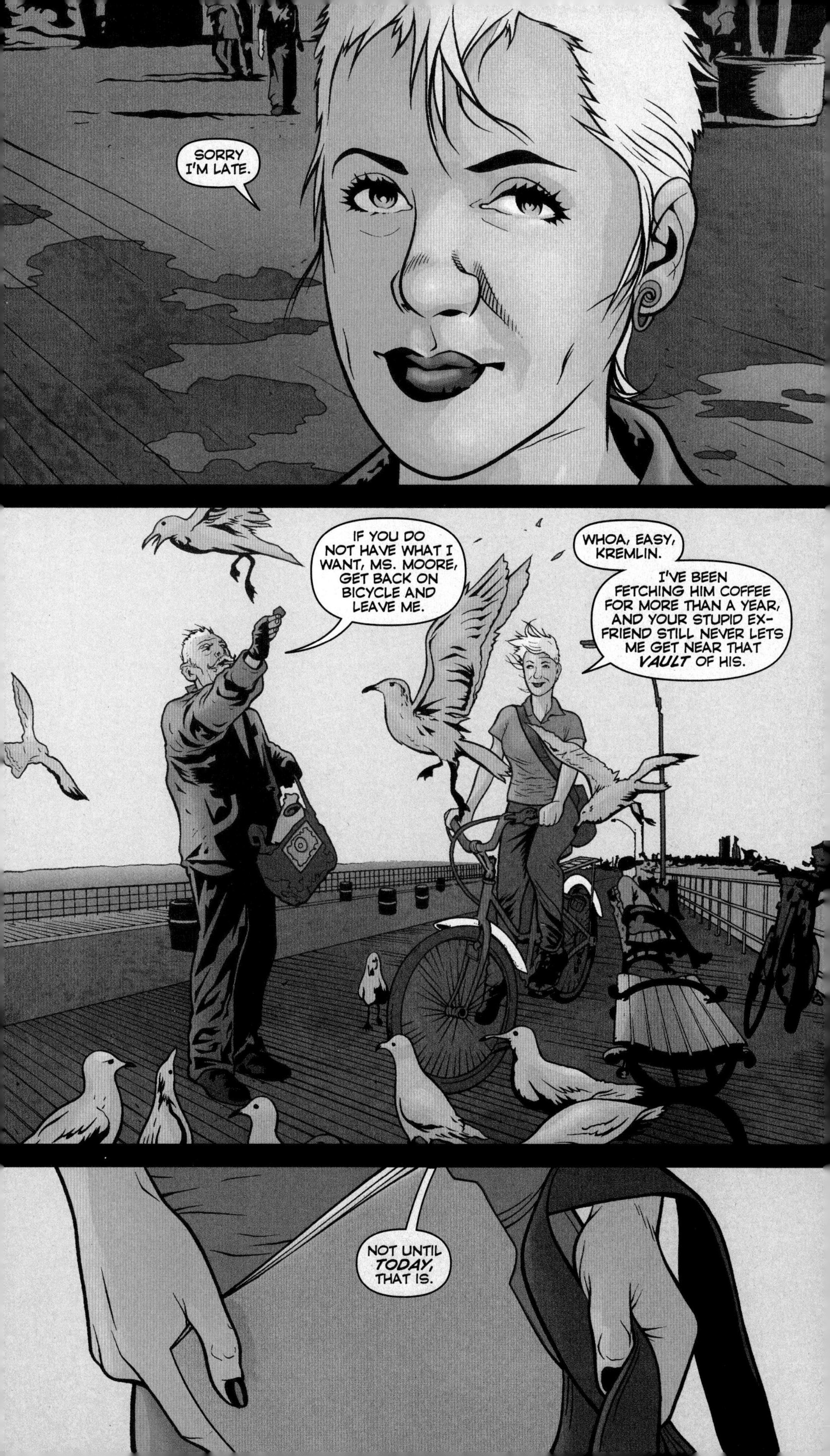
SORRY I'M LATE.
IF YOU DO NOT HAVE WHAT I WANT, MS. MOORE, GET BACK ON BICYCLE AND LEAVE ME.
WHOA, EASY, KREMLIN.
I'VE BEEN FETCHING HIM COFFEE FOR MORE THAN A YEAR, AND YOUR STUPID EX-FRIEND STILL NEVER LETS ME GET NEAR THAT *VAULT* OF HIS.
NOT UNTIL *TODAY*, THAT IS.

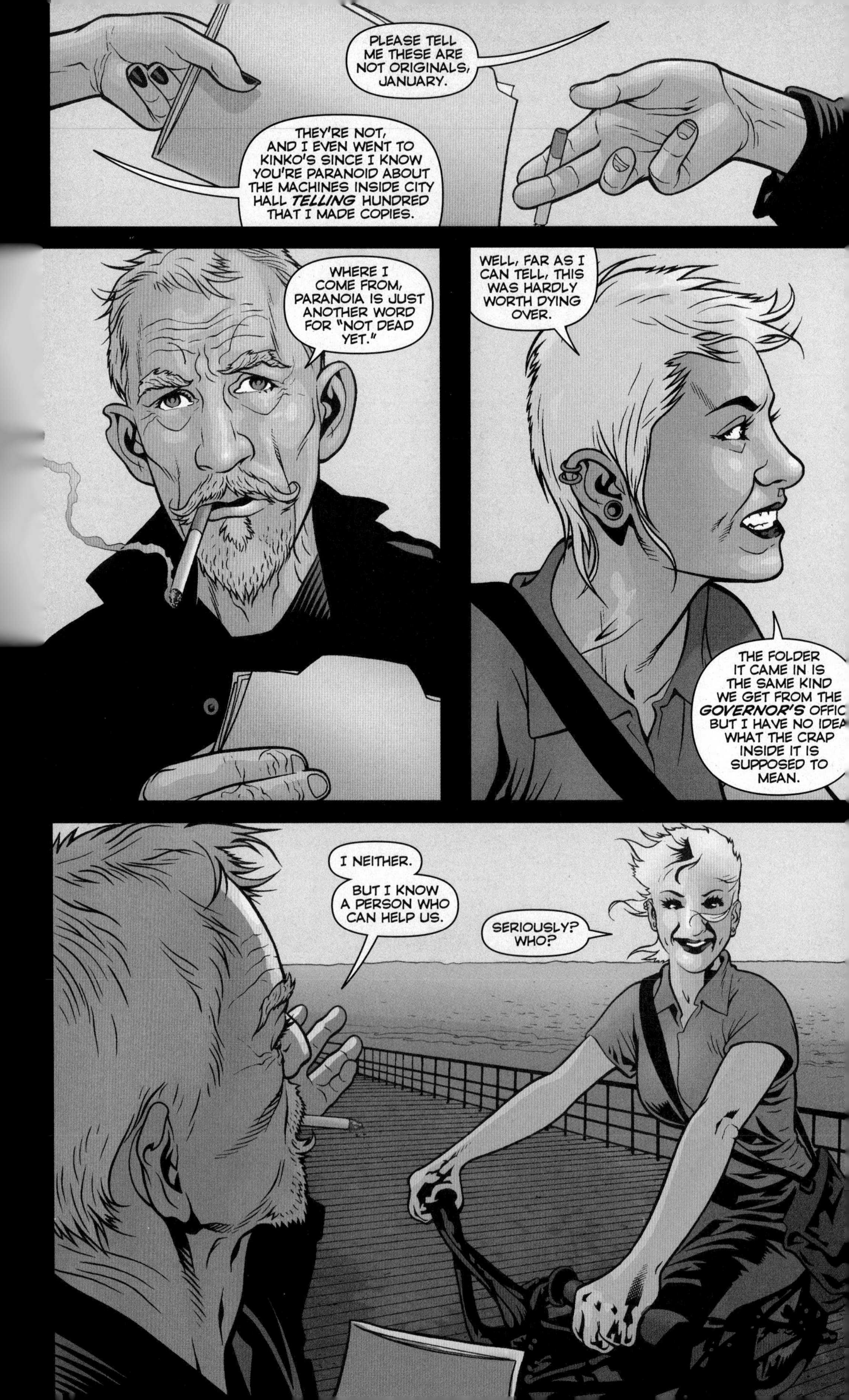
PLEASE TELL ME THESE ARE NOT ORIGINALS, JANUARY.
THEY'RE NOT, AND I EVEN WENT TO KINKO'S SINCE I KNOW YOU'RE PARANOID ABOUT THE MACHINES INSIDE CITY HALL *TELLING* HUNDRED THAT I MADE COPIES.
WHERE I COME FROM, PARANOIA IS JUST ANOTHER WORD FOR "NOT DEAD YET."
WELL, FAR AS I CAN TELL, THIS WAS HARDLY WORTH DYING OVER.
THE FOLDER IT CAME IN IS THE SAME KIND WE GET FROM THE *GOVERNOR'S* OFFIC BUT I HAVE NO IDEA WHAT THE CRAP INSIDE IT IS SUPPOSED TO MEAN.
I NEITHER.
BUT I KNOW A PERSON WHO CAN HELP US.
SERIOUSLY? WHO?

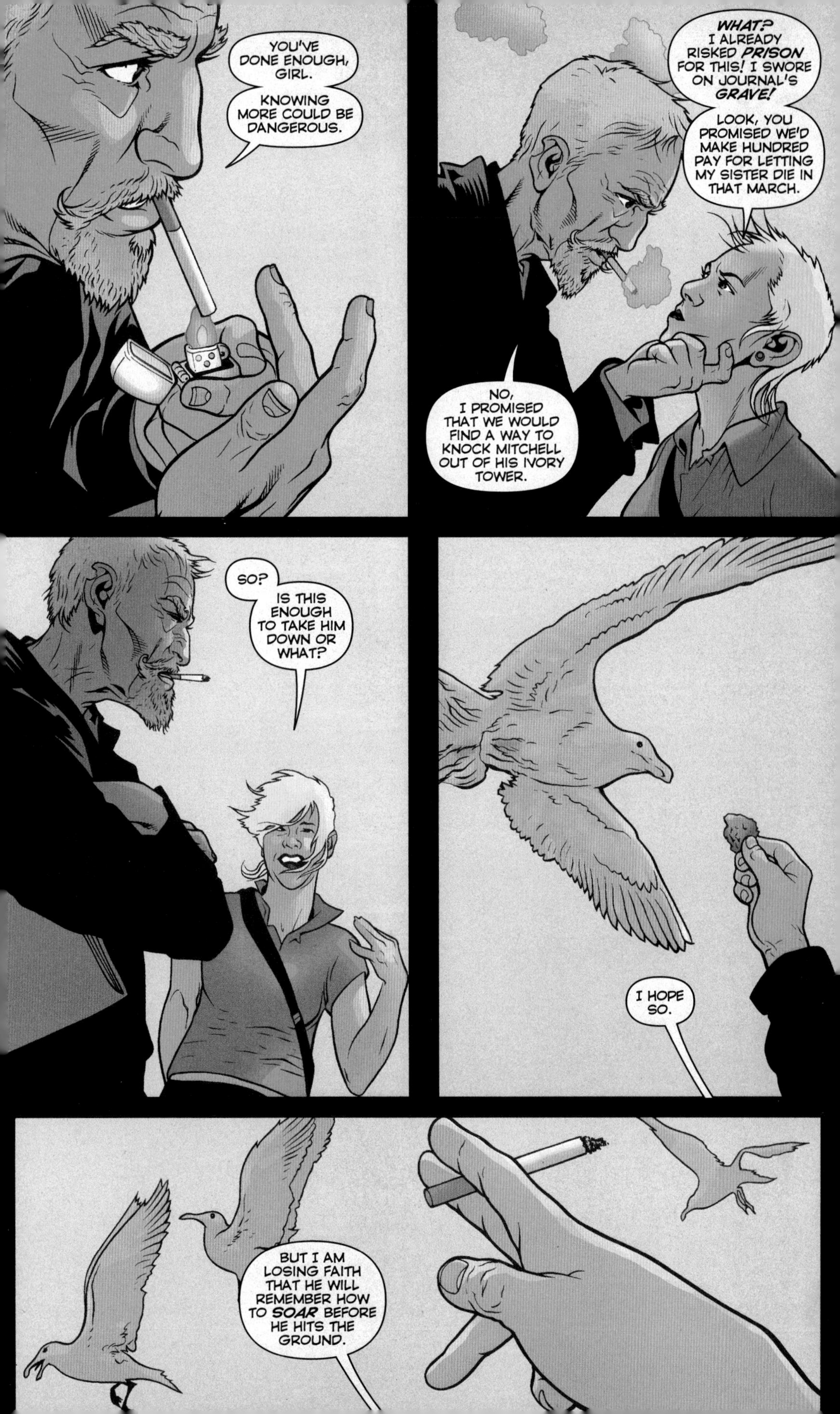
YOU'VE DONE ENOUGH, GIRL.
KNOWING MORE COULD BE DANGEROUS.
WHAT? I ALREADY RISKED PRISON FOR THIS! I SWORE ON JOURNAL'S GRAVE!
LOOK, YOU PROMISED WE'D MAKE HUNDRED PAY FOR LETTING MY SISTER DIE IN THAT MARCH.
NO, I PROMISED THAT WE WOULD FIND A WAY TO KNOCK MITCHELL OUT OF HIS IVORY TOWER.
SO?
IS THIS ENOUGH TO TAKE HIM DOWN OR WHAT?
I HOPE SO.
BUT I AM LOSING FAITH THAT HE WILL REMEMBER HOW TO SOAR BEFORE HE HITS THE GROUND.

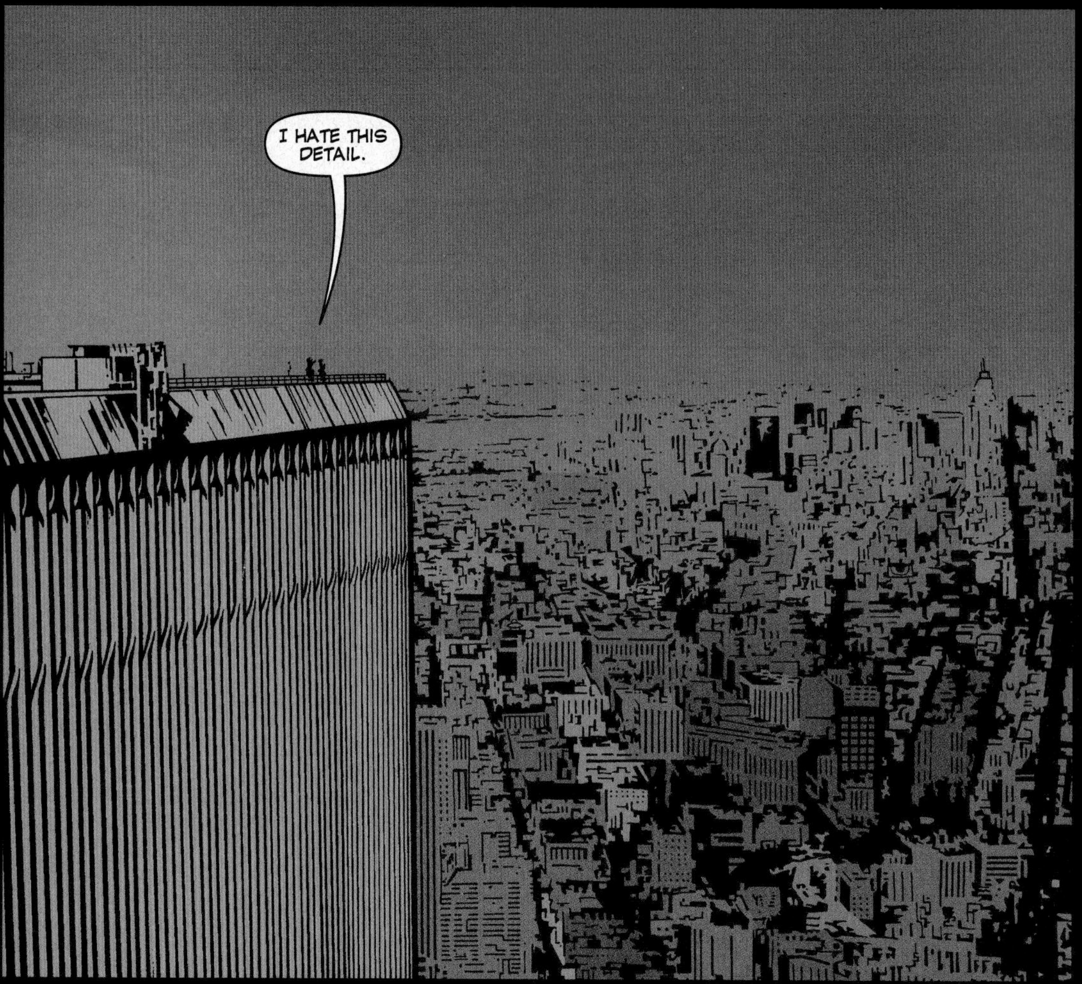
I HATE THIS DETAIL.

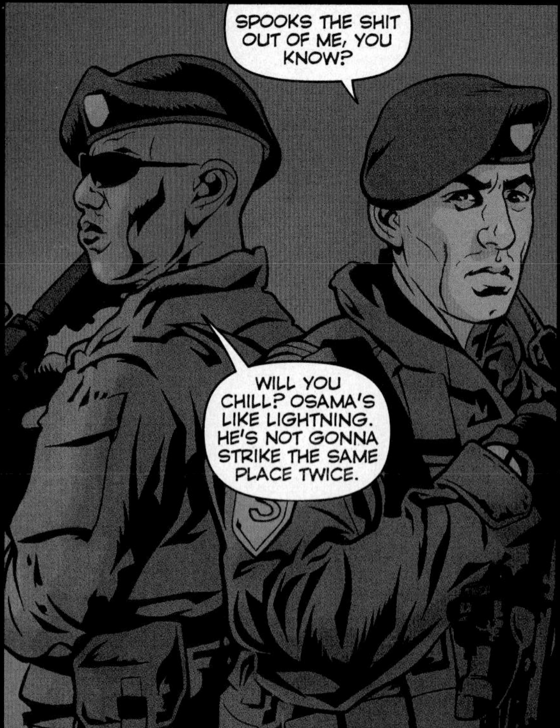
SPOOKS THE SHIT OUT OF ME, YOU KNOW?
WILL YOU CHILL? OSAMA'S LIKE LIGHTNING. HE'S NOT GONNA STRIKE THE SAME PLACE TWICE.

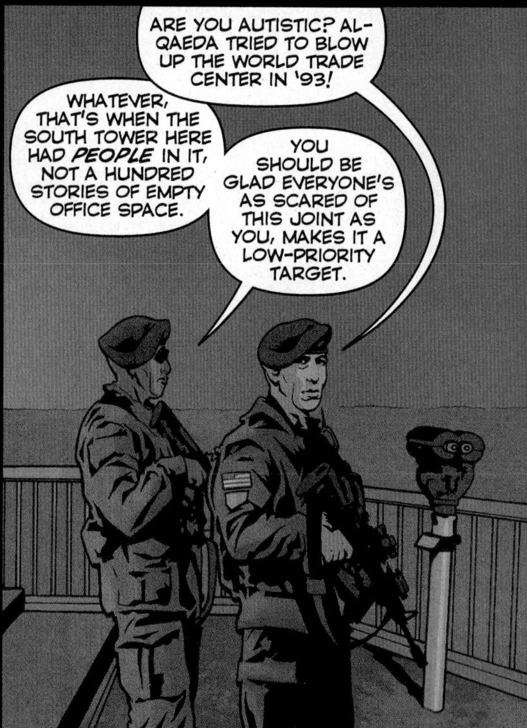
ARE YOU AUTISTIC? AL-QAEDA TRIED TO BLOW UP THE WORLD TRADE CENTER IN '93!
WHATEVER, THAT'S WHEN THE SOUTH TOWER HERE HAD *PEOPLE* IN IT, NOT A HUNDRED STORIES OF EMPTY OFFICE SPACE.
YOU SHOULD BE GLAD EVERYONE'S AS SCARED OF THIS JOINT AS YOU, MAKES IT A LOW-PRIORITY TARGET.

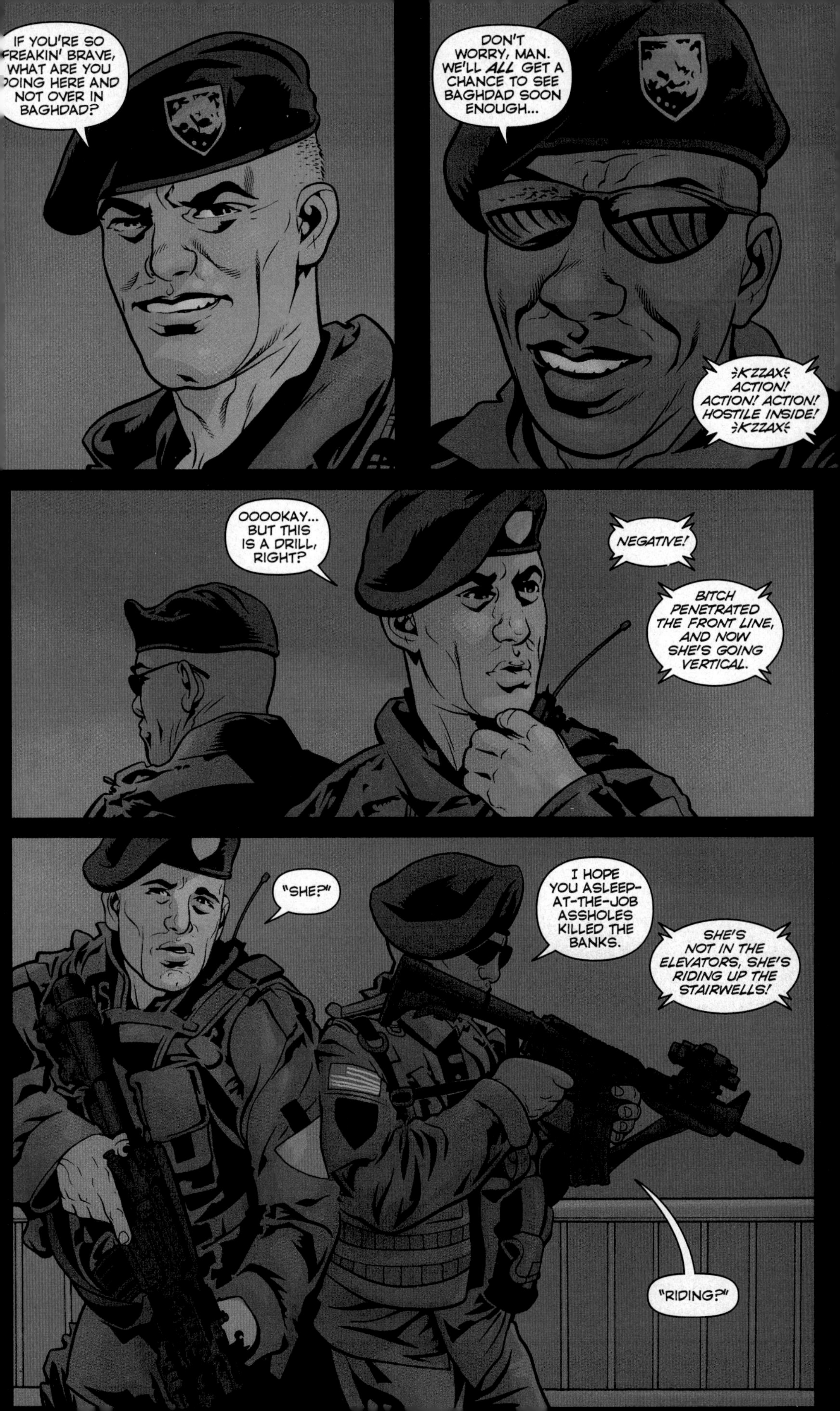
IF YOU'RE SO FREAKIN' BRAVE, WHAT ARE YOU DOING HERE AND NOT OVER IN BAGHDAD?
DON'T WORRY, MAN. WE'LL ALL GET A CHANCE TO SEE BAGHDAD SOON ENOUGH...
KZZAX ACTION! ACTION! ACTION! HOSTILE INSIDE! KZZAX
OOOOKAY... BUT THIS IS A DRILL, RIGHT?
NEGATIVE!
BITCH PENETRATED THE FRONT LINE, AND NOW SHE'S GOING VERTICAL.
"SHE?"
I HOPE YOU ASLEEP-AT-THE-JOB ASSHOLES KILLED THE BANKS.
SHE'S NOT IN THE ELEVATORS, SHE'S RIDING UP THE STAIRWELLS!
"RIDING?"

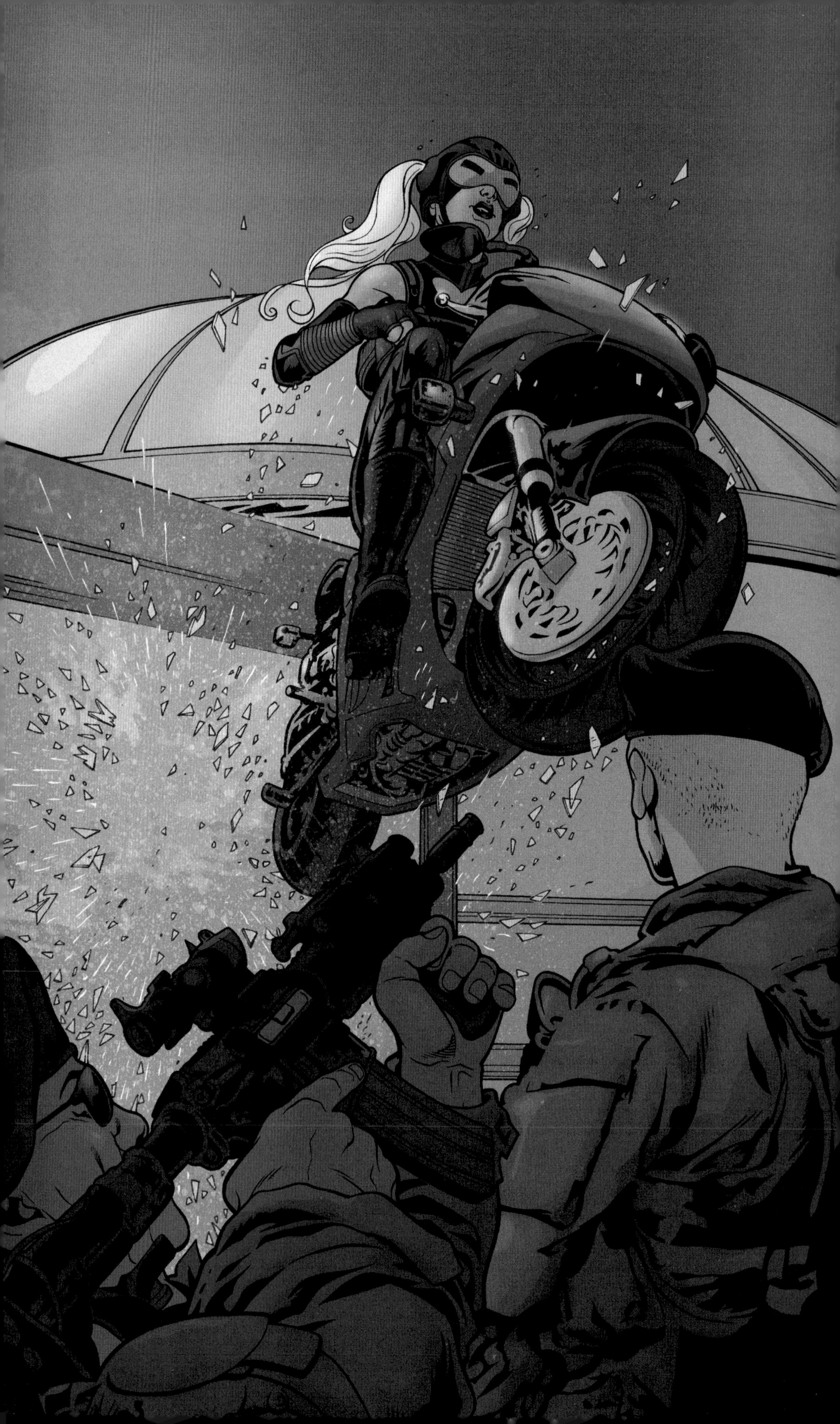

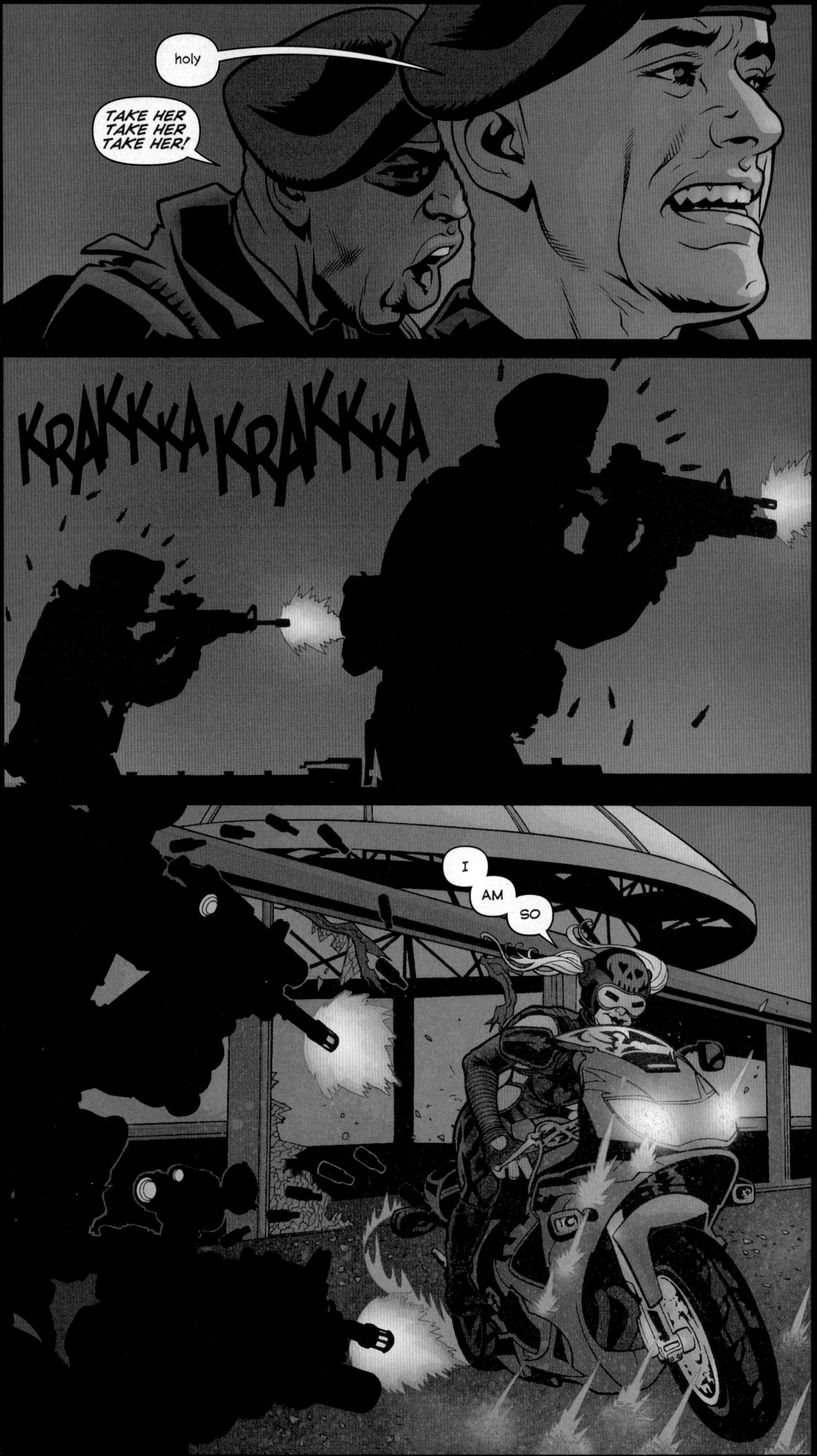
holy
TAKE HER TAKE HER TAKE HER!
KRAKKKA KRAKKKA
I
AM
SO

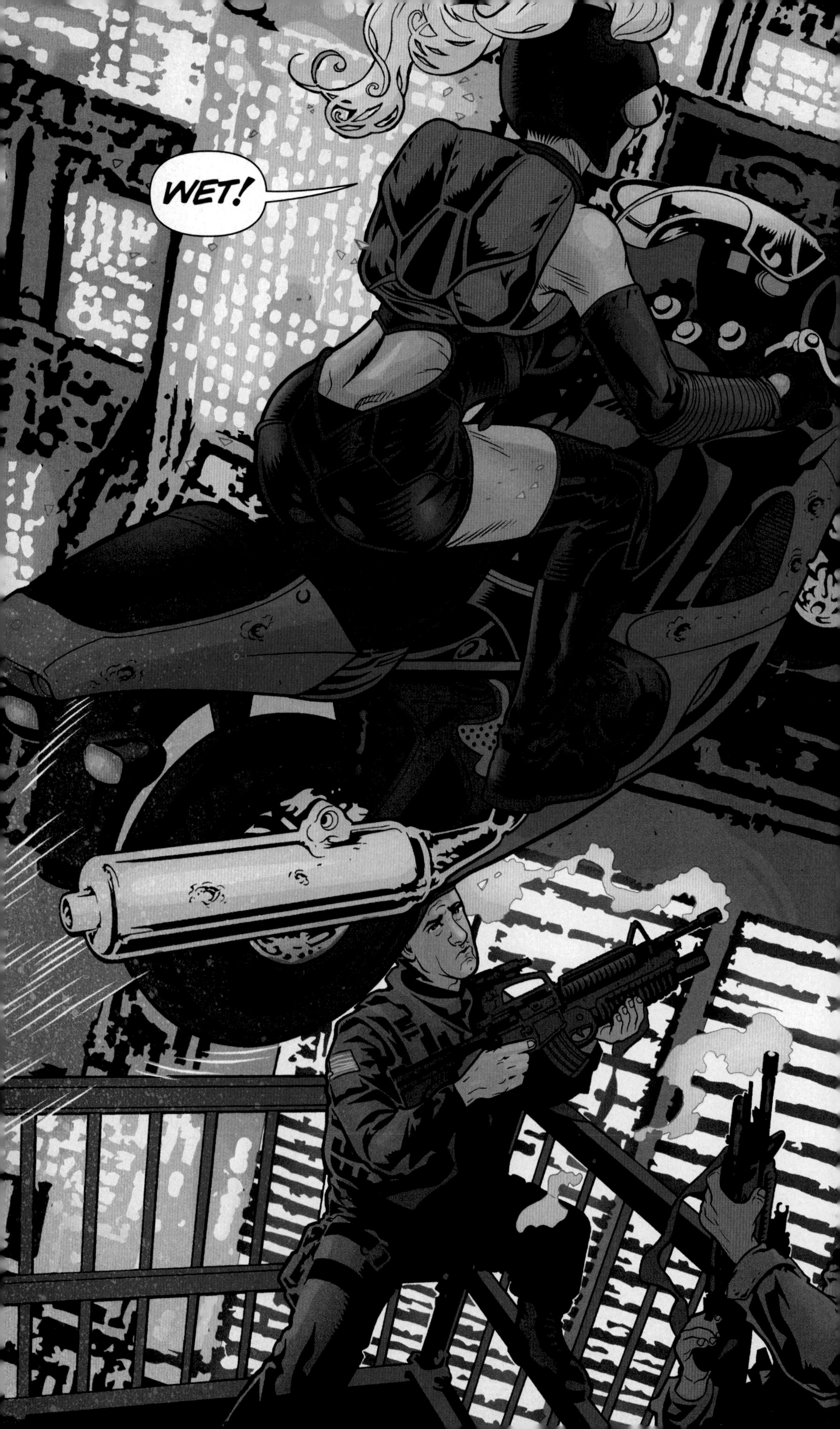
WET!

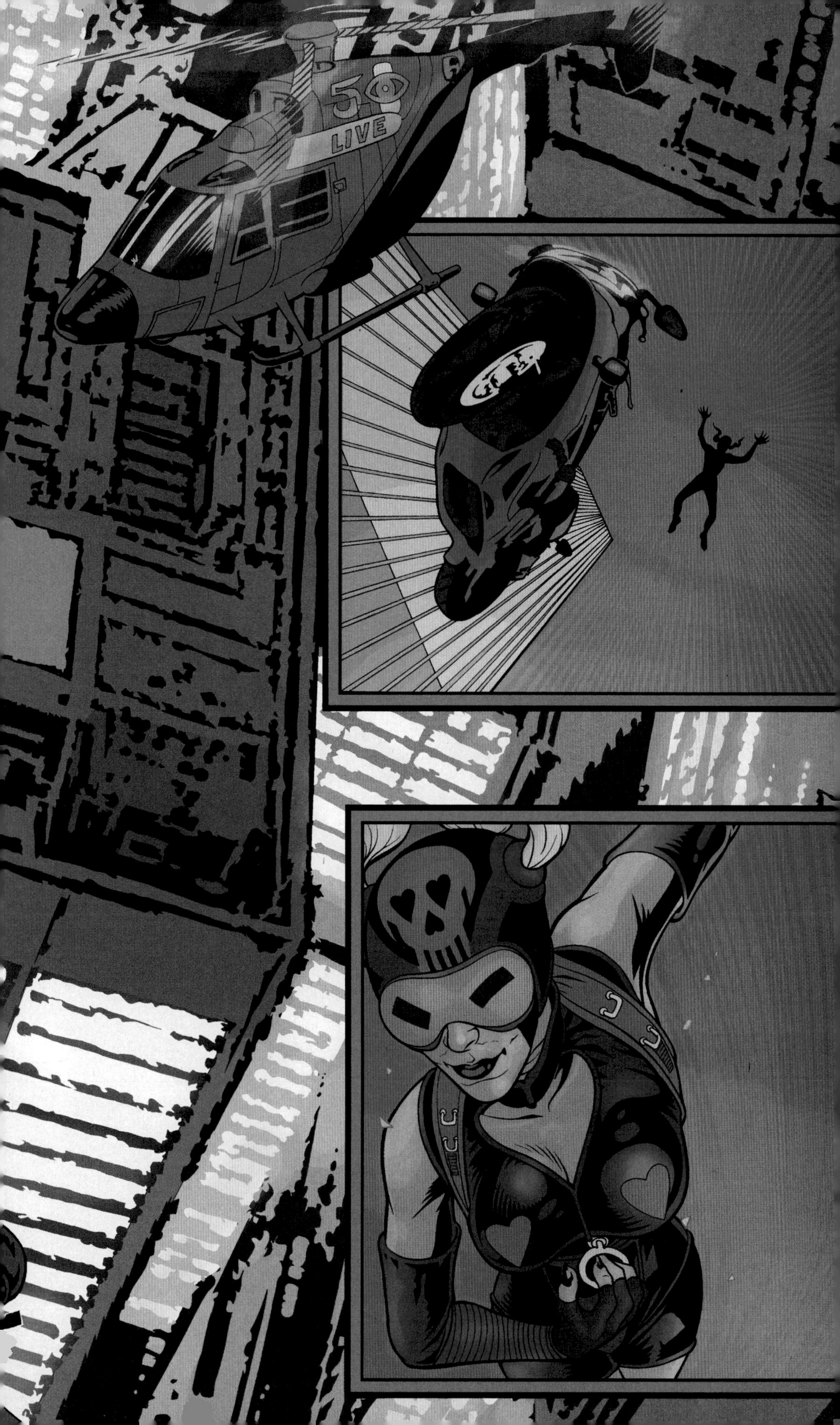
LIVE

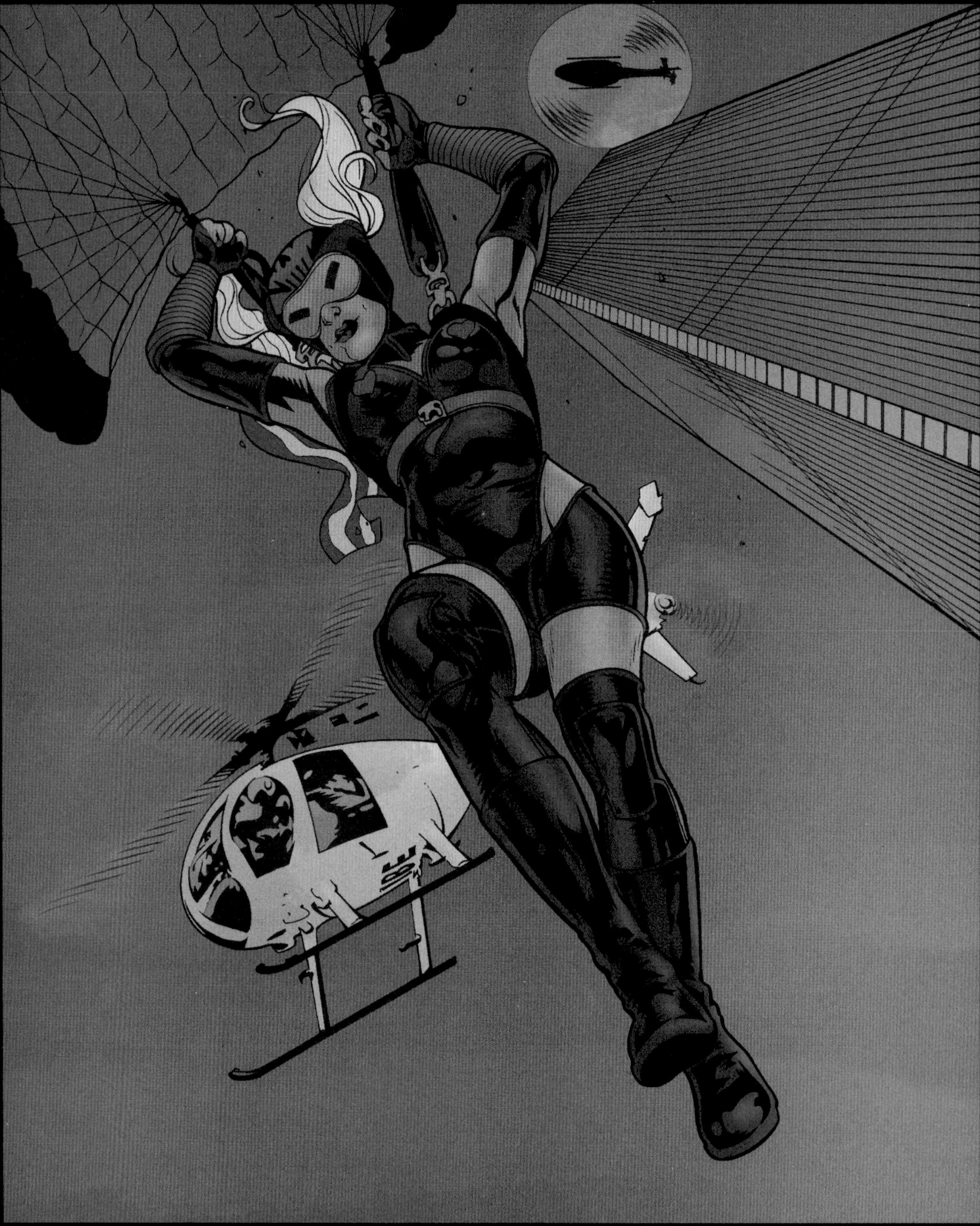

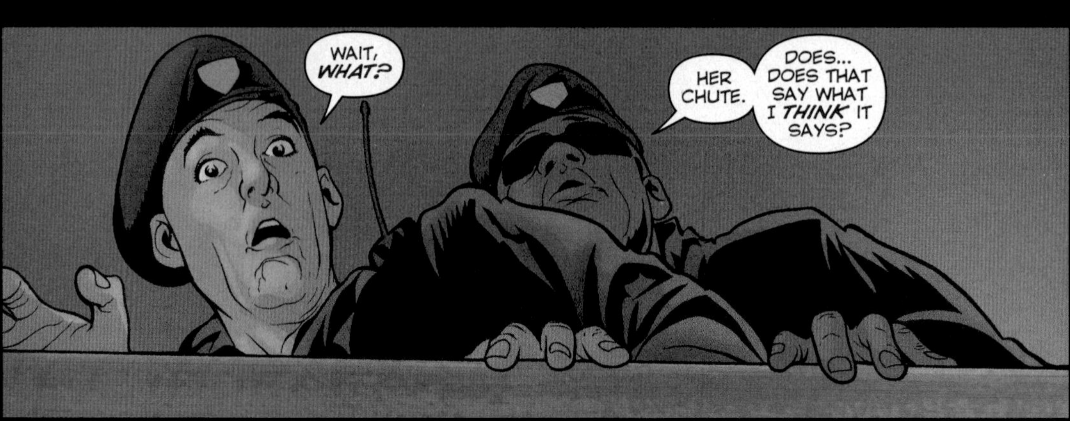
WAIT, *WHAT?*
HER CHUTE.
DOES... DOES THAT SAY WHAT I *THINK* IT SAYS?

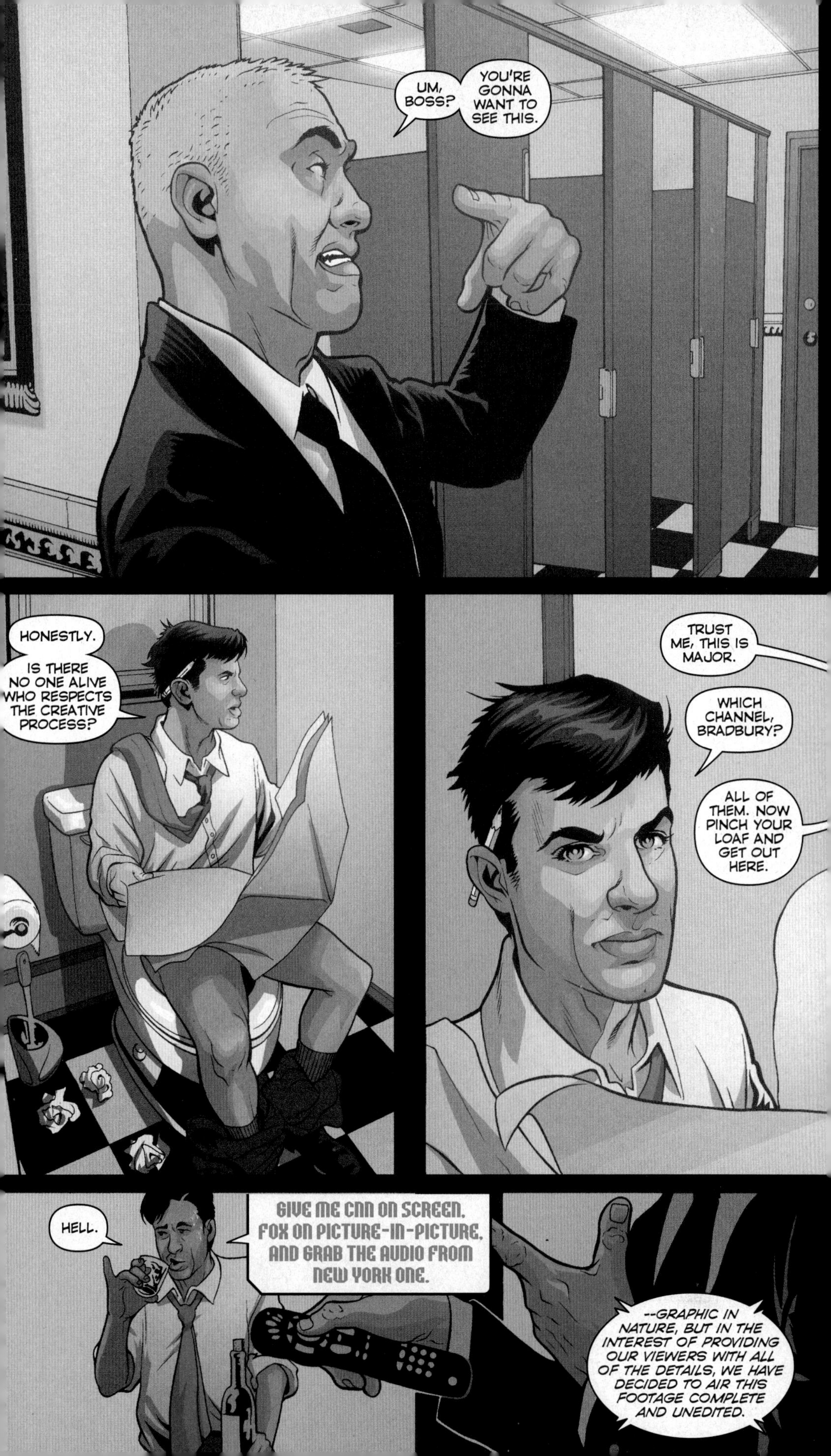
UM, BOSS?
YOU'RE GONNA WANT TO SEE THIS.
HONESTLY.
IS THERE NO ONE ALIVE WHO RESPECTS THE CREATIVE PROCESS?
TRUST ME, THIS IS MAJOR.
WHICH CHANNEL, BRADBURY?
ALL OF THEM. NOW PINCH YOUR LOAF AND GET OUT HERE.
HELL.
GIVE ME CNN ON SCREEN, FOX ON PICTURE-IN-PICTURE, AND GRAB THE AUDIO FROM NEW YORK ONE.
--GRAPHIC IN NATURE, BUT IN THE INTEREST OF PROVIDING OUR VIEWERS WITH ALL OF THE DETAILS, WE HAVE DECIDED TO AIR THIS FOOTAGE COMPLETE AND UNEDITED.

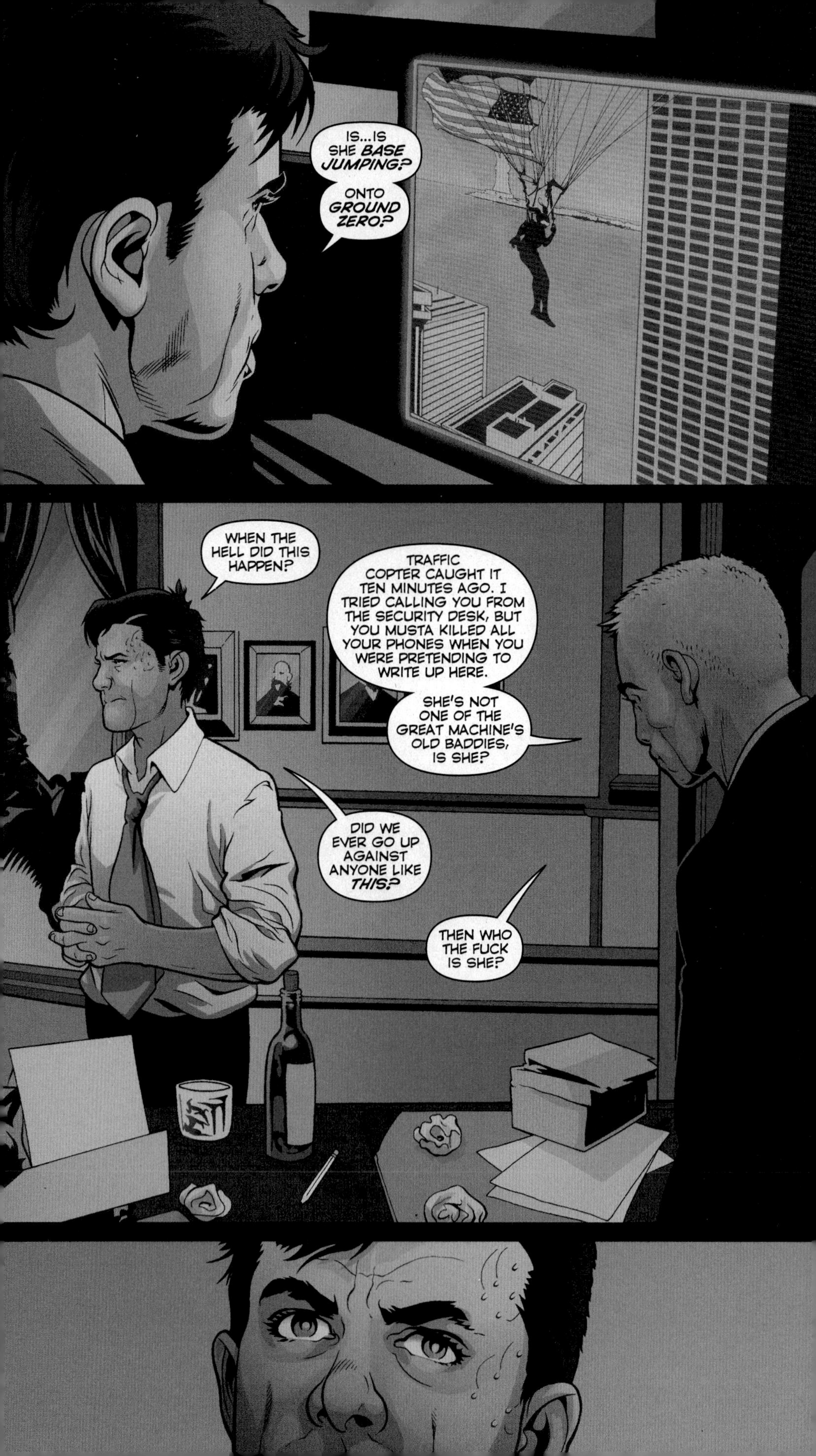

IS...IS SHE *BASE JUMPING?*
ONTO *GROUND ZERO?*
WHEN THE HELL DID THIS HAPPEN?
TRAFFIC COPTER CAUGHT IT TEN MINUTES AGO. I TRIED CALLING YOU FROM THE SECURITY DESK, BUT YOU MUSTA KILLED ALL YOUR PHONES WHEN YOU WERE PRETENDING TO WRITE UP HERE.
SHE'S NOT ONE OF THE GREAT MACHINE'S OLD BADDIES, IS SHE?
DID WE EVER GO UP AGAINST ANYONE LIKE *THIS?*
THEN WHO THE FUCK IS SHE?

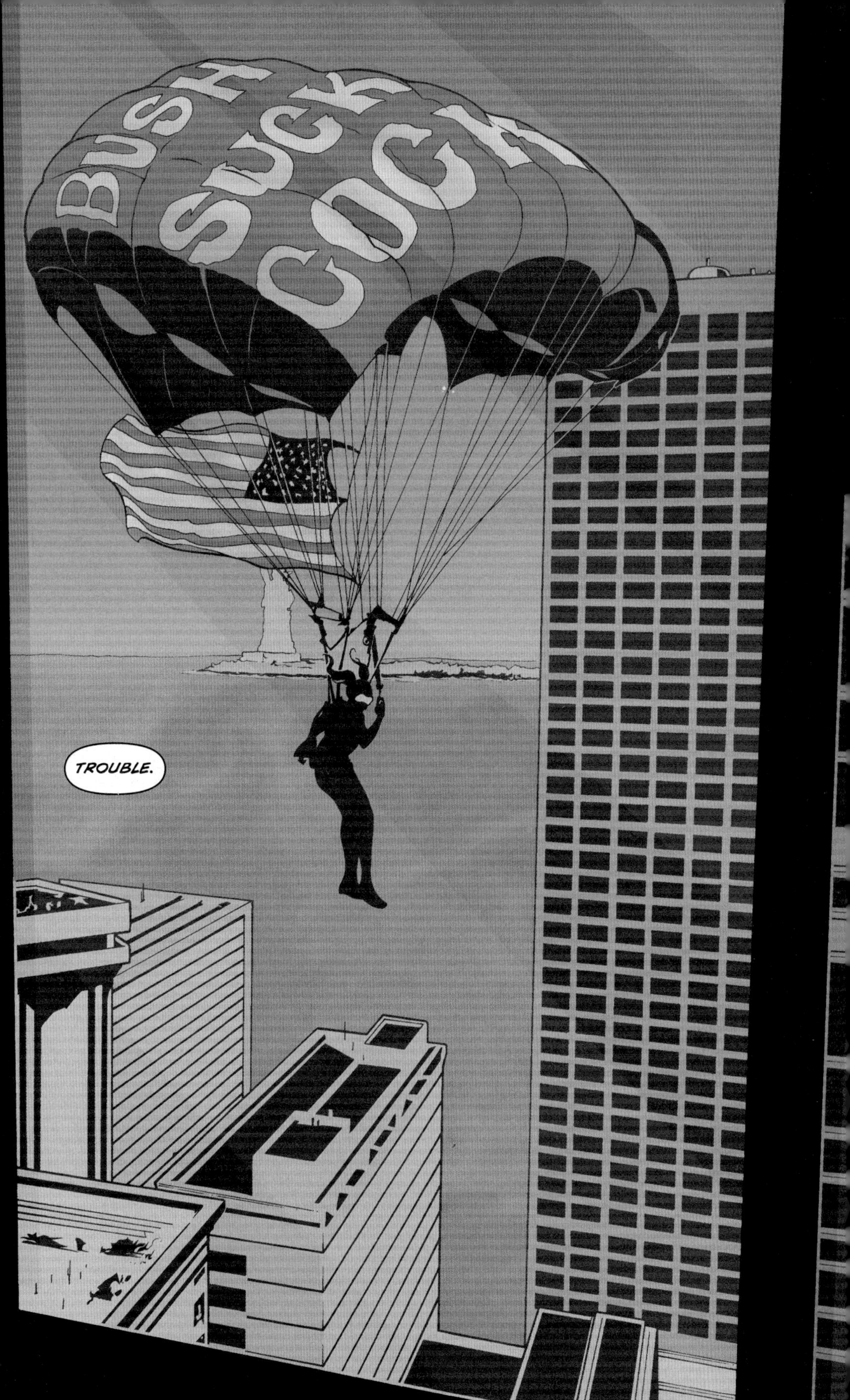
BUSH SUCK COCK
TROUBLE.

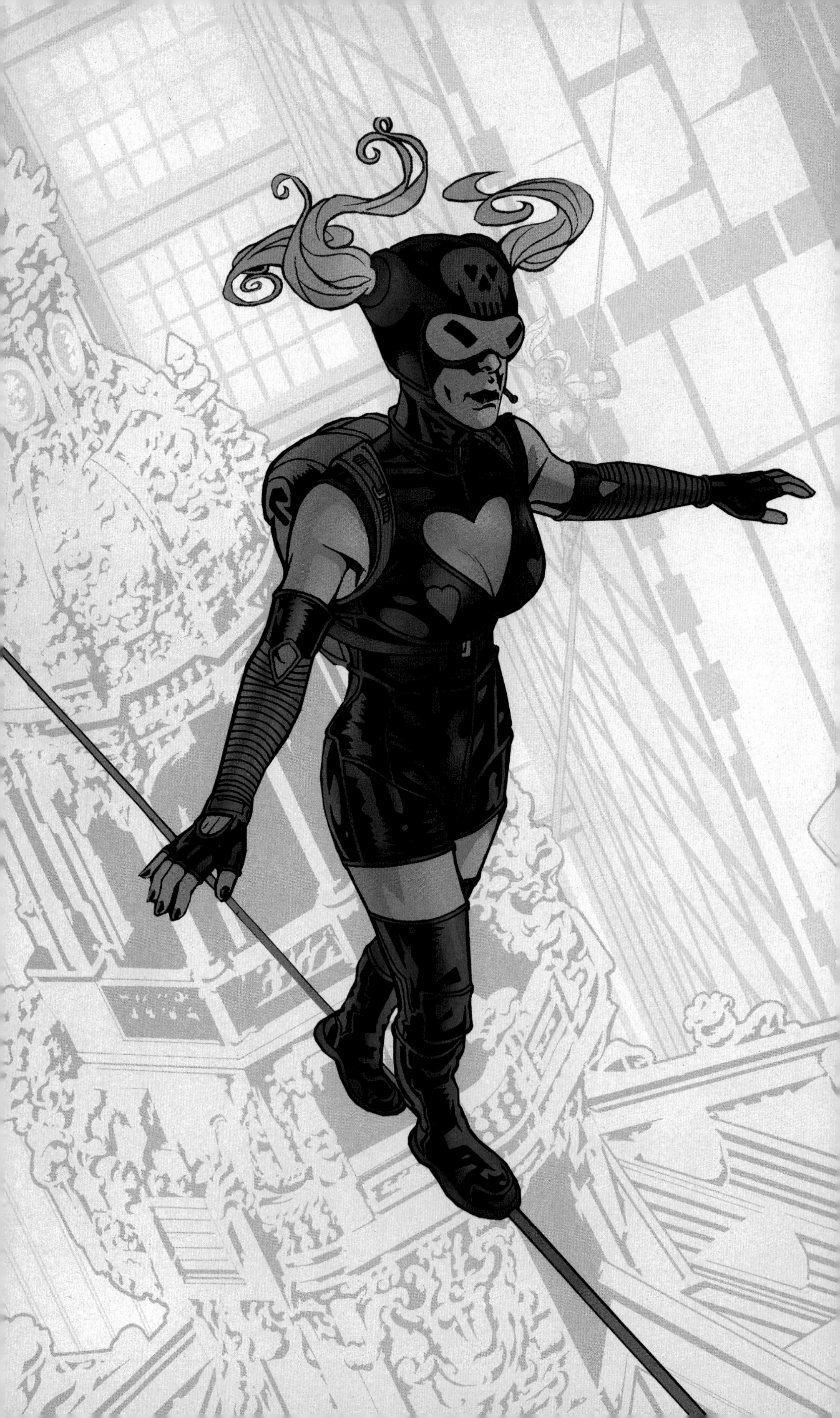

Dirty Tricks
part 2

Chapter 3

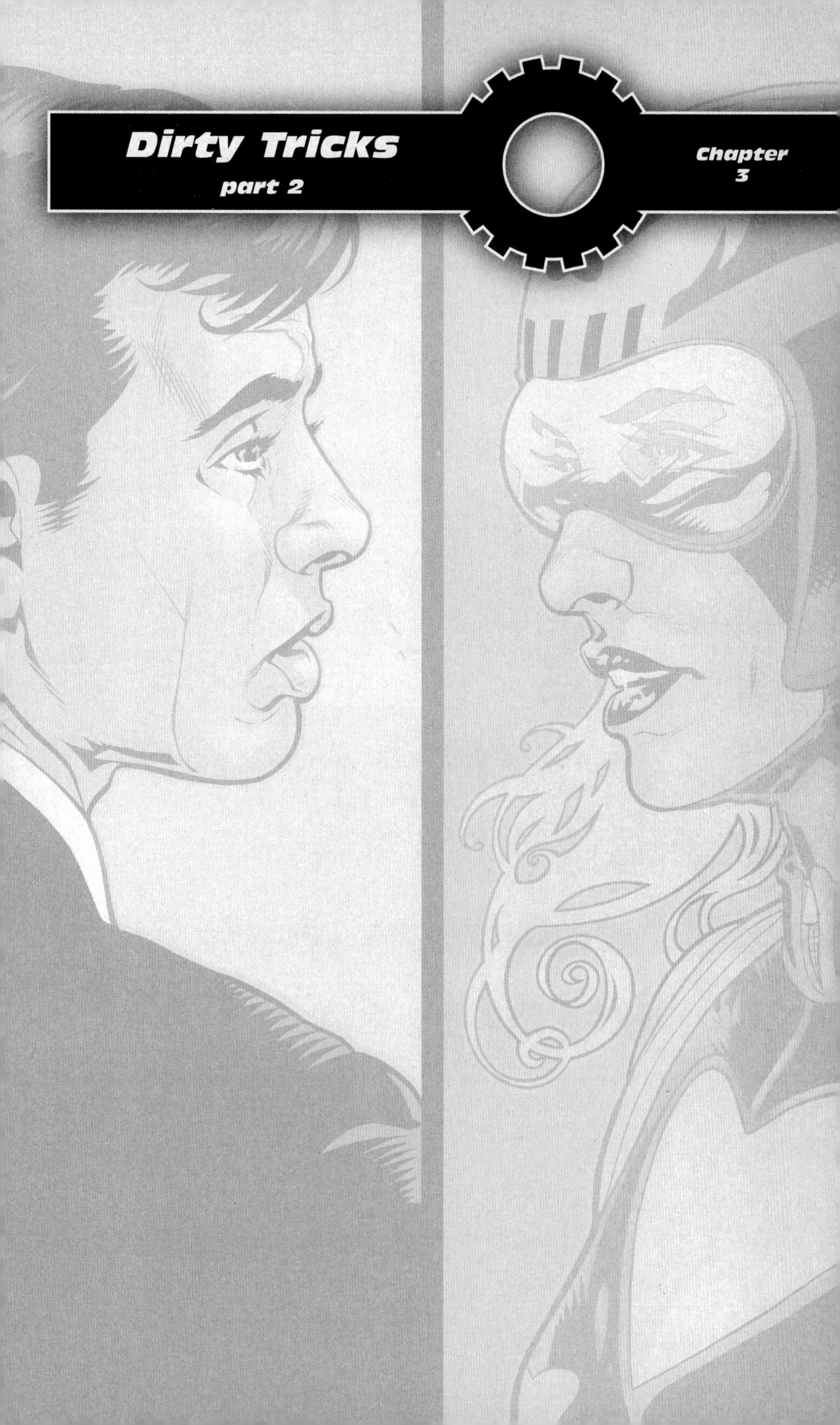

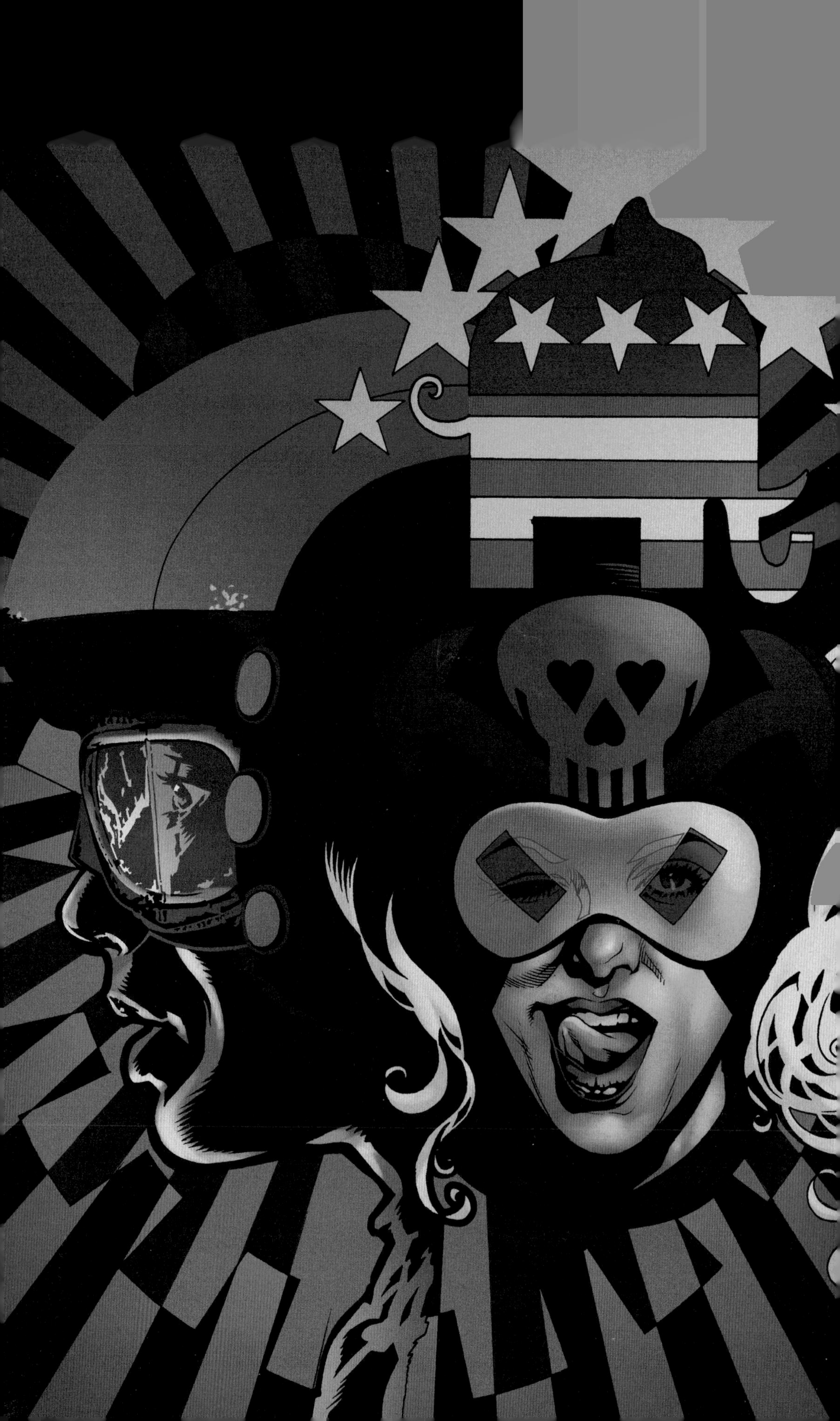

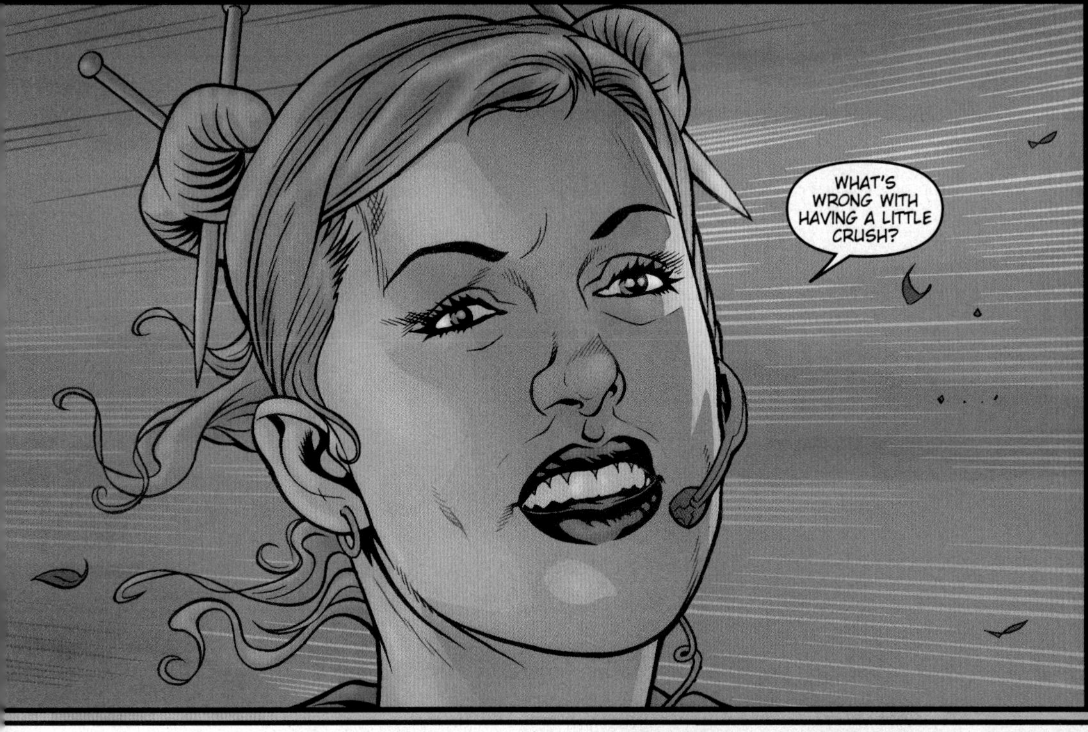
WHAT'S WRONG WITH HAVING A LITTLE CRUSH?

SATURDAY, JUNE 2, 2001

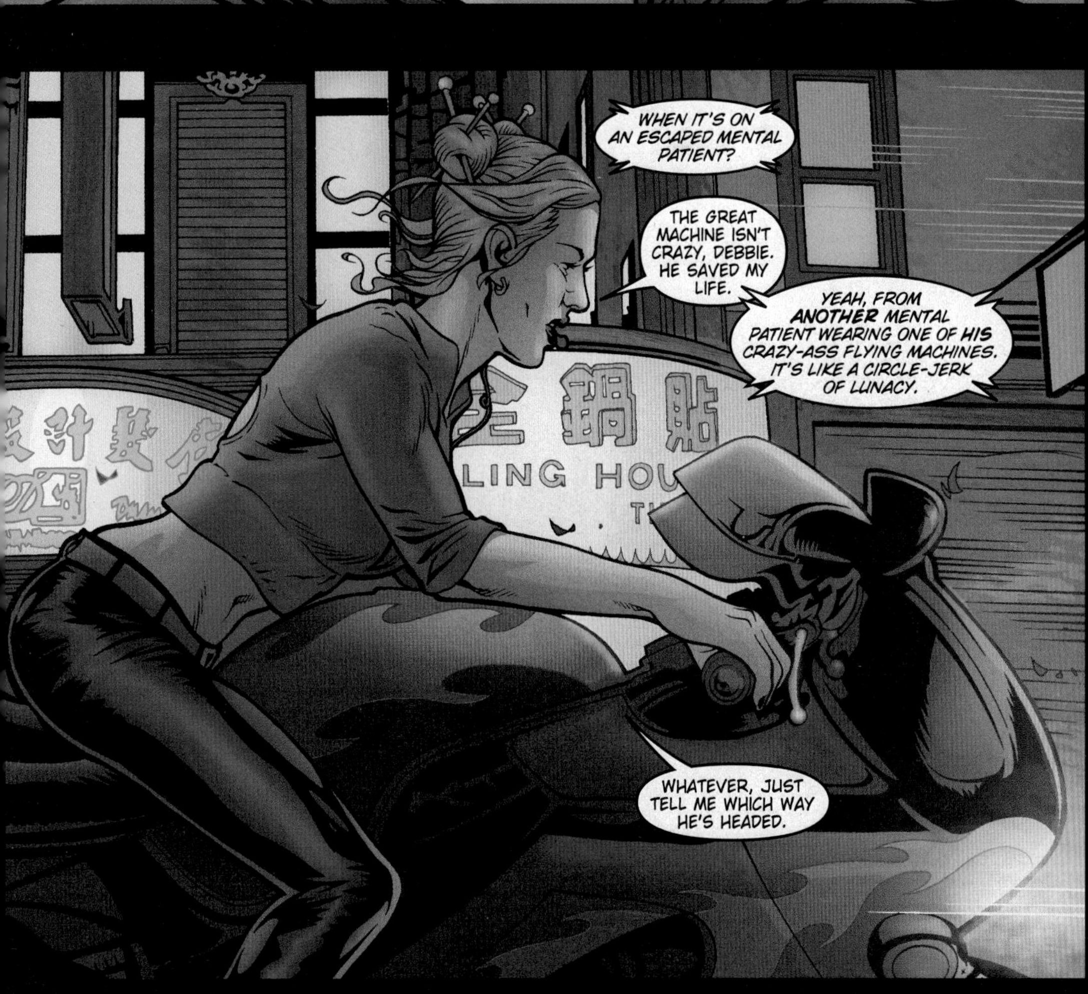
WHEN IT'S ON AN ESCAPED MENTAL PATIENT?
THE GREAT MACHINE ISN'T CRAZY, DEBBIE. HE SAVED MY LIFE.
YEAH, FROM ANOTHER MENTAL PATIENT WEARING ONE OF HIS CRAZY-ASS FLYING MACHINES. IT'S LIKE A CIRCLE-JERK OF LUNACY.
WHATEVER, JUST TELL ME WHICH WAY HE'S HEADED.

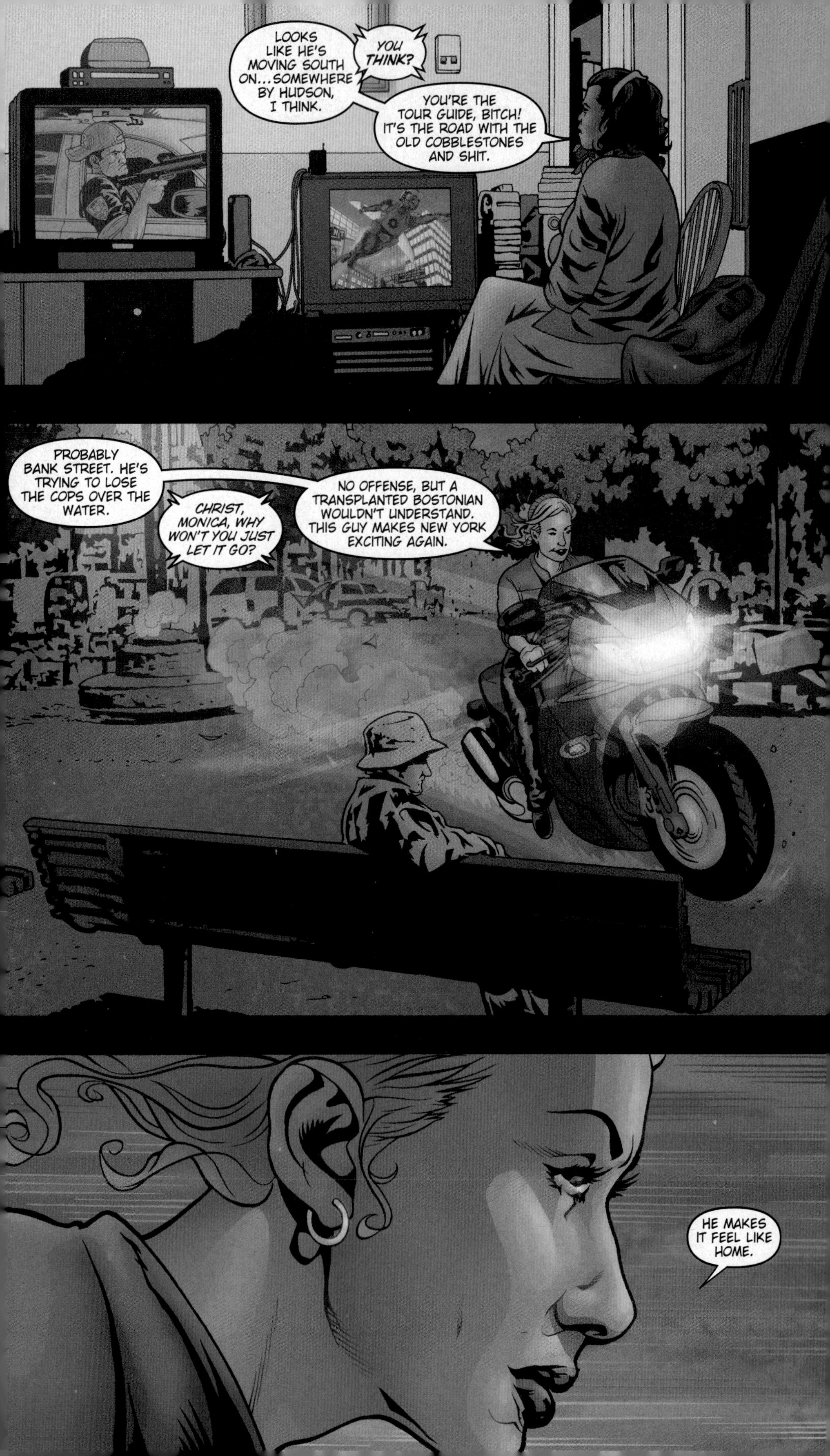
LOOKS LIKE HE'S MOVING SOUTH ON... SOMEWHERE BY HUDSON, I THINK.
YOU THINK?
YOU'RE THE TOUR GUIDE, BITCH! IT'S THE ROAD WITH THE OLD COBBLESTONES AND SHIT.
PROBABLY BANK STREET. HE'S TRYING TO LOSE THE COPS OVER THE WATER.
CHRIST, MONICA, WHY WON'T YOU JUST LET IT GO?
NO OFFENSE, BUT A TRANSPLANTED BOSTONIAN WOULDN'T UNDERSTAND. THIS GUY MAKES NEW YORK EXCITING AGAIN.
HE MAKES IT FEEL LIKE HOME.

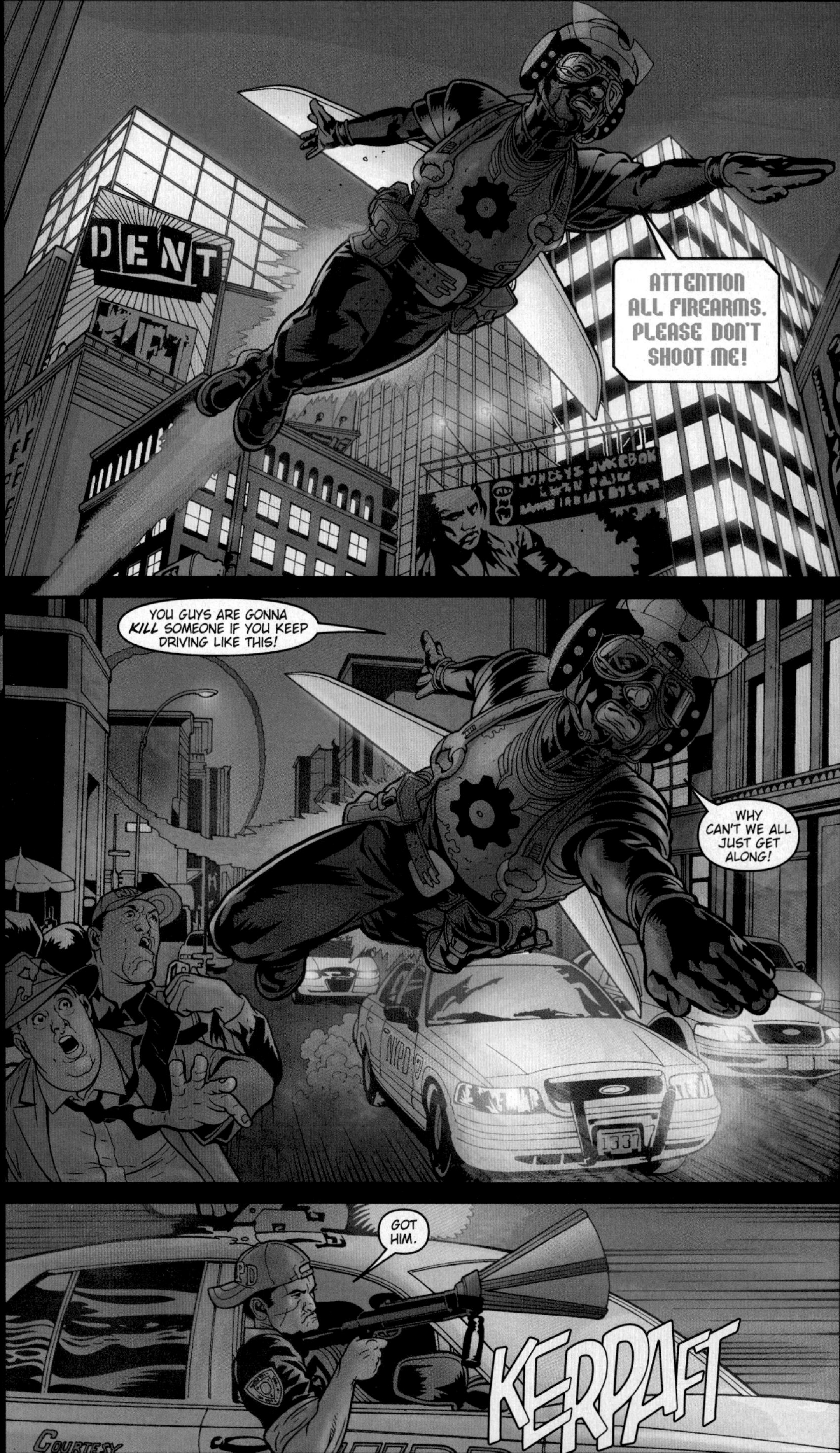
DENT
ATTENTION ALL FIREARMS. PLEASE DON'T SHOOT ME!
YOU GUYS ARE GONNA KILL SOMEONE IF YOU KEEP DRIVING LIKE THIS!
WHY CAN'T WE ALL JUST GET ALONG!
NYPD
GOT HIM.
KERPAFT
COURTESY

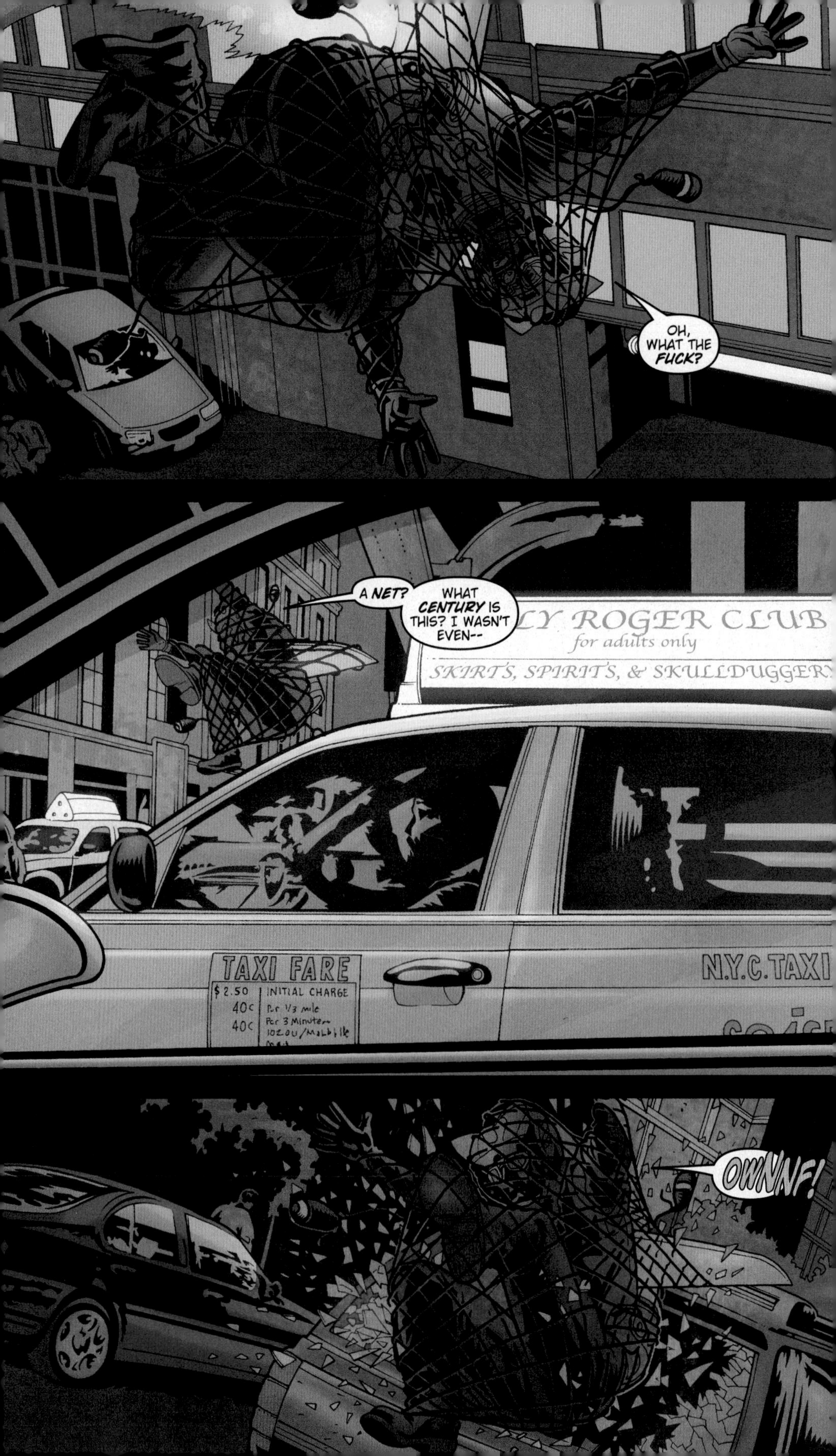
OH, WHAT THE FUCK?
A NET?
WHAT CENTURY IS THIS? I WASN'T EVEN--
LY ROGER CLUB
for adults only
SKIRTS, SPIRITS, & SKULLDUGGER
TAXI FARE
$2.50 INITIAL CHARGE
40¢ Per 1/3 mile
40¢ Per 3 Minutes
N.Y.C. TAXI
OWNNF!

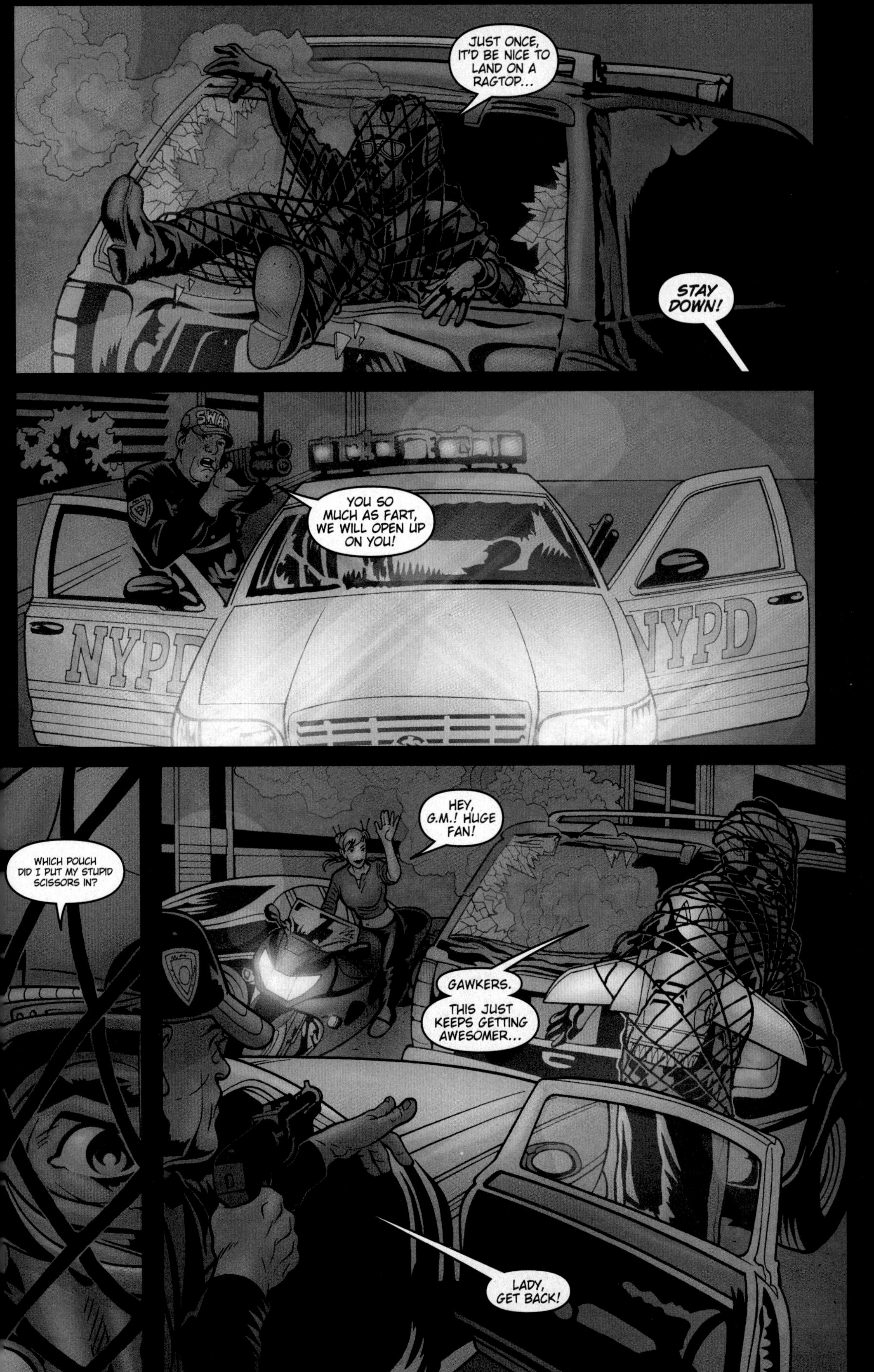
JUST ONCE, IT'D BE NICE TO LAND ON A RAGTOP...
STAY DOWN!
YOU SO MUCH AS FART, WE WILL OPEN UP ON YOU!
NYPD
NYPD
HEY, G.M.! HUGE FAN!
WHICH POUCH DID I PUT MY STUPID SCISSORS IN?
GAWKERS.
THIS JUST KEEPS GETTING AWESOMER...
LADY, GET BACK!

YOU GET BACK! HE ISN'T HURTING ANYONE!

LOOK, SISTER, DON'T MAKE ME CUFF YOU FOR INTERFERIN' WITH--

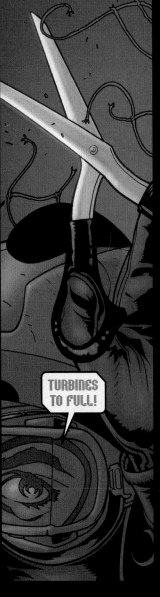

TURBINES TO FULL!

FOR THE LAST TIME, I'M NOT A VILLAIN, I'M A MOTHERFUCKING GOOD GUY!

YOU'RE WELCOME...

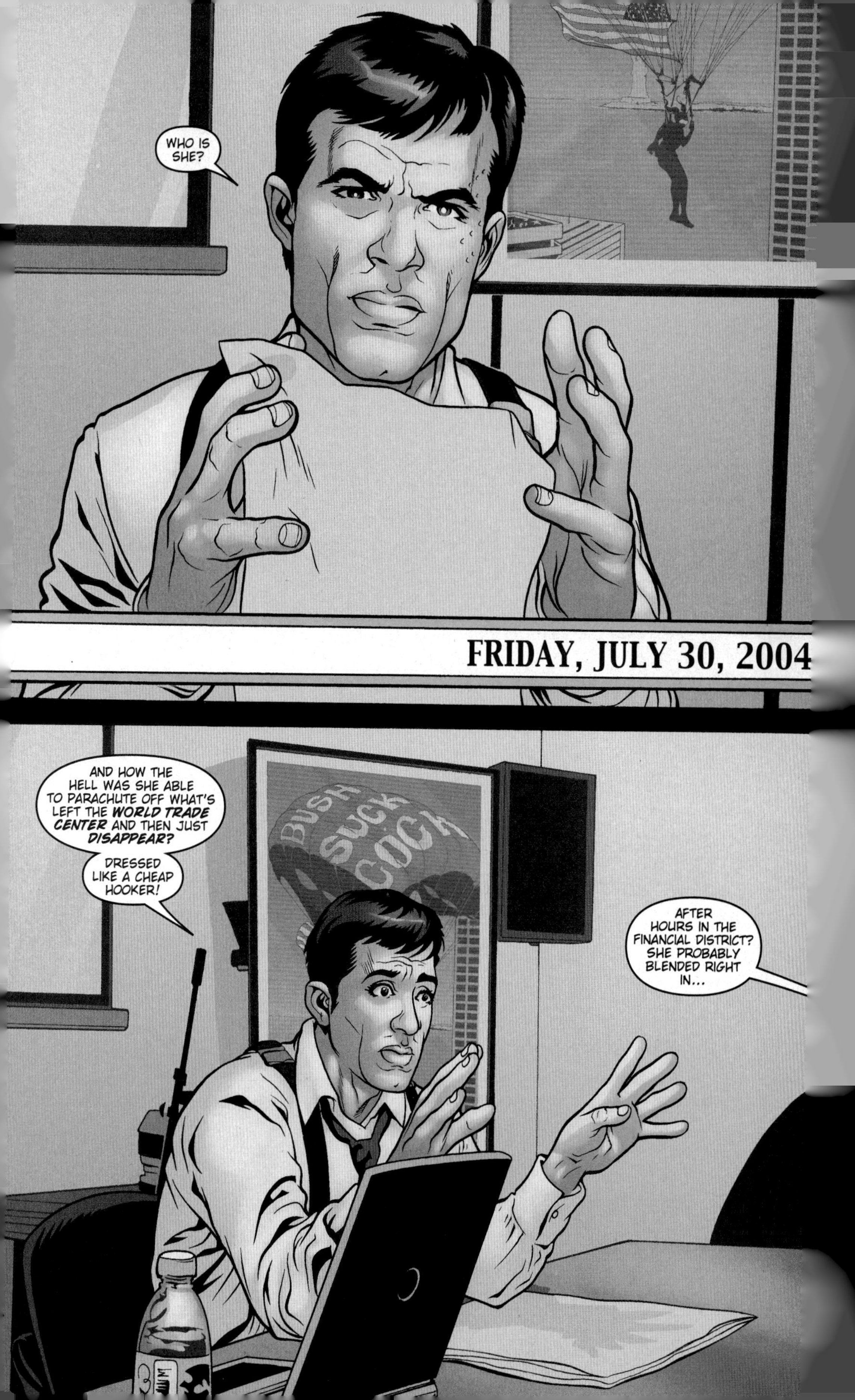
WHO IS SHE?
FRIDAY, JULY 30, 2004
AND HOW THE HELL WAS SHE ABLE TO PARACHUTE OFF WHAT'S LEFT THE WORLD TRADE CENTER AND THEN JUST DISAPPEAR?
DRESSED LIKE A CHEAP HOOKER!
BUSH SUCK COCK
AFTER HOURS IN THE FINANCIAL DISTRICT? SHE PROBABLY BLENDED RIGHT IN...

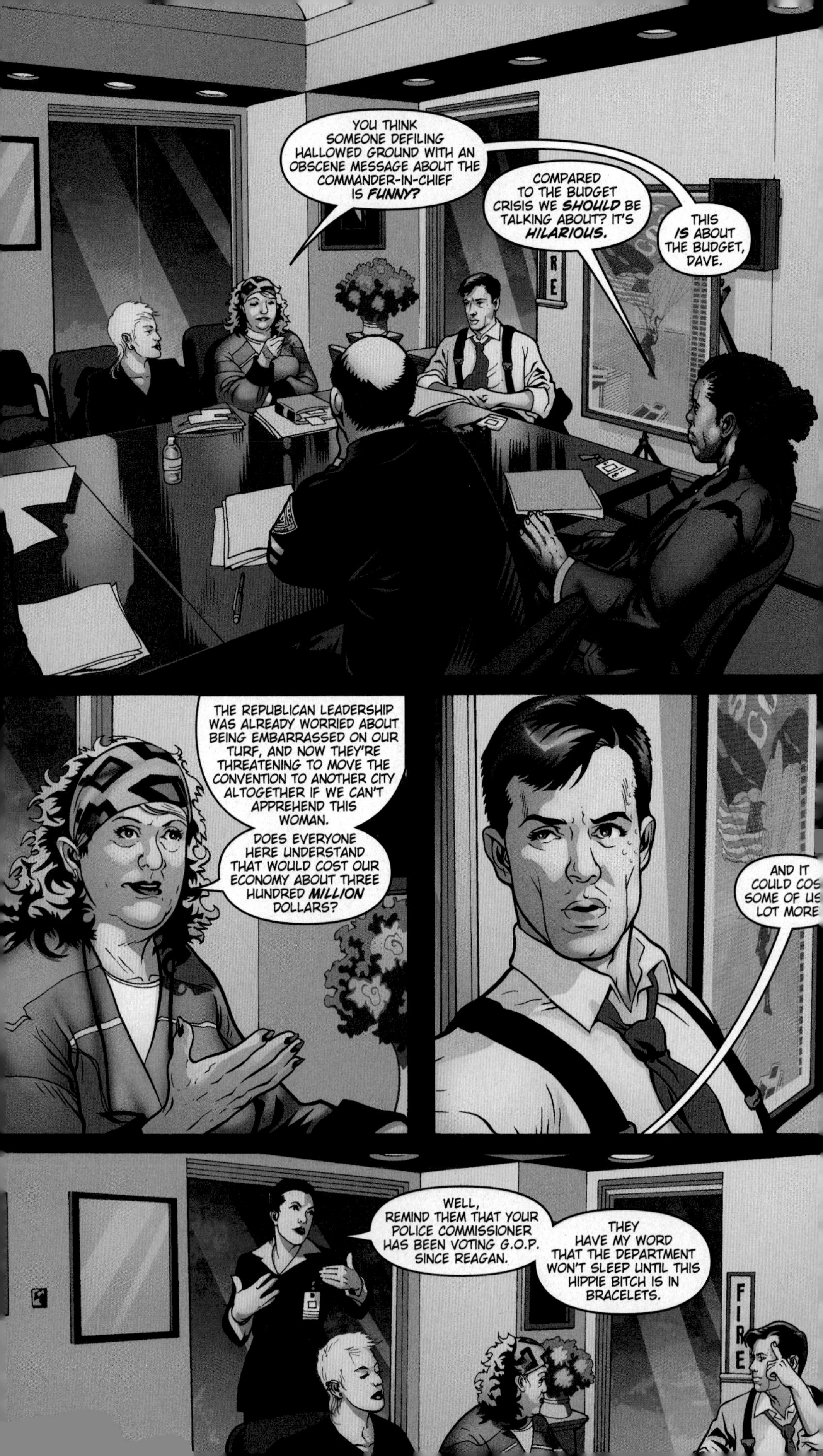
YOU THINK SOMEONE DEFILING HALLOWED GROUND WITH AN OBSCENE MESSAGE ABOUT THE COMMANDER-IN-CHIEF IS *FUNNY?*
COMPARED TO THE BUDGET CRISIS WE *SHOULD* BE TALKING ABOUT? IT'S *HILARIOUS.*
THIS *IS* ABOUT THE BUDGET, DAVE.
THE REPUBLICAN LEADERSHIP WAS ALREADY WORRIED ABOUT BEING EMBARRASSED ON OUR TURF, AND NOW THEY'RE THREATENING TO MOVE THE CONVENTION TO ANOTHER CITY ALTOGETHER IF WE CAN'T APPREHEND THIS WOMAN.
DOES EVERYONE HERE UNDERSTAND THAT WOULD COST OUR ECONOMY ABOUT THREE HUNDRED *MILLION* DOLLARS?
AND IT COULD COS SOME OF US LOT MORE
WELL, REMIND THEM THAT YOUR POLICE COMMISSIONER HAS BEEN VOTING G.O.P. SINCE REAGAN.
THEY HAVE MY WORD THAT THE DEPARTMENT WON'T SLEEP UNTIL THIS HIPPIE BITCH IS IN BRACELETS.
FIRE

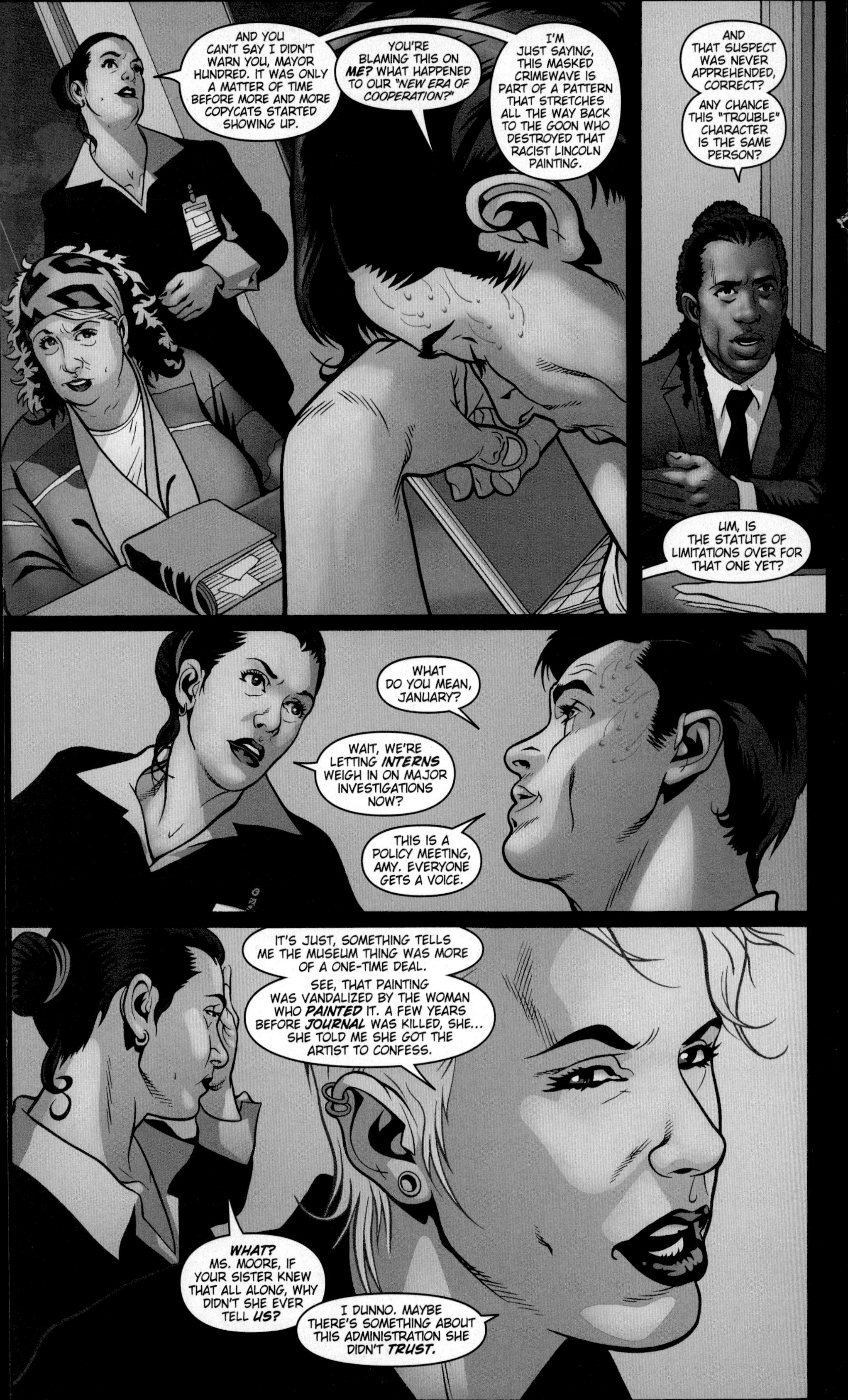
AND YOU CAN'T SAY I DIDN'T WARN YOU, MAYOR HUNDRED. IT WAS ONLY A MATTER OF TIME BEFORE MORE AND MORE COPYCATS STARTED SHOWING UP.
YOU'RE BLAMING THIS ON ME? WHAT HAPPENED TO OUR "NEW ERA OF COOPERATION?"
I'M JUST SAYING, THIS MASKED CRIMEWAVE IS PART OF A PATTERN THAT STRETCHES ALL THE WAY BACK TO THE GOON WHO DESTROYED THAT RACIST LINCOLN PAINTING.
AND THAT SUSPECT WAS NEVER APPREHENDED, CORRECT?
ANY CHANCE THIS "TROUBLE" CHARACTER IS THE SAME PERSON?
UM, IS THE STATUTE OF LIMITATIONS OVER FOR THAT ONE YET?
WHAT DO YOU MEAN, JANUARY?
WAIT, WE'RE LETTING INTERNS WEIGH IN ON MAJOR INVESTIGATIONS NOW?
THIS IS A POLICY MEETING, AMY. EVERYONE GETS A VOICE.
IT'S JUST, SOMETHING TELLS ME THE MUSEUM THING WAS MORE OF A ONE-TIME DEAL.
SEE, THAT PAINTING WAS VANDALIZED BY THE WOMAN WHO PAINTED IT. A FEW YEARS BEFORE JOURNAL WAS KILLED, SHE... SHE TOLD ME SHE GOT THE ARTIST TO CONFESS.
WHAT? MS. MOORE, IF YOUR SISTER KNEW THAT ALL ALONG, WHY DIDN'T SHE EVER TELL US?
I DUNNO. MAYBE THERE'S SOMETHING ABOUT THIS ADMINISTRATION SHE DIDN'T TRUST.

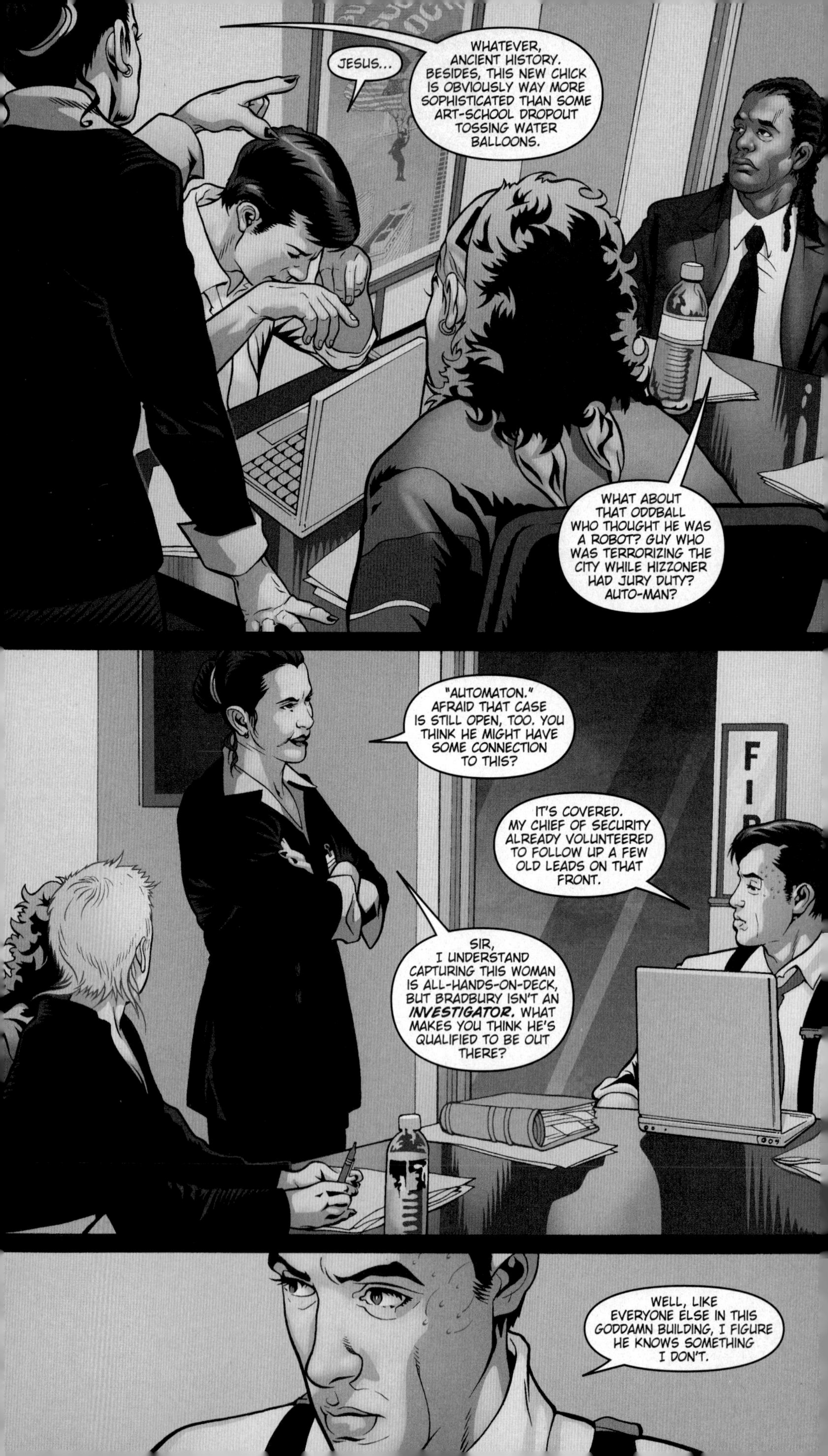
WHATEVER, ANCIENT HISTORY. BESIDES, THIS NEW CHICK IS OBVIOUSLY WAY MORE SOPHISTICATED THAN SOME ART-SCHOOL DROPOUT TOSSING WATER BALLOONS.
JESUS...
WHAT ABOUT THAT ODDBALL WHO THOUGHT HE WAS A ROBOT? GUY WHO WAS TERRORIZING THE CITY WHILE HIZZONER HAD JURY DUTY? AUTO-MAN?
"AUTOMATON." AFRAID THAT CASE IS STILL OPEN, TOO. YOU THINK HE MIGHT HAVE SOME CONNECTION TO THIS?
IT'S COVERED. MY CHIEF OF SECURITY ALREADY VOLUNTEERED TO FOLLOW UP A FEW OLD LEADS ON THAT FRONT.
SIR, I UNDERSTAND CAPTURING THIS WOMAN IS ALL-HANDS-ON-DECK, BUT BRADBURY ISN'T AN ***INVESTIGATOR.*** WHAT MAKES YOU THINK HE'S QUALIFIED TO BE OUT THERE?
WELL, LIKE EVERYONE ELSE IN THIS GODDAMN BUILDING, I FIGURE HE KNOWS SOMETHING I DON'T.

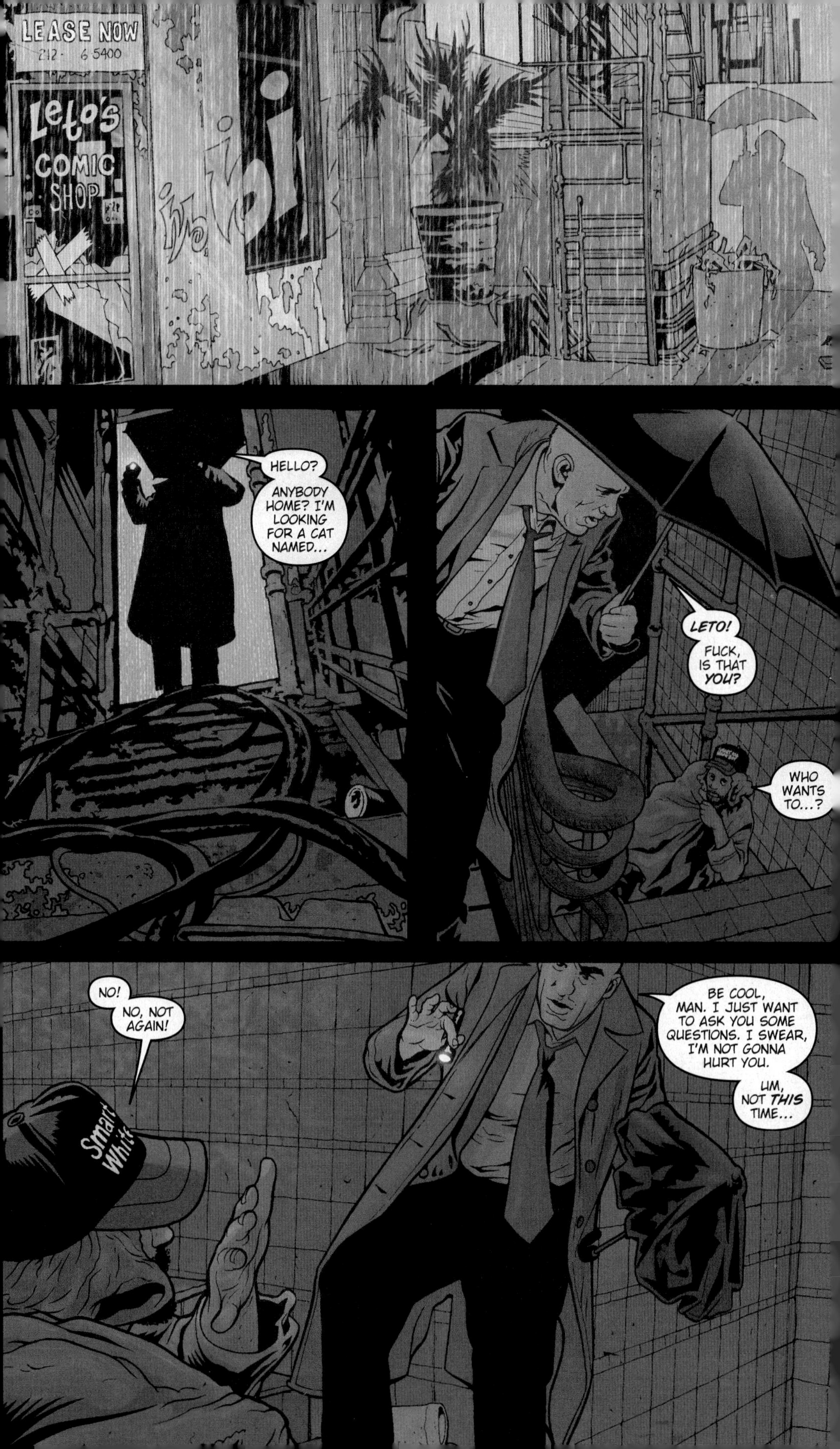
LEASE NOW
212- 6 5400
Leto's
COMIC
SHOP
HELLO?
ANYBODY HOME? I'M LOOKING FOR A CAT NAMED...
LETO!
FUCK, IS THAT YOU?
WHO WANTS TO...?
NO!
NO, NOT AGAIN!
BE COOL, MAN. I JUST WANT TO ASK YOU SOME QUESTIONS. I SWEAR, I'M NOT GONNA HURT YOU.
UM, NOT THIS TIME...

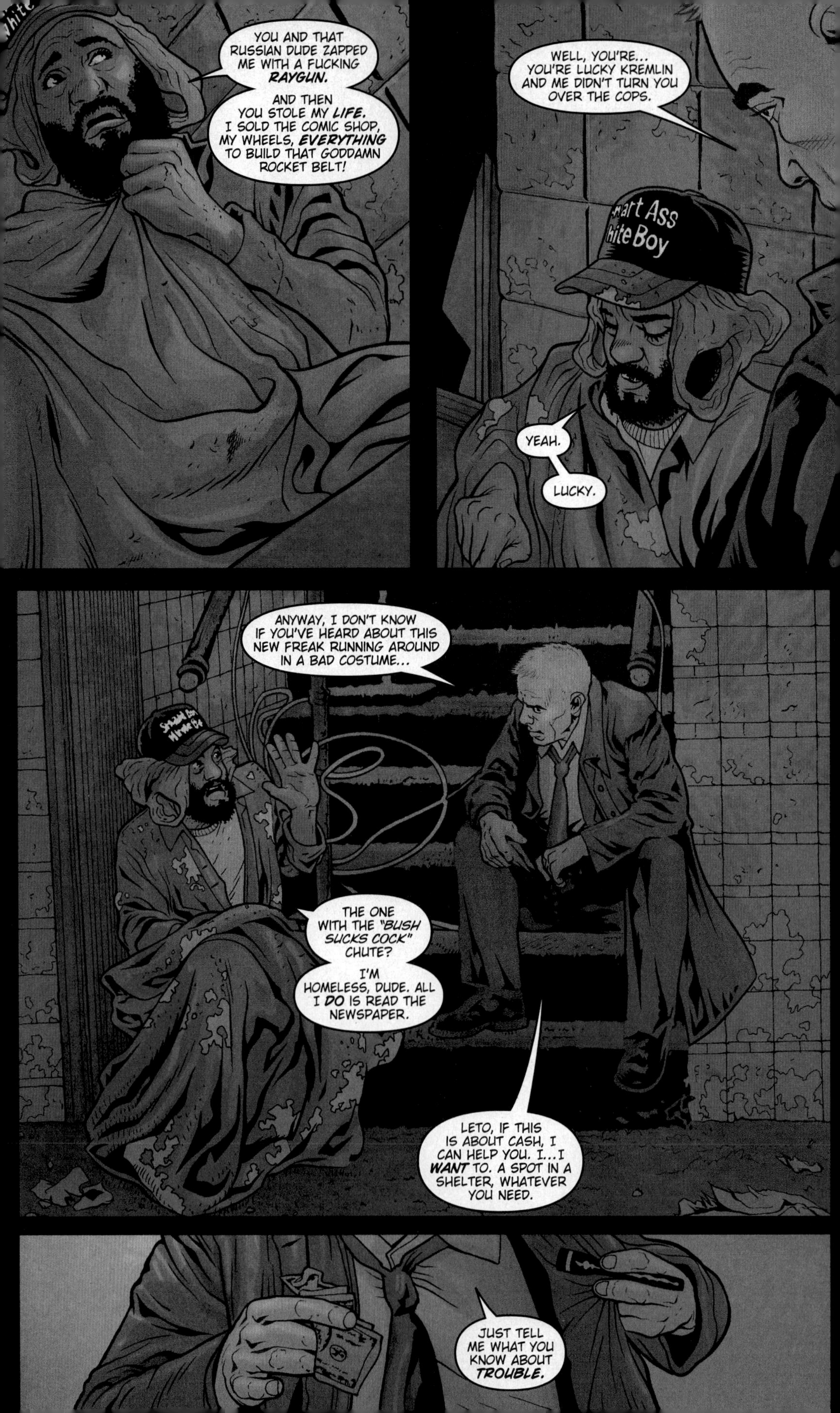
YOU AND THAT RUSSIAN DUDE ZAPPED ME WITH A FUCKING RAYGUN.
AND THEN YOU STOLE MY LIFE. I SOLD THE COMIC SHOP, MY WHEELS, EVERYTHING TO BUILD THAT GODDAMN ROCKET BELT!
WELL, YOU'RE... YOU'RE LUCKY KREMLIN AND ME DIDN'T TURN YOU OVER THE COPS.
Smart Ass White Boy
YEAH.
LUCKY.
ANYWAY, I DON'T KNOW IF YOU'VE HEARD ABOUT THIS NEW FREAK RUNNING AROUND IN A BAD COSTUME...
THE ONE WITH THE "BUSH SUCKS COCK" CHUTE?
I'M HOMELESS, DUDE. ALL I DO IS READ THE NEWSPAPER.
LETO, IF THIS IS ABOUT CASH, I CAN HELP YOU. I...I WANT TO. A SPOT IN A SHELTER, WHATEVER YOU NEED.
JUST TELL ME WHAT YOU KNOW ABOUT TROUBLE.

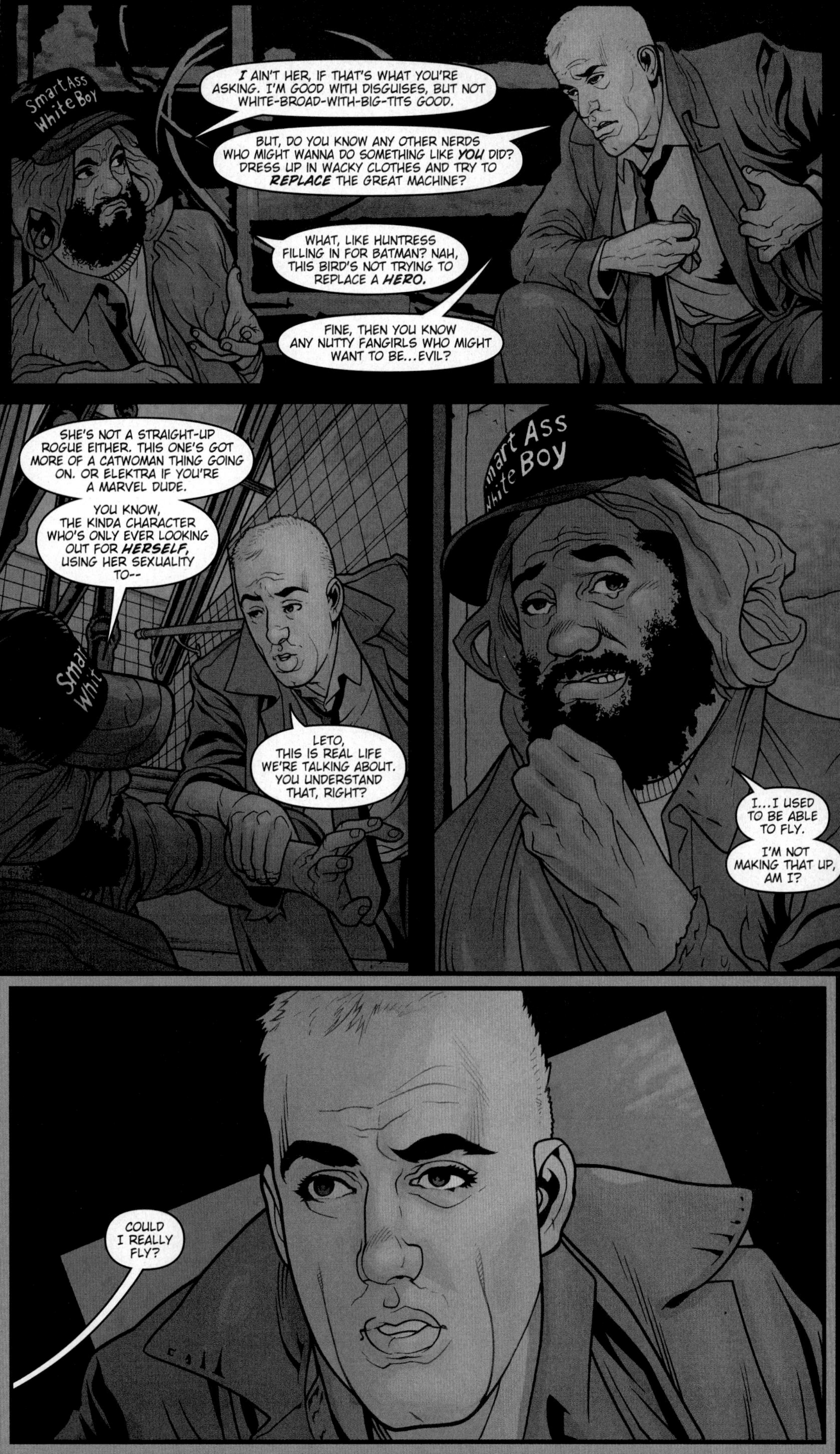
Smart Ass White Boy
I AIN'T HER, IF THAT'S WHAT YOU'RE ASKING. I'M GOOD WITH DISGUISES, BUT NOT WHITE-BROAD-WITH-BIG-TITS GOOD.
BUT, DO YOU KNOW ANY OTHER NERDS WHO MIGHT WANNA DO SOMETHING LIKE YOU DID? DRESS UP IN WACKY CLOTHES AND TRY TO REPLACE THE GREAT MACHINE?
WHAT, LIKE HUNTRESS FILLING IN FOR BATMAN? NAH, THIS BIRD'S NOT TRYING TO REPLACE A HERO.
FINE, THEN YOU KNOW ANY NUTTY FANGIRLS WHO MIGHT WANT TO BE...EVIL?
SHE'S NOT A STRAIGHT-UP ROGUE EITHER. THIS ONE'S GOT MORE OF A CATWOMAN THING GOING ON. OR ELEKTRA IF YOU'RE A MARVEL DUDE.
YOU KNOW, THE KINDA CHARACTER WHO'S ONLY EVER LOOKING OUT FOR HERSELF, USING HER SEXUALITY TO--
LETO, THIS IS REAL LIFE WE'RE TALKING ABOUT. YOU UNDERSTAND THAT, RIGHT?
Smart Ass White Boy
I...I USED TO BE ABLE TO FLY.
I'M NOT MAKING THAT UP, AM I?
COULD I REALLY FLY?

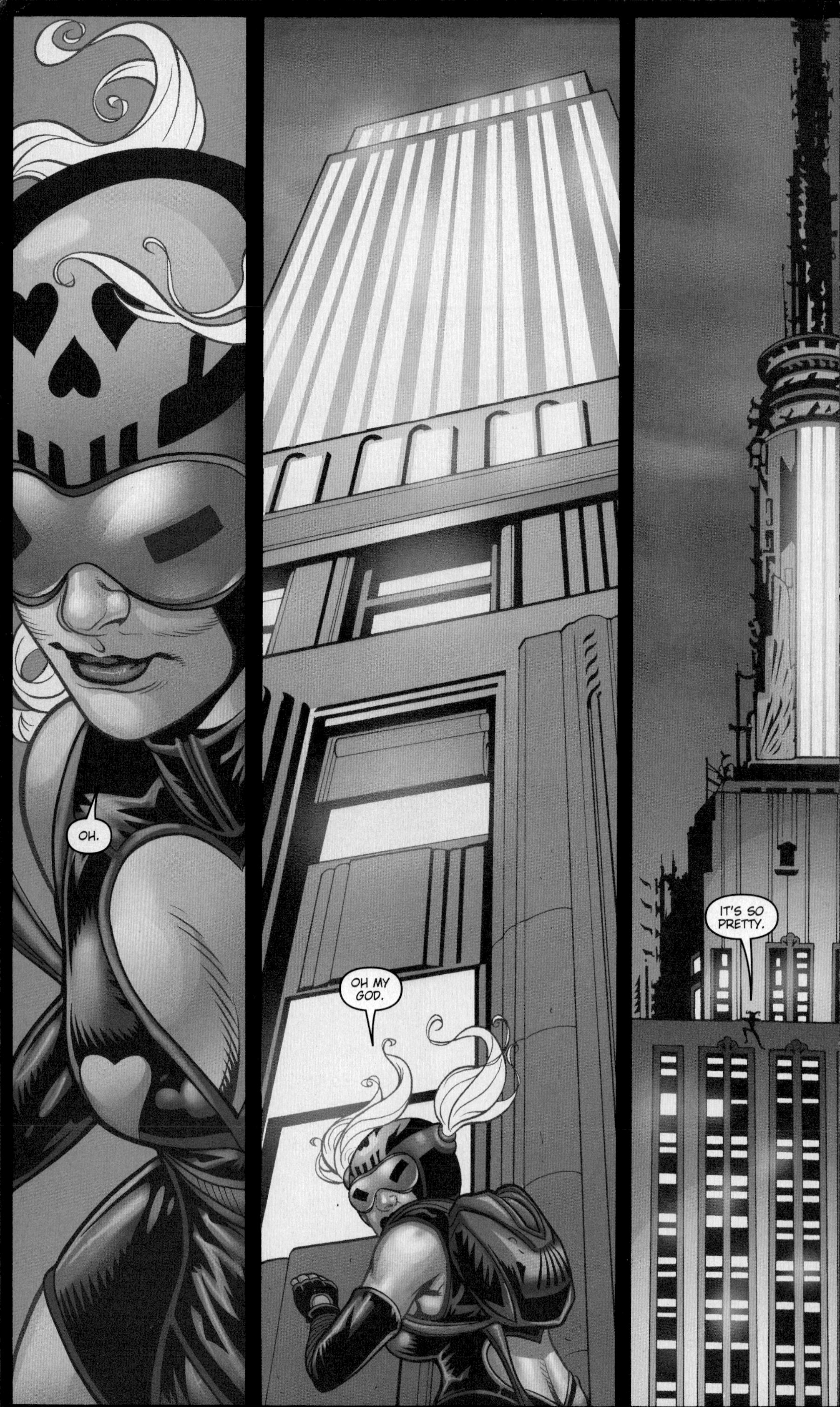
OH.
OH MY GOD.
IT'S SO PRETTY.

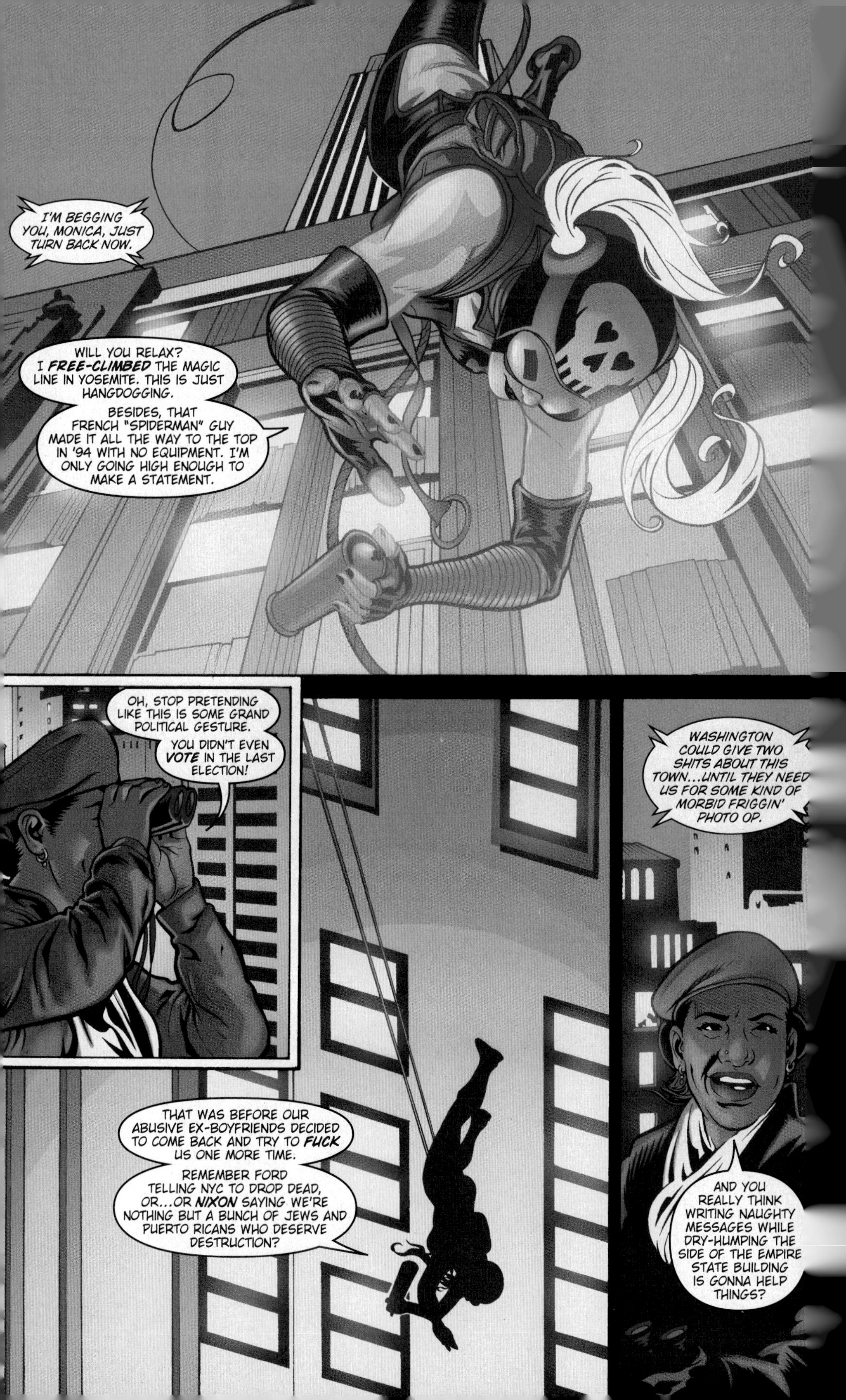
I'M BEGGING YOU, MONICA, JUST TURN BACK NOW.
WILL YOU RELAX? I FREE-CLIMBED THE MAGIC LINE IN YOSEMITE. THIS IS JUST HANGDOGGING.
BESIDES, THAT FRENCH "SPIDERMAN" GUY MADE IT ALL THE WAY TO THE TOP IN '94 WITH NO EQUIPMENT. I'M ONLY GOING HIGH ENOUGH TO MAKE A STATEMENT.
OH, STOP PRETENDING LIKE THIS IS SOME GRAND POLITICAL GESTURE.
YOU DIDN'T EVEN VOTE IN THE LAST ELECTION!
THAT WAS BEFORE OUR ABUSIVE EX-BOYFRIENDS DECIDED TO COME BACK AND TRY TO FUCK US ONE MORE TIME.
REMEMBER FORD TELLING NYC TO DROP DEAD, OR...OR NIXON SAYING WE'RE NOTHING BUT A BUNCH OF JEWS AND PUERTO RICANS WHO DESERVE DESTRUCTION?
WASHINGTON COULD GIVE TWO SHITS ABOUT THIS TOWN...UNTIL THEY NEED US FOR SOME KIND OF MORBID FRIGGIN' PHOTO OP.
AND YOU REALLY THINK WRITING NAUGHTY MESSAGES WHILE DRY-HUMPING THE SIDE OF THE EMPIRE STATE BUILDING IS GONNA HELP THINGS?

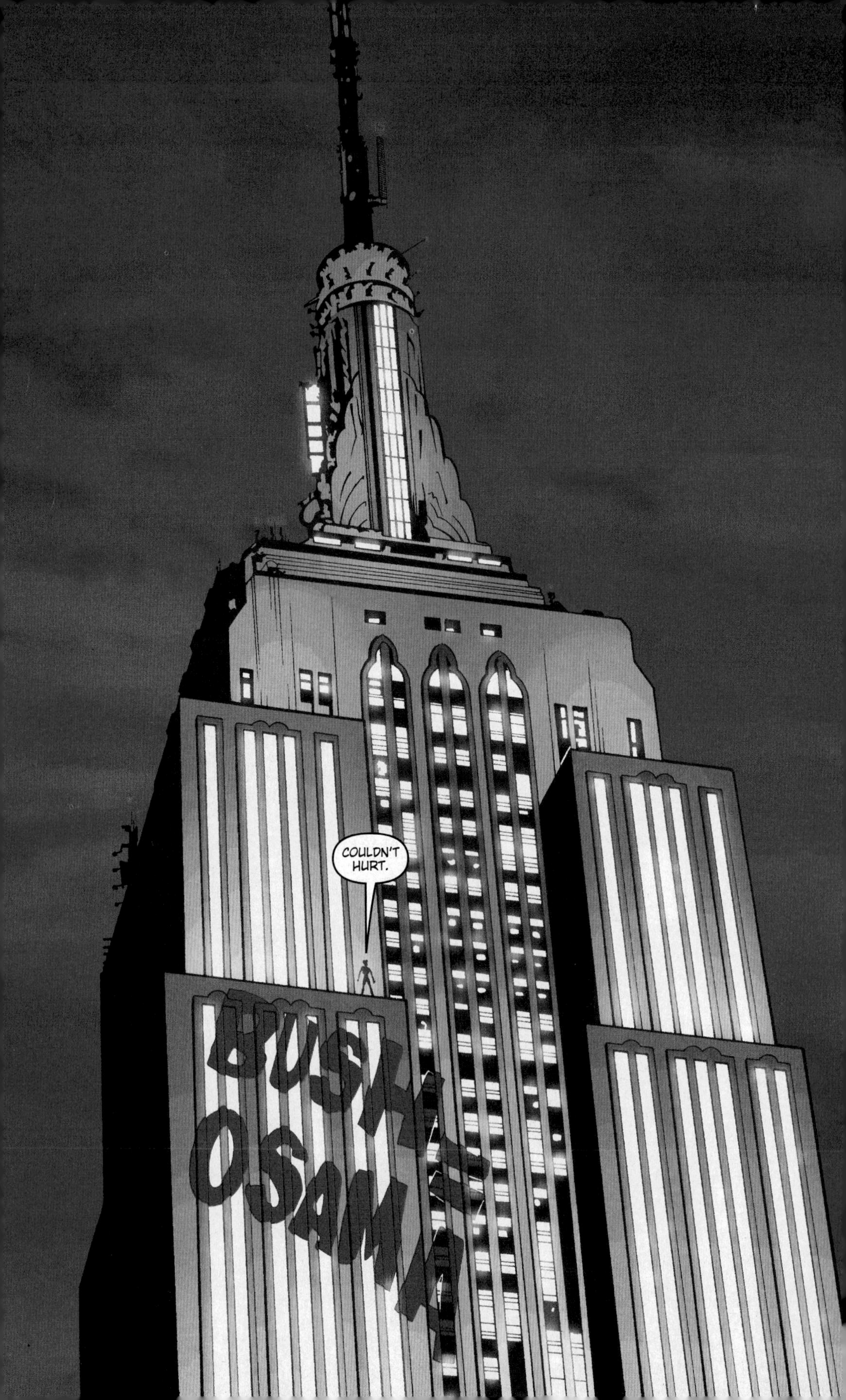
COULDN'T HURT.
BUSH

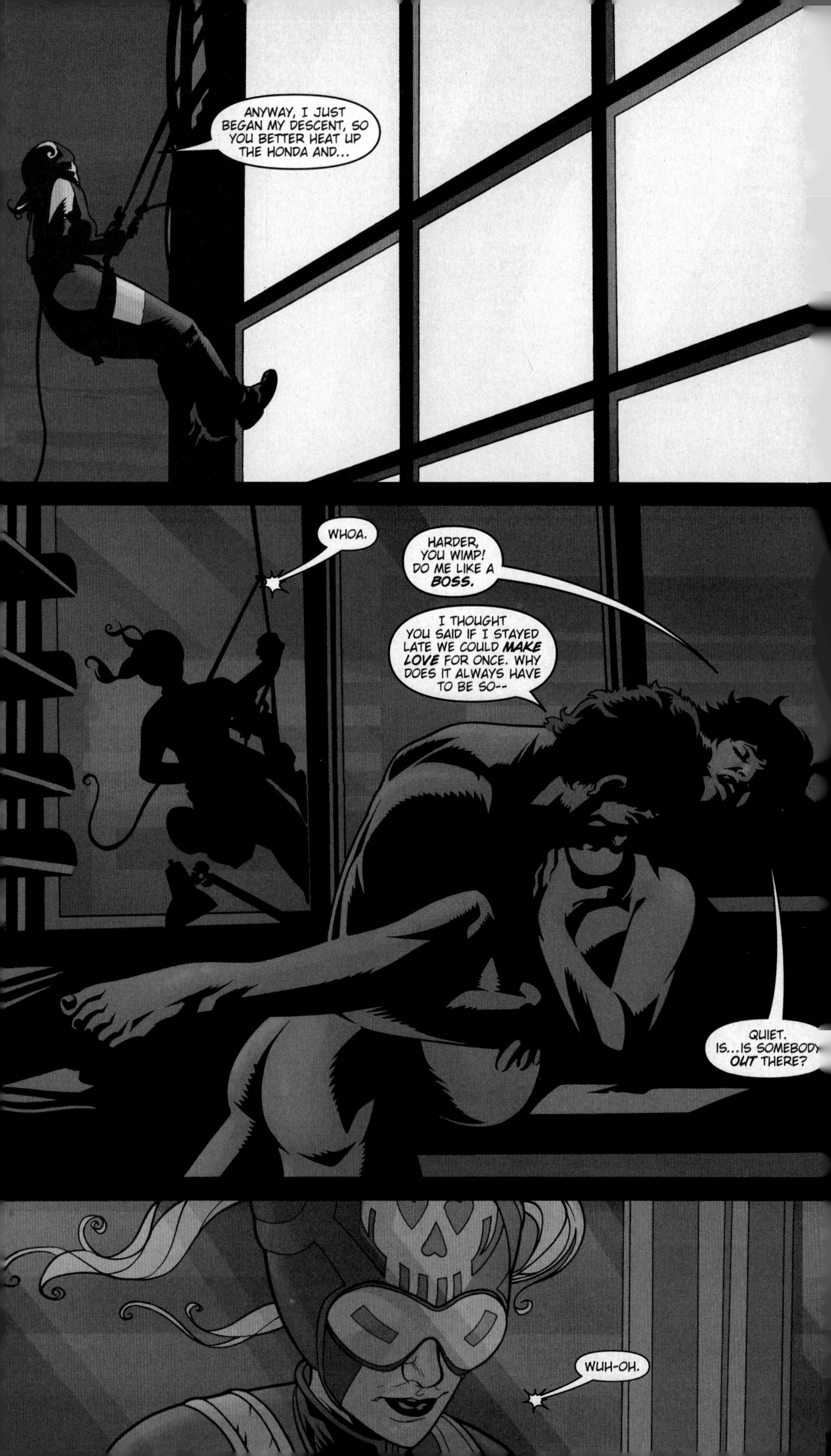
ANYWAY, I JUST BEGAN MY DESCENT, SO YOU BETTER HEAT UP THE HONDA AND...
WHOA.
HARDER, YOU WIMP! DO ME LIKE A ***BOSS.***
I THOUGHT YOU SAID IF I STAYED LATE WE COULD ***MAKE LOVE*** FOR ONCE. WHY DOES IT ALWAYS HAVE TO BE SO--
QUIET. IS...IS SOMEBODY ***OUT*** THERE?
WUH-OH.

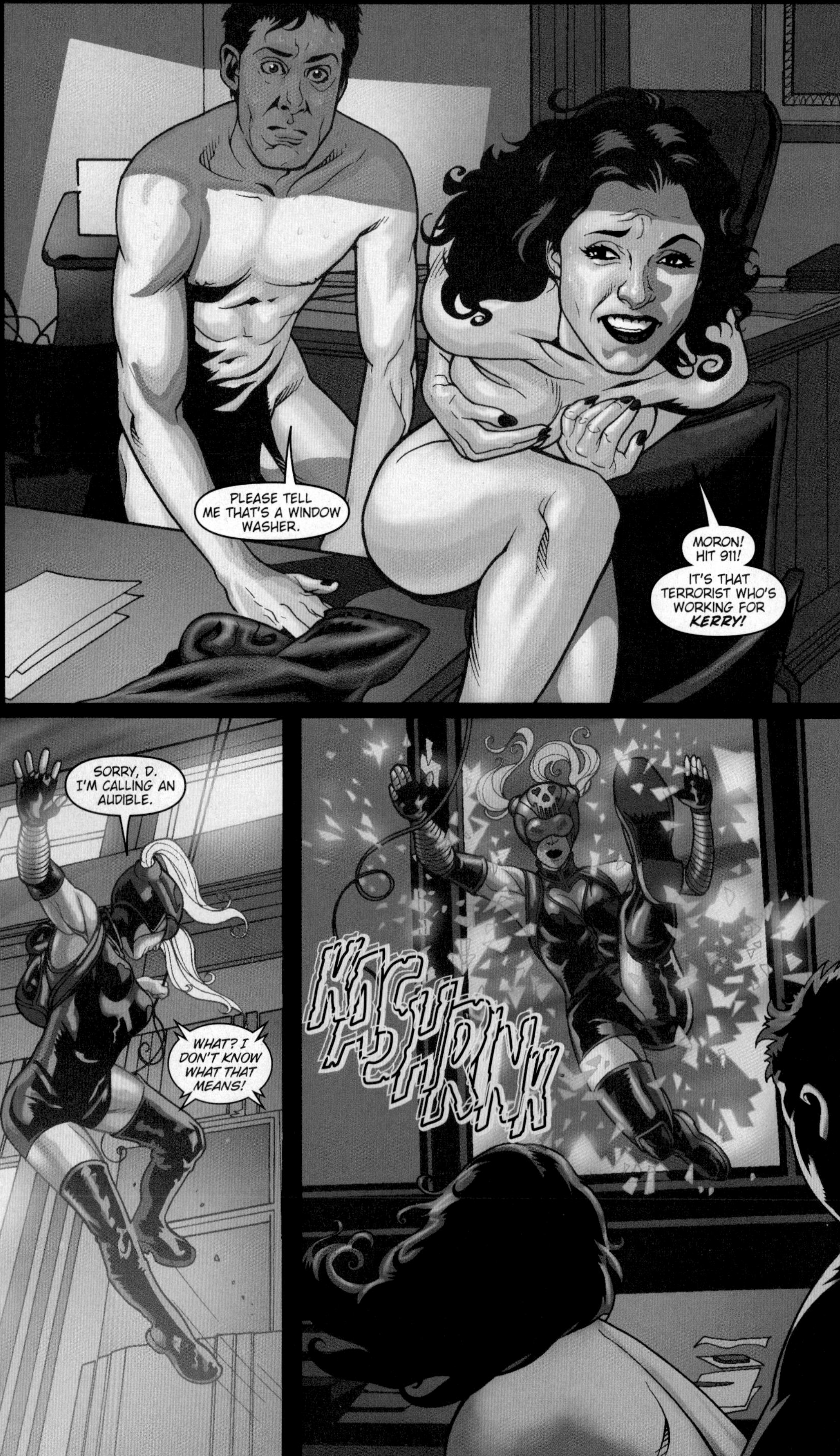
PLEASE TELL ME THAT'S A WINDOW WASHER.
MORON! HIT 911!
IT'S THAT TERRORIST WHO'S WORKING FOR **KERRY!**
SORRY, D. I'M CALLING AN AUDIBLE.
WHAT? I DON'T KNOW WHAT THAT MEANS!

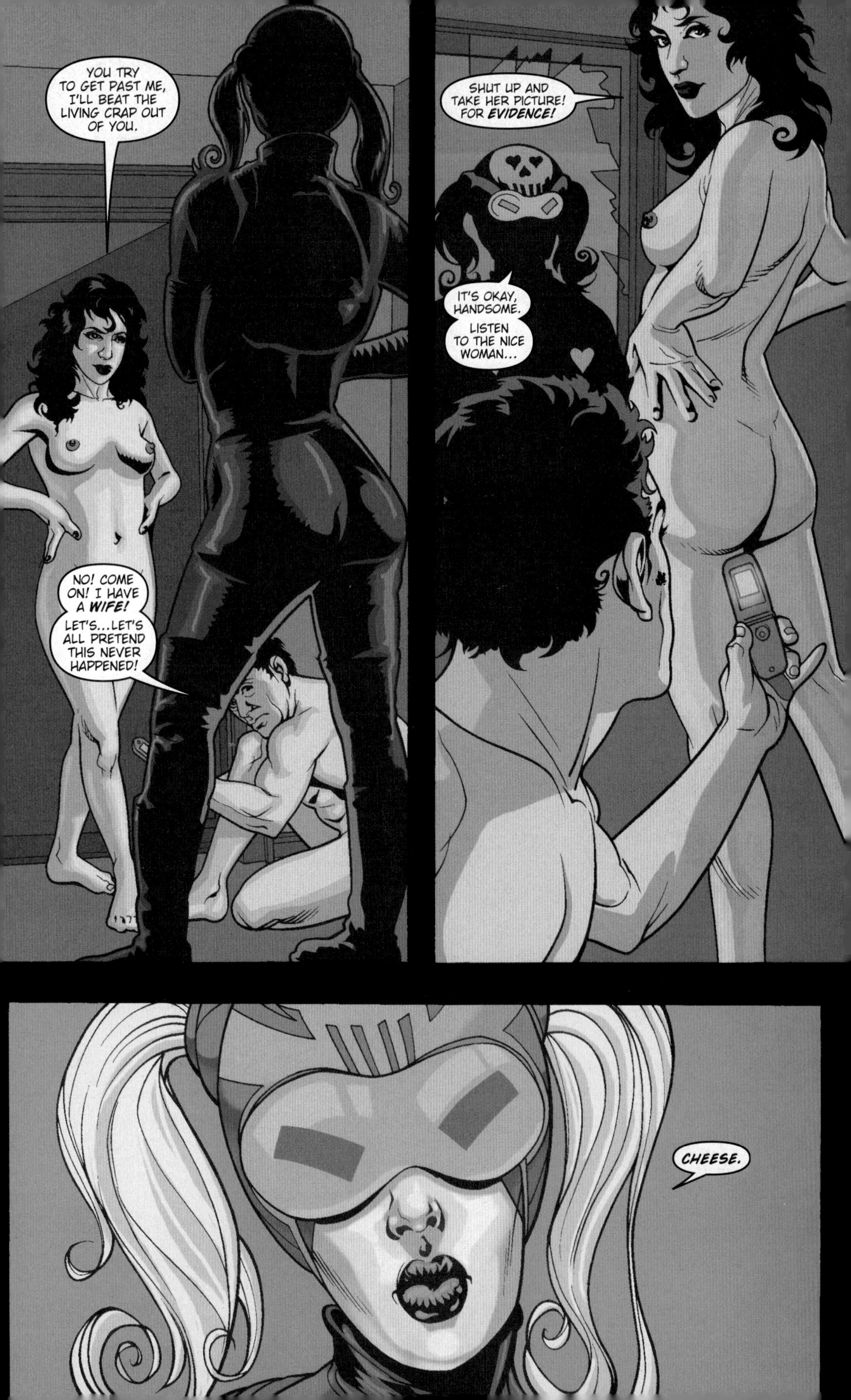
YOU TRY TO GET PAST ME, I'LL BEAT THE LIVING CRAP OUT OF YOU.
NO! COME ON! I HAVE A **WIFE!**
LET'S...LET'S ALL PRETEND THIS NEVER HAPPENED!
SHUT UP AND TAKE HER PICTURE! FOR **EVIDENCE!**
IT'S OKAY, HANDSOME.
LISTEN TO THE NICE WOMAN...
CHEESE.

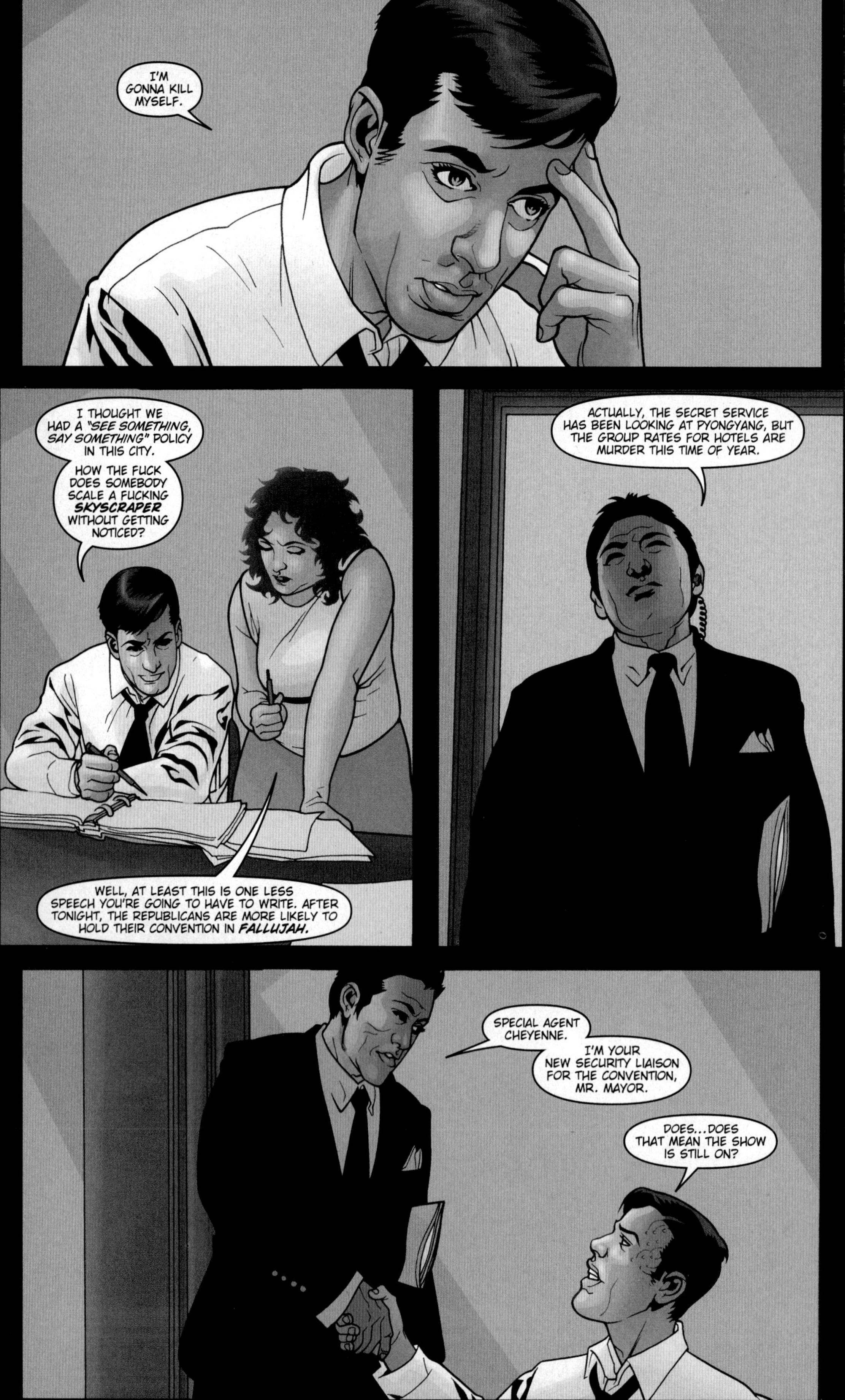
I'M GONNA KILL MYSELF.
I THOUGHT WE HAD A "SEE SOMETHING, SAY SOMETHING" POLICY IN THIS CITY.
HOW THE FUCK DOES SOMEBODY SCALE A FUCKING SKYSCRAPER WITHOUT GETTING NOTICED?
WELL, AT LEAST THIS IS ONE LESS SPEECH YOU'RE GOING TO HAVE TO WRITE. AFTER TONIGHT, THE REPUBLICANS ARE MORE LIKELY TO HOLD THEIR CONVENTION IN FALLUJAH.
ACTUALLY, THE SECRET SERVICE HAS BEEN LOOKING AT PYONGYANG, BUT THE GROUP RATES FOR HOTELS ARE MURDER THIS TIME OF YEAR.
SPECIAL AGENT CHEYENNE.
I'M YOUR NEW SECURITY LIAISON FOR THE CONVENTION, MR. MAYOR.
DOES...DOES THAT MEAN THE SHOW IS STILL ON?

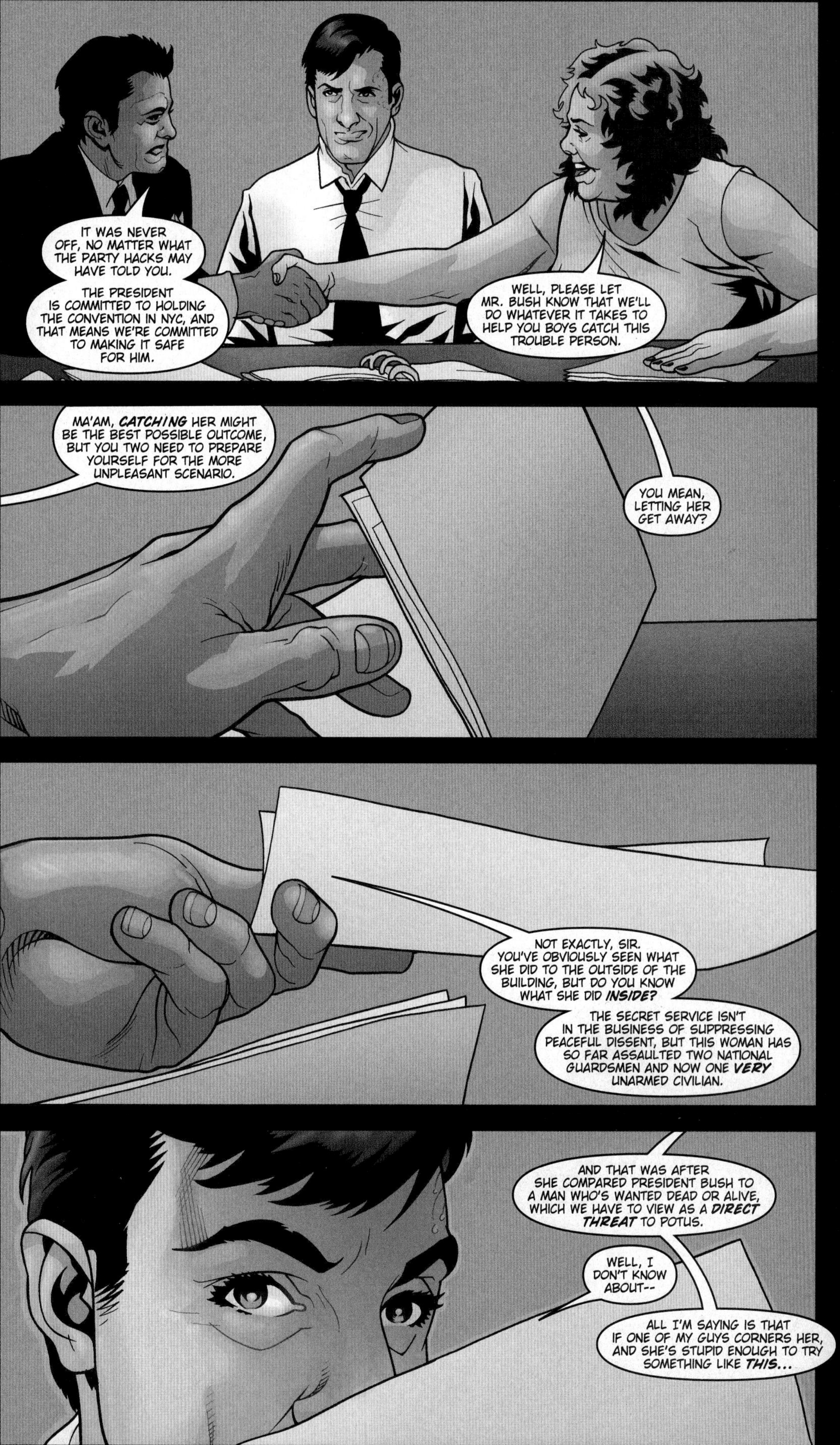
IT WAS NEVER OFF, NO MATTER WHAT THE PARTY HACKS MAY HAVE TOLD YOU.
THE PRESIDENT IS COMMITTED TO HOLDING THE CONVENTION IN NYC, AND THAT MEANS WE'RE COMMITTED TO MAKING IT SAFE FOR HIM.
WELL, PLEASE LET MR. BUSH KNOW THAT WE'LL DO WHATEVER IT TAKES TO HELP YOU BOYS CATCH THIS TROUBLE PERSON.
MA'AM, *CATCHING* HER MIGHT BE THE BEST POSSIBLE OUTCOME, BUT YOU TWO NEED TO PREPARE YOURSELF FOR THE MORE UNPLEASANT SCENARIO.
YOU MEAN, LETTING HER GET AWAY?
NOT EXACTLY, SIR. YOU'VE OBVIOUSLY SEEN WHAT SHE DID TO THE OUTSIDE OF THE BUILDING, BUT DO YOU KNOW WHAT SHE DID *INSIDE?*
THE SECRET SERVICE ISN'T IN THE BUSINESS OF SUPPRESSING PEACEFUL DISSENT, BUT THIS WOMAN HAS SO FAR ASSAULTED TWO NATIONAL GUARDSMEN AND NOW ONE *VERY* UNARMED CIVILIAN.
AND THAT WAS AFTER SHE COMPARED PRESIDENT BUSH TO A MAN WHO'S WANTED DEAD OR ALIVE, WHICH WE HAVE TO VIEW AS A *DIRECT THREAT* TO POTUS.
WELL, I DON'T KNOW ABOUT--
ALL I'M SAYING IS THAT IF ONE OF MY GUYS CORNERS HER, AND SHE'S STUPID ENOUGH TO TRY SOMETHING LIKE *THIS...*

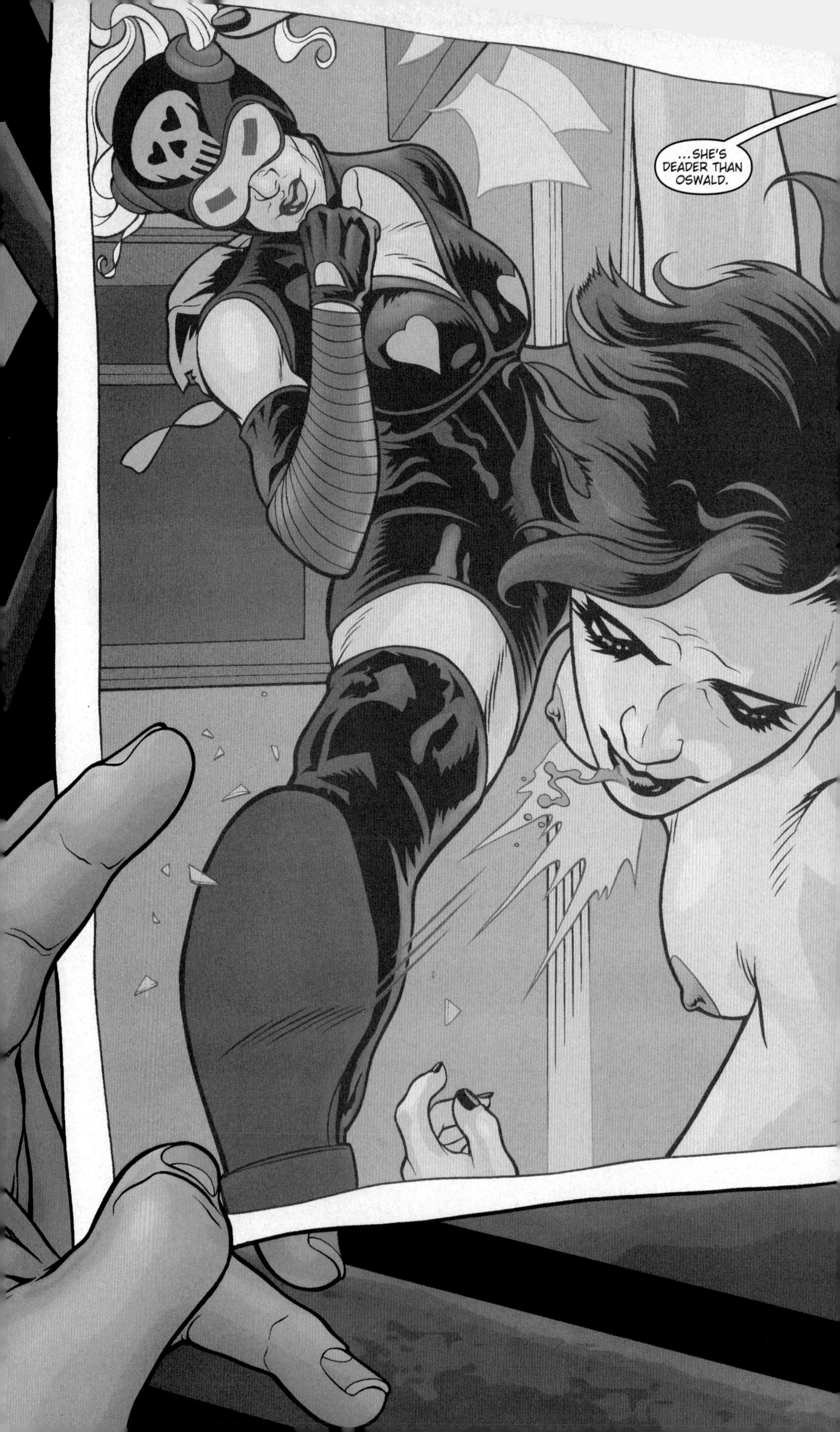
...SHE'S DEADER THAN OSWALD.

Dirty Tricks

part 3

Chapter 4

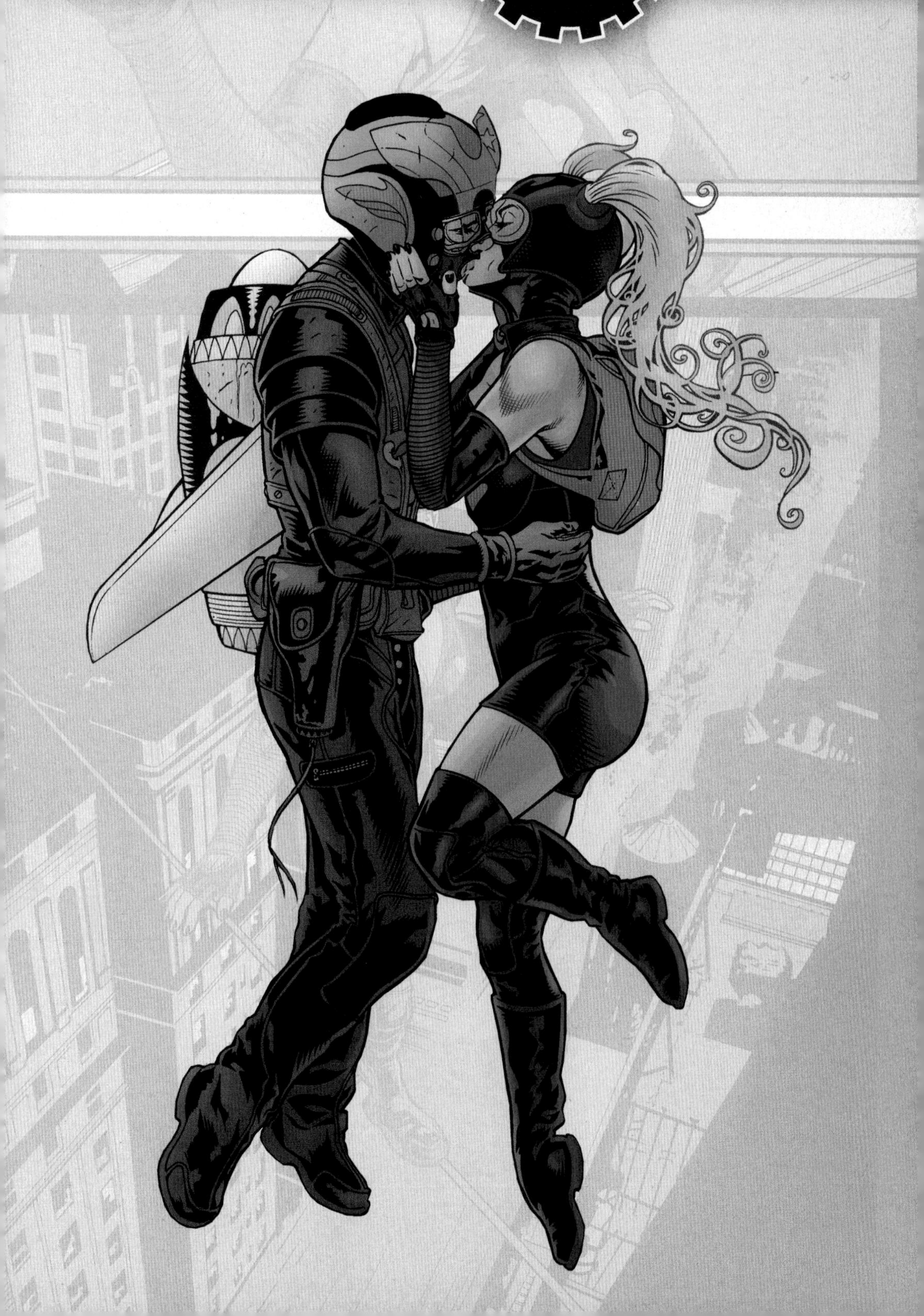

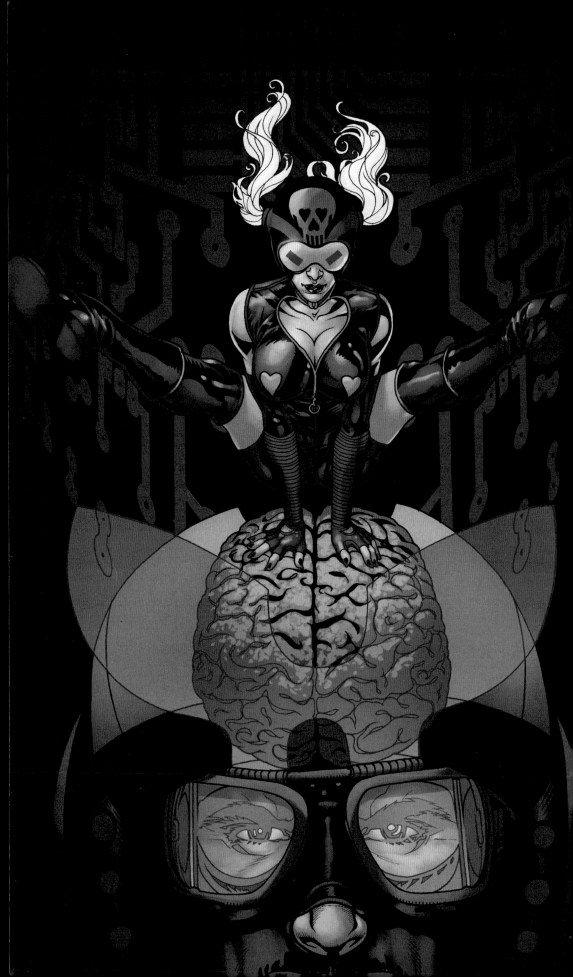

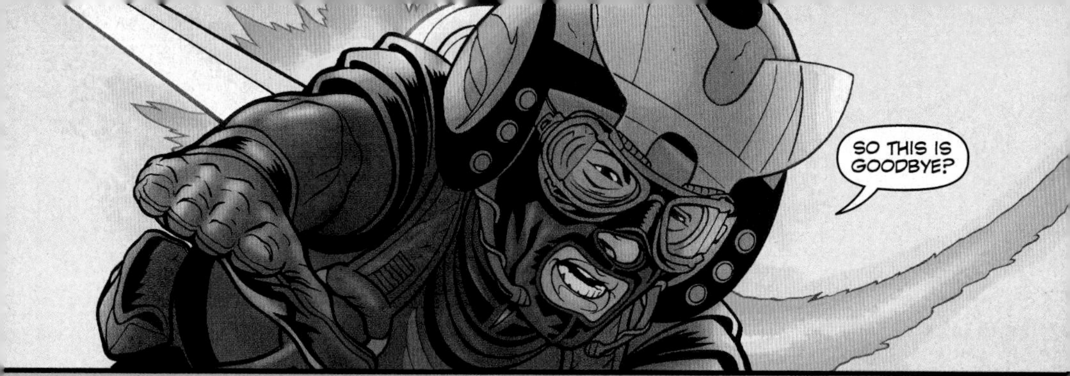
SO THIS IS GOODBYE?

WEDNESDAY, JULY 4, 2001

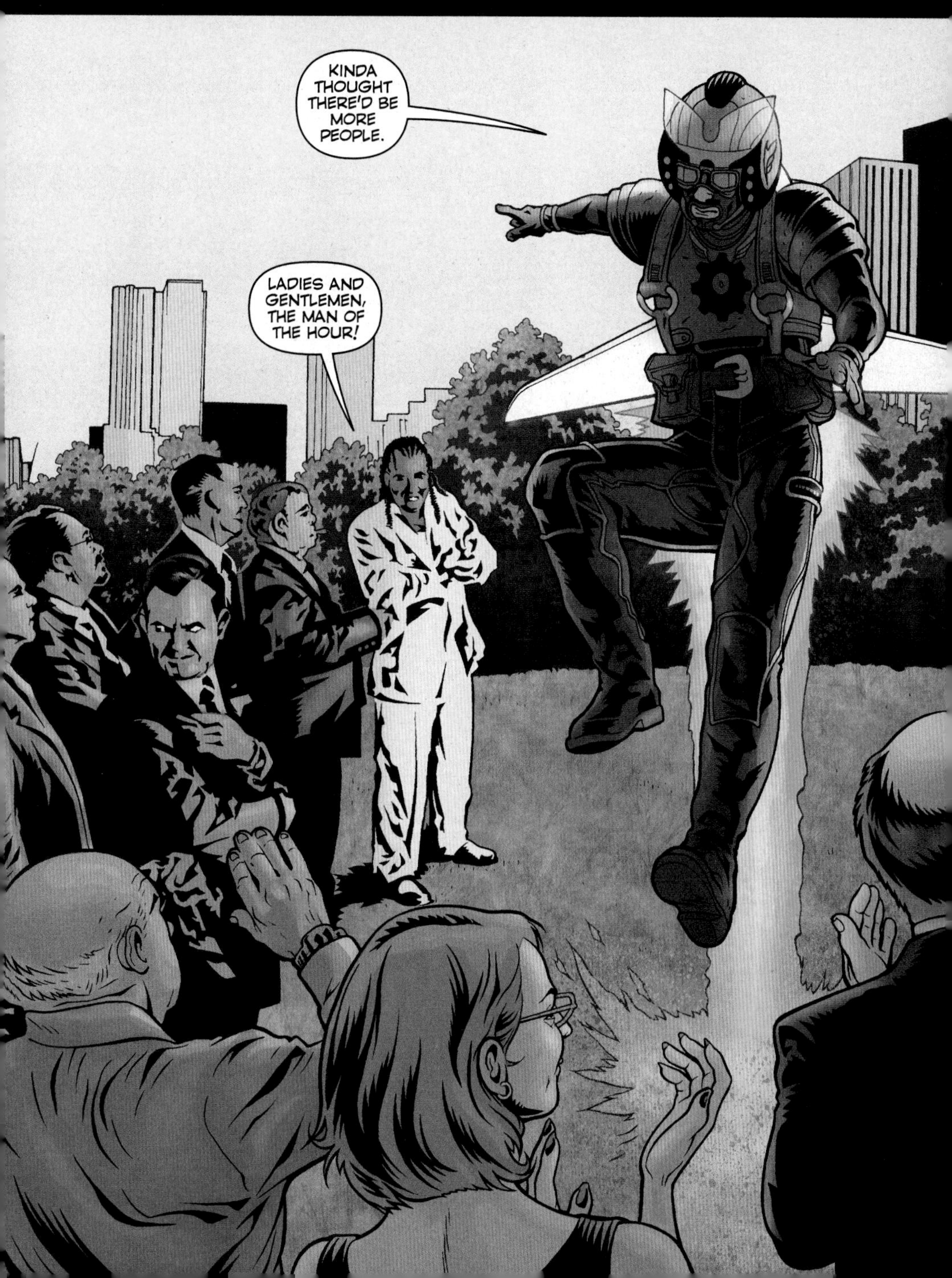
KINDA THOUGHT THERE'D BE MORE PEOPLE.
LADIES AND GENTLEMEN, THE MAN OF THE HOUR!

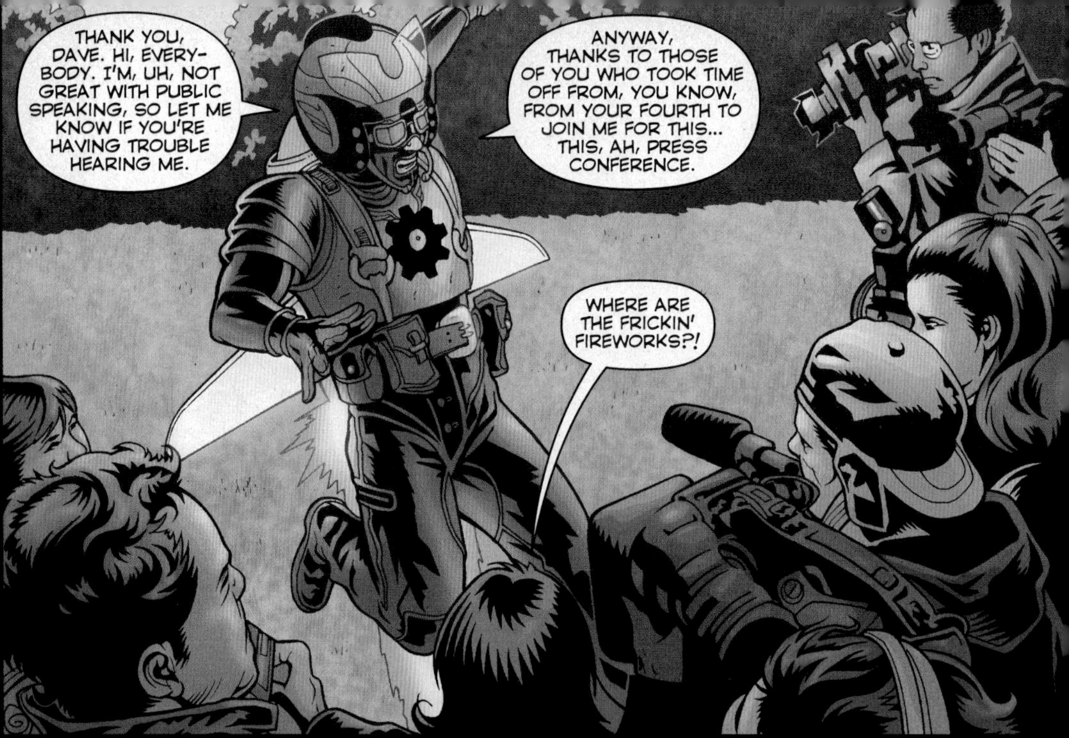
THANK YOU, DAVE. HI, EVERY-BODY. I'M, UH, NOT GREAT WITH PUBLIC SPEAKING, SO LET ME KNOW IF YOU'RE HAVING TROUBLE HEARING ME.
ANYWAY, THANKS TO THOSE OF YOU WHO TOOK TIME OFF FROM, YOU KNOW, FROM YOUR FOURTH TO JOIN ME FOR THIS... THIS, AH, PRESS CONFERENCE.
WHERE ARE THE FRICKIN' FIREWORKS?!

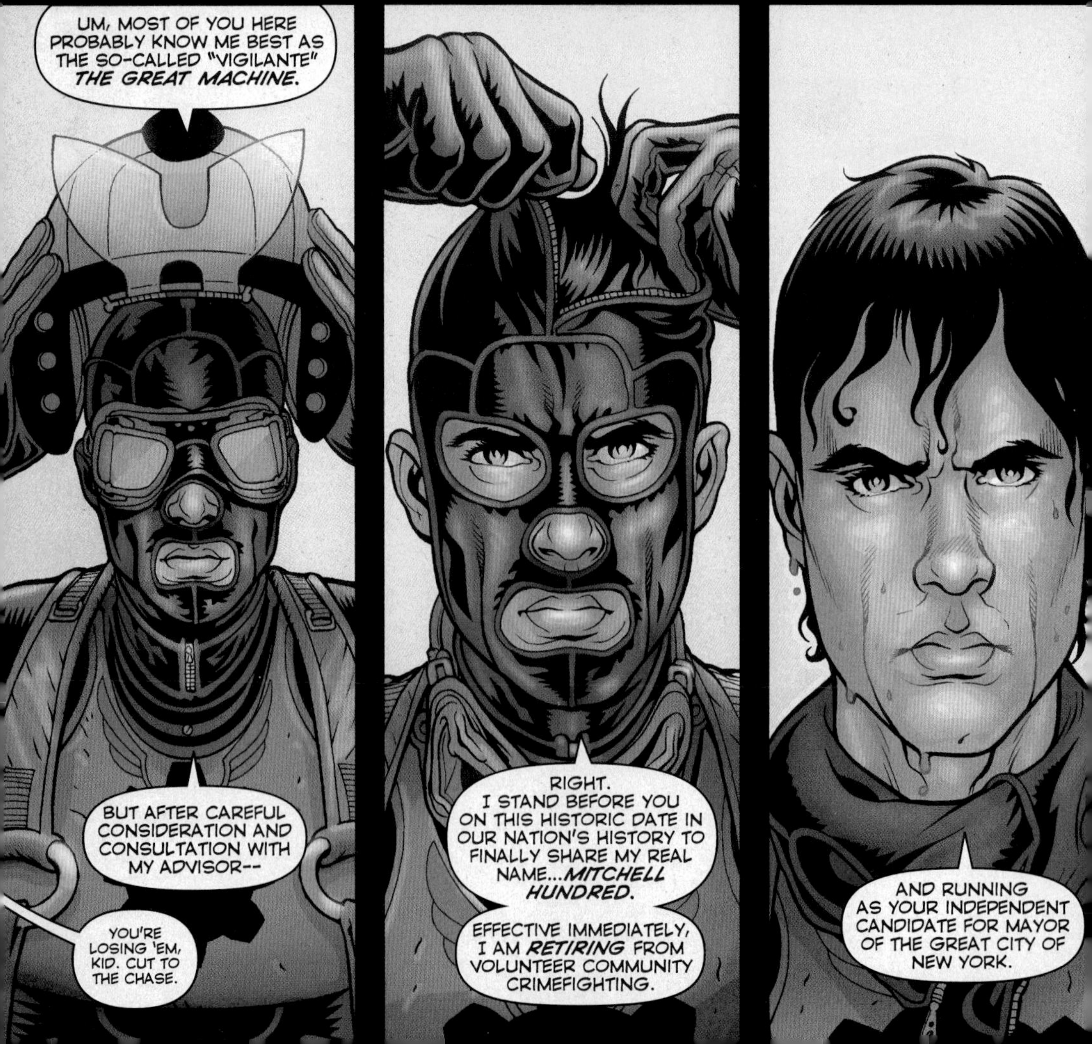
UM, MOST OF YOU HERE PROBABLY KNOW ME BEST AS THE SO-CALLED "VIGILANTE" ***THE GREAT MACHINE***.
BUT AFTER CAREFUL CONSIDERATION AND CONSULTATION WITH MY ADVISOR--
YOU'RE LOSING 'EM, KID. CUT TO THE CHASE.
RIGHT. I STAND BEFORE YOU ON THIS HISTORIC DATE IN OUR NATION'S HISTORY TO FINALLY SHARE MY REAL NAME...***MITCHELL HUNDRED***.
EFFECTIVE IMMEDIATELY, I AM ***RETIRING*** FROM VOLUNTEER COMMUNITY CRIMEFIGHTING.
AND RUNNING AS YOUR INDEPENDENT CANDIDATE FOR MAYOR OF THE GREAT CITY OF NEW YORK.

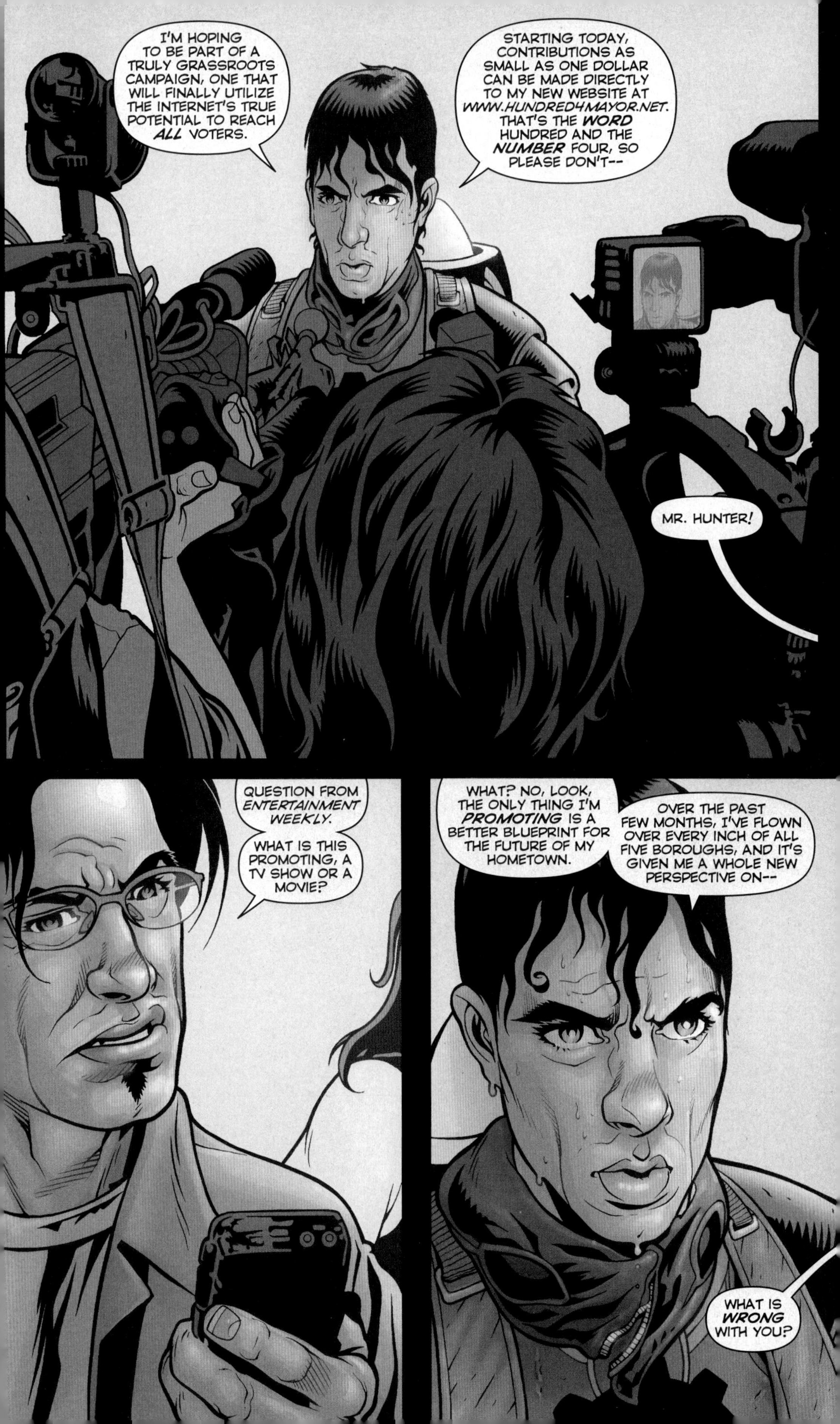

I'M HOPING TO BE PART OF A TRULY GRASSROOTS CAMPAIGN, ONE THAT WILL FINALLY UTILIZE THE INTERNET'S TRUE POTENTIAL TO REACH ALL VOTERS.
STARTING TODAY, CONTRIBUTIONS AS SMALL AS ONE DOLLAR CAN BE MADE DIRECTLY TO MY NEW WEBSITE AT WWW.HUNDRED4MAYOR.NET. THAT'S THE WORD HUNDRED AND THE NUMBER FOUR, SO PLEASE DON'T--
MR. HUNTER!
QUESTION FROM ENTERTAINMENT WEEKLY.
WHAT IS THIS PROMOTING, A TV SHOW OR A MOVIE?
WHAT? NO, LOOK, THE ONLY THING I'M PROMOTING IS A BETTER BLUEPRINT FOR THE FUTURE OF MY HOMETOWN.
OVER THE PAST FEW MONTHS, I'VE FLOWN OVER EVERY INCH OF ALL FIVE BOROUGHS, AND IT'S GIVEN ME A WHOLE NEW PERSPECTIVE ON--
WHAT IS WRONG WITH YOU?

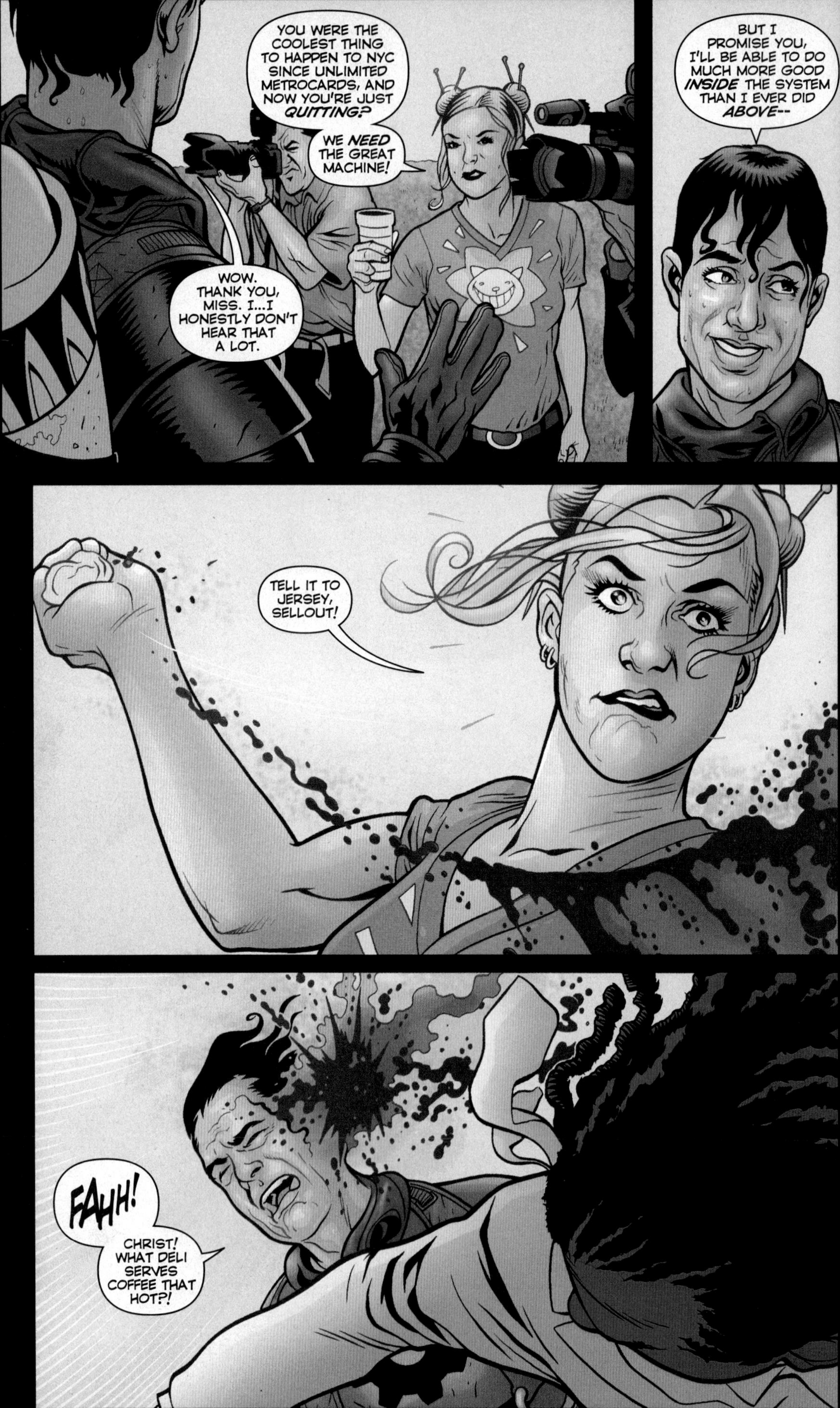
YOU WERE THE COOLEST THING TO HAPPEN TO NYC SINCE UNLIMITED METROCARDS, AND NOW YOU'RE JUST QUITTING?
WE NEED THE GREAT MACHINE!
WOW. THANK YOU, MISS. I...I HONESTLY DON'T HEAR THAT A LOT.
BUT I PROMISE YOU, I'LL BE ABLE TO DO MUCH MORE GOOD INSIDE THE SYSTEM THAN I EVER DID ABOVE--
TELL IT TO JERSEY, SELLOUT!
FAHH!
CHRIST! WHAT DELI SERVES COFFEE THAT HOT?!

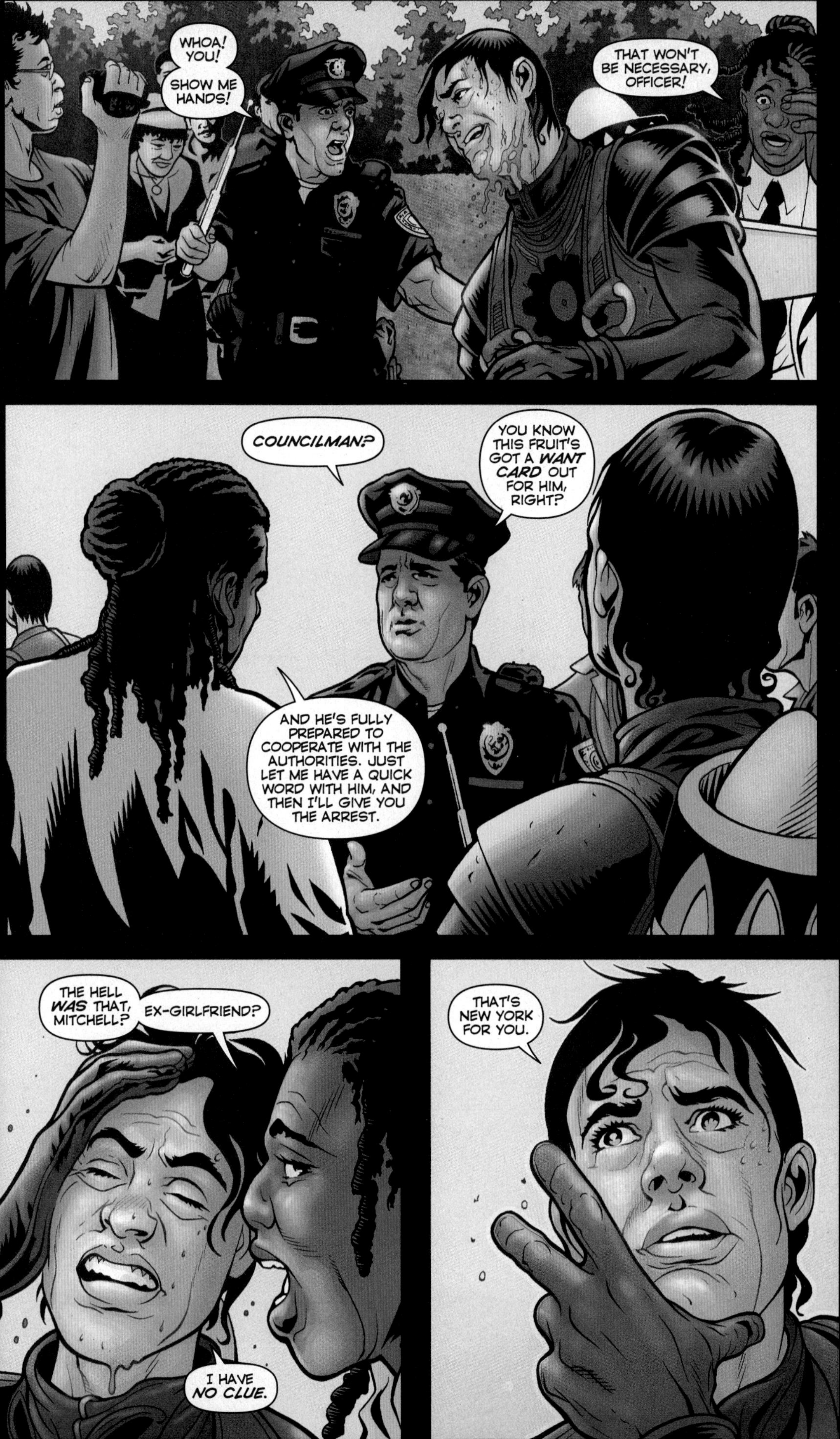
WHOA! YOU!
SHOW ME HANDS!
THAT WON'T BE NECESSARY, OFFICER!
COUNCILMAN?
YOU KNOW THIS FRUIT'S GOT A WANT CARD OUT FOR HIM, RIGHT?
AND HE'S FULLY PREPARED TO COOPERATE WITH THE AUTHORITIES. JUST LET ME HAVE A QUICK WORD WITH HIM, AND THEN I'LL GIVE YOU THE ARREST.
THE HELL WAS THAT, MITCHELL?
EX-GIRLFRIEND?
I HAVE NO CLUE.
THAT'S NEW YORK FOR YOU.

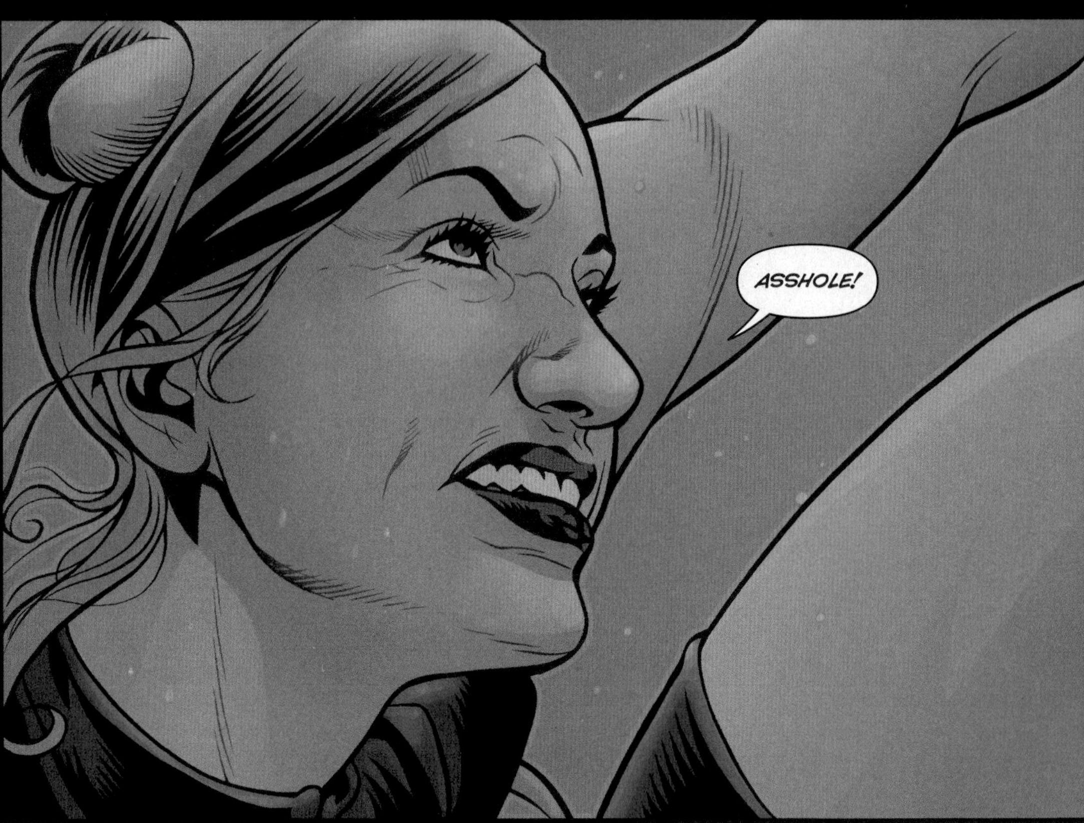
ASSHOLE!

FRIDAY, AUGUST 27, 2004

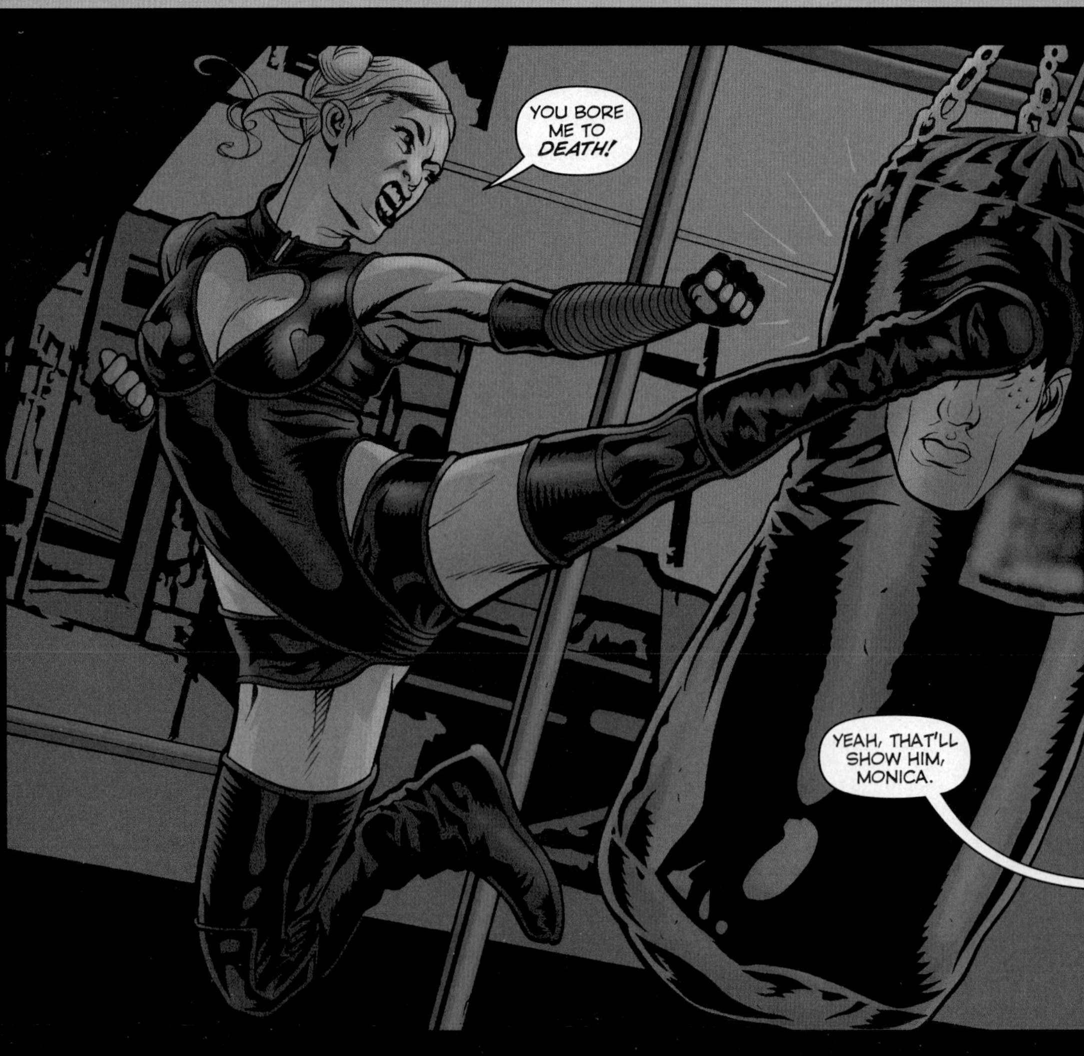
YOU BORE ME TO DEATH!
YEAH, THAT'LL SHOW HIM, MONICA.

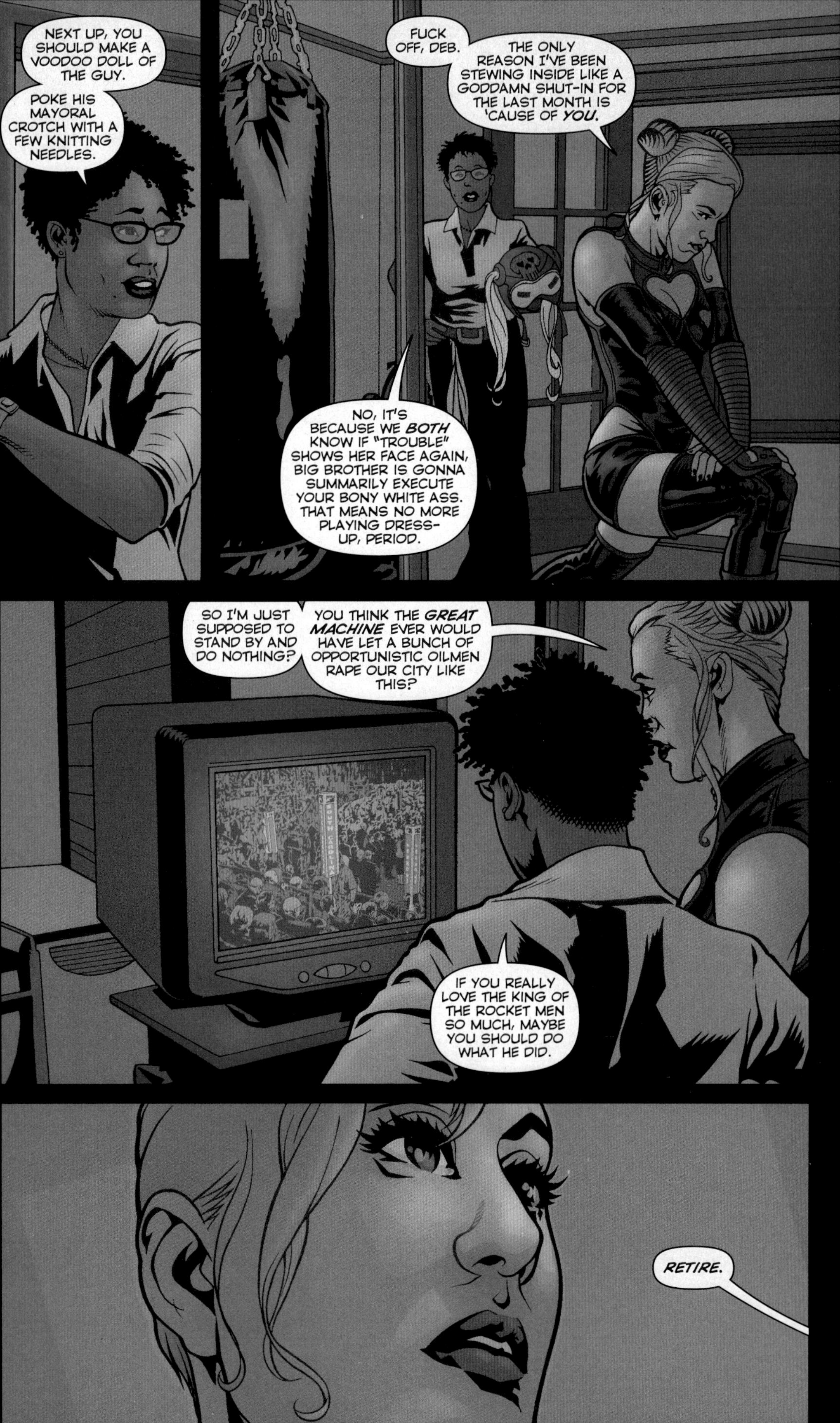
NEXT UP, YOU SHOULD MAKE A VOODOO DOLL OF THE GUY.
POKE HIS MAYORAL CROTCH WITH A FEW KNITTING NEEDLES.
FUCK OFF, DEB.
THE ONLY REASON I'VE BEEN STEWING INSIDE LIKE A GODDAMN SHUT-IN FOR THE LAST MONTH IS 'CAUSE OF *YOU.*
NO, IT'S BECAUSE WE *BOTH* KNOW IF "TROUBLE" SHOWS HER FACE AGAIN, BIG BROTHER IS GONNA SUMMARILY EXECUTE YOUR BONY WHITE ASS. THAT MEANS NO MORE PLAYING DRESS-UP, PERIOD.
SO I'M JUST SUPPOSED TO STAND BY AND DO NOTHING?
YOU THINK THE *GREAT MACHINE* EVER WOULD HAVE LET A BUNCH OF OPPORTUNISTIC OILMEN RAPE OUR CITY LIKE THIS?
IF YOU REALLY LOVE THE KING OF THE ROCKET MEN SO MUCH, MAYBE YOU SHOULD DO WHAT HE DID.
RETIRE.

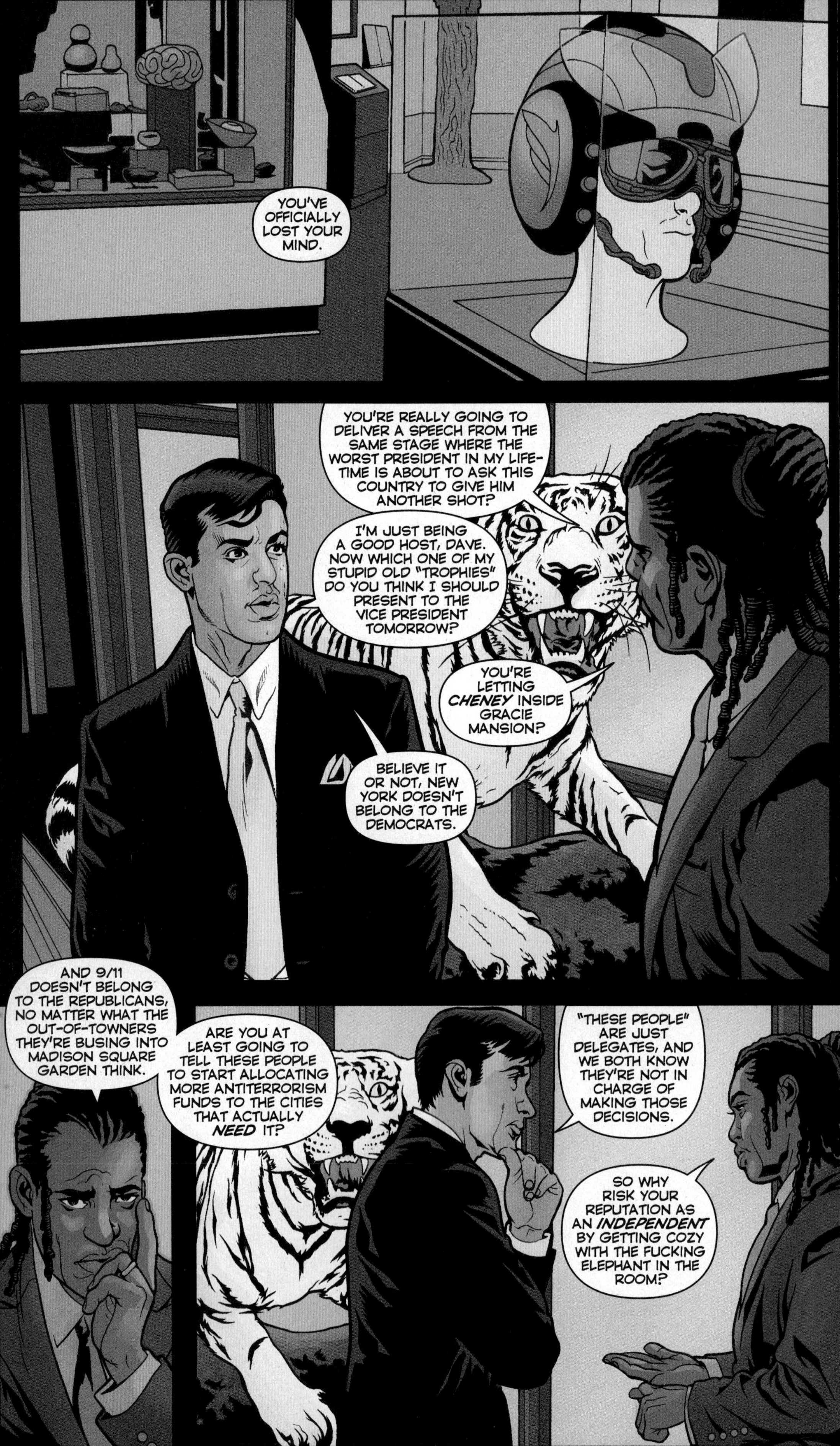
YOU'VE OFFICIALLY LOST YOUR MIND.
YOU'RE REALLY GOING TO DELIVER A SPEECH FROM THE SAME STAGE WHERE THE WORST PRESIDENT IN MY LIFE-TIME IS ABOUT TO ASK THIS COUNTRY TO GIVE HIM ANOTHER SHOT?
I'M JUST BEING A GOOD HOST, DAVE. NOW WHICH ONE OF MY STUPID OLD "TROPHIES" DO YOU THINK I SHOULD PRESENT TO THE VICE PRESIDENT TOMORROW?
YOU'RE LETTING *CHENEY* INSIDE GRACIE MANSION?
BELIEVE IT OR NOT, NEW YORK DOESN'T BELONG TO THE DEMOCRATS.
AND 9/11 DOESN'T BELONG TO THE REPUBLICANS, NO MATTER WHAT THE OUT-OF-TOWNERS THEY'RE BUSING INTO MADISON SQUARE GARDEN THINK.
ARE YOU AT LEAST GOING TO TELL THESE PEOPLE TO START ALLOCATING MORE ANTITERRORISM FUNDS TO THE CITIES THAT ACTUALLY *NEED* IT?
"THESE PEOPLE" ARE JUST DELEGATES, AND WE BOTH KNOW THEY'RE NOT IN CHARGE OF MAKING THOSE DECISIONS.
SO WHY RISK YOUR REPUTATION AS AN *INDEPENDENT* BY GETTING COZY WITH THE FUCKING ELEPHANT IN THE ROOM?

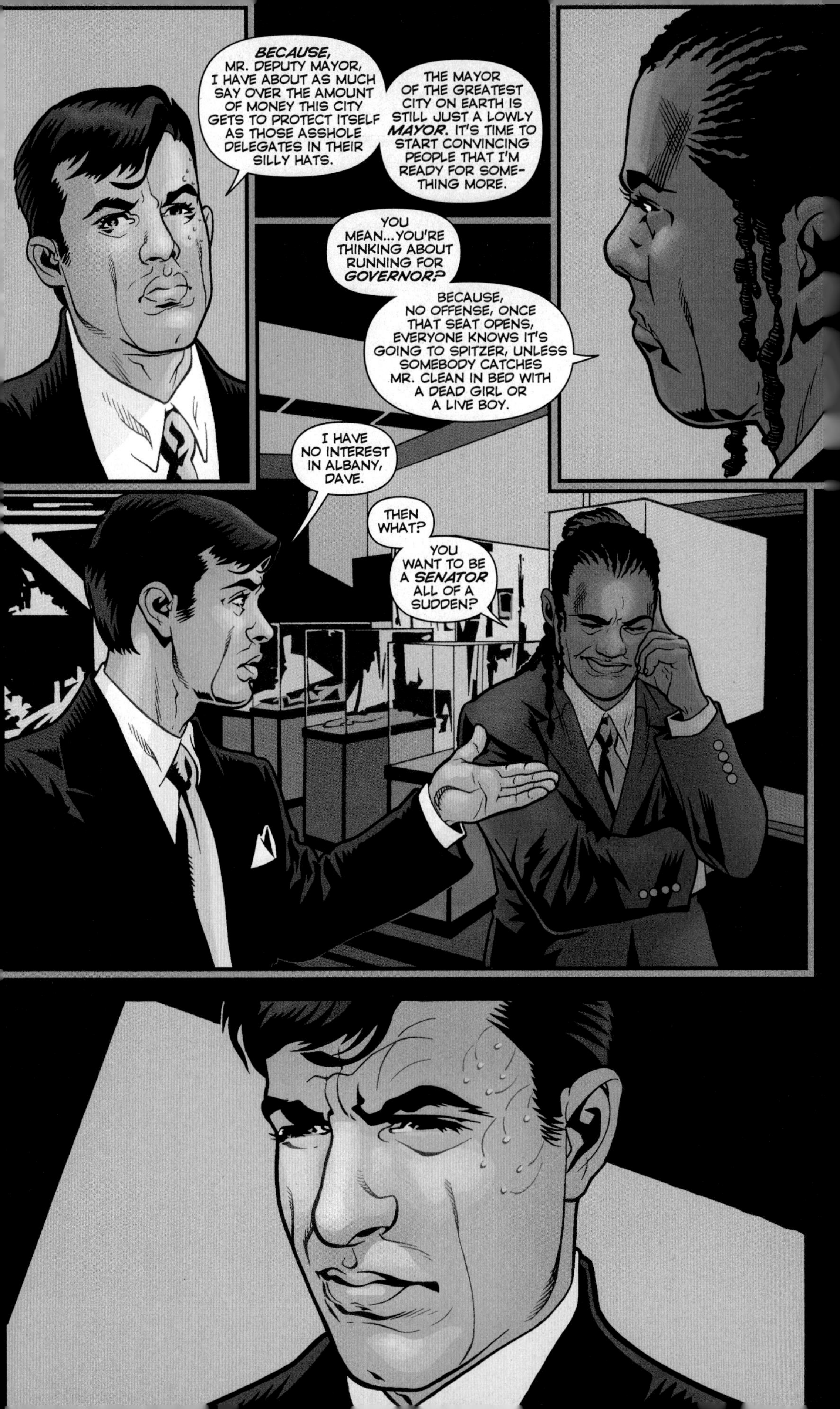
BECAUSE, MR. DEPUTY MAYOR, I HAVE ABOUT AS MUCH SAY OVER THE AMOUNT OF MONEY THIS CITY GETS TO PROTECT ITSELF AS THOSE ASSHOLE DELEGATES IN THEIR SILLY HATS.
THE MAYOR OF THE GREATEST CITY ON EARTH IS STILL JUST A LOWLY MAYOR. IT'S TIME TO START CONVINCING PEOPLE THAT I'M READY FOR SOMETHING MORE.
YOU MEAN...YOU'RE THINKING ABOUT RUNNING FOR GOVERNOR?
BECAUSE, NO OFFENSE, ONCE THAT SEAT OPENS, EVERYONE KNOWS IT'S GOING TO SPITZER, UNLESS SOMEBODY CATCHES MR. CLEAN IN BED WITH A DEAD GIRL OR A LIVE BOY.
I HAVE NO INTEREST IN ALBANY, DAVE.
THEN WHAT?
YOU WANT TO BE A SENATOR ALL OF A SUDDEN?

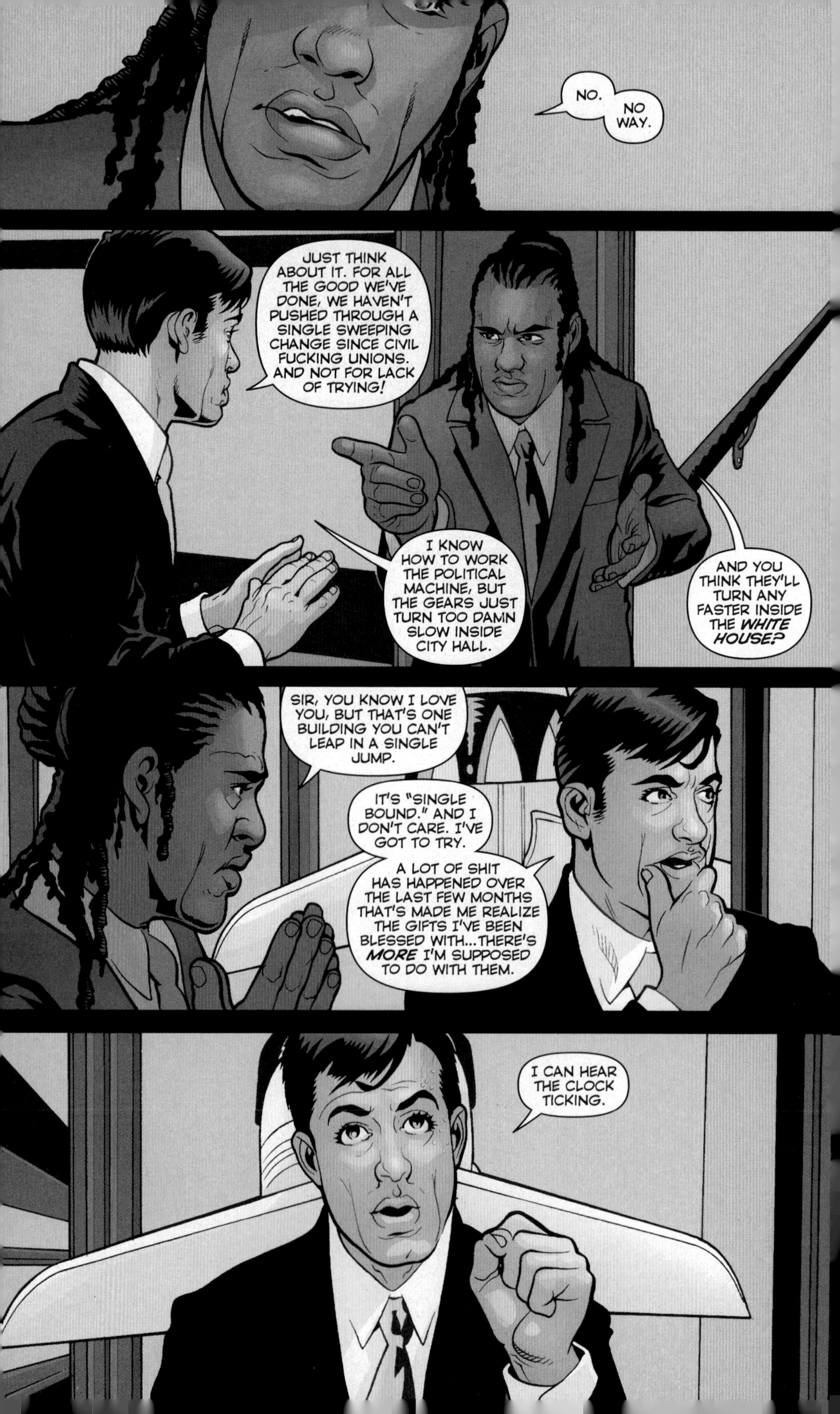
NO.
NO WAY.
JUST THINK ABOUT IT. FOR ALL THE GOOD WE'VE DONE, WE HAVEN'T PUSHED THROUGH A SINGLE SWEEPING CHANGE SINCE CIVIL FUCKING UNIONS. AND NOT FOR LACK OF TRYING!
I KNOW HOW TO WORK THE POLITICAL MACHINE, BUT THE GEARS JUST TURN TOO DAMN SLOW INSIDE CITY HALL.
AND YOU THINK THEY'LL TURN ANY FASTER INSIDE THE WHITE HOUSE?
SIR, YOU KNOW I LOVE YOU, BUT THAT'S ONE BUILDING YOU CAN'T LEAP IN A SINGLE JUMP.
IT'S "SINGLE BOUND." AND I DON'T CARE. I'VE GOT TO TRY.
A LOT OF SHIT HAS HAPPENED OVER THE LAST FEW MONTHS THAT'S MADE ME REALIZE THE GIFTS I'VE BEEN BLESSED WITH...THERE'S MORE I'M SUPPOSED TO DO WITH THEM.
I CAN HEAR THE CLOCK TICKING.

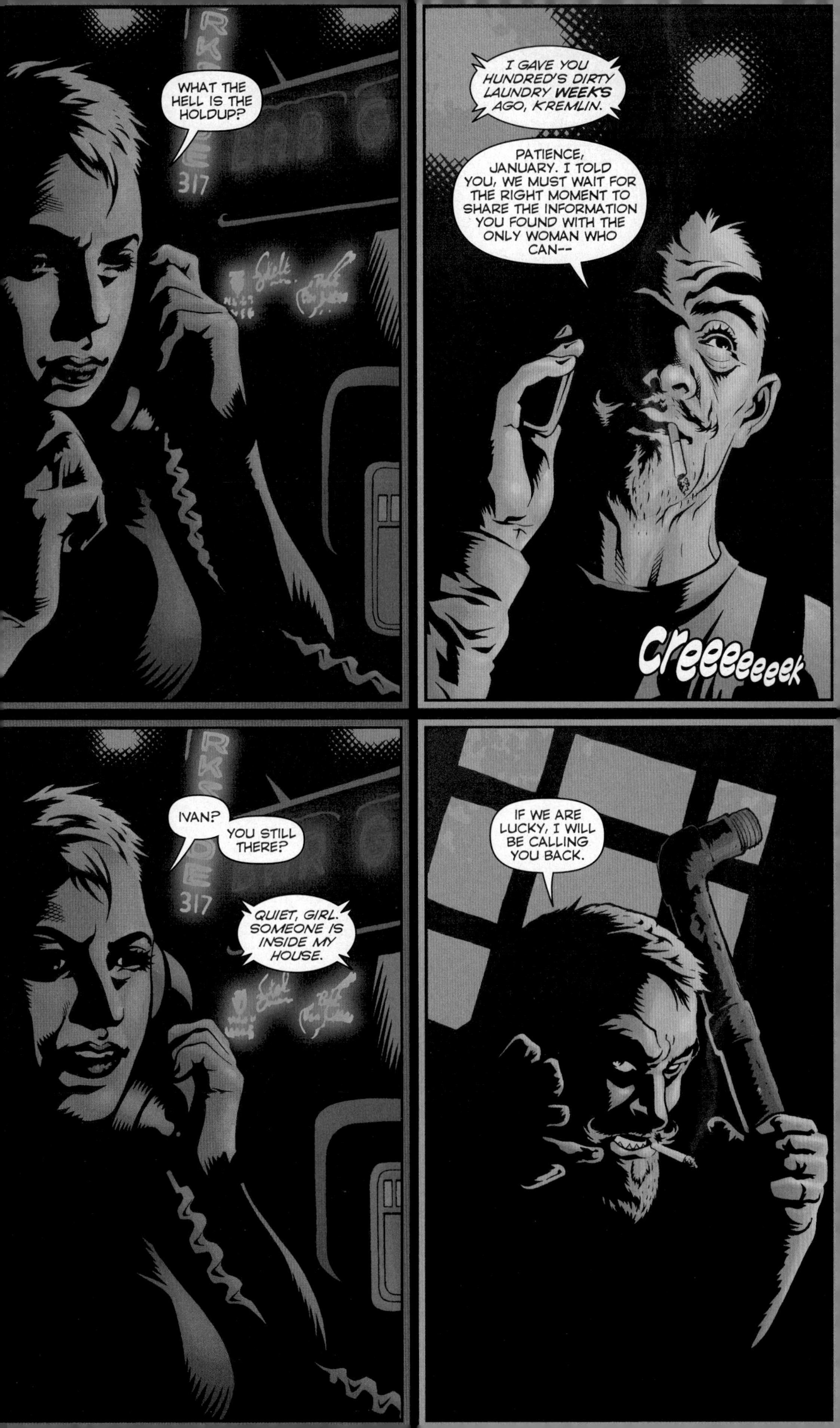
WHAT THE HELL IS THE HOLDUP?
I GAVE YOU HUNDRED'S DIRTY LAUNDRY WEEKS AGO, KREMLIN.
PATIENCE, JANUARY. I TOLD YOU, WE MUST WAIT FOR THE RIGHT MOMENT TO SHARE THE INFORMATION YOU FOUND WITH THE ONLY WOMAN WHO CAN--
Creeeeeeeek
IVAN?
YOU STILL THERE?
QUIET, GIRL. SOMEONE IS INSIDE MY HOUSE.
IF WE ARE LUCKY, I WILL BE CALLING YOU BACK.

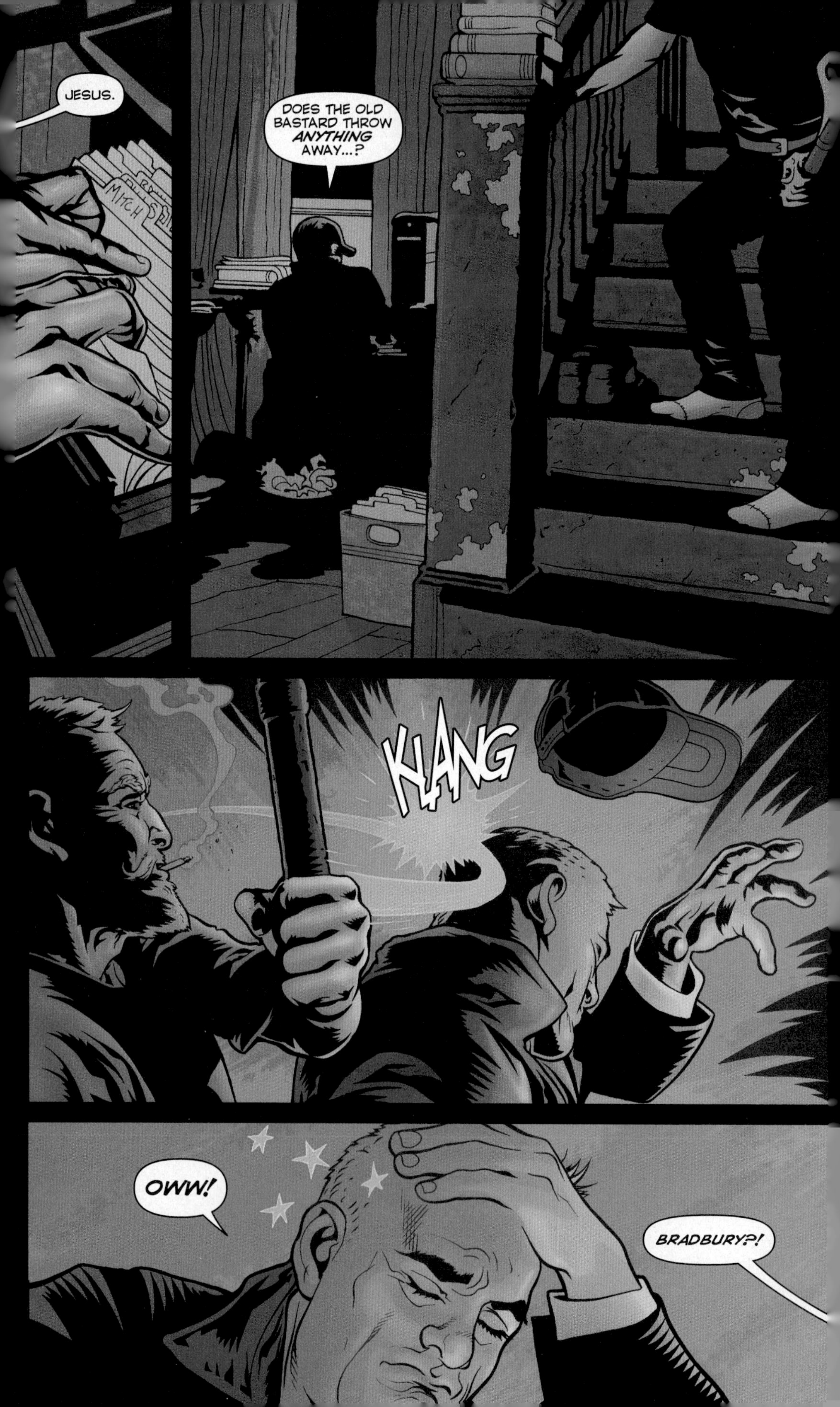
JESUS.
MITCH
DOES THE OLD BASTARD THROW *ANYTHING* AWAY...?
KLANG
OWW!
BRADBURY?!

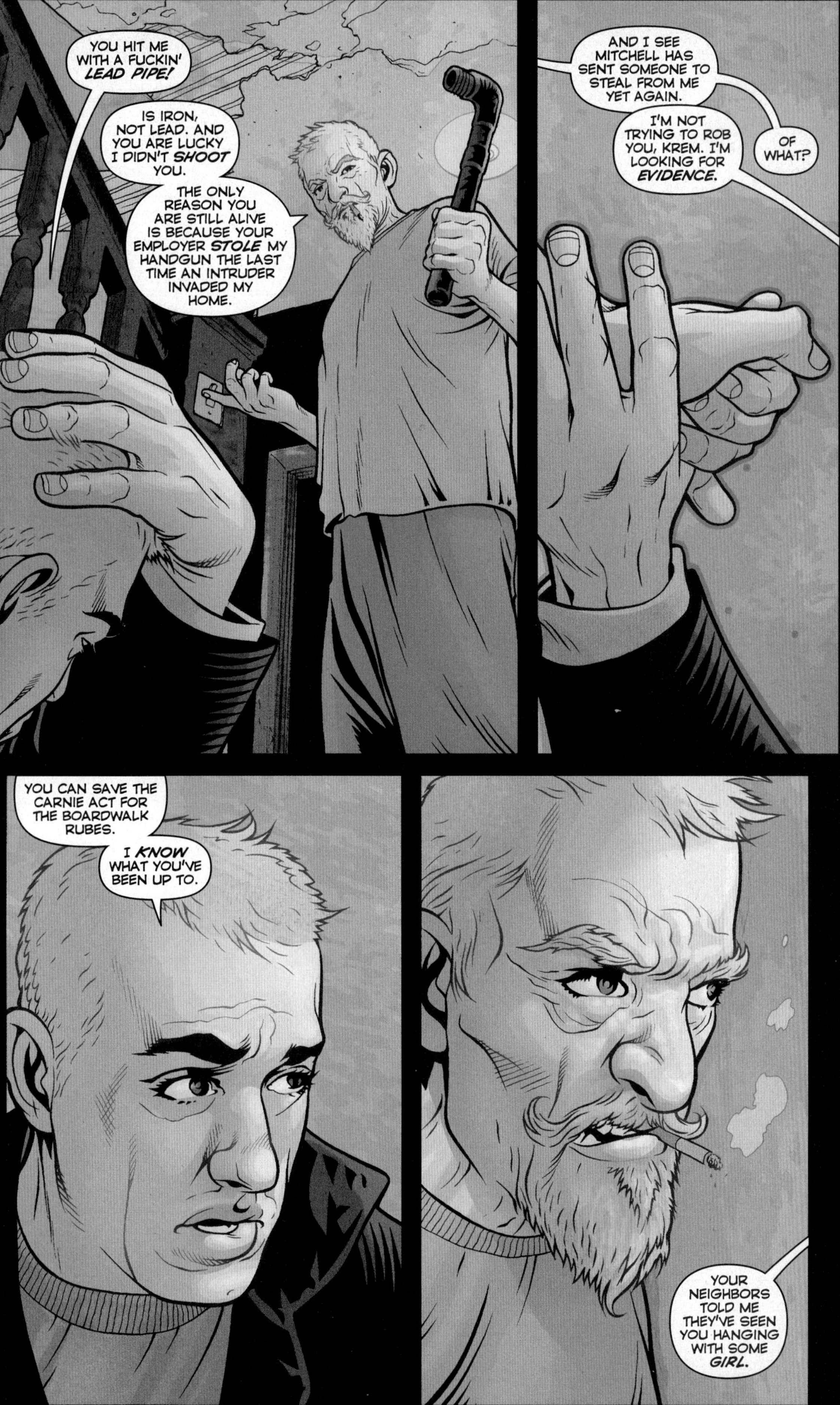
YOU HIT ME WITH A FUCKIN' LEAD PIPE!
IS IRON, NOT LEAD. AND YOU ARE LUCKY I DIDN'T SHOOT YOU.
THE ONLY REASON YOU ARE STILL ALIVE IS BECAUSE YOUR EMPLOYER STOLE MY HANDGUN THE LAST TIME AN INTRUDER INVADED MY HOME.
AND I SEE MITCHELL HAS SENT SOMEONE TO STEAL FROM ME YET AGAIN.
OF WHAT?
I'M NOT TRYING TO ROB YOU, KREM. I'M LOOKING FOR EVIDENCE.
YOU CAN SAVE THE CARNIE ACT FOR THE BOARDWALK RUBES.
I KNOW WHAT YOU'VE BEEN UP TO.
YOUR NEIGHBORS TOLD ME THEY'VE SEEN YOU HANGING WITH SOME GIRL.

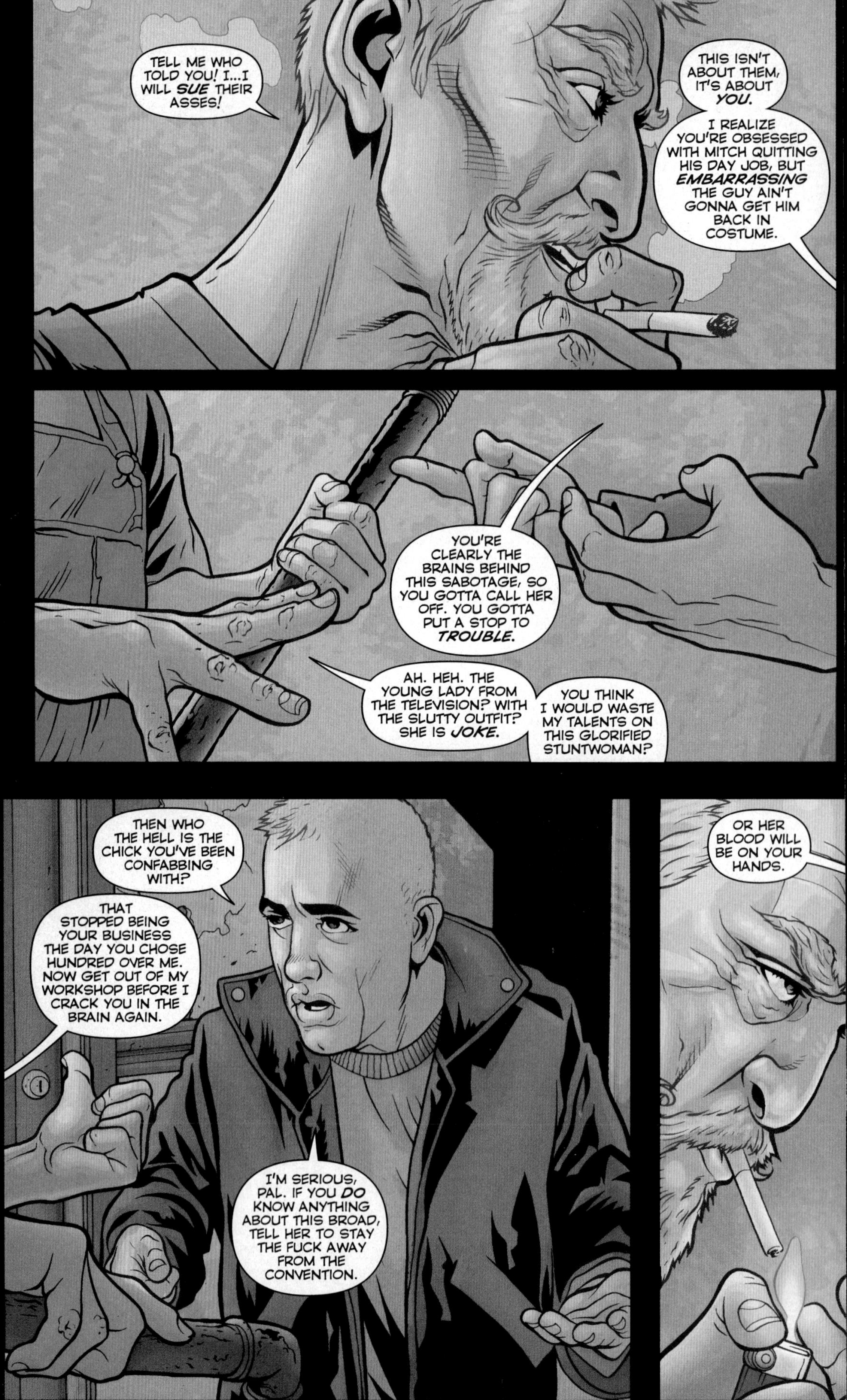
TELL ME WHO TOLD YOU! I...I WILL SUE THEIR ASSES!
THIS ISN'T ABOUT THEM, IT'S ABOUT YOU.
I REALIZE YOU'RE OBSESSED WITH MITCH QUITTING HIS DAY JOB, BUT EMBARRASSING THE GUY AIN'T GONNA GET HIM BACK IN COSTUME.
YOU'RE CLEARLY THE BRAINS BEHIND THIS SABOTAGE, SO YOU GOTTA CALL HER OFF. YOU GOTTA PUT A STOP TO TROUBLE.
AH. HEH. THE YOUNG LADY FROM THE TELEVISION? WITH THE SLUTTY OUTFIT? SHE IS JOKE.
YOU THINK I WOULD WASTE MY TALENTS ON THIS GLORIFIED STUNTWOMAN?
THEN WHO THE HELL IS THE CHICK YOU'VE BEEN CONFABBING WITH?
THAT STOPPED BEING YOUR BUSINESS THE DAY YOU CHOSE HUNDRED OVER ME. NOW GET OUT OF MY WORKSHOP BEFORE I CRACK YOU IN THE BRAIN AGAIN.
I'M SERIOUS, PAL. IF YOU DO KNOW ANYTHING ABOUT THIS BROAD, TELL HER TO STAY THE FUCK AWAY FROM THE CONVENTION.
OR HER BLOOD WILL BE ON YOUR HANDS.

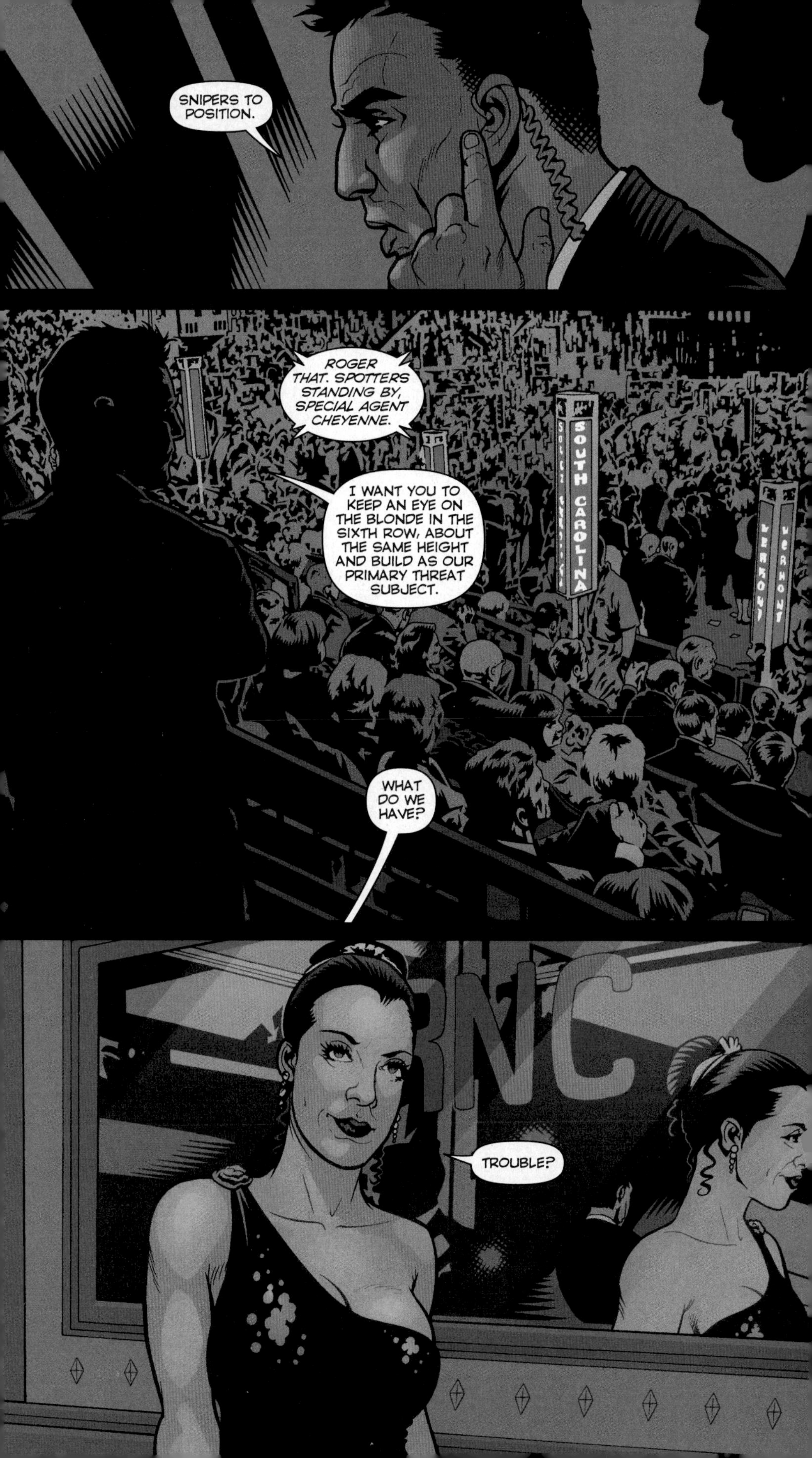
SNIPERS TO POSITION.
ROGER THAT. SPOTTERS STANDING BY, SPECIAL AGENT CHEYENNE.
SOUTH CAROLINA
I WANT YOU TO KEEP AN EYE ON THE BLONDE IN THE SIXTH ROW, ABOUT THE SAME HEIGHT AND BUILD AS OUR PRIMARY THREAT SUBJECT.
WHAT DO WE HAVE?
RNC
TROUBLE?

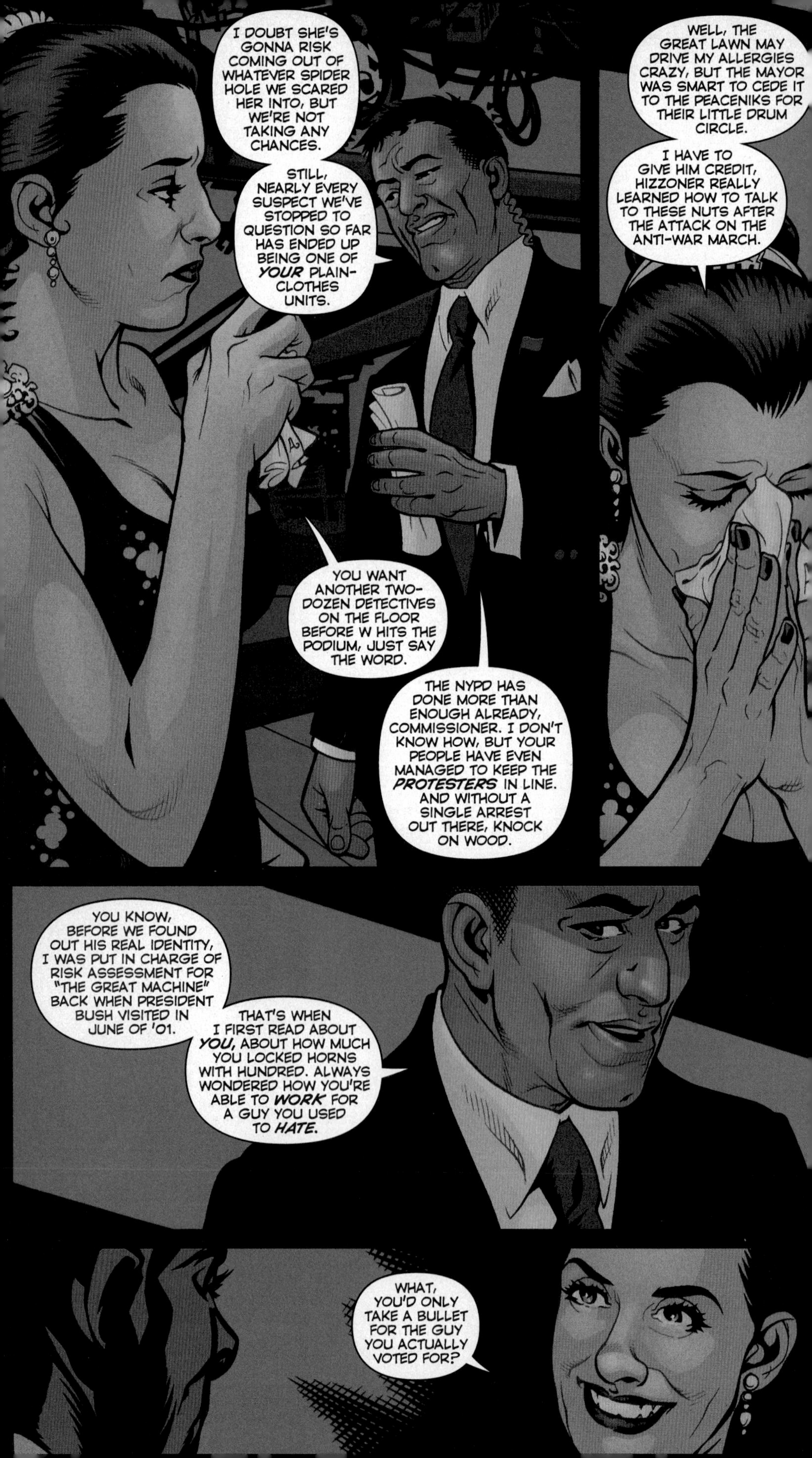
I DOUBT SHE'S GONNA RISK COMING OUT OF WHATEVER SPIDER HOLE WE SCARED HER INTO, BUT WE'RE NOT TAKING ANY CHANCES.
STILL, NEARLY EVERY SUSPECT WE'VE STOPPED TO QUESTION SO FAR HAS ENDED UP BEING ONE OF *YOUR* PLAIN-CLOTHES UNITS.
YOU WANT ANOTHER TWO-DOZEN DETECTIVES ON THE FLOOR BEFORE W HITS THE PODIUM, JUST SAY THE WORD.
THE NYPD HAS DONE MORE THAN ENOUGH ALREADY, COMMISSIONER. I DON'T KNOW HOW, BUT YOUR PEOPLE HAVE EVEN MANAGED TO KEEP THE *PROTESTERS* IN LINE. AND WITHOUT A SINGLE ARREST OUT THERE, KNOCK ON WOOD.
WELL, THE GREAT LAWN MAY DRIVE MY ALLERGIES CRAZY, BUT THE MAYOR WAS SMART TO CEDE IT TO THE PEACENIKS FOR THEIR LITTLE DRUM CIRCLE.
I HAVE TO GIVE HIM CREDIT, HIZZONER REALLY LEARNED HOW TO TALK TO THESE NUTS AFTER THE ATTACK ON THE ANTI-WAR MARCH.
YOU KNOW, BEFORE WE FOUND OUT HIS REAL IDENTITY, I WAS PUT IN CHARGE OF RISK ASSESSMENT FOR "THE GREAT MACHINE" BACK WHEN PRESIDENT BUSH VISITED IN JUNE OF '01.
THAT'S WHEN I FIRST READ ABOUT *YOU*, ABOUT HOW MUCH YOU LOCKED HORNS WITH HUNDRED. ALWAYS WONDERED HOW YOU'RE ABLE TO *WORK* FOR A GUY YOU USED TO *HATE*.
WHAT, YOU'D ONLY TAKE A BULLET FOR THE GUY YOU ACTUALLY VOTED FOR?

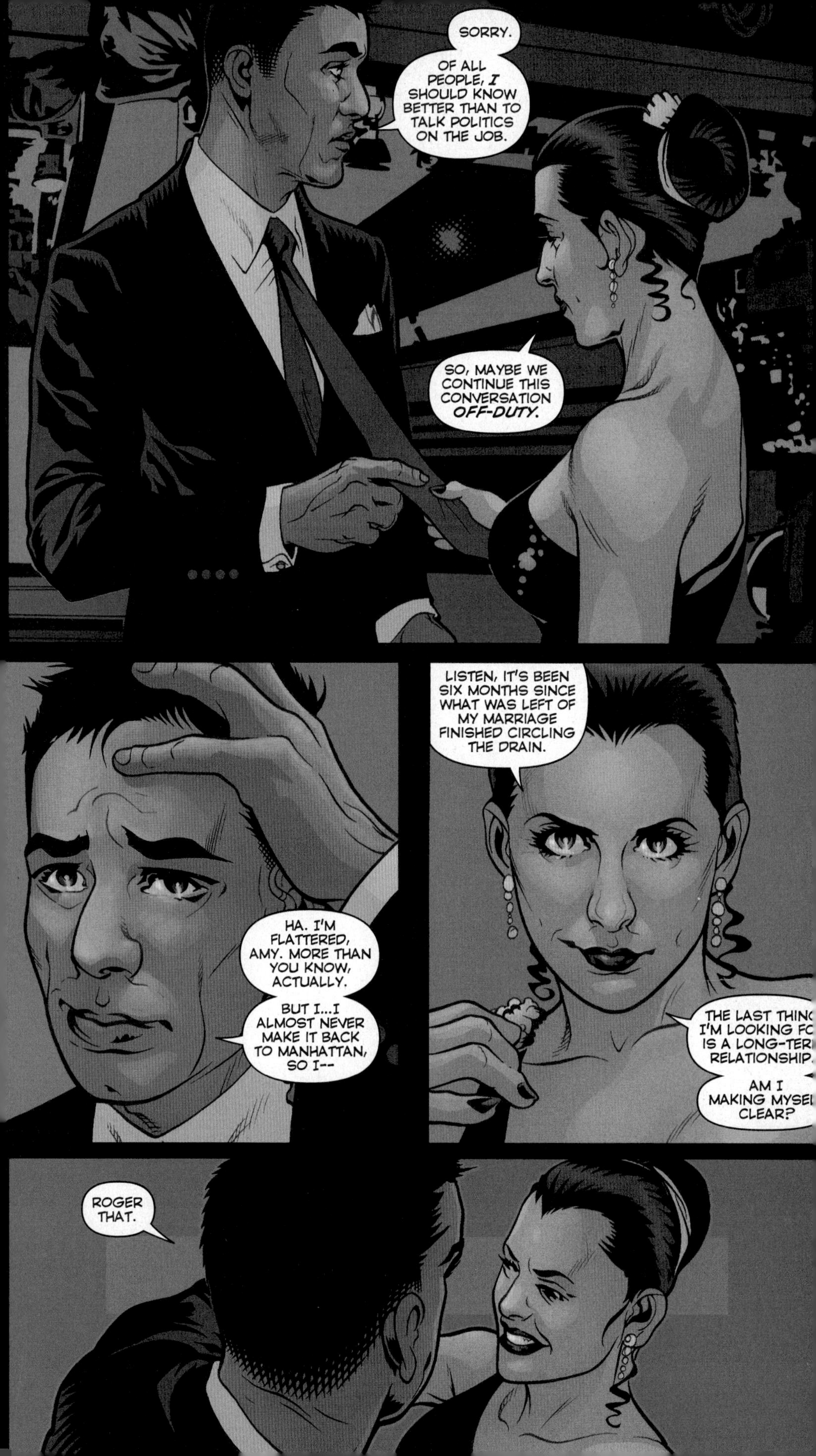
SORRY.
OF ALL PEOPLE, *I* SHOULD KNOW BETTER THAN TO TALK POLITICS ON THE JOB.
SO, MAYBE WE CONTINUE THIS CONVERSATION ***OFF-DUTY.***
HA. I'M FLATTERED, AMY. MORE THAN YOU KNOW, ACTUALLY.
BUT I...I ALMOST NEVER MAKE IT BACK TO MANHATTAN, SO I--
LISTEN, IT'S BEEN SIX MONTHS SINCE WHAT WAS LEFT OF MY MARRIAGE FINISHED CIRCLING THE DRAIN.
THE LAST THIN I'M LOOKING FO IS A LONG-TER RELATIONSHIP.
AM I MAKING MYSE CLEAR?
ROGER THAT.

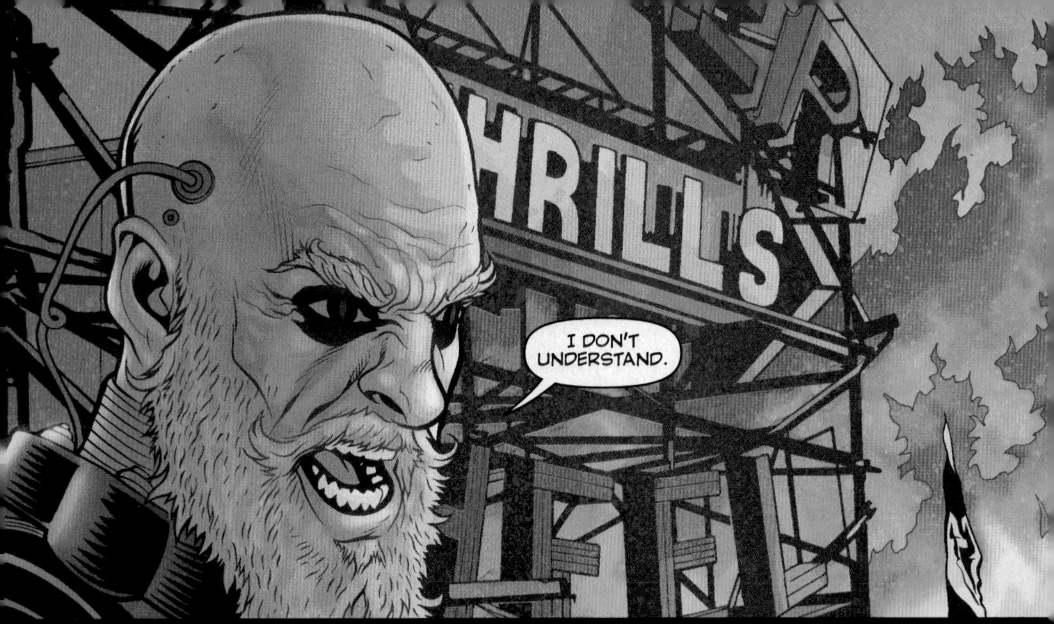
I DON'T UNDERSTAND.

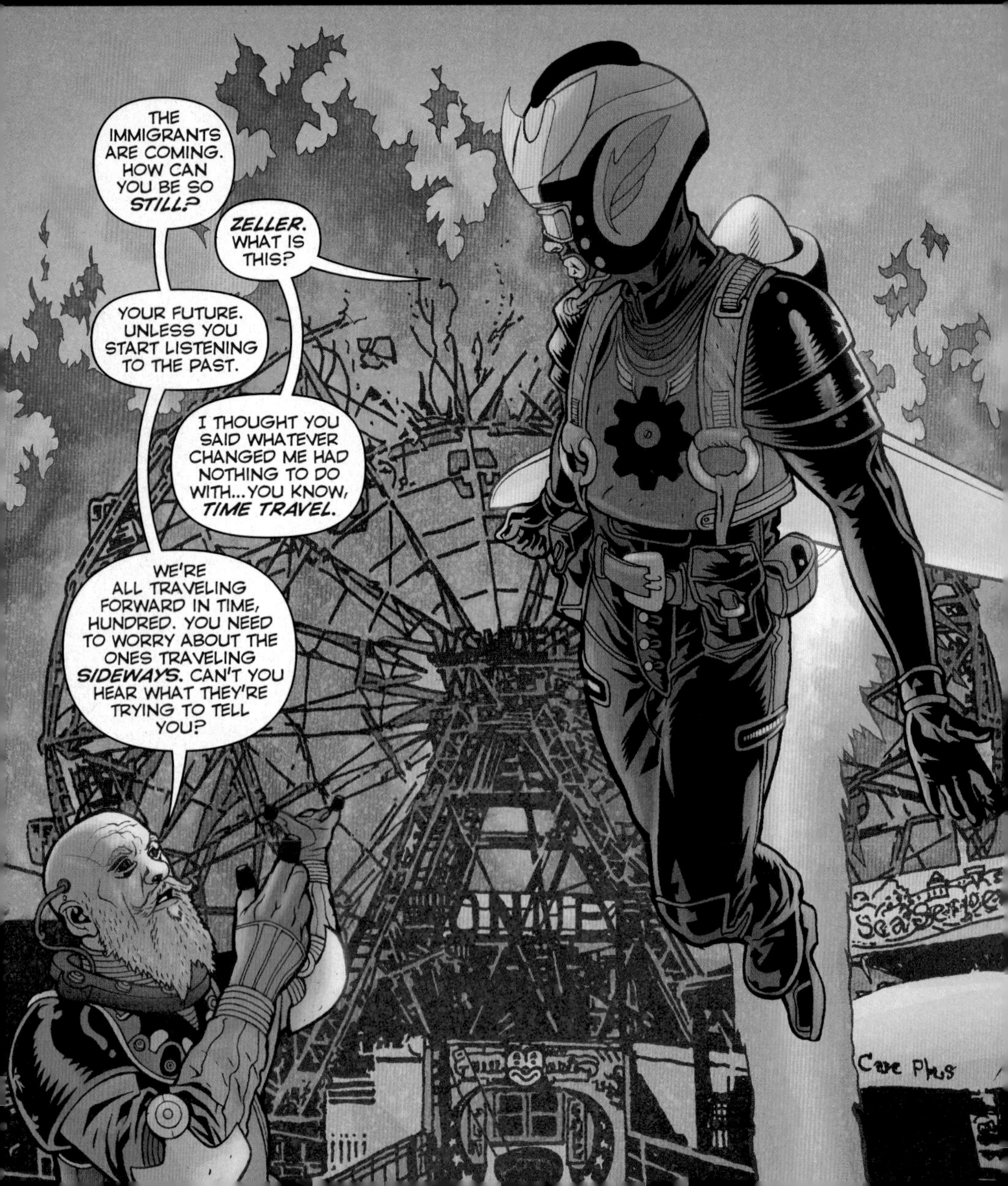
THE IMMIGRANTS ARE COMING. HOW CAN YOU BE SO *STILL?*
ZELLER. WHAT IS THIS?
YOUR FUTURE. UNLESS YOU START LISTENING TO THE PAST.
I THOUGHT YOU SAID WHATEVER CHANGED ME HAD NOTHING TO DO WITH...YOU KNOW, *TIME TRAVEL.*
WE'RE ALL TRAVELING FORWARD IN TIME, HUNDRED. YOU NEED TO WORRY ABOUT THE ONES TRAVELING *SIDEWAYS.* CAN'T YOU HEAR WHAT THEY'RE TRYING TO TELL YOU?

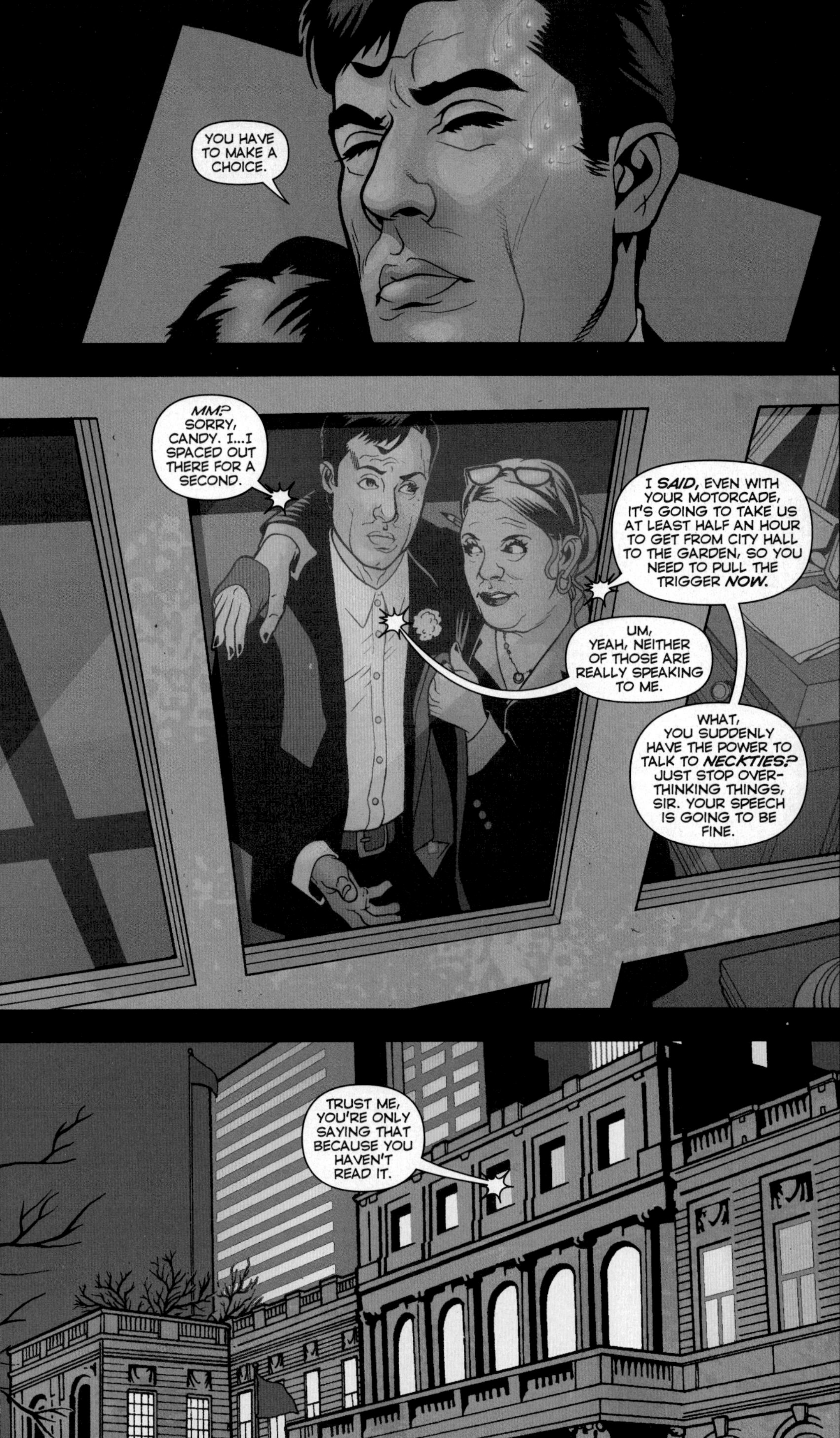
YOU HAVE TO MAKE A CHOICE.
MM? SORRY, CANDY. I...I SPACED OUT THERE FOR A SECOND.
I SAID, EVEN WITH YOUR MOTORCADE, IT'S GOING TO TAKE US AT LEAST HALF AN HOUR TO GET FROM CITY HALL TO THE GARDEN, SO YOU NEED TO PULL THE TRIGGER NOW.
UM, YEAH, NEITHER OF THOSE ARE REALLY SPEAKING TO ME.
WHAT, YOU SUDDENLY HAVE THE POWER TO TALK TO NECKTIES? JUST STOP OVER-THINKING THINGS, SIR. YOUR SPEECH IS GOING TO BE FINE.
TRUST ME, YOU'RE ONLY SAYING THAT BECAUSE YOU HAVEN'T READ IT.

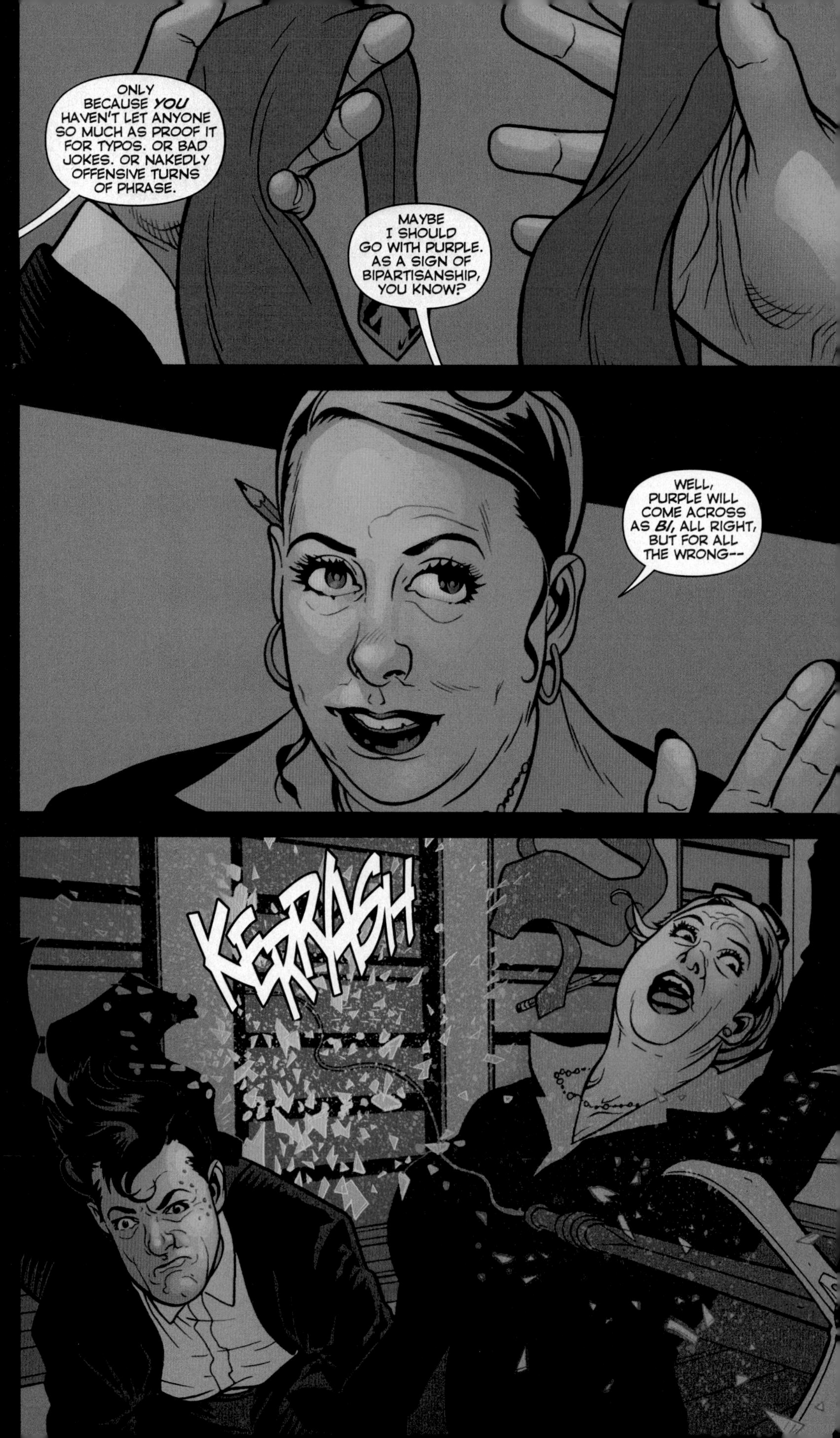

ONLY BECAUSE *YOU* HAVEN'T LET ANYONE SO MUCH AS PROOF IT FOR TYPOS. OR BAD JOKES. OR NAKEDLY OFFENSIVE TURNS OF PHRASE.
MAYBE I SHOULD GO WITH PURPLE. AS A SIGN OF BIPARTISANSHIP, YOU KNOW?
WELL, PURPLE WILL COME ACROSS AS *BI*, ALL RIGHT, BUT FOR ALL THE WRONG--
KRRASH

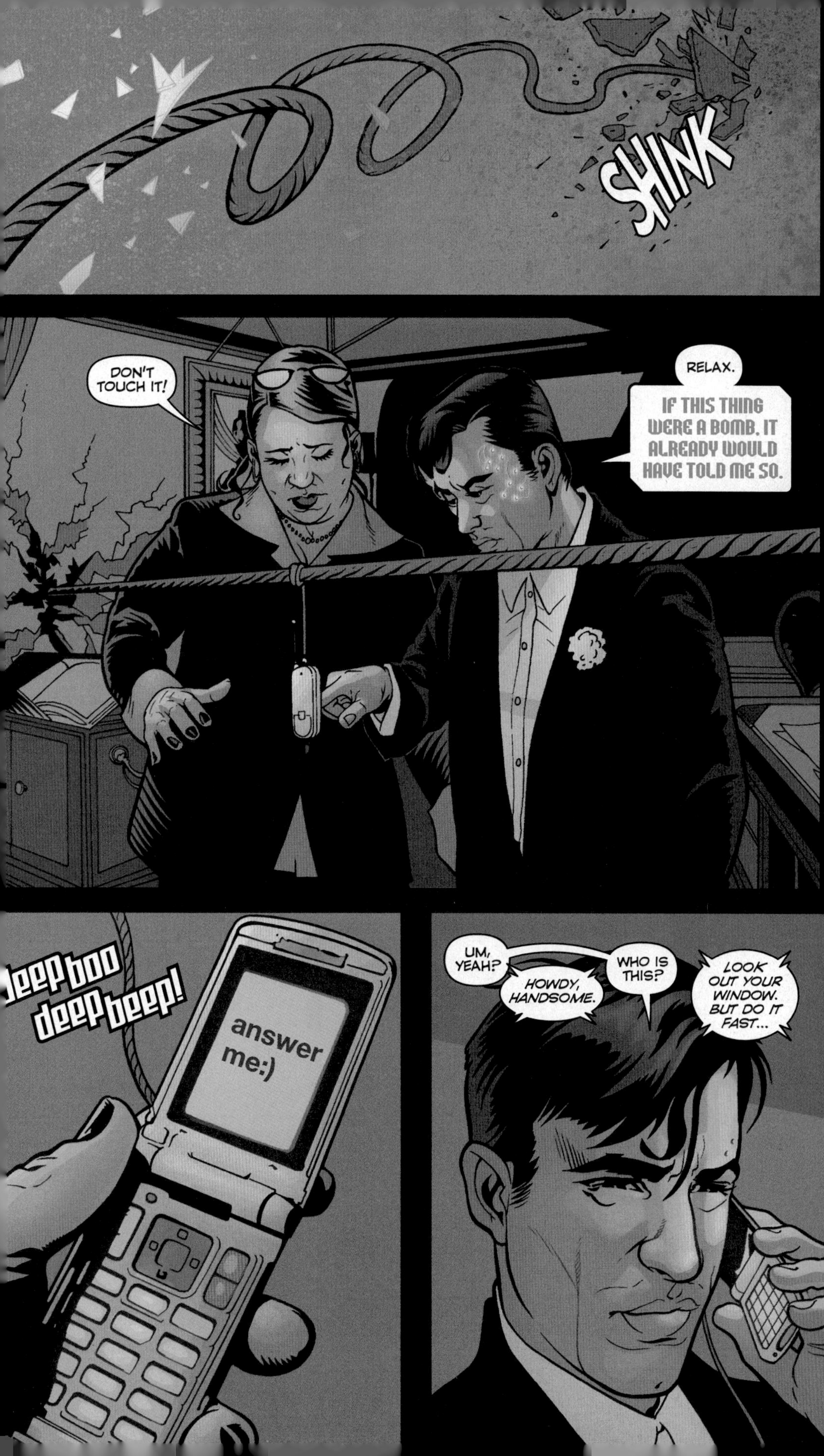
SHINK
DON'T TOUCH IT!
RELAX.
IF THIS THING WERE A BOMB, IT ALREADY WOULD HAVE TOLD ME SO.
beep boo deep beep!
answer me:)
UM, YEAH?
HOWDY, HANDSOME.
WHO IS THIS?
LOOK OUT YOUR WINDOW. BUT DO IT FAST...

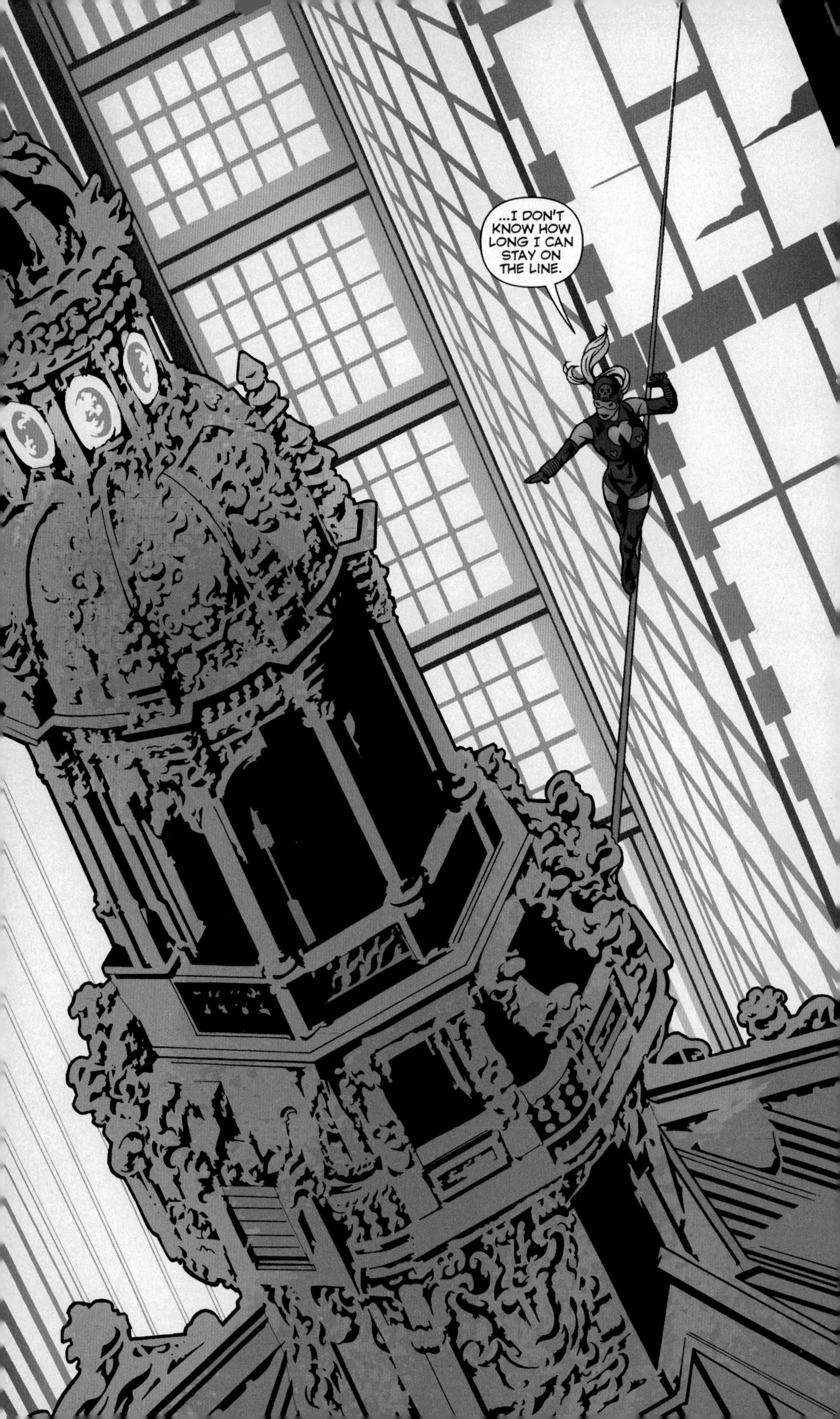
...I DON'T KNOW HOW LONG I CAN STAY ON THE LINE.

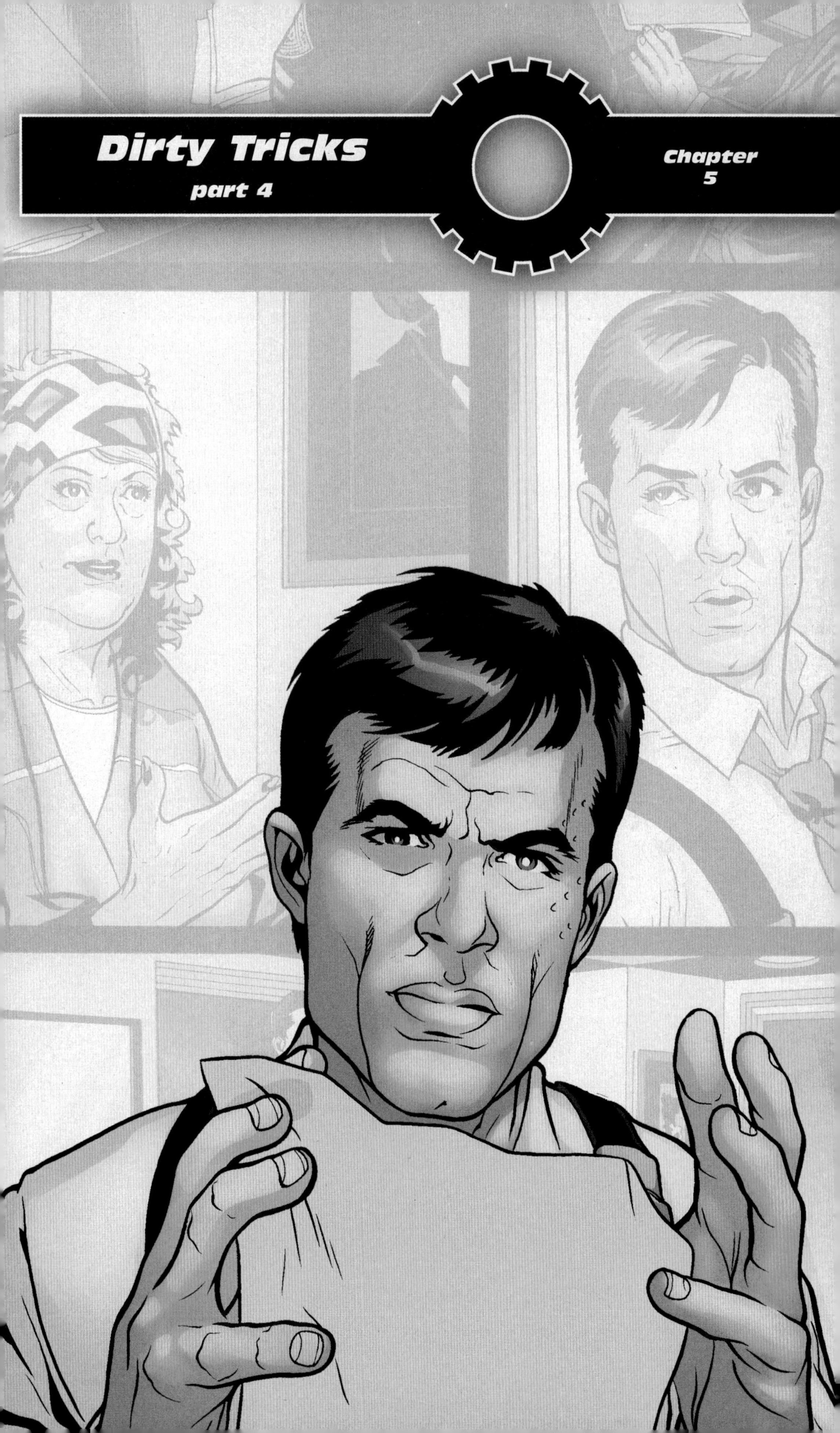

Dirty Tricks
part 4
Chapter
5

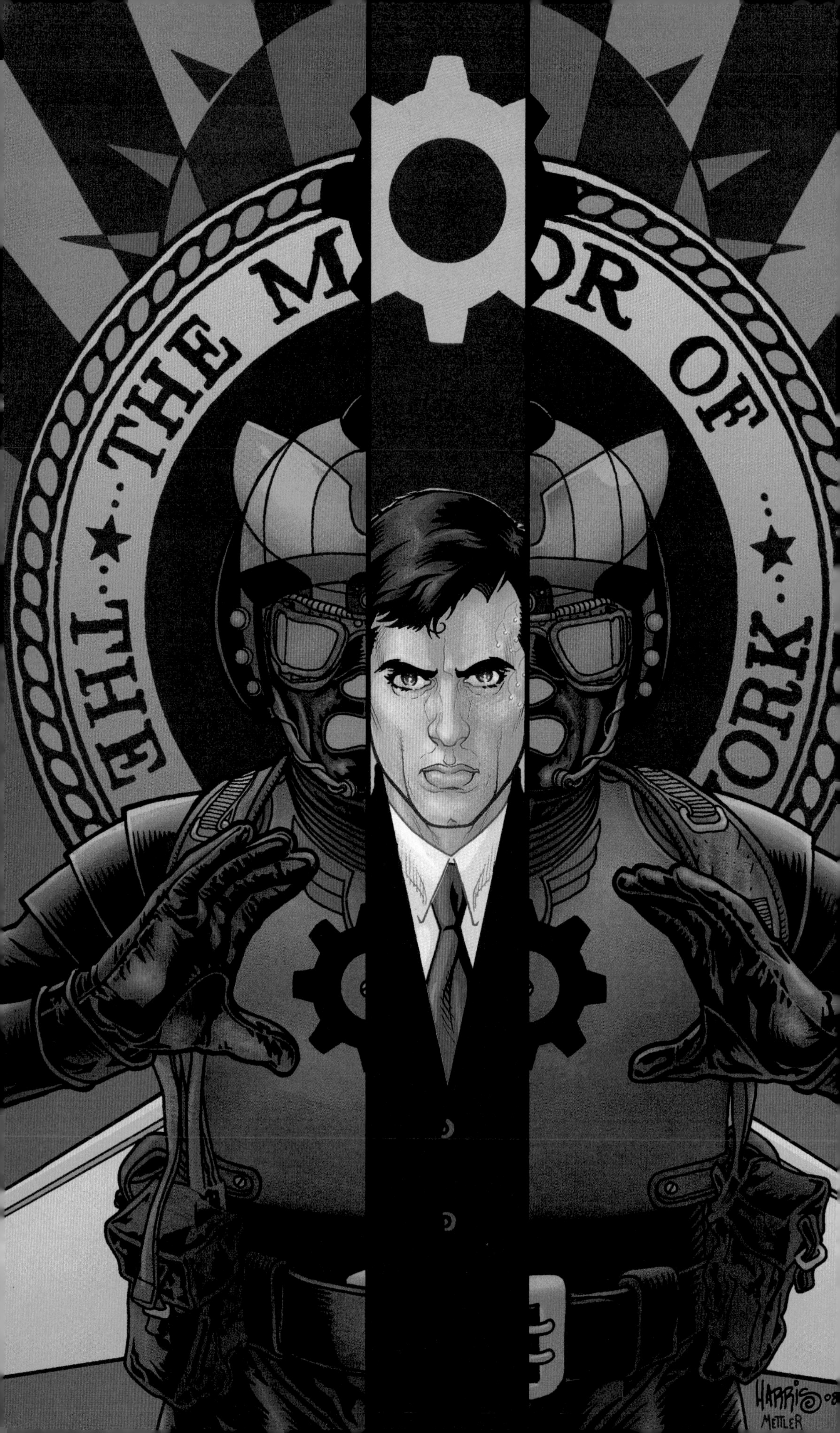
THE...★...THE M
OR OF
...★...ORK
HARRIS '08
METTLER

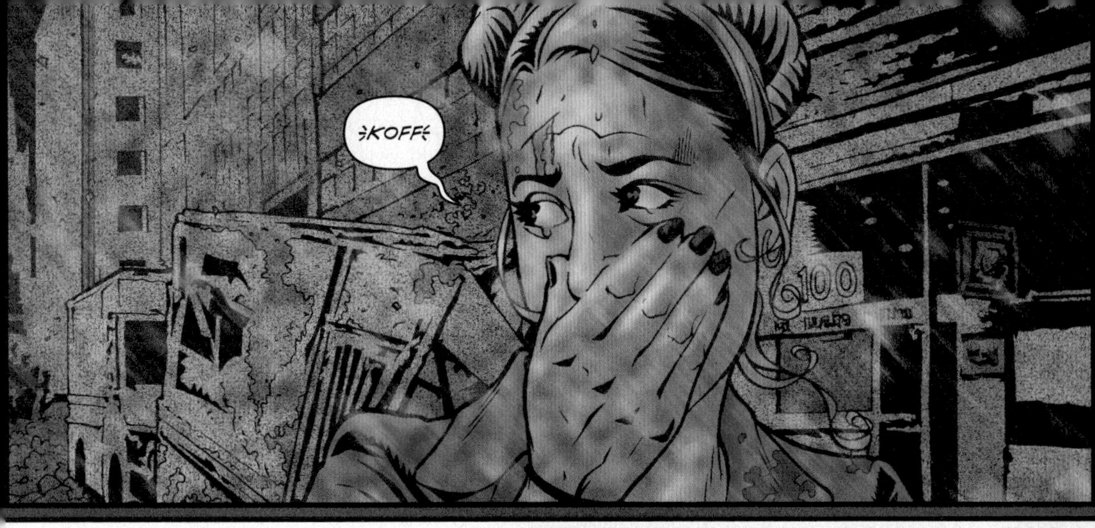
KOFF
100

TUESDAY, SEPTEMBER 11, 2001

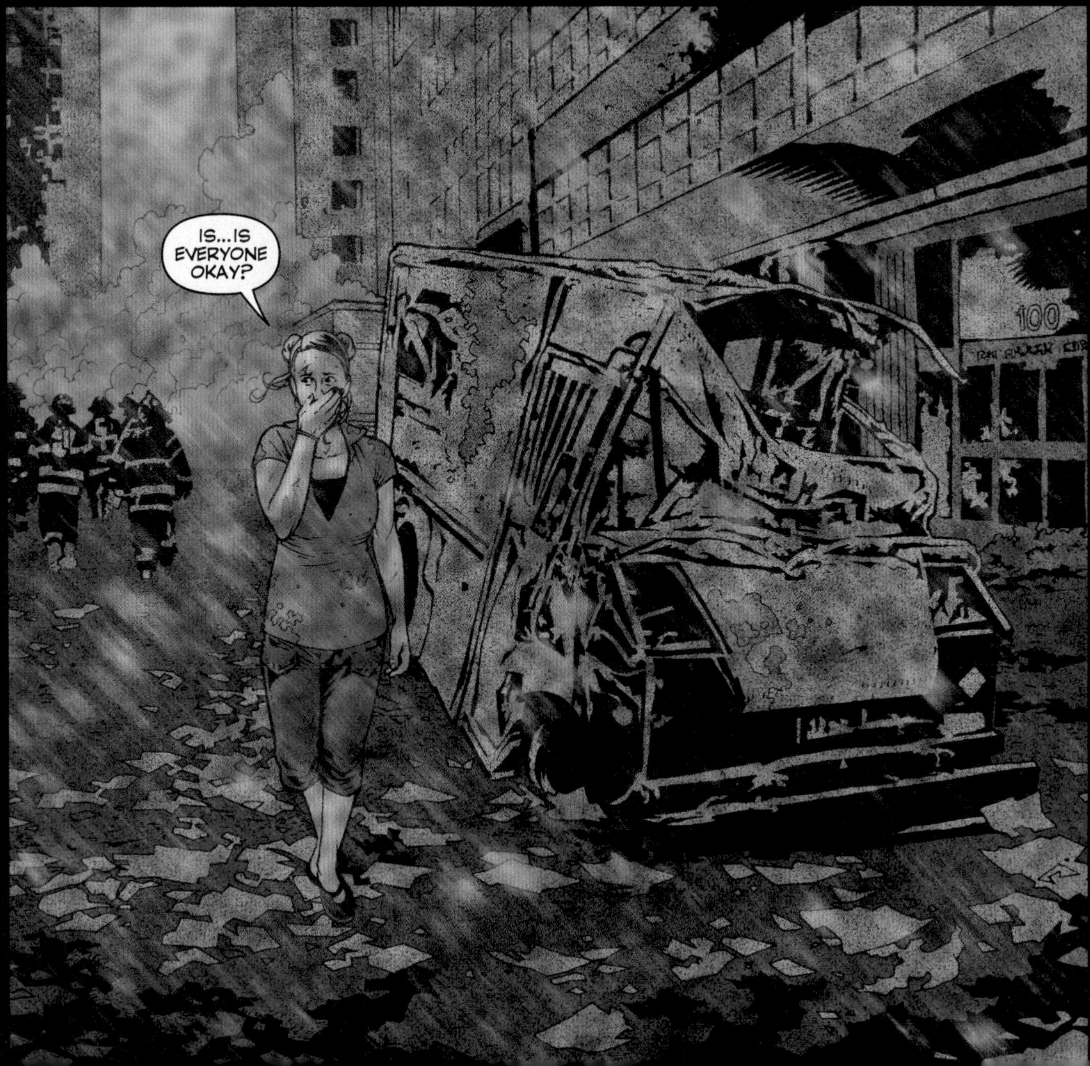
IS...IS EVERYONE OKAY?
100

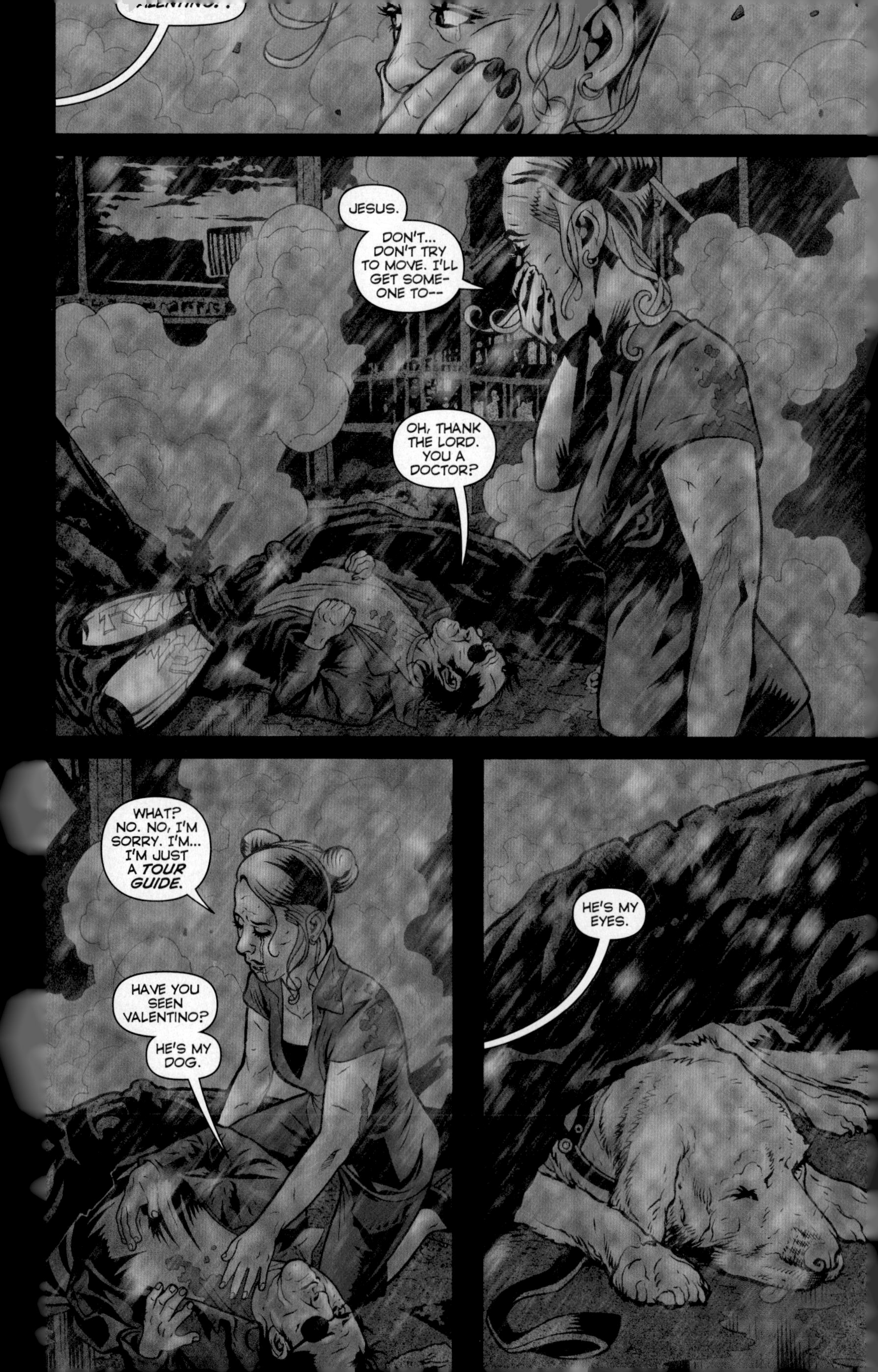
JESUS.
DON'T... DON'T TRY TO MOVE. I'LL GET SOME-ONE TO--
OH, THANK THE LORD. YOU A DOCTOR?
WHAT? NO. NO, I'M SORRY. I'M... I'M JUST A TOUR GUIDE.
HAVE YOU SEEN VALENTINO?
HE'S MY DOG.
HE'S MY EYES.

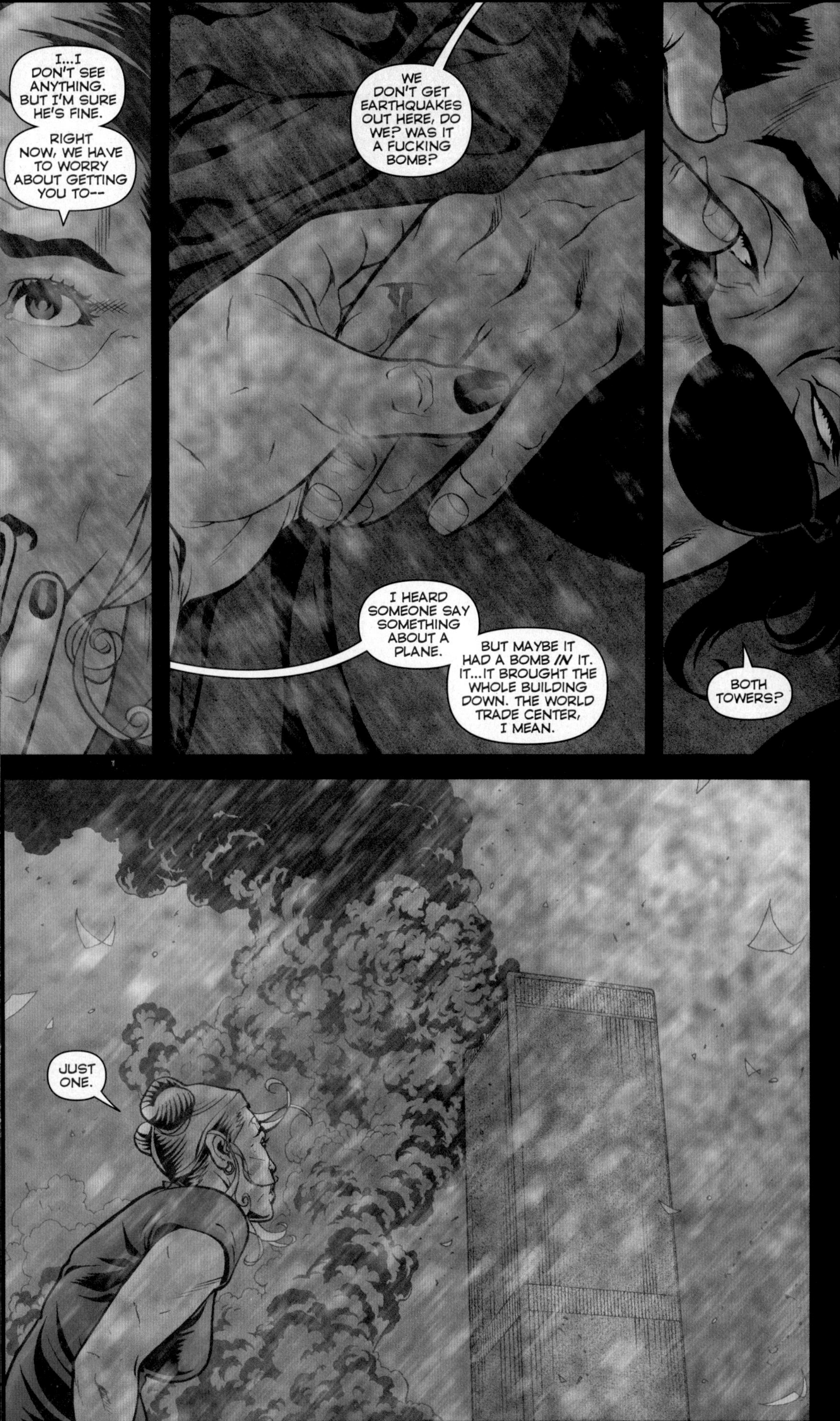
I...I DON'T SEE ANYTHING. BUT I'M SURE HE'S FINE.
RIGHT NOW, WE HAVE TO WORRY ABOUT GETTING YOU TO--
WE DON'T GET EARTHQUAKES OUT HERE, DO WE? WAS IT A FUCKING BOMB?
I HEARD SOMEONE SAY SOMETHING ABOUT A PLANE.
BUT MAYBE IT HAD A BOMB *IN* IT. IT...IT BROUGHT THE WHOLE BUILDING DOWN. THE WORLD TRADE CENTER, I MEAN.
BOTH TOWERS?
JUST ONE.

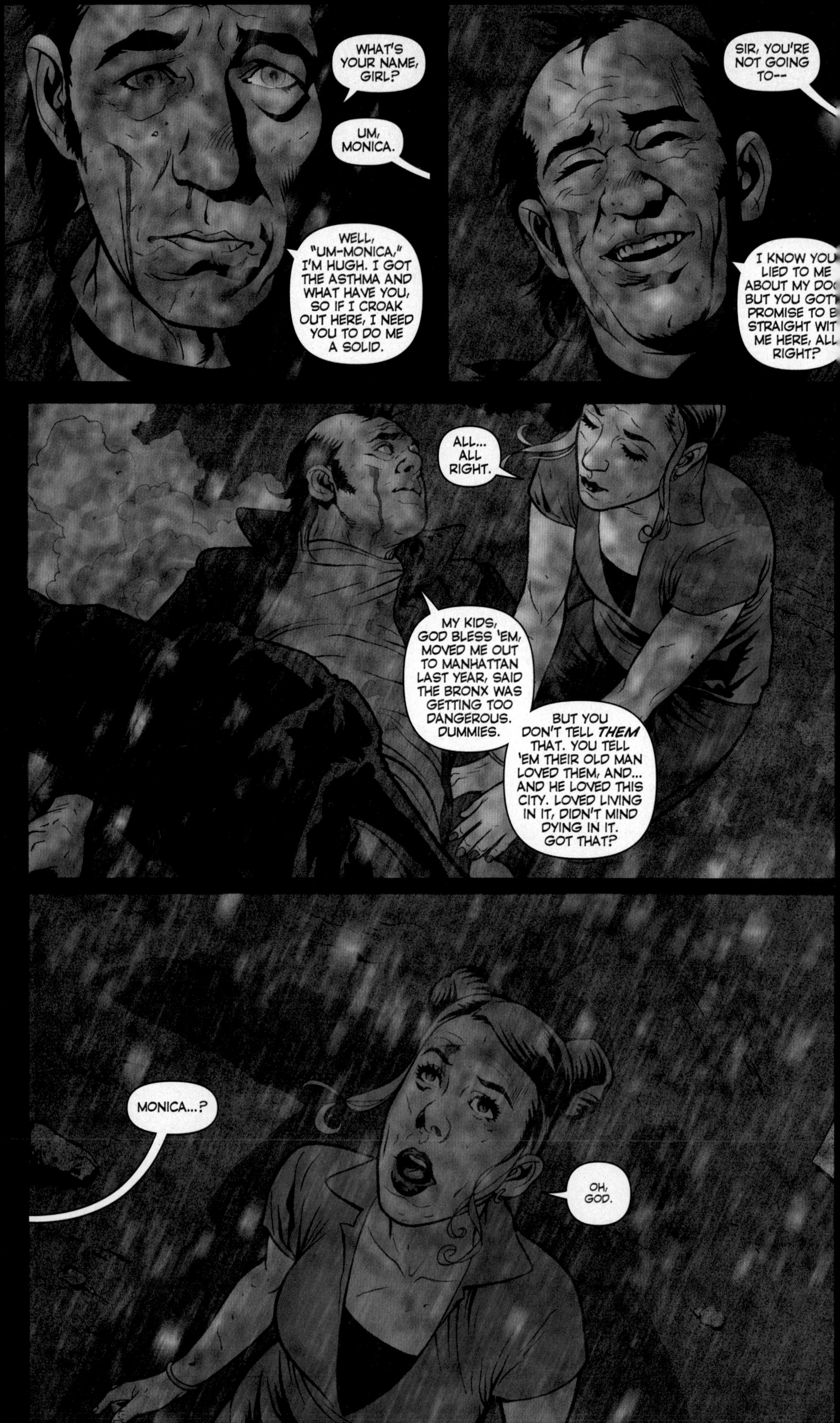
WHAT'S YOUR NAME, GIRL?
UM, MONICA.
WELL, "UM-MONICA," I'M HUGH. I GOT THE ASTHMA AND WHAT HAVE YOU, SO IF I CROAK OUT HERE, I NEED YOU TO DO ME A SOLID.
SIR, YOU'RE NOT GOING TO--
ALL... ALL RIGHT.
MY KIDS, GOD BLESS 'EM, MOVED ME OUT TO MANHATTAN LAST YEAR, SAID THE BRONX WAS GETTING TOO DANGEROUS. DUMMIES.
BUT YOU DON'T TELL *THEM* THAT. YOU TELL 'EM THEIR OLD MAN LOVED THEM, AND... AND HE LOVED THIS CITY. LOVED LIVING IN IT, DIDN'T MIND DYING IN IT. GOT THAT?
MONICA...?
OH, GOD.

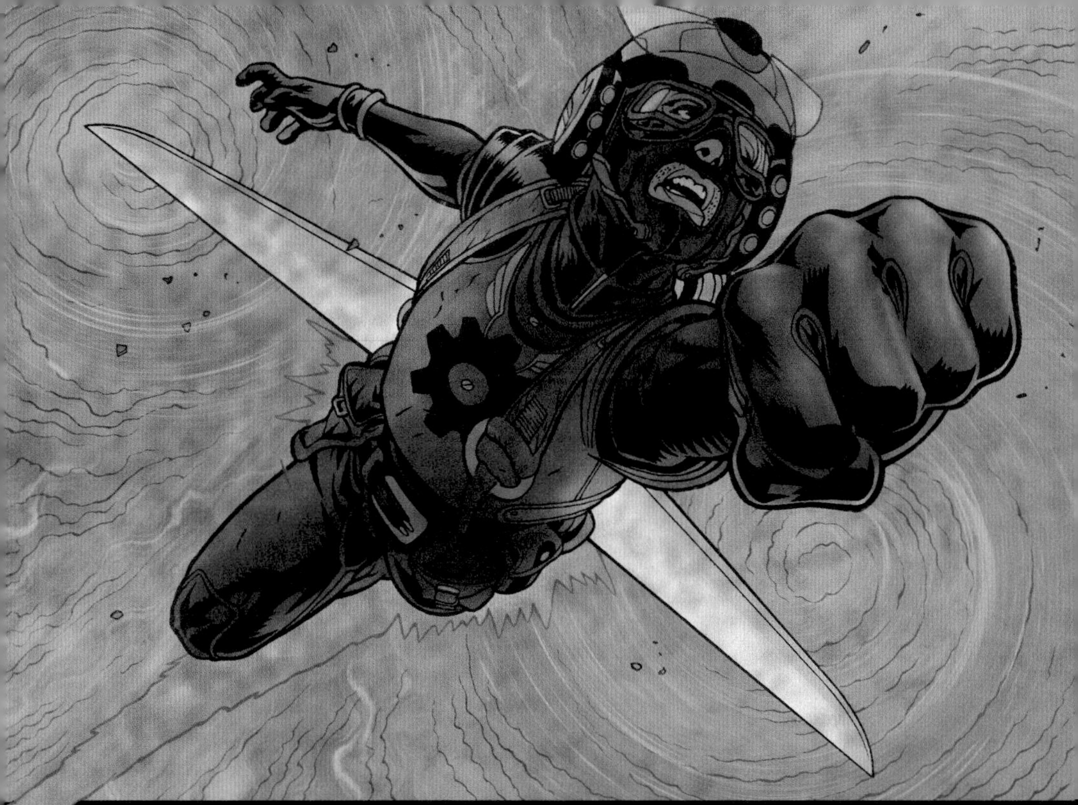

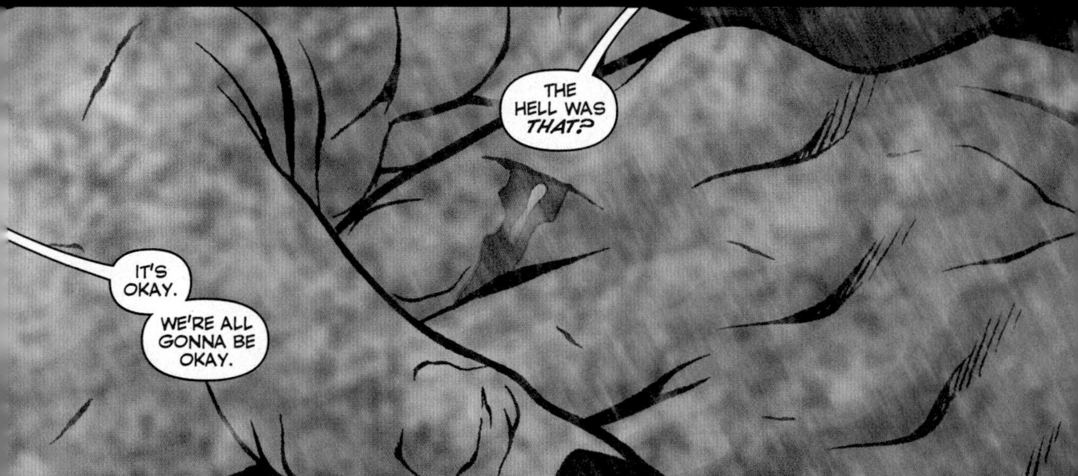
THE HELL WAS THAT?
IT'S OKAY.
WE'RE ALL GONNA BE OKAY.

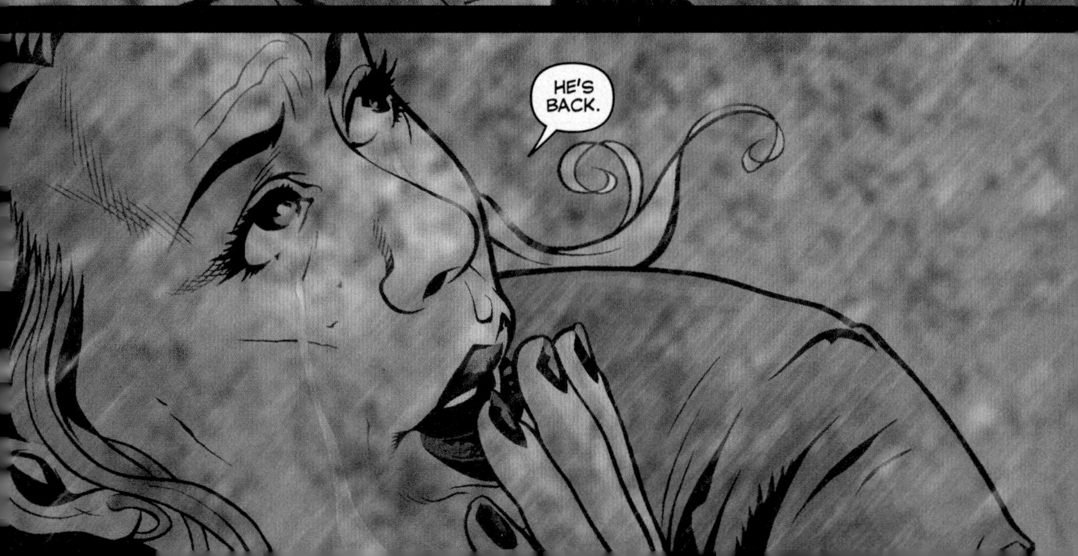
HE'S BACK.

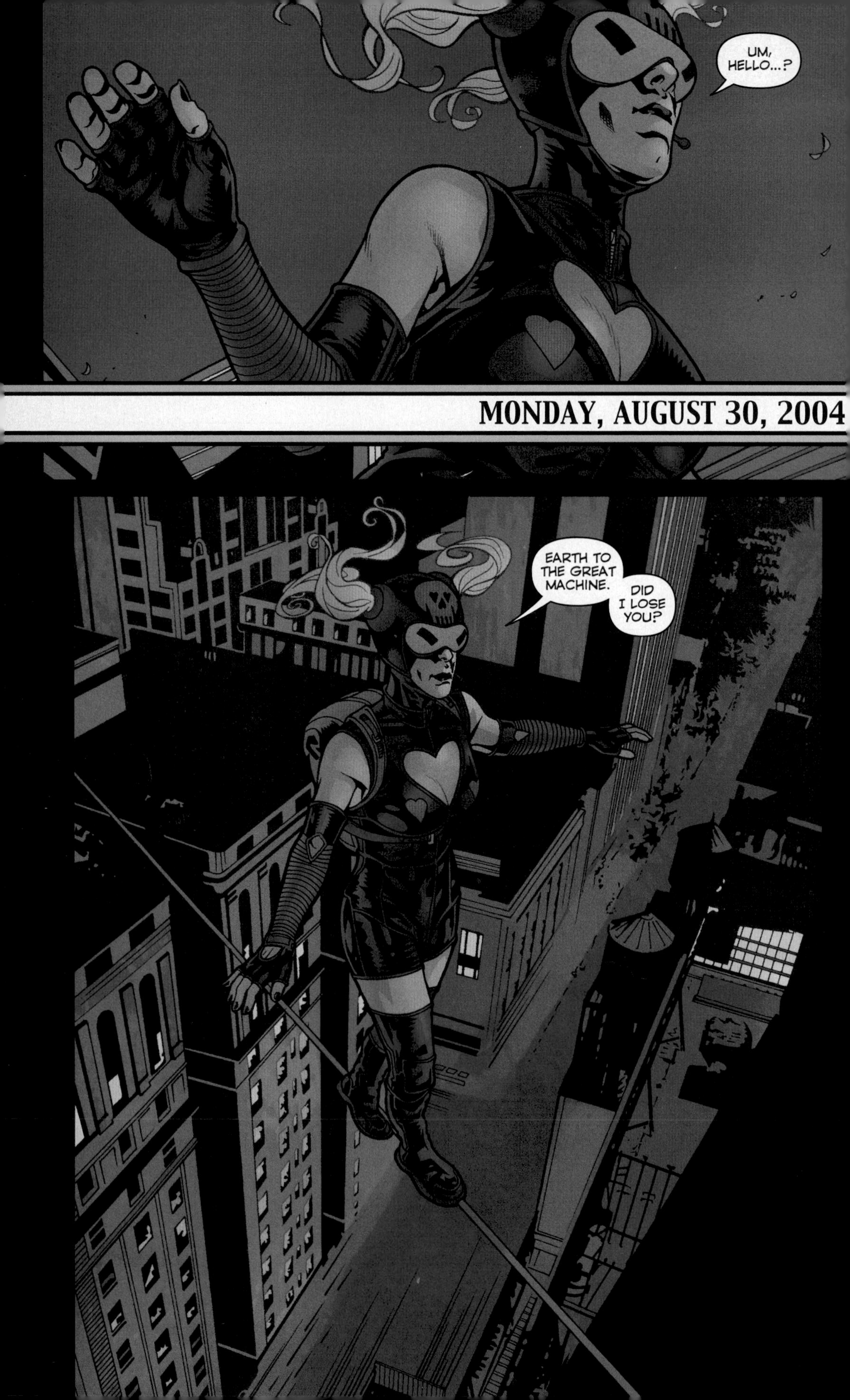
UM, HELLO...?
MONDAY, AUGUST 30, 2004
EARTH TO THE GREAT MACHINE.
DID I LOSE YOU?

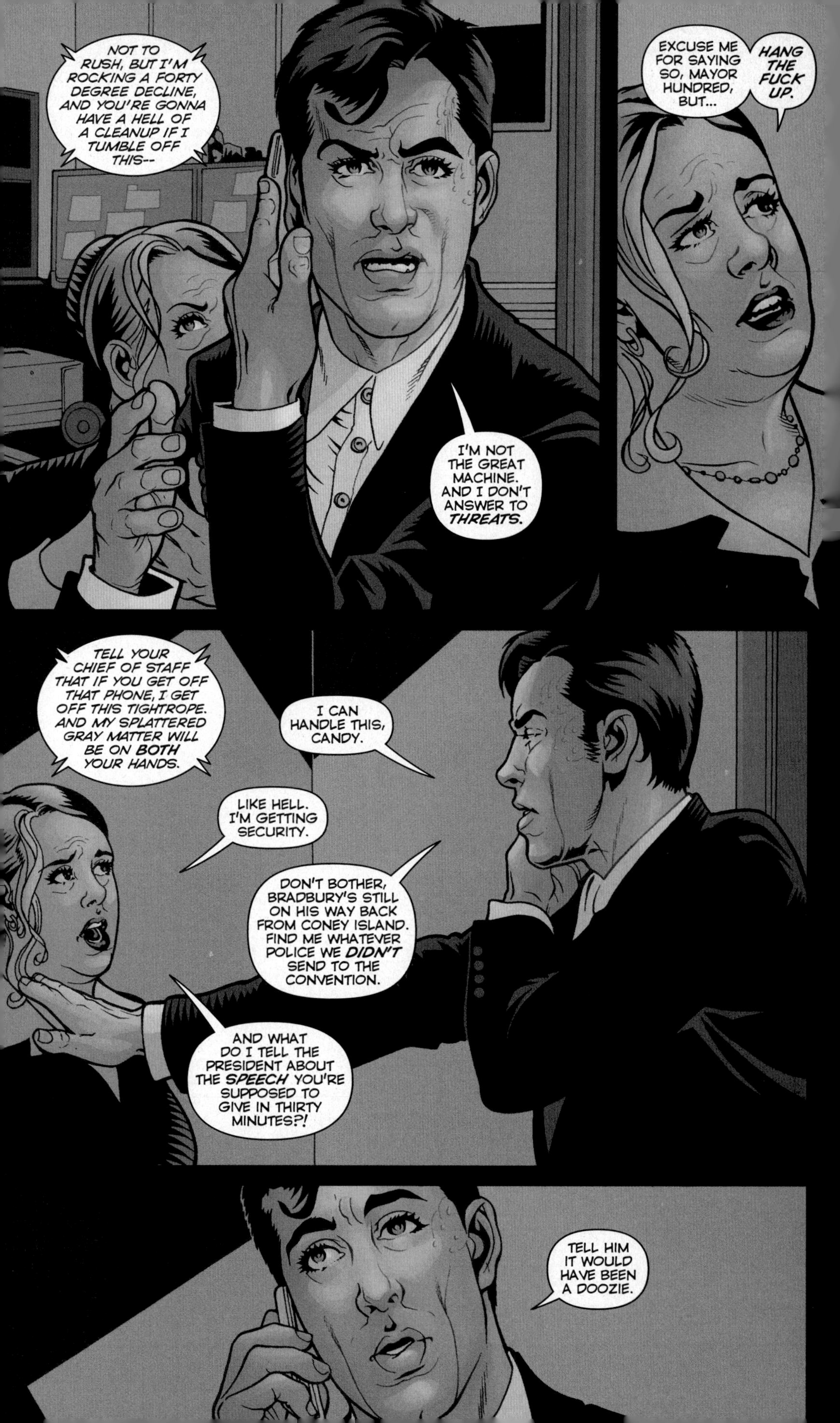
NOT TO RUSH, BUT I'M ROCKING A FORTY DEGREE DECLINE, AND YOU'RE GONNA HAVE A HELL OF A CLEANUP IF I TUMBLE OFF THIS--
I'M NOT THE GREAT MACHINE. AND I DON'T ANSWER TO THREATS.
EXCUSE ME FOR SAYING SO, MAYOR HUNDRED, BUT...
HANG THE FUCK UP.
TELL YOUR CHIEF OF STAFF THAT IF YOU GET OFF THAT PHONE, I GET OFF THIS TIGHTROPE. AND MY SPLATTERED GRAY MATTER WILL BE ON BOTH YOUR HANDS.
I CAN HANDLE THIS, CANDY.
LIKE HELL. I'M GETTING SECURITY.
DON'T BOTHER, BRADBURY'S STILL ON HIS WAY BACK FROM CONEY ISLAND. FIND ME WHATEVER POLICE WE DIDN'T SEND TO THE CONVENTION.
AND WHAT DO I TELL THE PRESIDENT ABOUT THE SPEECH YOU'RE SUPPOSED TO GIVE IN THIRTY MINUTES?!
TELL HIM IT WOULD HAVE BEEN A DOOZIE.

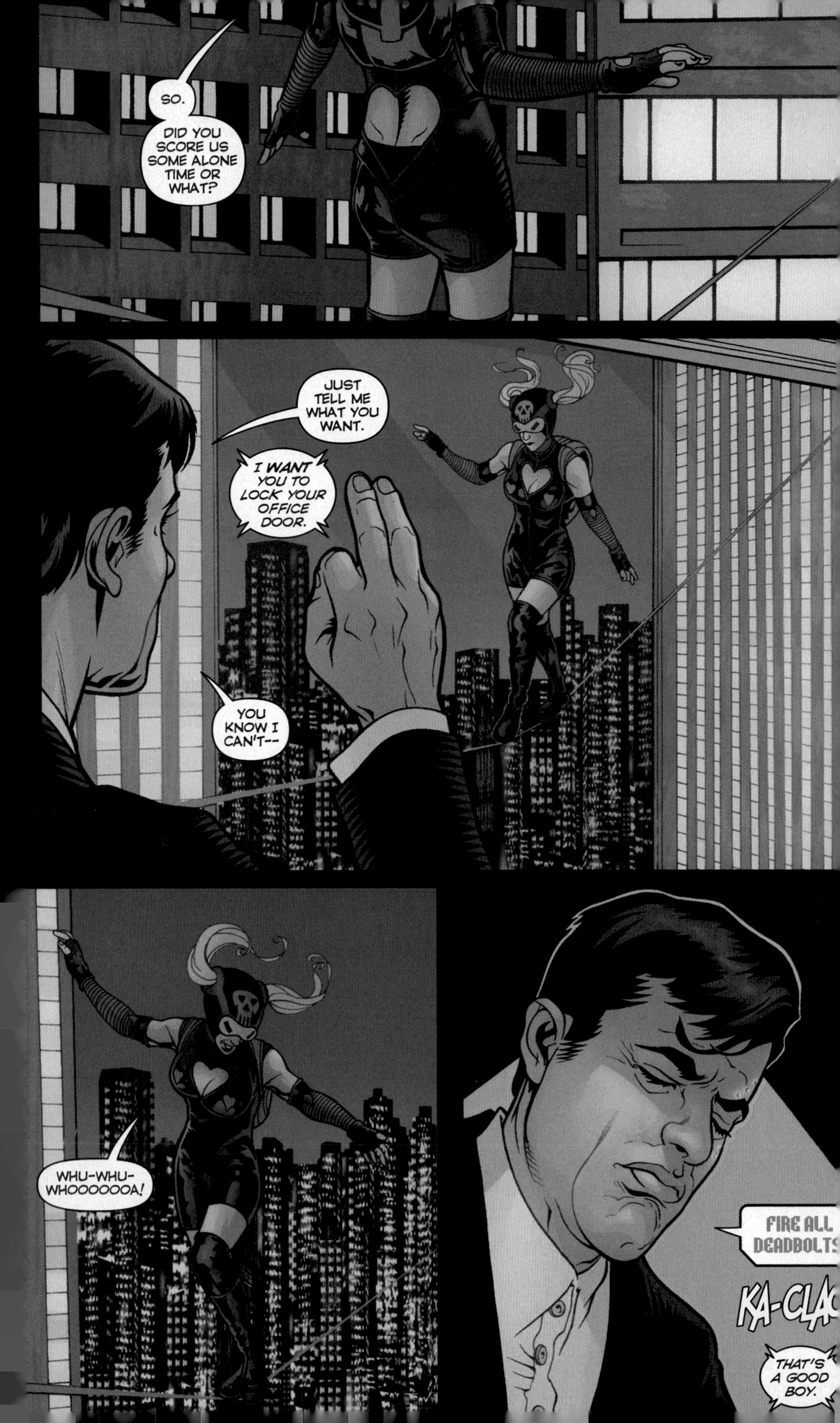

SO.
DID YOU SCORE US SOME ALONE TIME OR WHAT?
JUST TELL ME WHAT YOU WANT.
I *WANT* YOU TO LOCK YOUR OFFICE DOOR.
YOU KNOW I CAN'T--
WHU-WHU-WHOOOOOOA!
FIRE ALL DEADBOLTS
KA-CLAC
THAT'S A GOOD BOY.

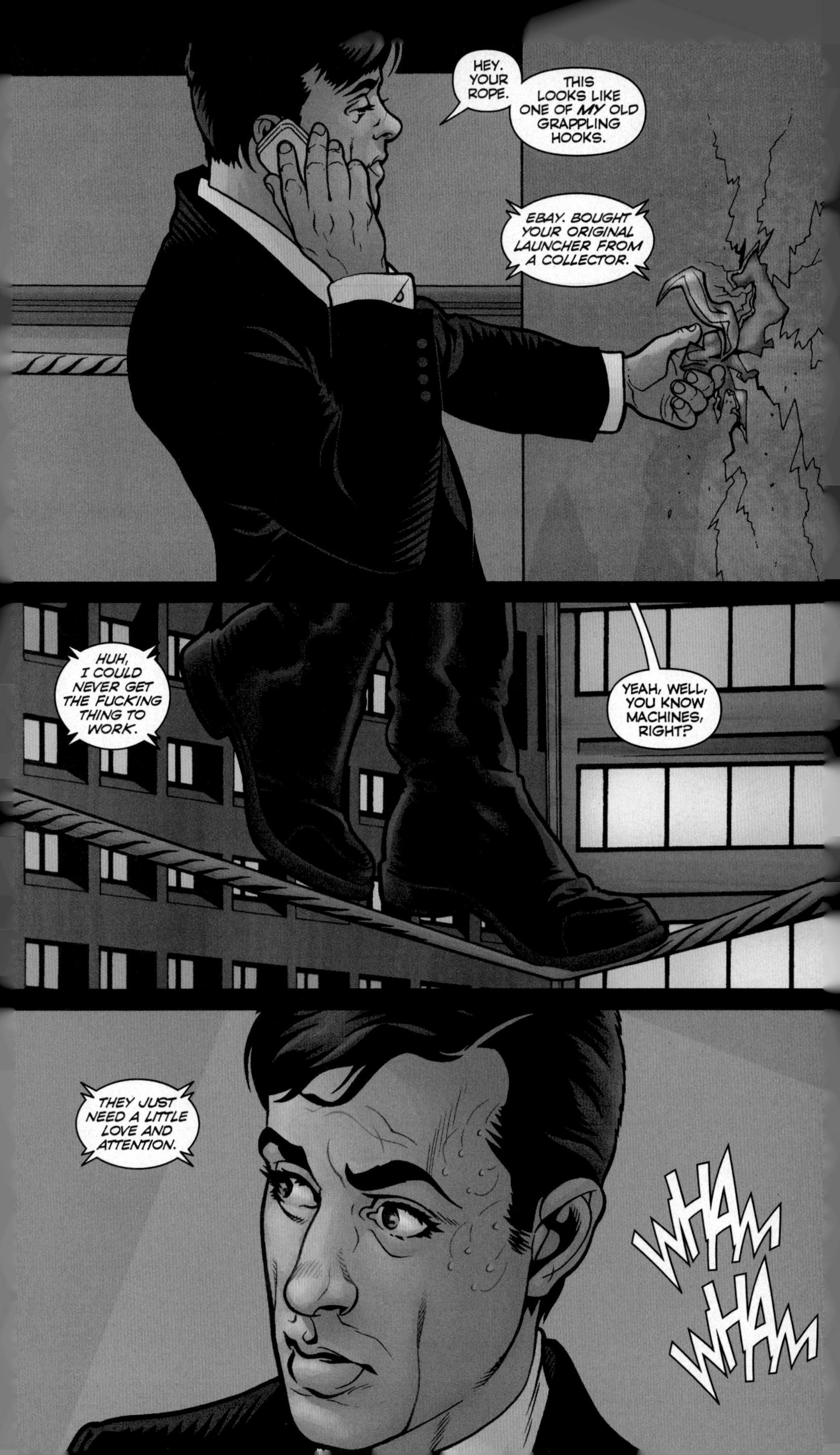
HEY. YOUR ROPE.
THIS LOOKS LIKE ONE OF MY OLD GRAPPLING HOOKS.
EBAY. BOUGHT YOUR ORIGINAL LAUNCHER FROM A COLLECTOR.
HUH, I COULD NEVER GET THE FUCKING THING TO WORK.
YEAH, WELL, YOU KNOW MACHINES, RIGHT?
THEY JUST NEED A LITTLE LOVE AND ATTENTION.
WHAM
WHAM

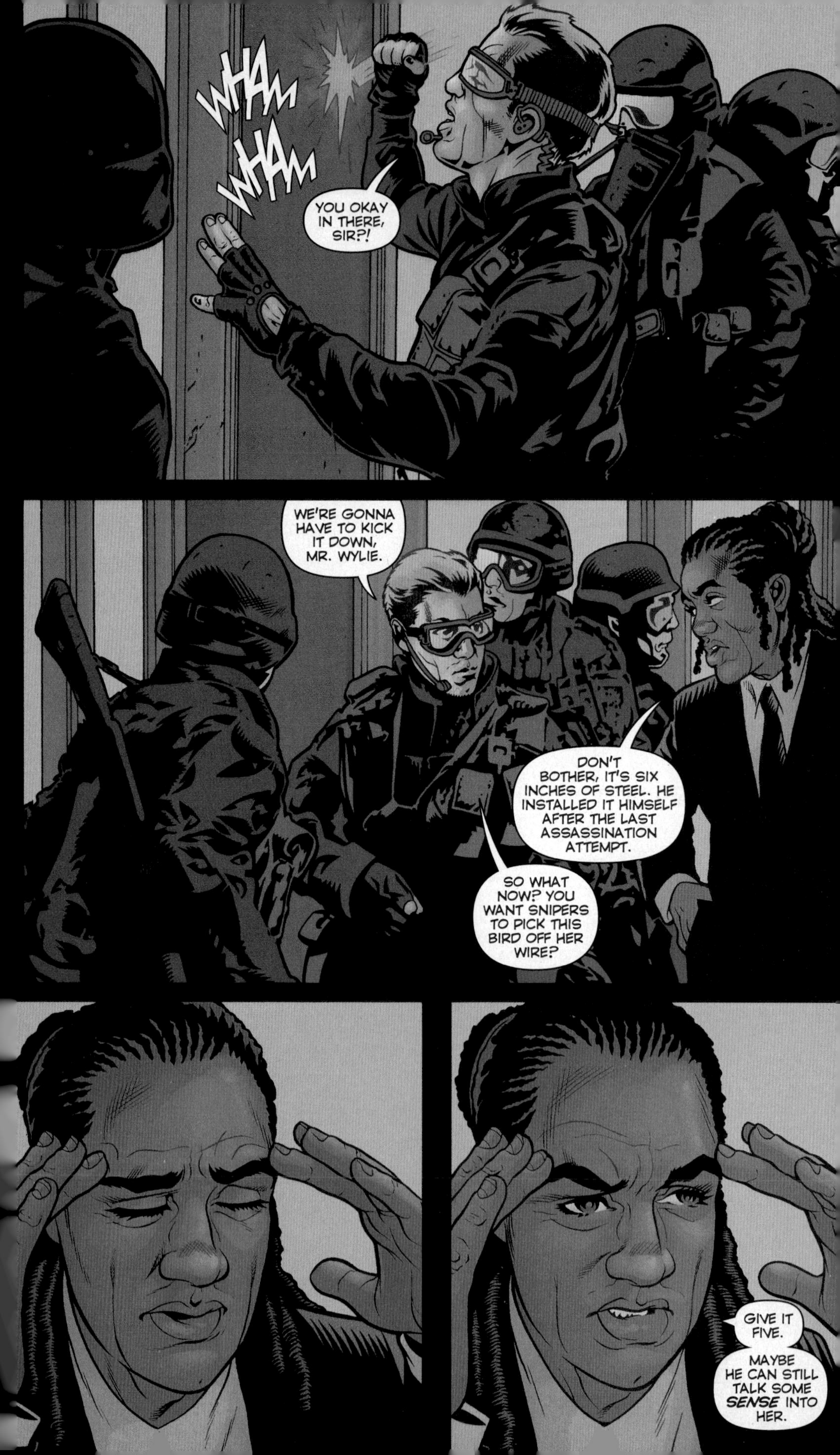
WHAM WHAM
YOU OKAY IN THERE, SIR?!
WE'RE GONNA HAVE TO KICK IT DOWN, MR. WYLIE.
DON'T BOTHER, IT'S SIX INCHES OF STEEL. HE INSTALLED IT HIMSELF AFTER THE LAST ASSASSINATION ATTEMPT.
SO WHAT NOW? YOU WANT SNIPERS TO PICK THIS BIRD OFF HER WIRE?
GIVE IT FIVE.
MAYBE HE CAN STILL TALK SOME SENSE INTO HER.

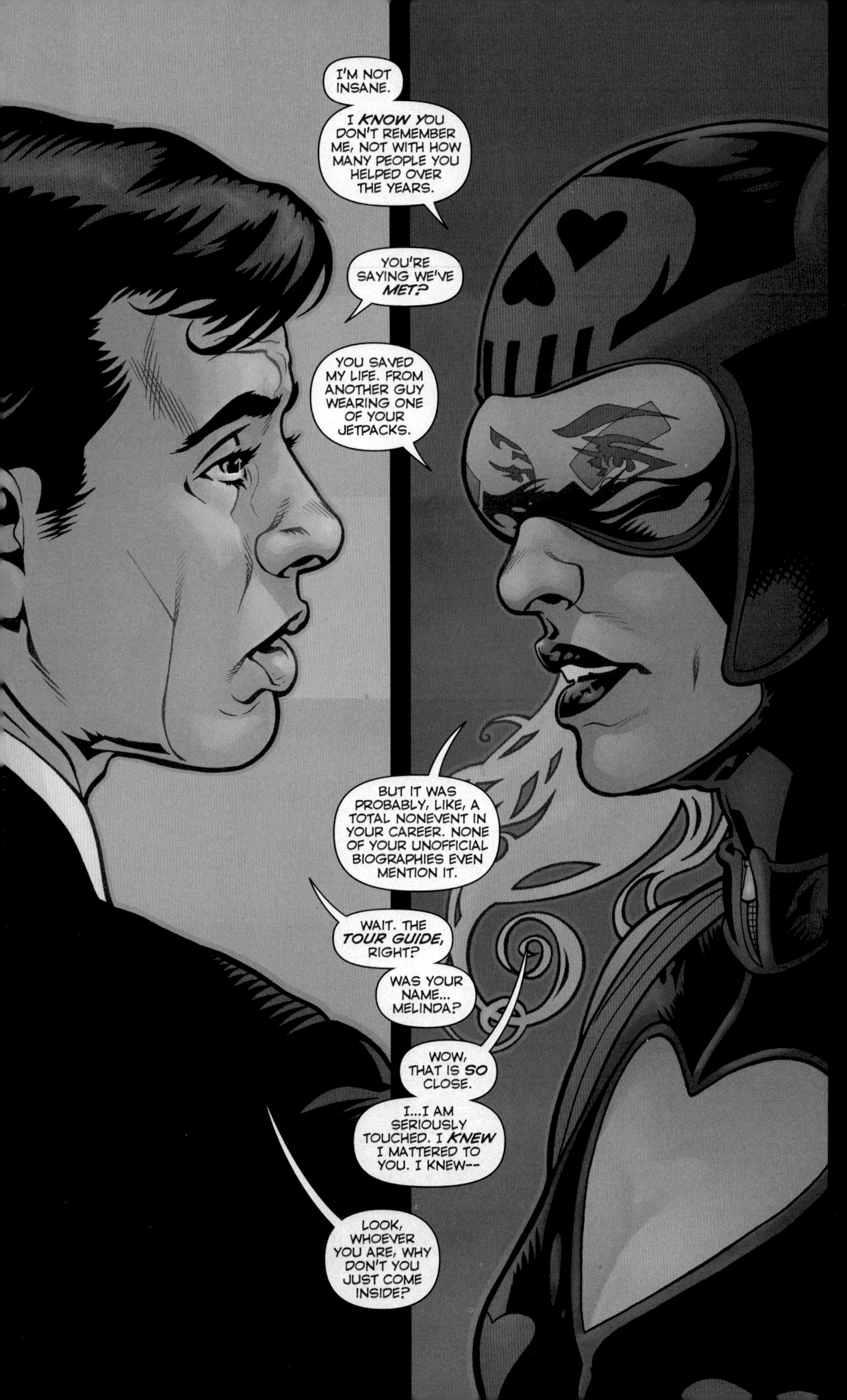
I'M NOT INSANE.
I *KNOW* YOU DON'T REMEMBER ME, NOT WITH HOW MANY PEOPLE YOU HELPED OVER THE YEARS.
YOU'RE SAYING WE'VE *MET?*
YOU SAVED MY LIFE. FROM ANOTHER GUY WEARING ONE OF YOUR JETPACKS.
BUT IT WAS PROBABLY, LIKE, A TOTAL NONEVENT IN YOUR CAREER. NONE OF YOUR UNOFFICIAL BIOGRAPHIES EVEN MENTION IT.
WAIT. THE *TOUR GUIDE,* RIGHT?
WAS YOUR NAME... MELINDA?
WOW, THAT IS *SO* CLOSE.
I...I AM SERIOUSLY TOUCHED. I *KNEW* I MATTERED TO YOU. I KNEW--
LOOK, WHOEVER YOU ARE, WHY DON'T YOU JUST COME INSIDE?

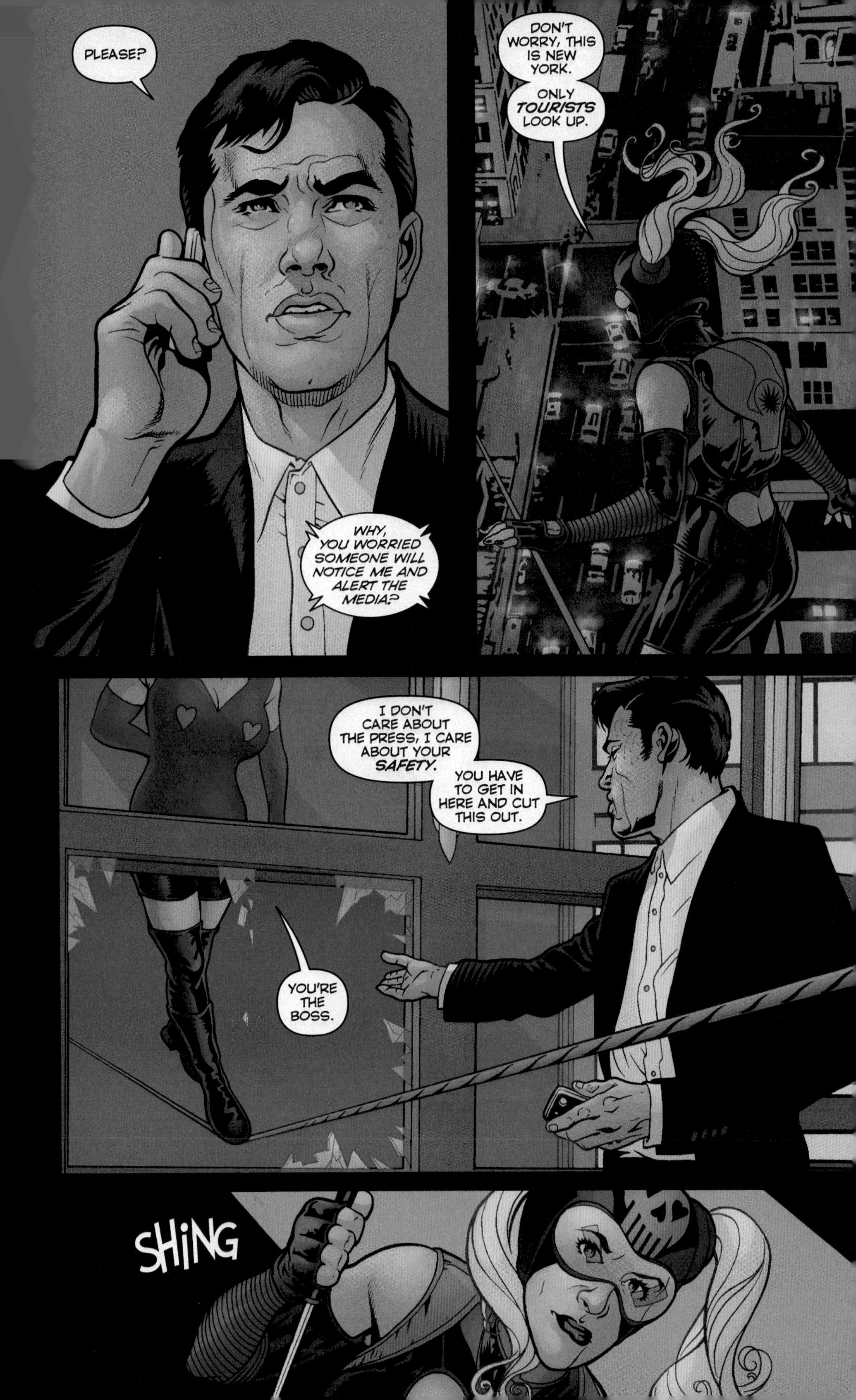
PLEASE?
DON'T WORRY, THIS IS NEW YORK.
ONLY TOURISTS LOOK UP.
WHY, YOU WORRIED SOMEONE WILL NOTICE ME AND ALERT THE MEDIA?
I DON'T CARE ABOUT THE PRESS, I CARE ABOUT YOUR SAFETY.
YOU HAVE TO GET IN HERE AND CUT THIS OUT.
YOU'RE THE BOSS.
SHING

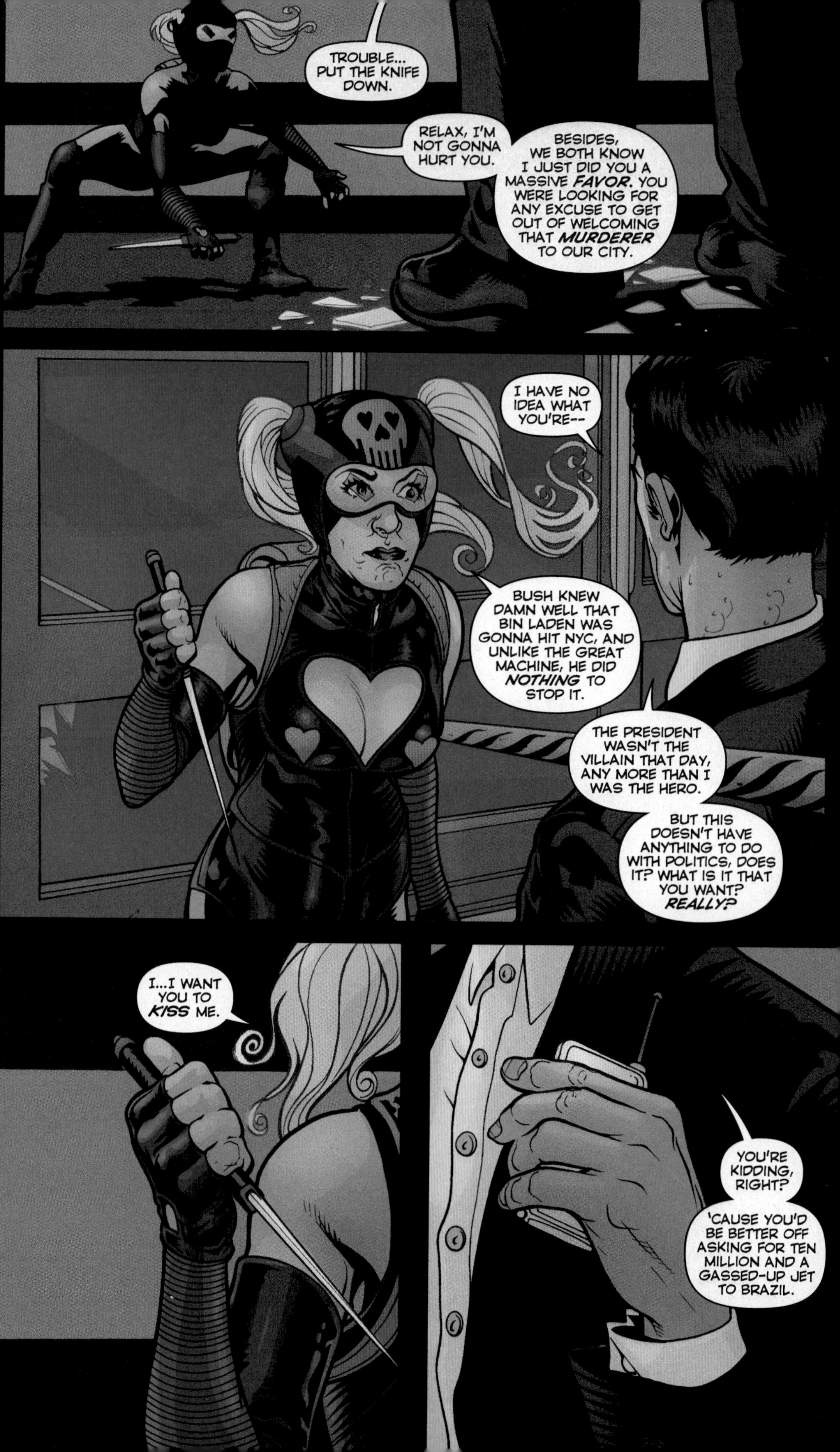
TROUBLE... PUT THE KNIFE DOWN.
RELAX, I'M NOT GONNA HURT YOU.
BESIDES, WE BOTH KNOW I JUST DID YOU A MASSIVE *FAVOR*. YOU WERE LOOKING FOR ANY EXCUSE TO GET OUT OF WELCOMING THAT *MURDERER* TO OUR CITY.
I HAVE NO IDEA WHAT YOU'RE--
BUSH KNEW DAMN WELL THAT BIN LADEN WAS GONNA HIT NYC, AND UNLIKE THE GREAT MACHINE, HE DID *NOTHING* TO STOP IT.
THE PRESIDENT WASN'T THE VILLAIN THAT DAY, ANY MORE THAN I WAS THE HERO.
BUT THIS DOESN'T HAVE ANYTHING TO DO WITH POLITICS, DOES IT? WHAT IS IT THAT YOU WANT? *REALLY?*
I...I WANT YOU TO *KISS* ME.
YOU'RE KIDDING, RIGHT?
'CAUSE YOU'D BE BETTER OFF ASKING FOR TEN MILLION AND A GASSED-UP JET TO BRAZIL.

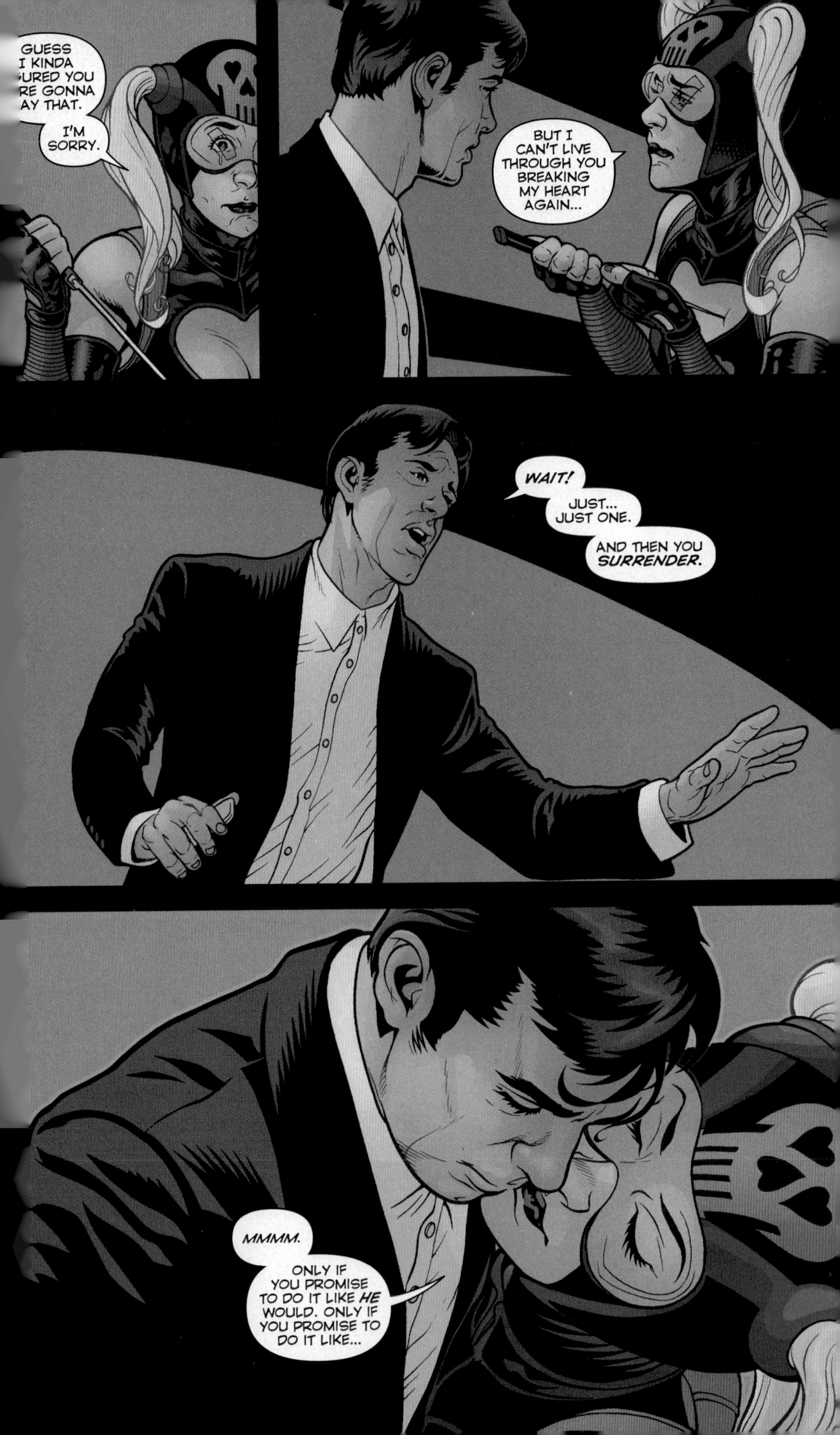
GUESS I KINDA GURED YOU RE GONNA AY THAT.
I'M SORRY.
BUT I CAN'T LIVE THROUGH YOU BREAKING MY HEART AGAIN...
WAIT!
JUST... JUST ONE.
AND THEN YOU *SURRENDER.*
MMMM.
ONLY IF YOU PROMISE TO DO IT LIKE *HE* WOULD. ONLY IF YOU PROMISE TO DO IT LIKE...

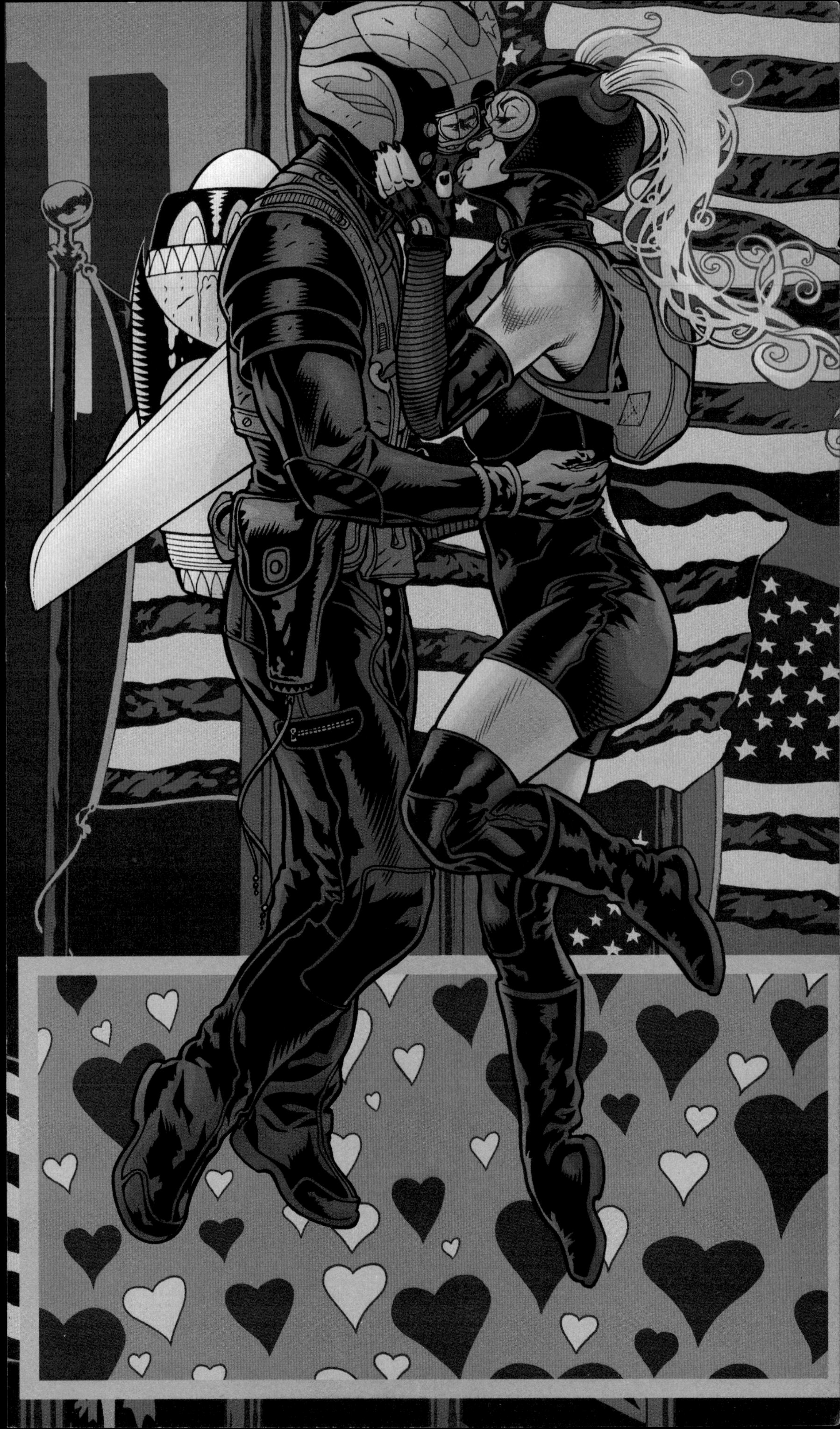

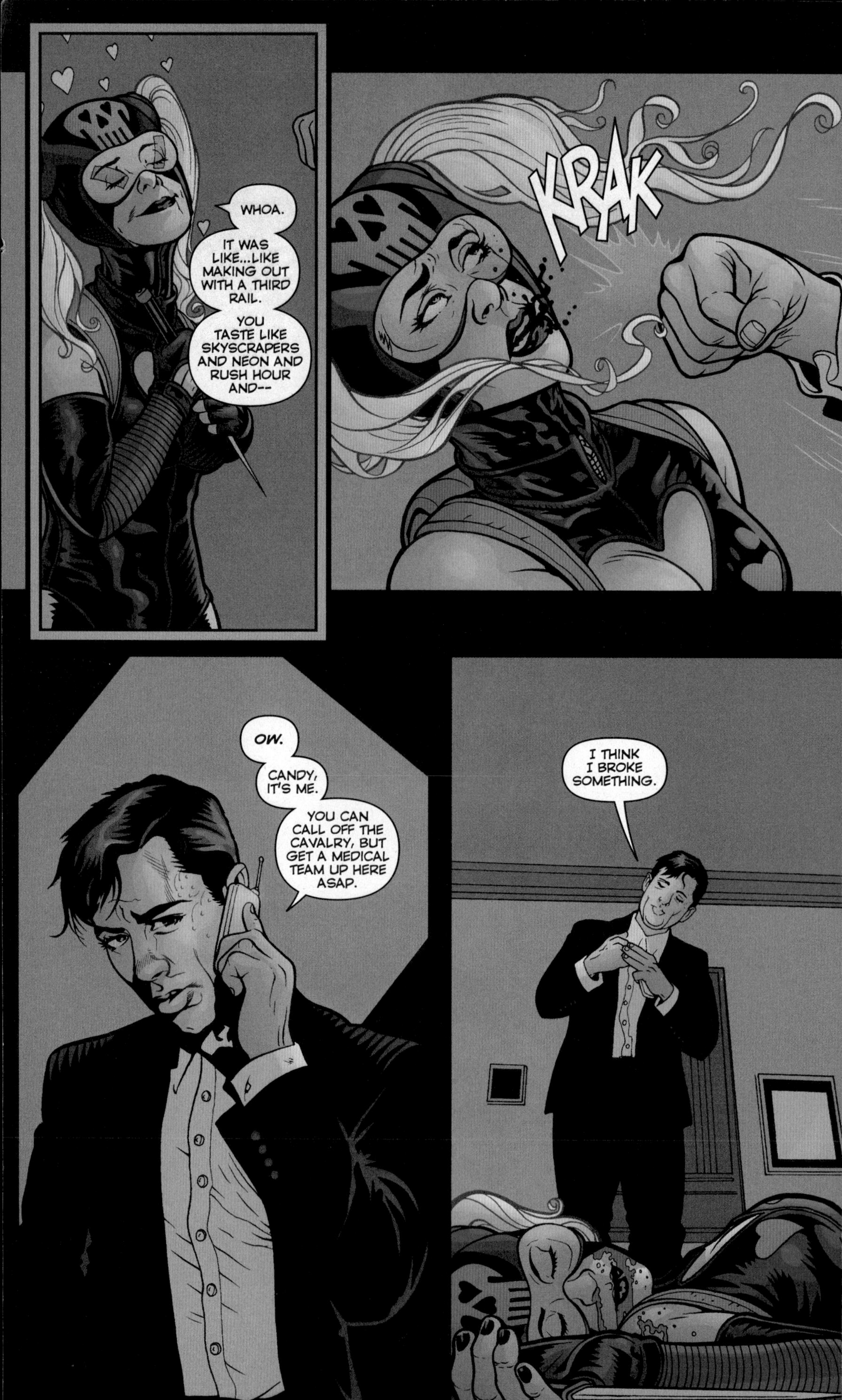
WHOA.
IT WAS LIKE...LIKE MAKING OUT WITH A THIRD RAIL.
YOU TASTE LIKE SKYSCRAPERS AND NEON AND RUSH HOUR AND--
KRAK
OW.
CANDY, IT'S ME.
YOU CAN CALL OFF THE CAVALRY, BUT GET A MEDICAL TEAM UP HERE ASAP.
I THINK I BROKE SOMETHING.

TROUBLE NO MORE!
Hizzoner helps nab G.O.P. nightmare
by SUZANNE PADILLA

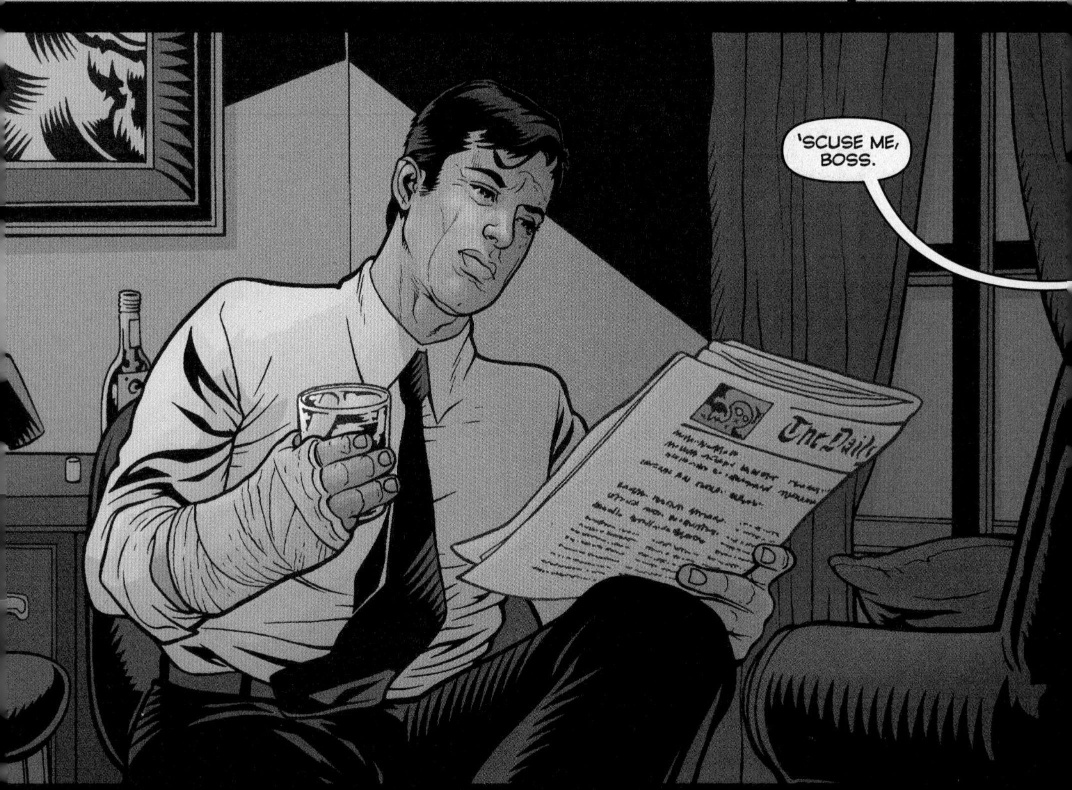
'SCUSE ME, BOSS.

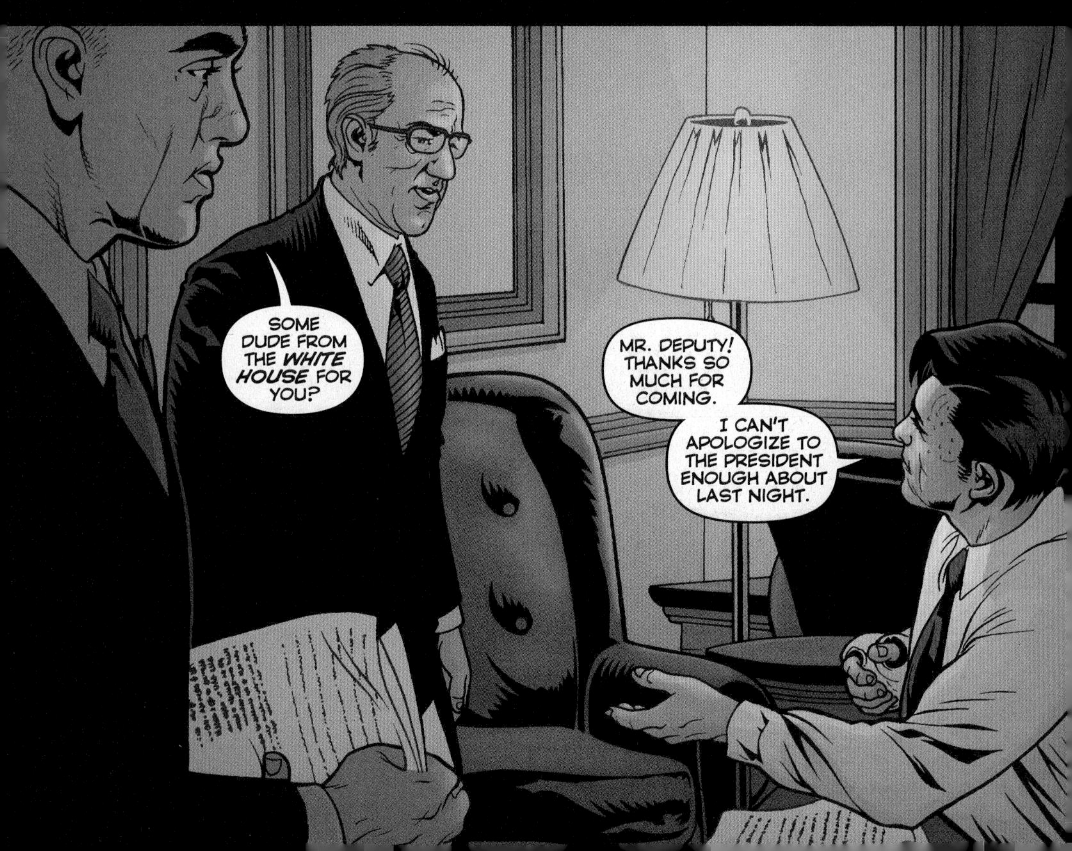
SOME DUDE FROM THE *WHITE HOUSE* FOR YOU?
MR. DEPUTY! THANKS SO MUCH FOR COMING.
I CAN'T APOLOGIZE TO THE PRESIDENT ENOUGH ABOUT LAST NIGHT.

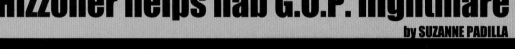

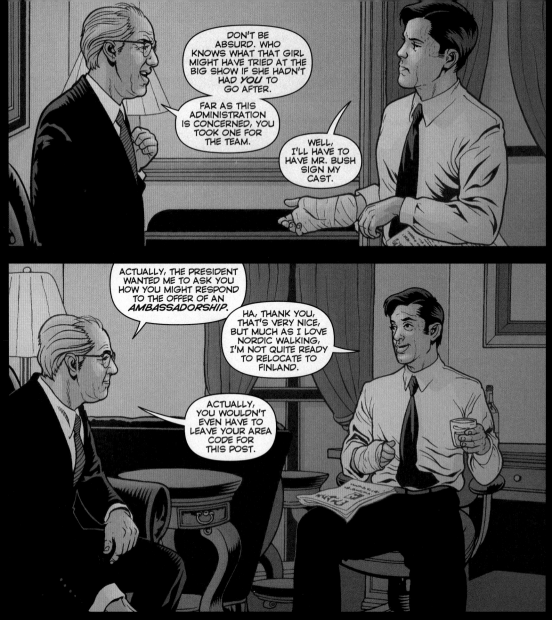

DON'T BE ABSURD. WHO KNOWS WHAT THAT GIRL MIGHT HAVE TRIED AT THE BIG SHOW IF SHE HADN'T HAD *YOU* TO GO AFTER.

FAR AS THIS ADMINISTRATION IS CONCERNED, YOU TOOK ONE FOR THE TEAM.

WELL, I'LL HAVE TO HAVE MR. BUSH SIGN MY CAST.

ACTUALLY, THE PRESIDENT WANTED ME TO ASK YOU HOW YOU MIGHT RESPOND TO THE OFFER OF AN *AMBASSADORSHIP*.

HA, THANK YOU, THAT'S VERY NICE, BUT MUCH AS I LOVE NORDIC WALKING, I'M NOT QUITE READY TO RELOCATE TO FINLAND.

ACTUALLY, YOU WOULDN'T EVEN HAVE TO LEAVE YOUR AREA CODE FOR THIS POST.

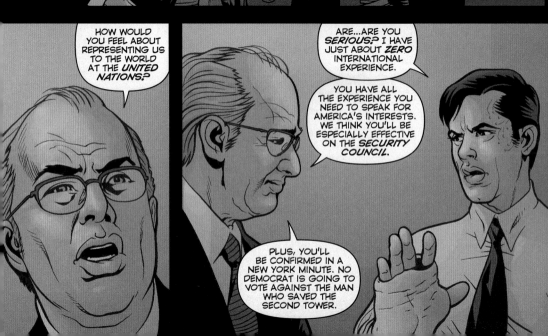

HOW WOULD YOU FEEL ABOUT REPRESENTING US TO THE WORLD AT THE *UNITED NATIONS*?

ARE...ARE YOU *SERIOUS?* I HAVE JUST ABOUT *ZERO* INTERNATIONAL EXPERIENCE.

YOU HAVE ALL THE EXPERIENCE YOU NEED TO SPEAK FOR AMERICA'S INTERESTS. WE THINK YOU'LL BE ESPECIALLY EFFECTIVE ON THE *SECURITY COUNCIL*.

PLUS, YOU'LL BE CONFIRMED IN A NEW YORK MINUTE. NO DEMOCRAT IS GOING TO VOTE AGAINST THE MAN WHO SAVED THE SECOND TOWER.

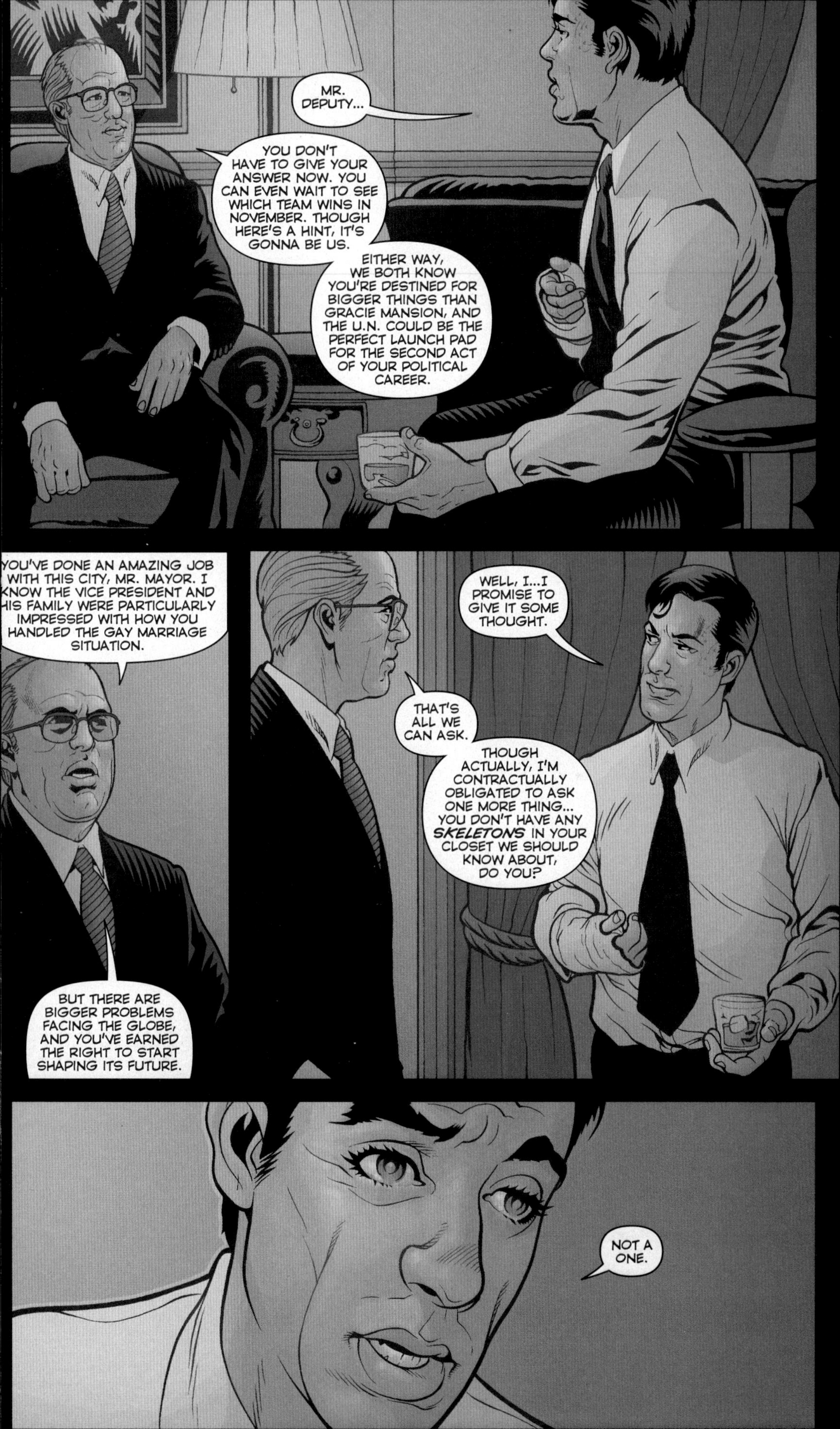
MR. DEPUTY...
YOU DON'T HAVE TO GIVE YOUR ANSWER NOW. YOU CAN EVEN WAIT TO SEE WHICH TEAM WINS IN NOVEMBER. THOUGH HERE'S A HINT, IT'S GONNA BE US.
EITHER WAY, WE BOTH KNOW YOU'RE DESTINED FOR BIGGER THINGS THAN GRACIE MANSION, AND THE U.N. COULD BE THE PERFECT LAUNCH PAD FOR THE SECOND ACT OF YOUR POLITICAL CAREER.
YOU'VE DONE AN AMAZING JOB WITH THIS CITY, MR. MAYOR. I KNOW THE VICE PRESIDENT AND HIS FAMILY WERE PARTICULARLY IMPRESSED WITH HOW YOU HANDLED THE GAY MARRIAGE SITUATION.
BUT THERE ARE BIGGER PROBLEMS FACING THE GLOBE, AND YOU'VE EARNED THE RIGHT TO START SHAPING ITS FUTURE.
WELL, I...I PROMISE TO GIVE IT SOME THOUGHT.
THAT'S ALL WE CAN ASK.
THOUGH ACTUALLY, I'M CONTRACTUALLY OBLIGATED TO ASK ONE MORE THING... YOU DON'T HAVE ANY *SKELETONS* IN YOUR CLOSET WE SHOULD KNOW ABOUT, DO YOU?
NOT A ONE.

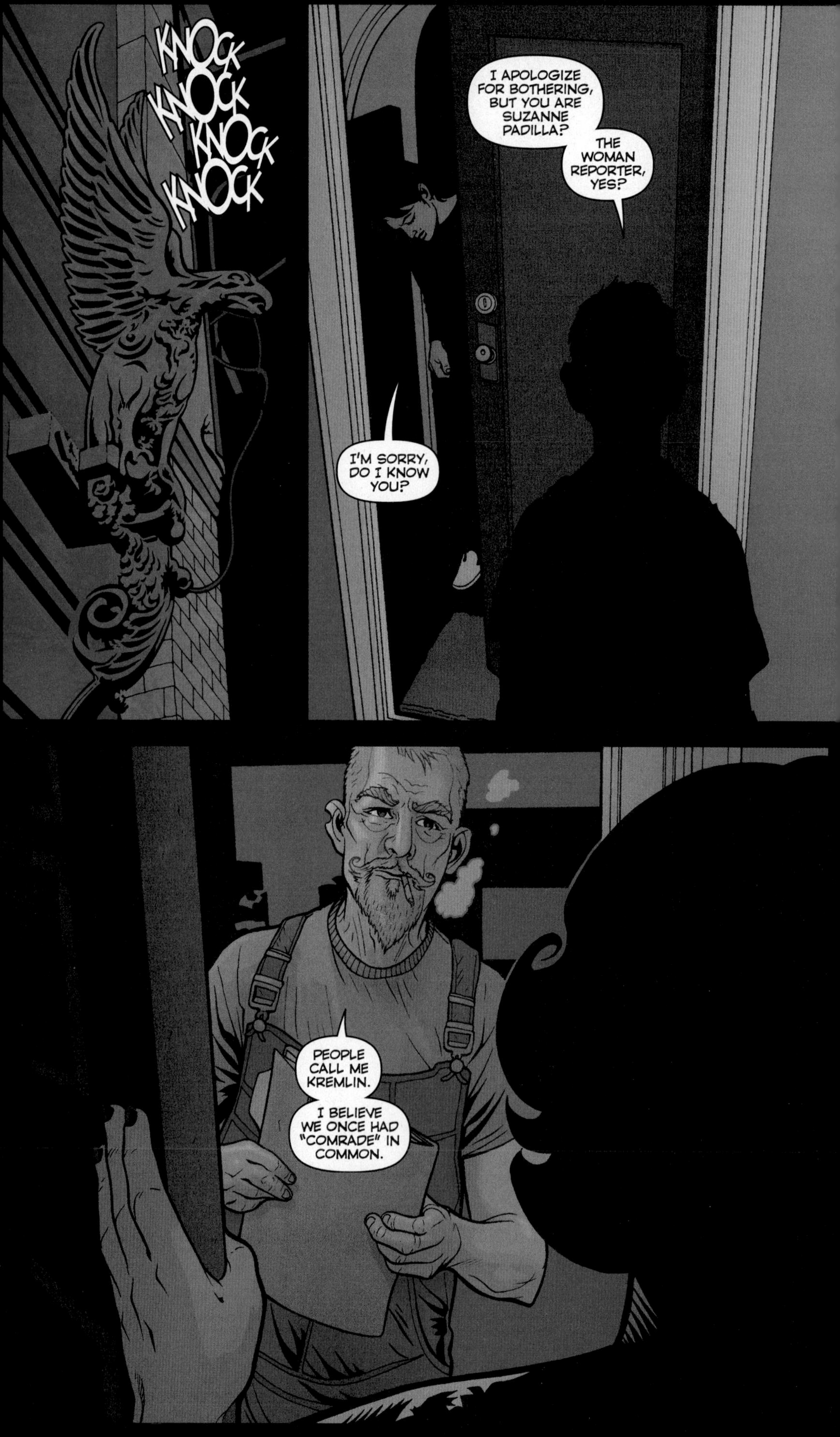
KNOCK KNOCK KNOCK KNOCK
I APOLOGIZE FOR BOTHERING, BUT YOU ARE SUZANNE PADILLA?
THE WOMAN REPORTER, YES?
I'M SORRY, DO I KNOW YOU?
PEOPLE CALL ME KREMLIN.
I BELIEVE WE ONCE HAD "COMRADE" IN COMMON.

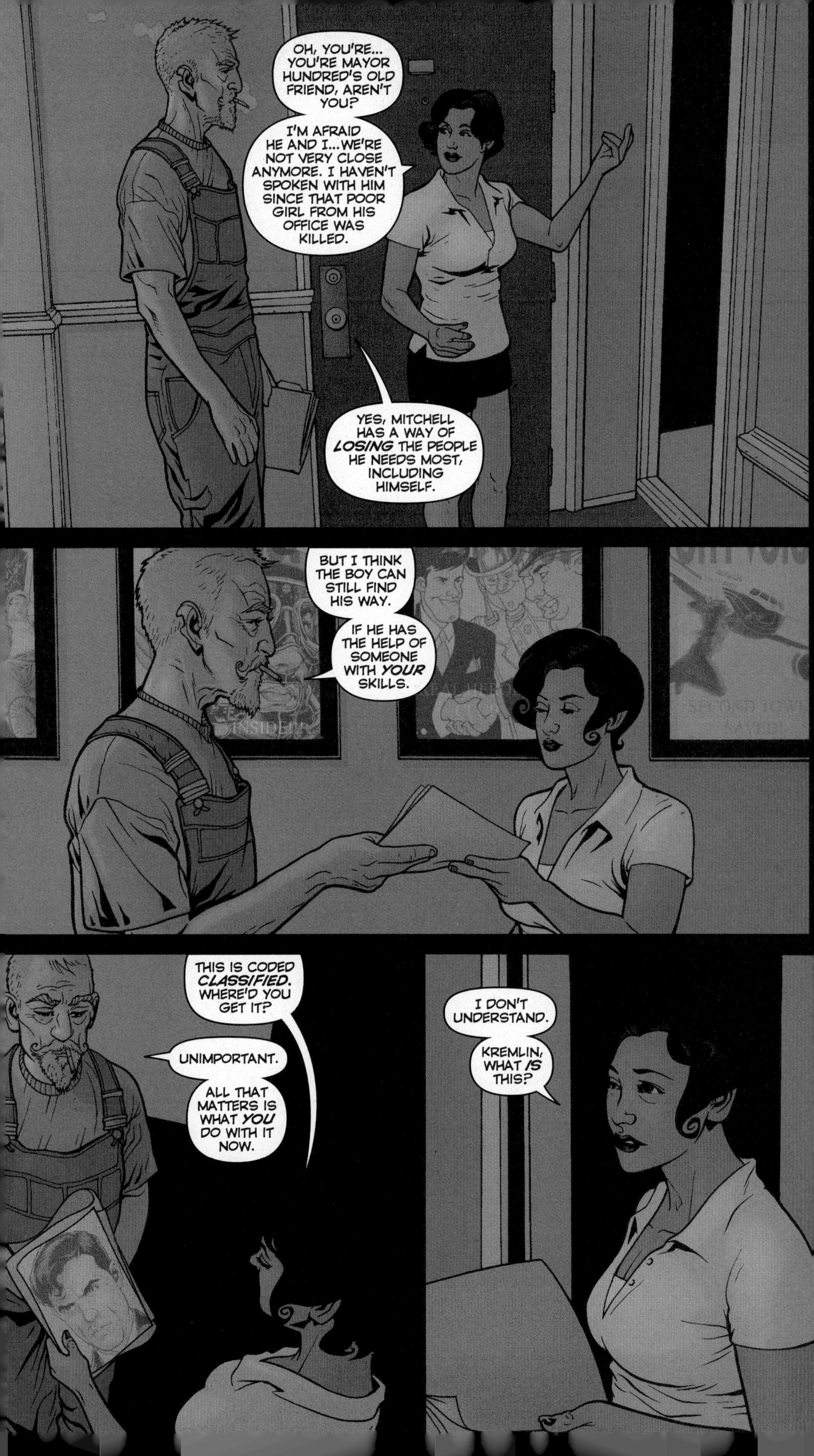
OH, YOU'RE... YOU'RE MAYOR HUNDRED'S OLD FRIEND, AREN'T YOU?
I'M AFRAID HE AND I...WE'RE NOT VERY CLOSE ANYMORE. I HAVEN'T SPOKEN WITH HIM SINCE THAT POOR GIRL FROM HIS OFFICE WAS KILLED.
YES, MITCHELL HAS A WAY OF *LOSING* THE PEOPLE HE NEEDS MOST, INCLUDING HIMSELF.
BUT I THINK THE BOY CAN STILL FIND HIS WAY.
IF HE HAS THE HELP OF SOMEONE WITH *YOUR* SKILLS.
THIS IS CODED *CLASSIFIED*. WHERE'D YOU GET IT?
UNIMPORTANT.
ALL THAT MATTERS IS WHAT *YOU* DO WITH IT NOW.
I DON'T UNDERSTAND.
KREMLIN, WHAT *IS* THIS?

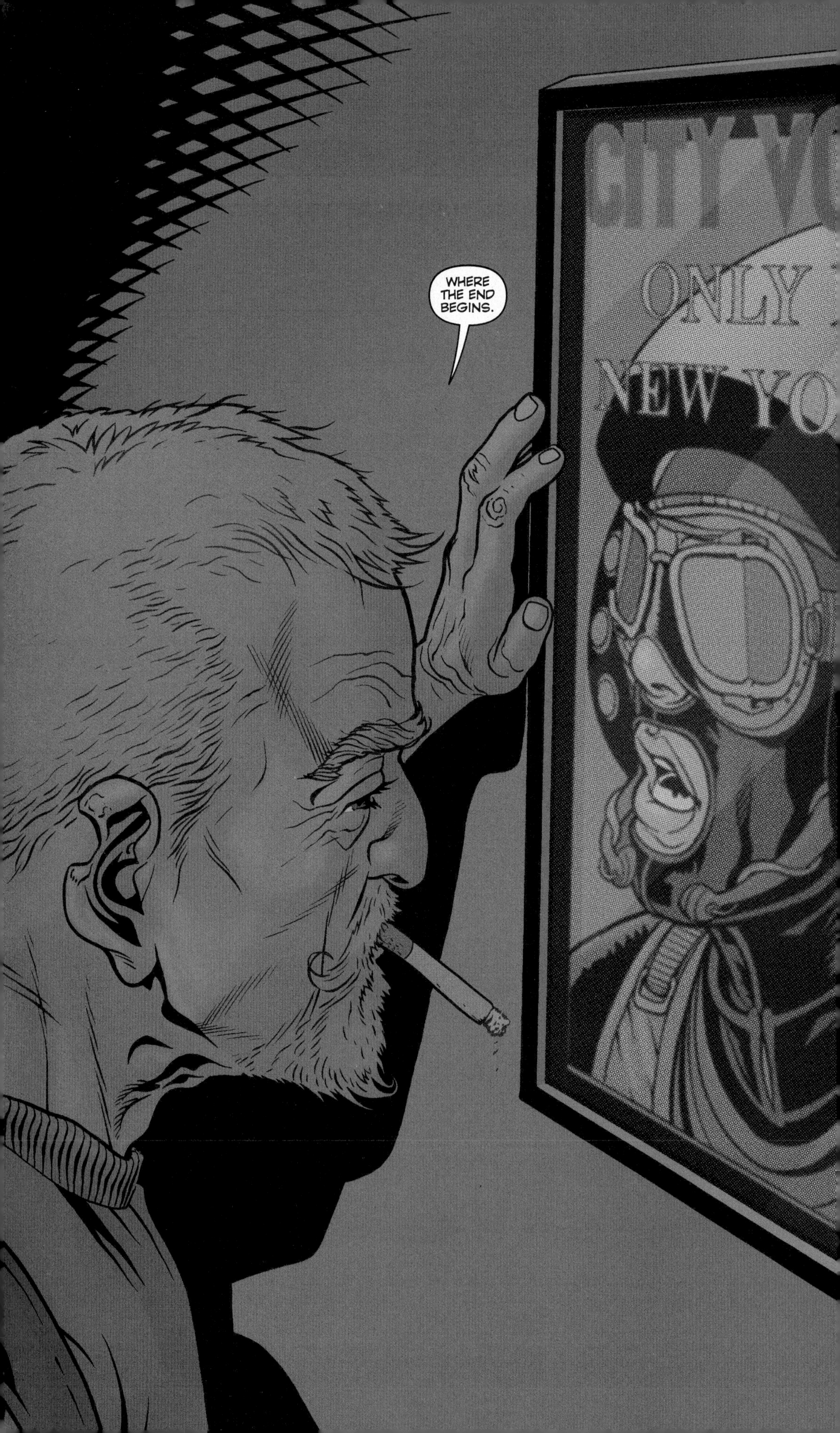
WHERE THE END BEGINS.

Masquerade

Chapter 6

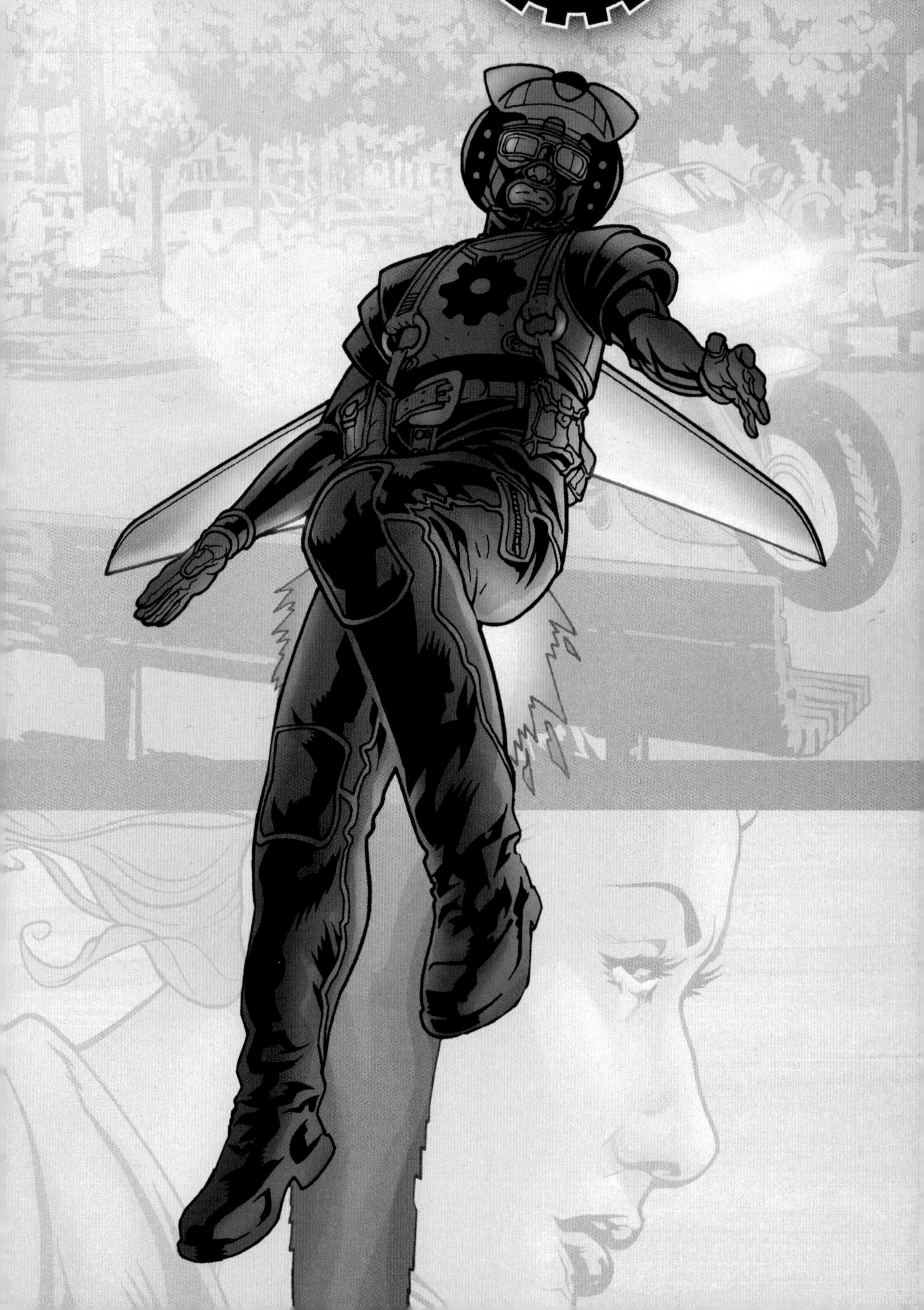

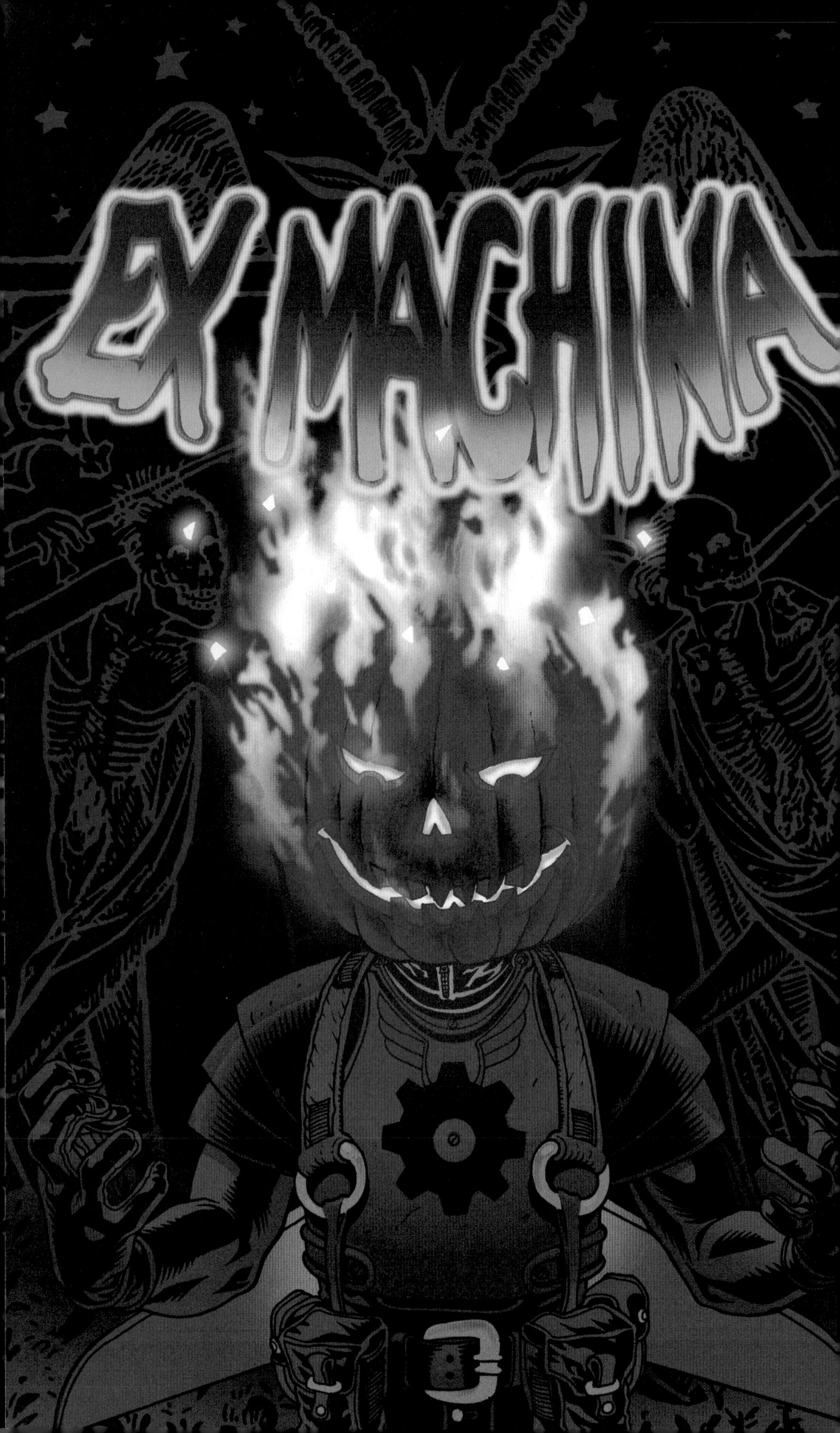
EX MACHINA

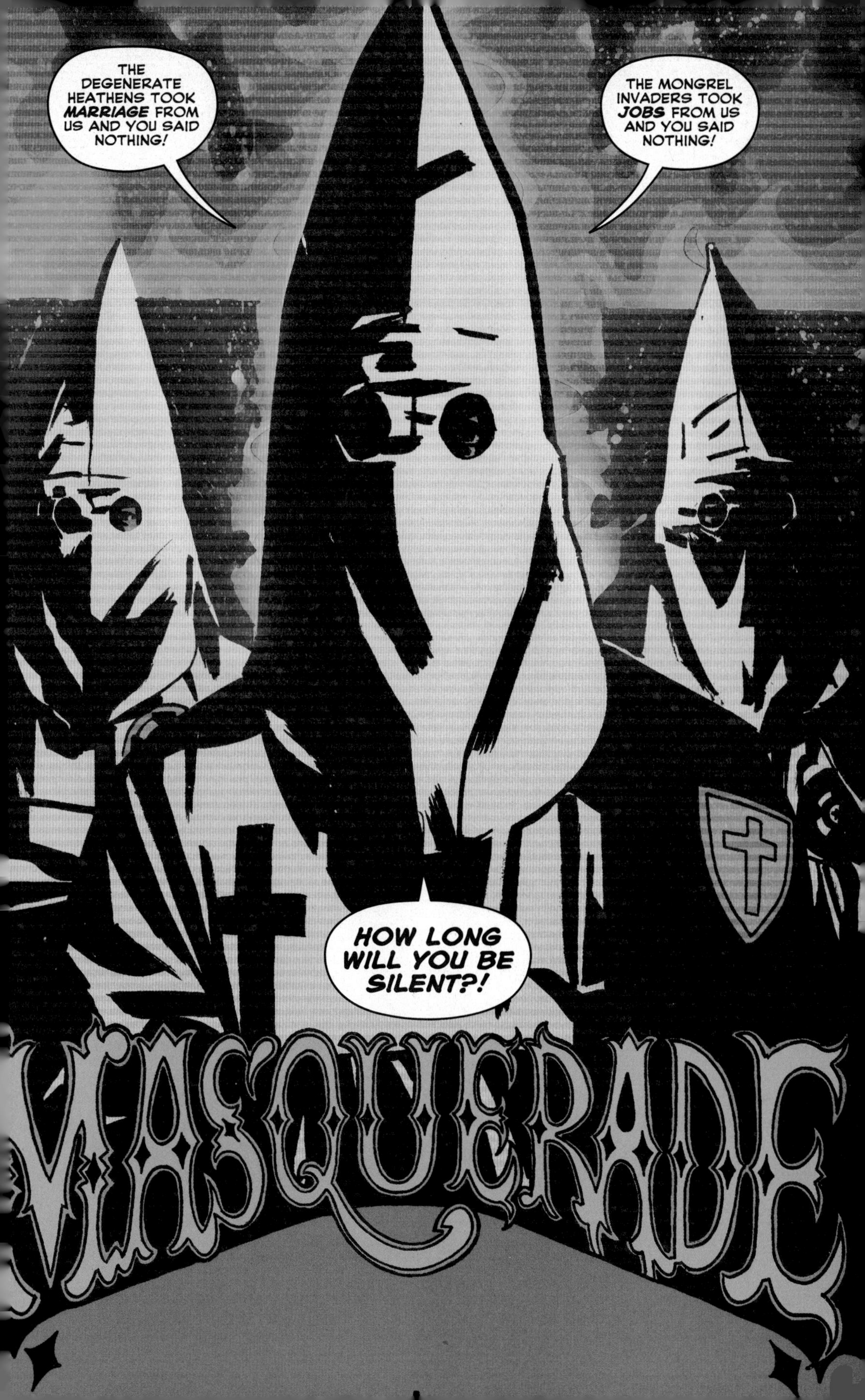
THE DEGENERATE HEATHENS TOOK **MARRIAGE** FROM US AND YOU SAID NOTHING!
THE MONGREL INVADERS TOOK **JOBS** FROM US AND YOU SAID NOTHING!
HOW LONG WILL YOU BE SILENT?!
MASQUERADE

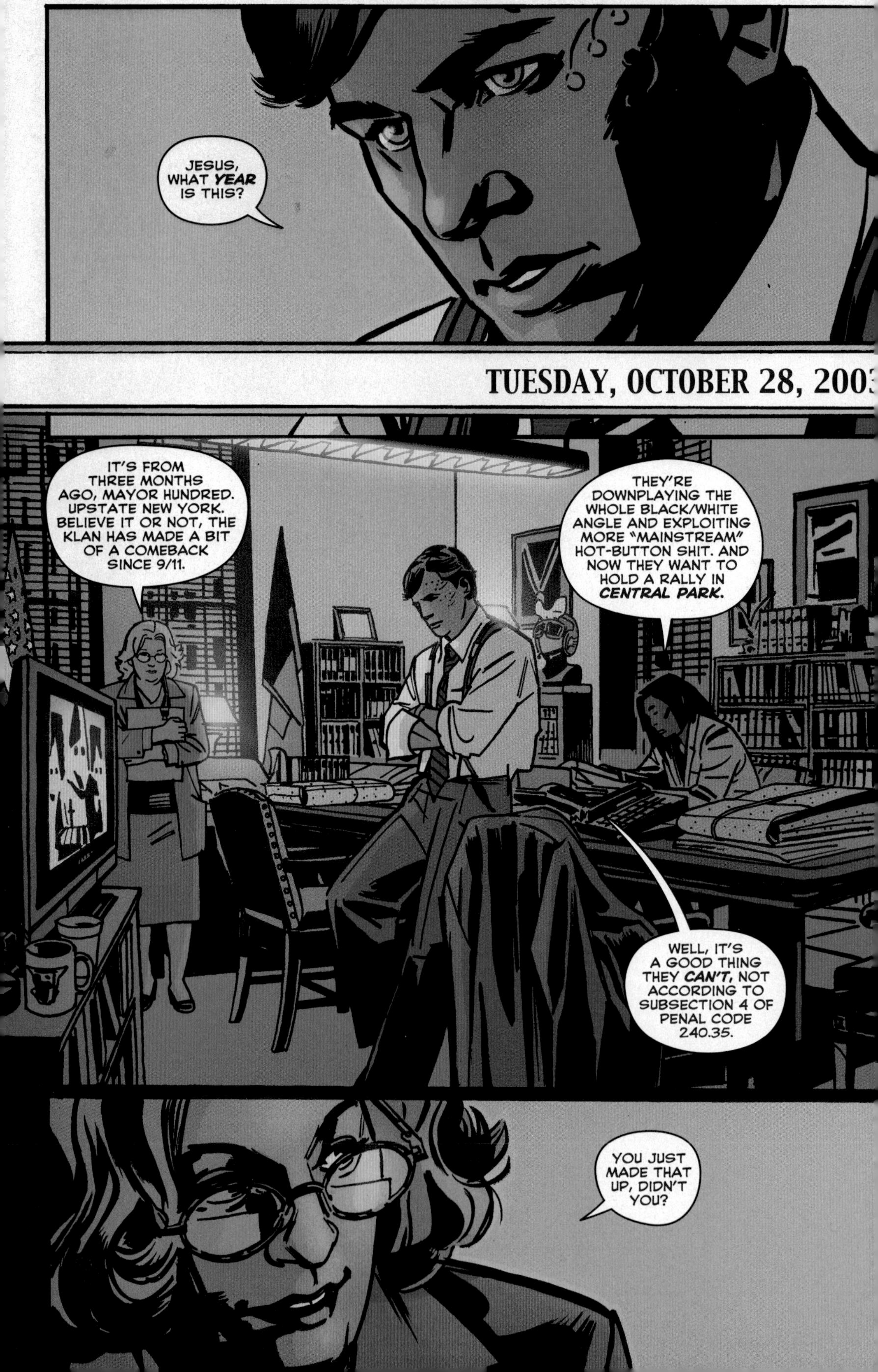
JESUS, WHAT YEAR IS THIS?
TUESDAY, OCTOBER 28, 200
IT'S FROM THREE MONTHS AGO, MAYOR HUNDRED. UPSTATE NEW YORK. BELIEVE IT OR NOT, THE KLAN HAS MADE A BIT OF A COMEBACK SINCE 9/11.
THEY'RE DOWNPLAYING THE WHOLE BLACK/WHITE ANGLE AND EXPLOITING MORE "MAINSTREAM" HOT-BUTTON SHIT. AND NOW THEY WANT TO HOLD A RALLY IN CENTRAL PARK.
WELL, IT'S A GOOD THING THEY CAN'T, NOT ACCORDING TO SUBSECTION 4 OF PENAL CODE 240.35.
YOU JUST MADE THAT UP, DIDN'T YOU?

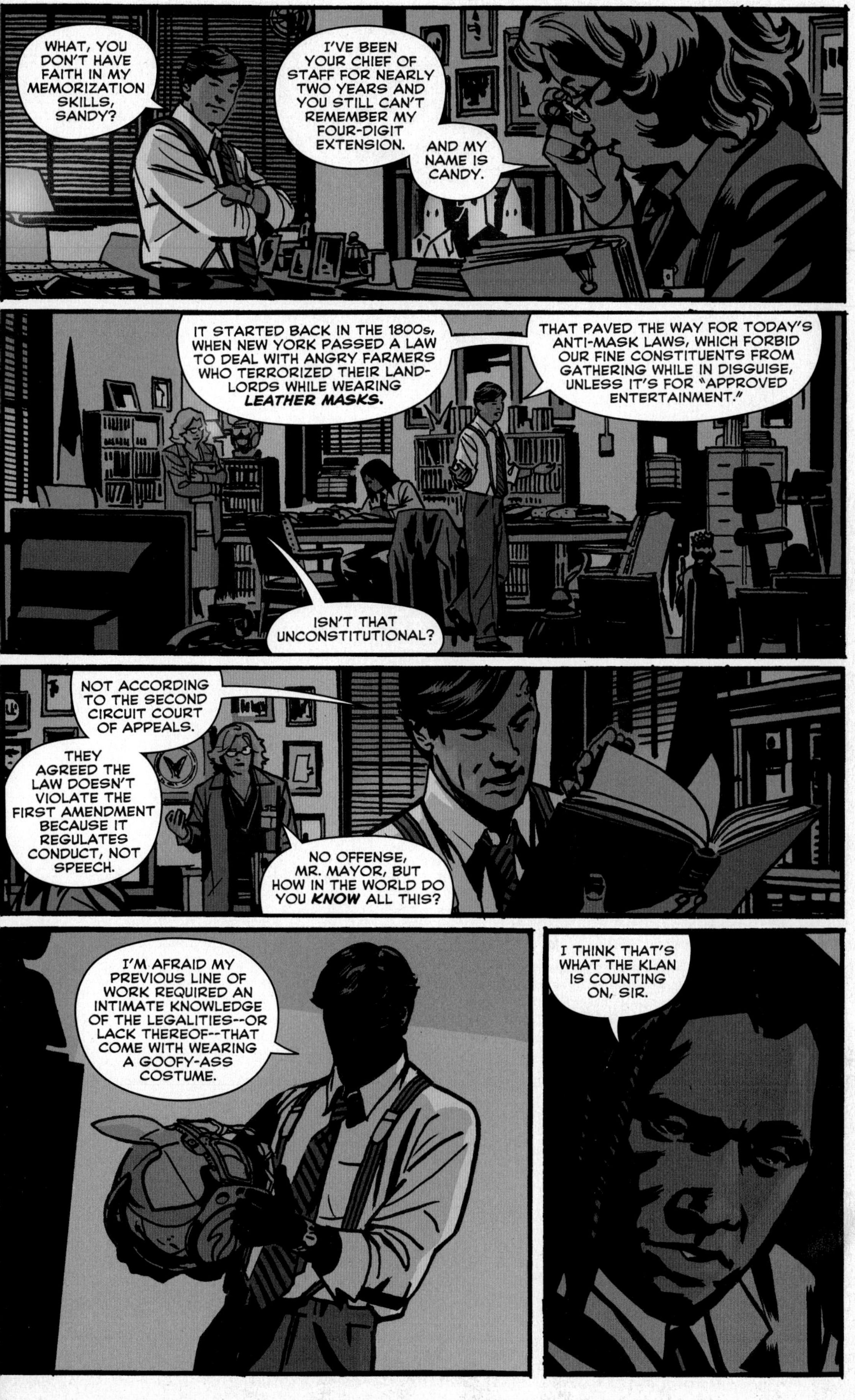
WHAT, YOU DON'T HAVE FAITH IN MY MEMORIZATION SKILLS, SANDY?
I'VE BEEN YOUR CHIEF OF STAFF FOR NEARLY TWO YEARS AND YOU STILL CAN'T REMEMBER MY FOUR-DIGIT EXTENSION.
AND MY NAME IS CANDY.
IT STARTED BACK IN THE 1800s, WHEN NEW YORK PASSED A LAW TO DEAL WITH ANGRY FARMERS WHO TERRORIZED THEIR LAND-LORDS WHILE WEARING ***LEATHER MASKS.***
THAT PAVED THE WAY FOR TODAY'S ANTI-MASK LAWS, WHICH FORBID OUR FINE CONSTITUENTS FROM GATHERING WHILE IN DISGUISE, UNLESS IT'S FOR "APPROVED ENTERTAINMENT."
ISN'T THAT UNCONSTITUTIONAL?
NOT ACCORDING TO THE SECOND CIRCUIT COURT OF APPEALS.
THEY AGREED THE LAW DOESN'T VIOLATE THE FIRST AMENDMENT BECAUSE IT REGULATES CONDUCT, NOT SPEECH.
NO OFFENSE, MR. MAYOR, BUT HOW IN THE WORLD DO YOU ***KNOW*** ALL THIS?
I'M AFRAID MY PREVIOUS LINE OF WORK REQUIRED AN INTIMATE KNOWLEDGE OF THE LEGALITIES--OR LACK THEREOF--THAT COME WITH WEARING A GOOFY-ASS COSTUME.
I THINK THAT'S WHAT THE KLAN IS COUNTING ON, SIR.

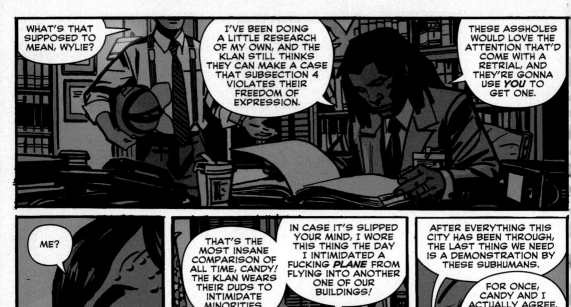

WHAT'S THAT SUPPOSED TO MEAN, WYLIE?

I'VE BEEN DOING A LITTLE RESEARCH OF MY OWN, AND THE KLAN STILL THINKS THEY CAN MAKE A CASE THAT SUBSECTION 4 VIOLATES THEIR FREEDOM OF EXPRESSION.

THESE ASSHOLES WOULD LOVE THE ATTENTION THAT'D COME WITH A RETRIAL, AND THEY'RE GONNA USE *YOU* TO GET ONE.

ME?

OH MY GOD, THE DEPUTY MAYOR IS RIGHT. IF YOU OF ALL PEOPLE EXPLOIT AN "ANTI-MASK LAW" TO DENY THE KKK A PERMIT, THEY'RE GOING TO PAINT YOU AS A MASSIVE HYPOCRITE.

THAT'S THE MOST INSANE COMPARISON OF ALL TIME, CANDY! THE KLAN WEARS THEIR DUDS TO INTIMIDATE MINORITIES.

IN CASE IT'S SLIPPED YOUR MIND, I WORE THIS THING THE DAY I INTIMIDATED A FUCKING *PLANE* FROM FLYING INTO ANOTHER ONE OF OUR BUILDINGS!

AND THE KKK WILL ARGUE THAT THEY'RE *ALSO* TRYING TO DEFEND THIS COUNTRY, THAT THEY DESERVE THE SAME ANONYMITY YOU ENJOYED IN YOUR "SUPERHERO" DAYS.

AFTER EVERYTHING THIS CITY HAS BEEN THROUGH, THE LAST THING WE NEED IS A DEMONSTRATION BY THESE SUBHUMANS.

FOR ONCE, CANDY AND I ACTUALLY AGREE. FIGHTING THIS RALLY MIGHT COST ME MY ACLU CARD, BUT I'D MUCH RATHER KEEP MY CREDENTIALS WITH THE NAACP.

HOW THE HELL DO WE WIN THIS ONE, SIR?

SIR?

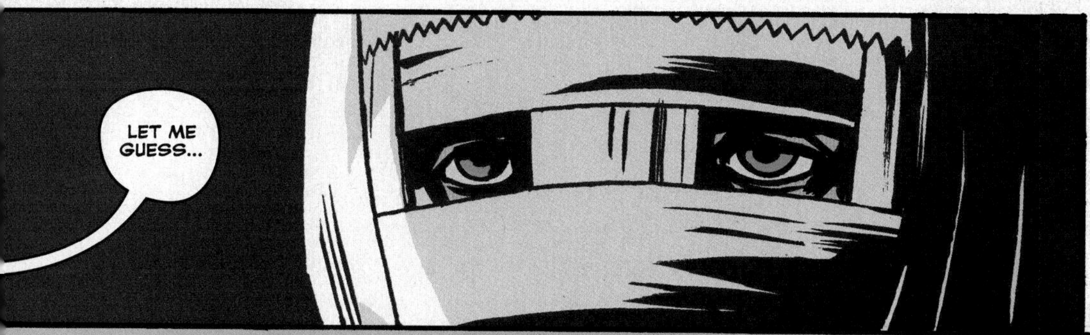
LET ME GUESS...

SUNDAY, OCTOBER 31, 1999

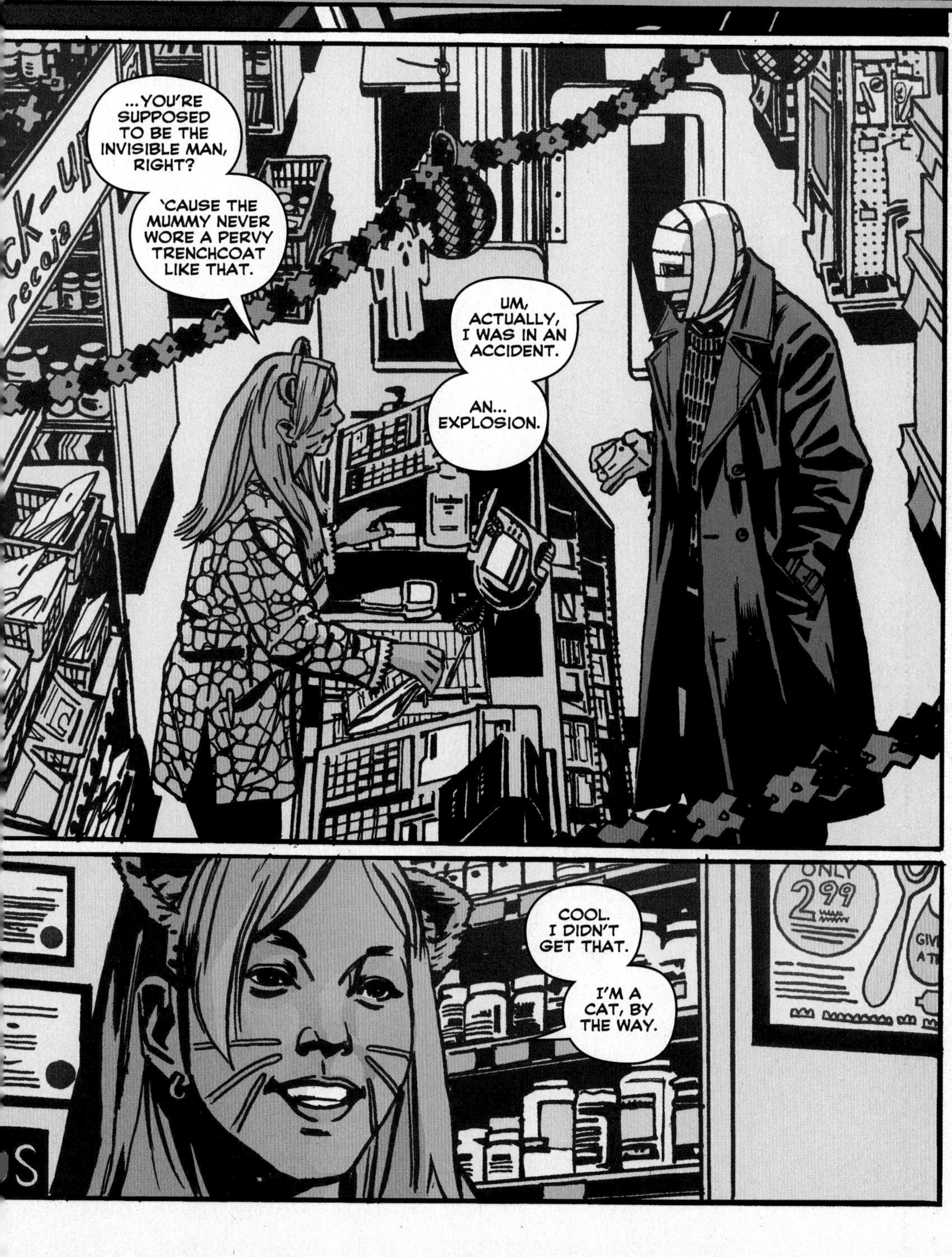
...YOU'RE SUPPOSED TO BE THE INVISIBLE MAN, RIGHT?
'CAUSE THE MUMMY NEVER WORE A PERVY TRENCHCOAT LIKE THAT.
UM, ACTUALLY, I WAS IN AN ACCIDENT.
AN... EXPLOSION.
ONLY
COOL. I DIDN'T GET THAT.
I'M A CAT, BY THE WAY.

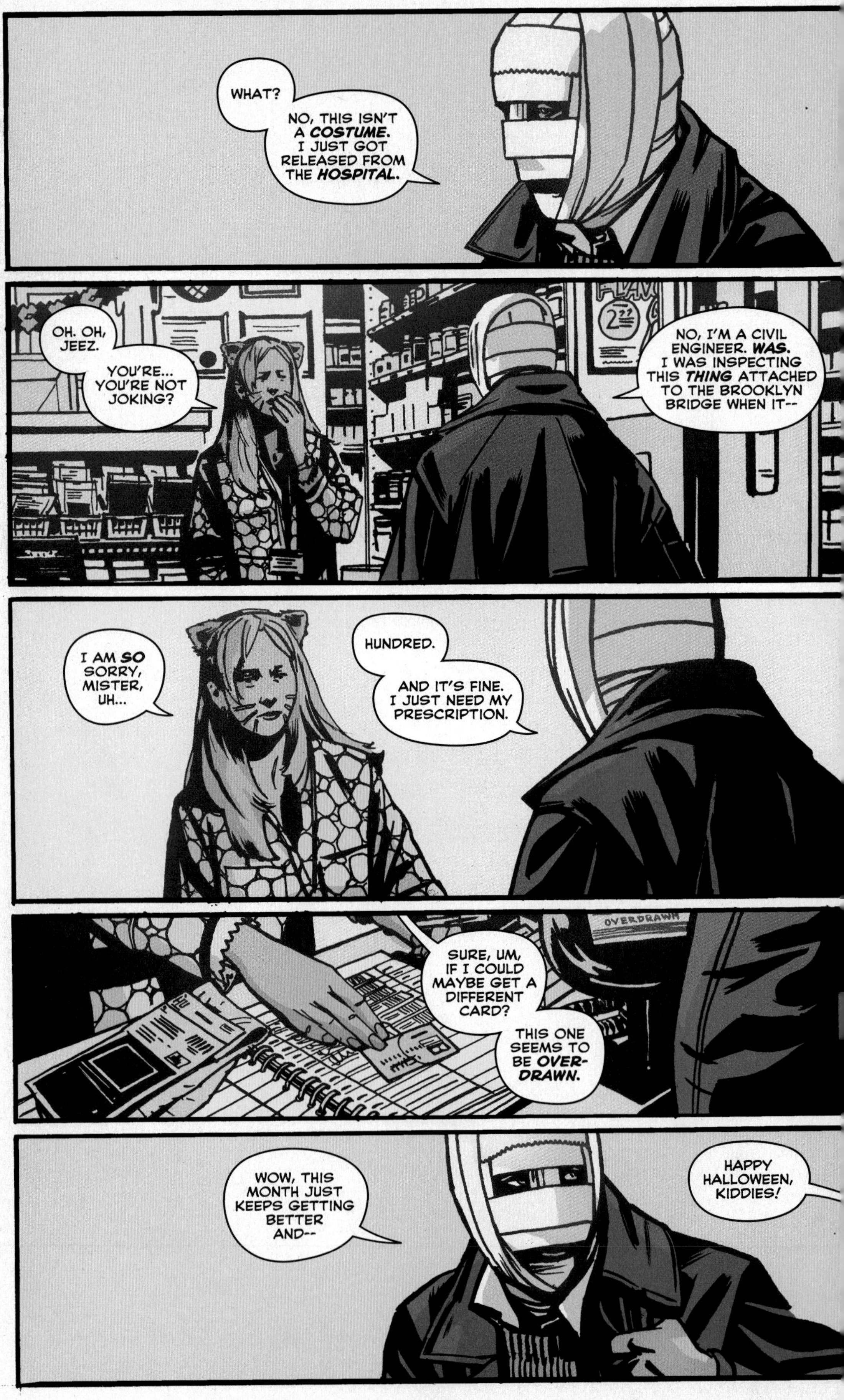
WHAT?
NO, THIS ISN'T A **COSTUME**. I JUST GOT RELEASED FROM THE **HOSPITAL**.
OH. OH, JEEZ.
YOU'RE... YOU'RE NOT JOKING?
NO, I'M A CIVIL ENGINEER. **WAS.** I WAS INSPECTING THIS **THING** ATTACHED TO THE BROOKLYN BRIDGE WHEN IT--
I AM **SO** SORRY, MISTER, UH...
HUNDRED.
AND IT'S FINE. I JUST NEED MY PRESCRIPTION.
OVERDRAWN
SURE, UM, IF I COULD MAYBE GET A DIFFERENT CARD?
THIS ONE SEEMS TO BE **OVER-DRAWN.**
WOW, THIS MONTH JUST KEEPS GETTING BETTER AND--
HAPPY HALLOWEEN, KIDDIES!

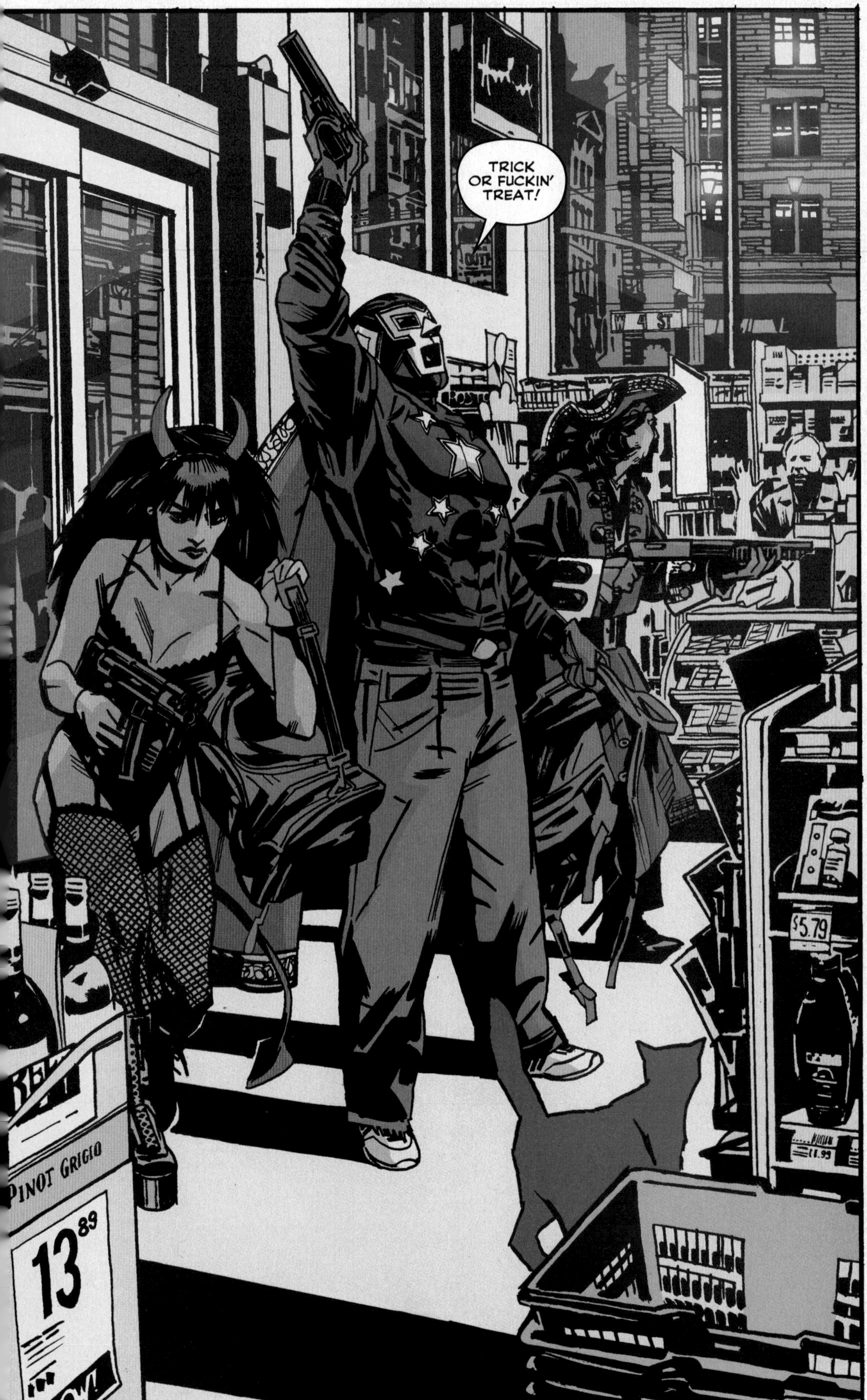
TRICK OR FUCKIN' TREAT!
W 4 ST
PINOT GRIGIO
13.89
$5.79

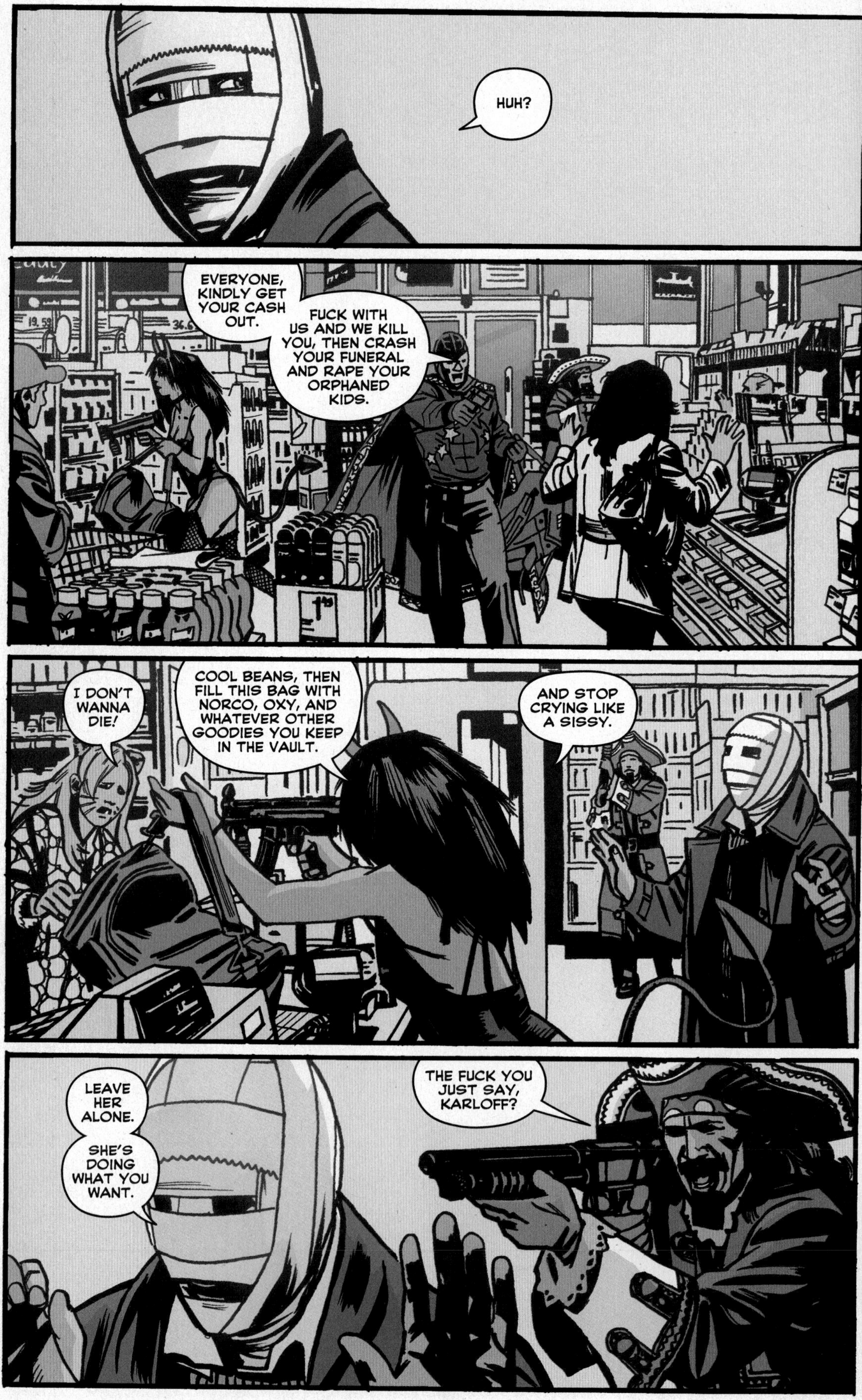
HUH?
EVERYONE, KINDLY GET YOUR CASH OUT.
FUCK WITH US AND WE KILL YOU, THEN CRASH YOUR FUNERAL AND RAPE YOUR ORPHANED KIDS.
I DON'T WANNA DIE!
COOL BEANS, THEN FILL THIS BAG WITH NORCO, OXY, AND WHATEVER OTHER GOODIES YOU KEEP IN THE VAULT.
AND STOP CRYING LIKE A SISSY.
LEAVE HER ALONE.
SHE'S DOING WHAT YOU WANT.
THE FUCK YOU JUST SAY, KARLOFF?

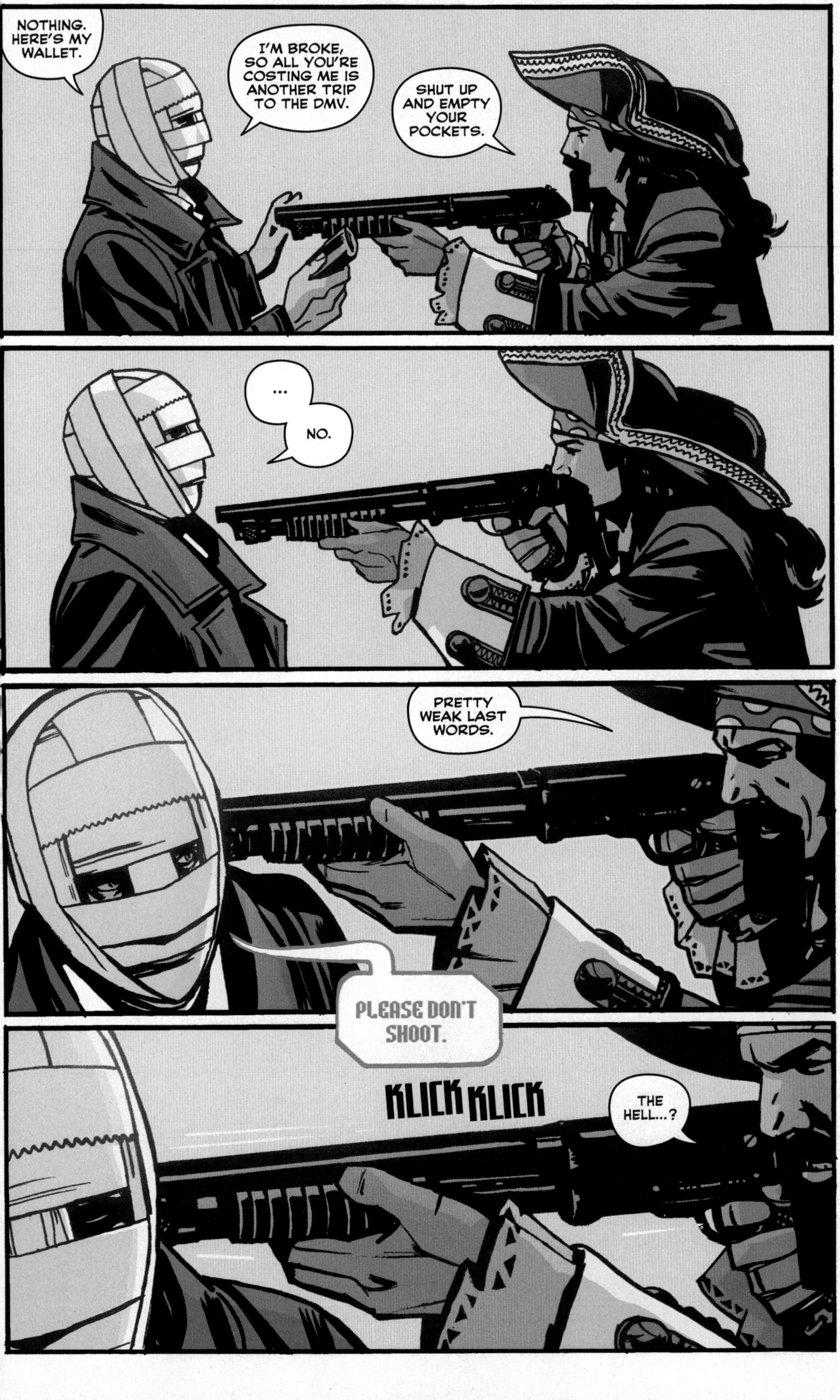
NOTHING. HERE'S MY WALLET.
I'M BROKE, SO ALL YOU'RE COSTING ME IS ANOTHER TRIP TO THE DMV.
SHUT UP AND EMPTY YOUR POCKETS.
...
NO.
PRETTY WEAK LAST WORDS.
PLEASE DON'T SHOOT.
KLICK KLICK
THE HELL...?

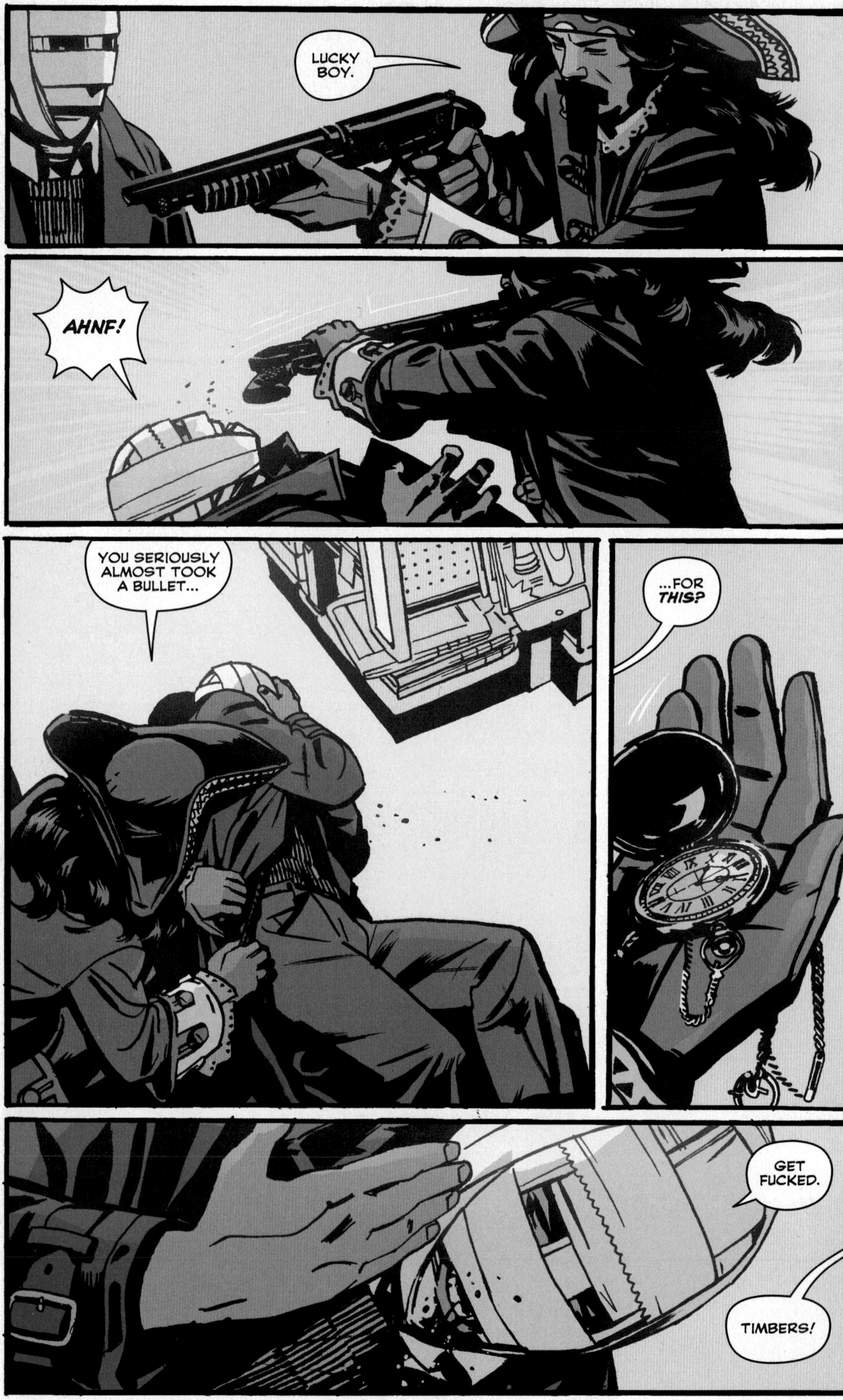
LUCKY BOY.
AHNF!
YOU SERIOUSLY ALMOST TOOK A BULLET...
...FOR THIS?
GET FUCKED.
TIMBERS!

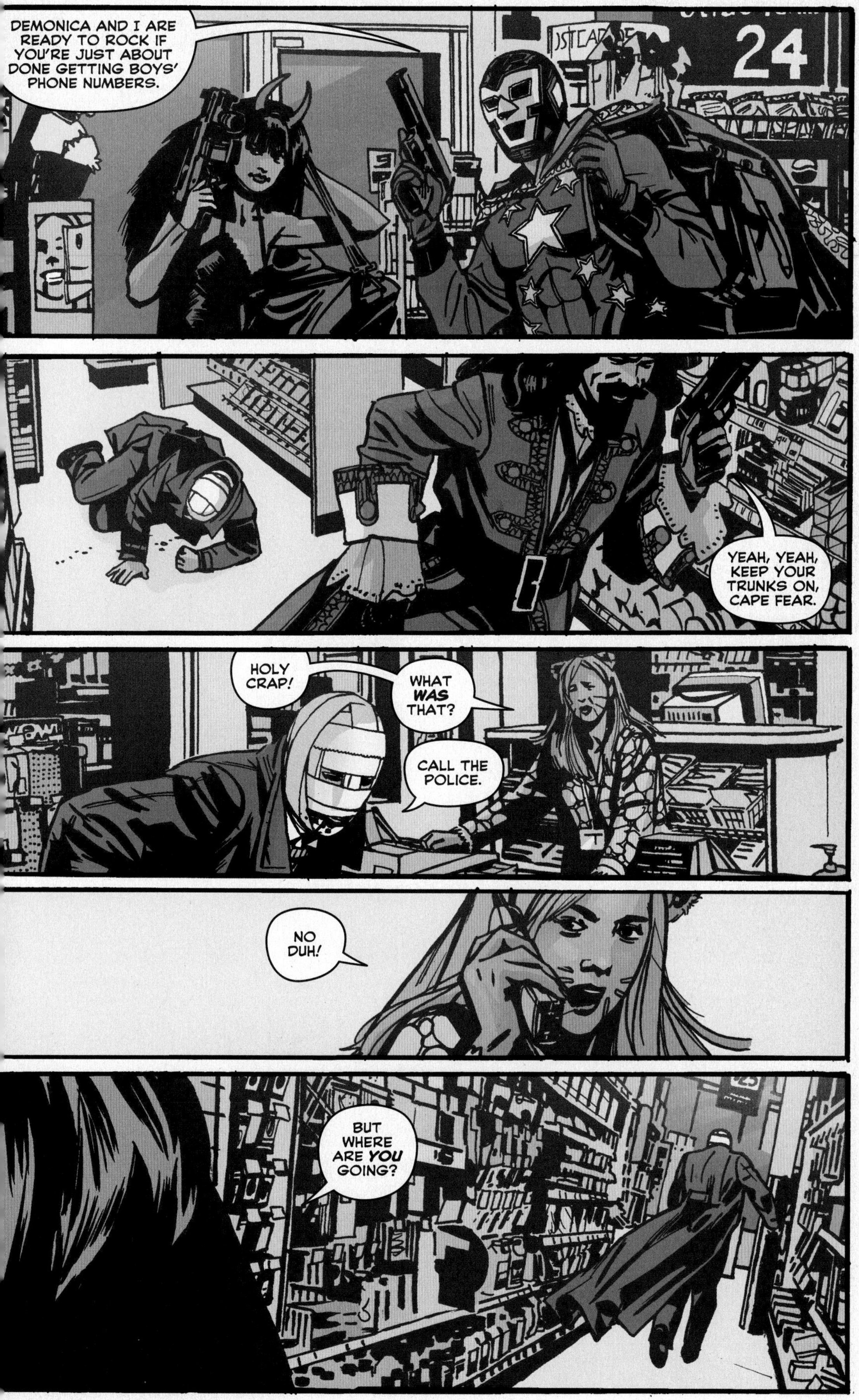
DEMONICA AND I ARE READY TO ROCK IF YOU'RE JUST ABOUT DONE GETTING BOYS' PHONE NUMBERS.
24
YEAH, YEAH, KEEP YOUR TRUNKS ON, CAPE FEAR.
HOLY CRAP!
WHAT *WAS* THAT?
CALL THE POLICE.
NO DUH!
BUT WHERE ARE *YOU* GOING?

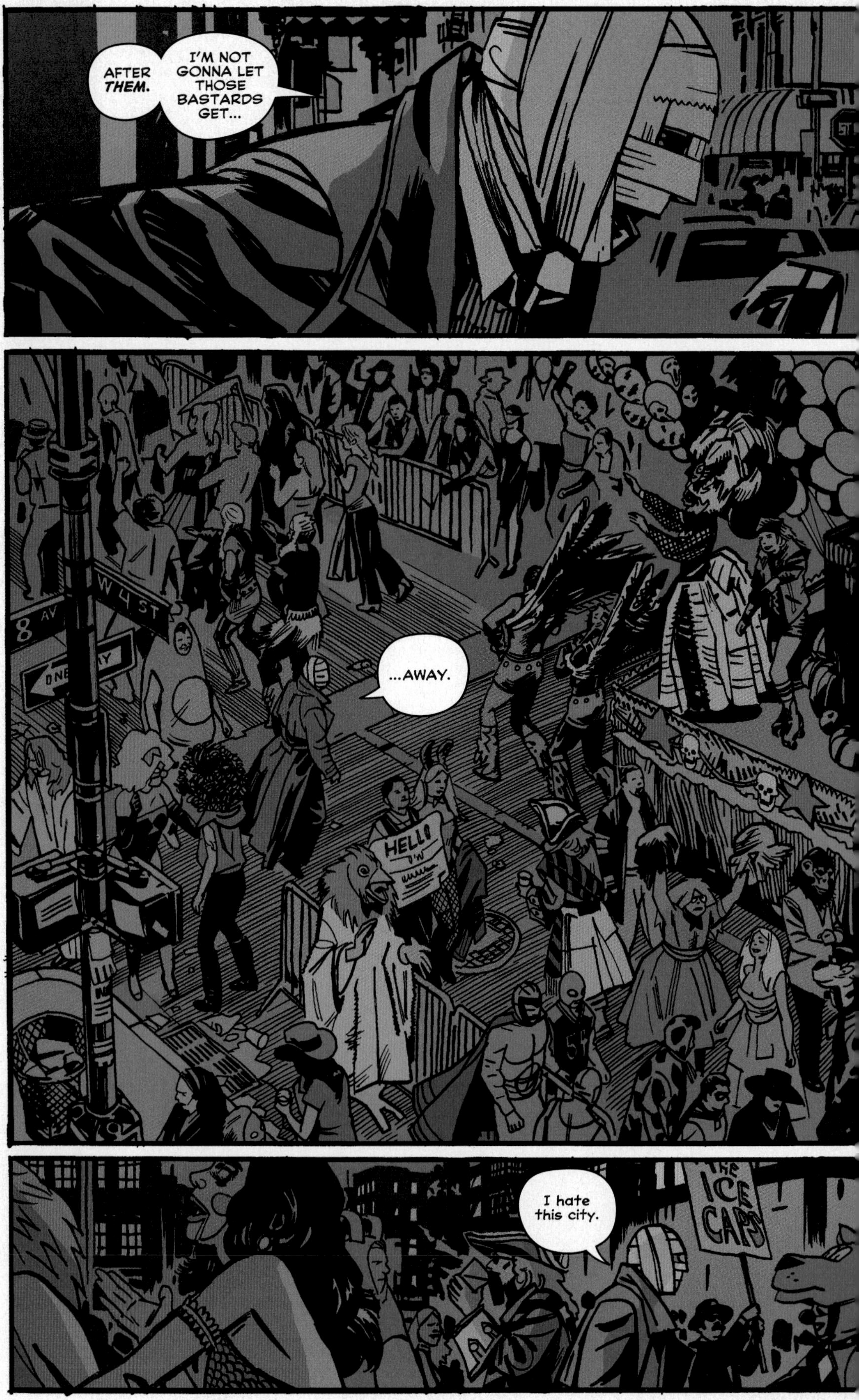
AFTER *THEM*.
I'M NOT GONNA LET THOSE BASTARDS GET...
8 AV
W 4 ST
...AWAY.
HELLO
I hate this city.
ICE CAPS

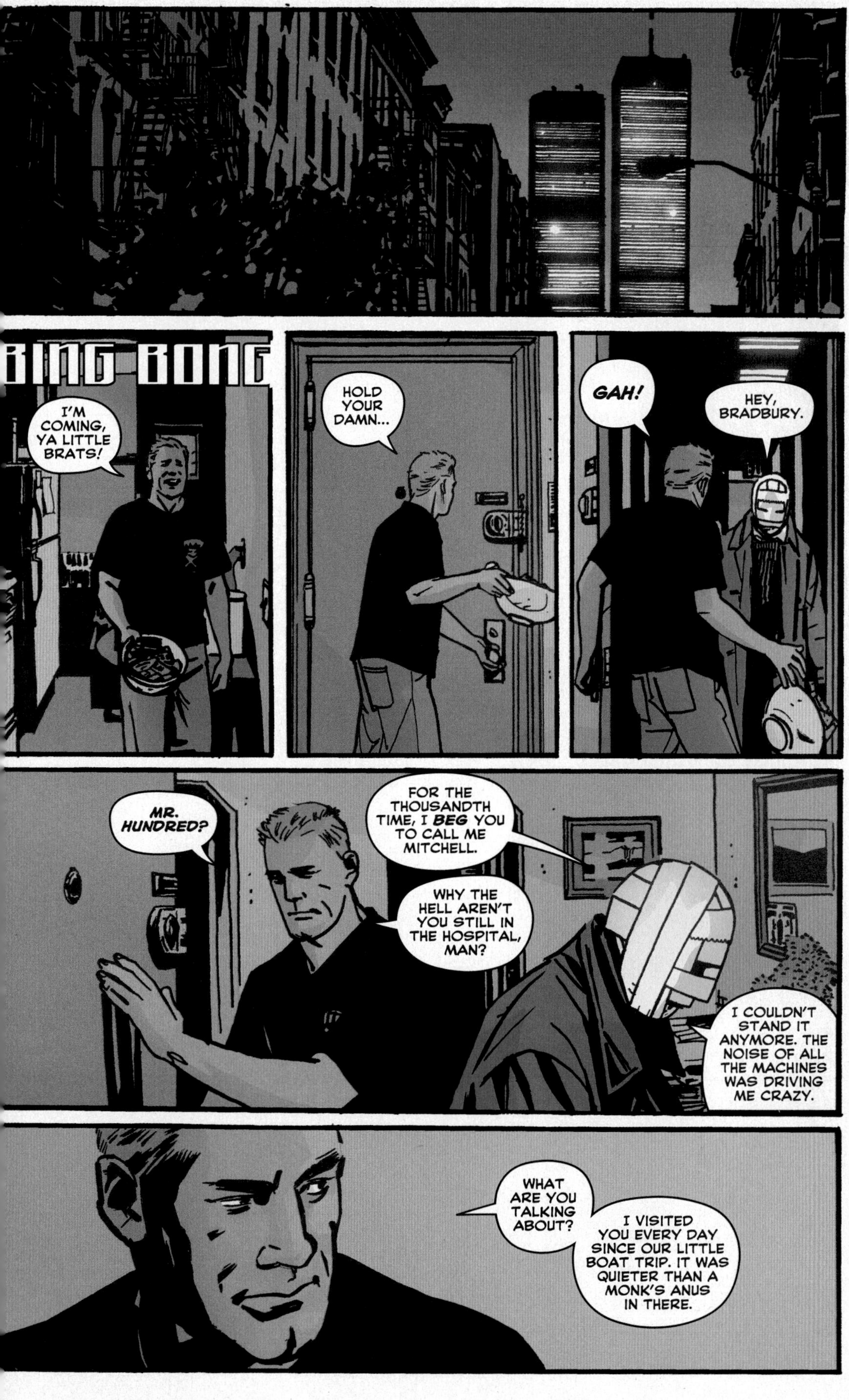
BING BONG
I'M COMING, YA LITTLE BRATS!
HOLD YOUR DAMN...
GAH!
HEY, BRADBURY.
MR. HUNDRED?
FOR THE THOUSANDTH TIME, I BEG YOU TO CALL ME MITCHELL.
WHY THE HELL AREN'T YOU STILL IN THE HOSPITAL, MAN?
I COULDN'T STAND IT ANYMORE. THE NOISE OF ALL THE MACHINES WAS DRIVING ME CRAZY.
WHAT ARE YOU TALKING ABOUT?
I VISITED YOU EVERY DAY SINCE OUR LITTLE BOAT TRIP. IT WAS QUIETER THAN A MONK'S ANUS IN THERE.

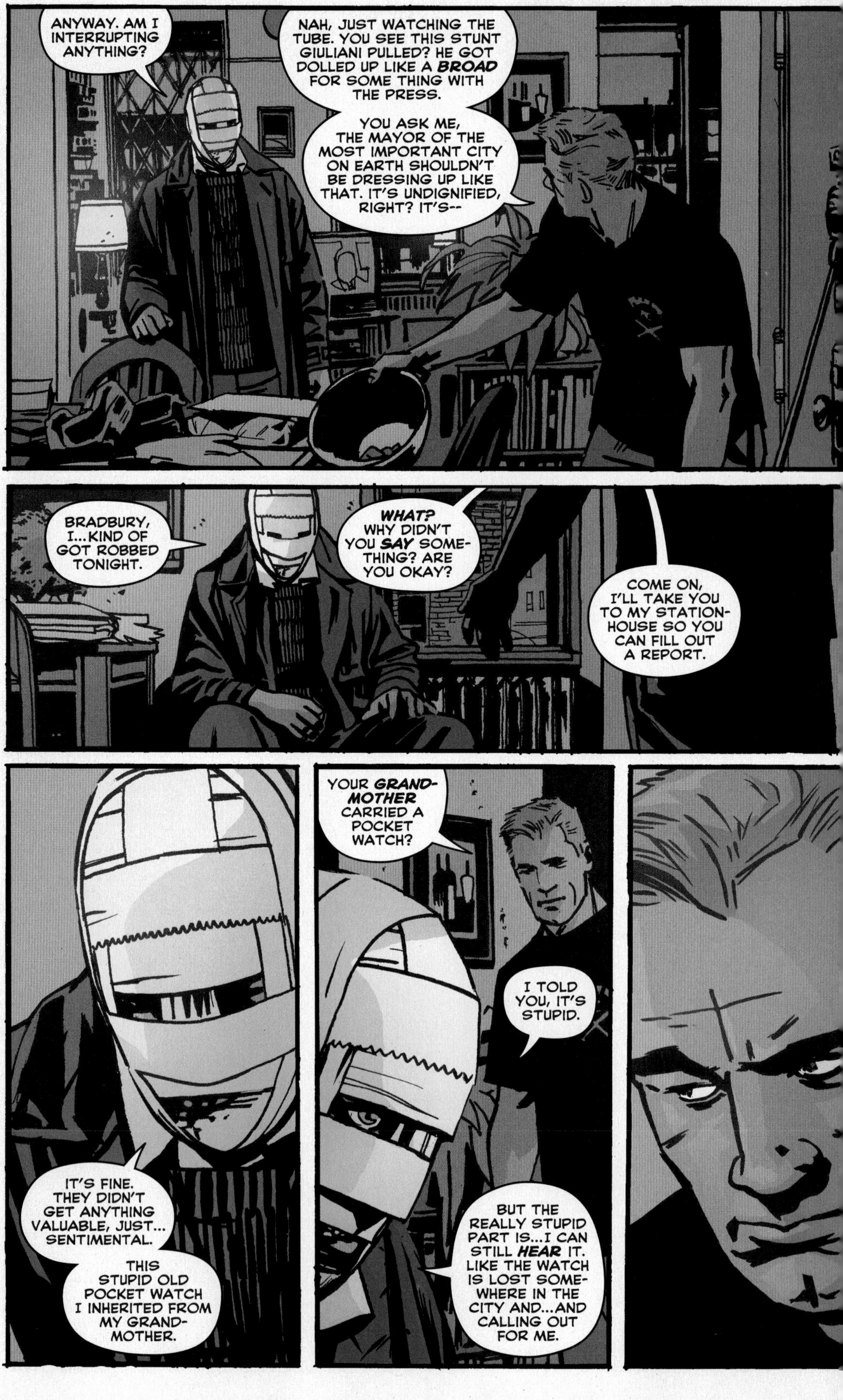
ANYWAY. AM I INTERRUPTING ANYTHING?
NAH, JUST WATCHING THE TUBE. YOU SEE THIS STUNT GIULIANI PULLED? HE GOT DOLLED UP LIKE A ***BROAD*** FOR SOME THING WITH THE PRESS.
YOU ASK ME, THE MAYOR OF THE MOST IMPORTANT CITY ON EARTH SHOULDN'T BE DRESSING UP LIKE THAT. IT'S UNDIGNIFIED, RIGHT? IT'S--
BRADBURY, I...KIND OF GOT ROBBED TONIGHT.
WHAT? WHY DIDN'T YOU ***SAY*** SOME-THING? ARE YOU OKAY?
COME ON, I'LL TAKE YOU TO MY STATION-HOUSE SO YOU CAN FILL OUT A REPORT.
IT'S FINE. THEY DIDN'T GET ANYTHING VALUABLE, JUST... SENTIMENTAL.
THIS STUPID OLD POCKET WATCH I INHERITED FROM MY GRAND-MOTHER.
YOUR ***GRAND-MOTHER*** CARRIED A POCKET WATCH?
I TOLD YOU, IT'S STUPID.
BUT THE REALLY STUPID PART IS...I CAN STILL ***HEAR*** IT. LIKE THE WATCH IS LOST SOME-WHERE IN THE CITY AND...AND CALLING OUT FOR ME.

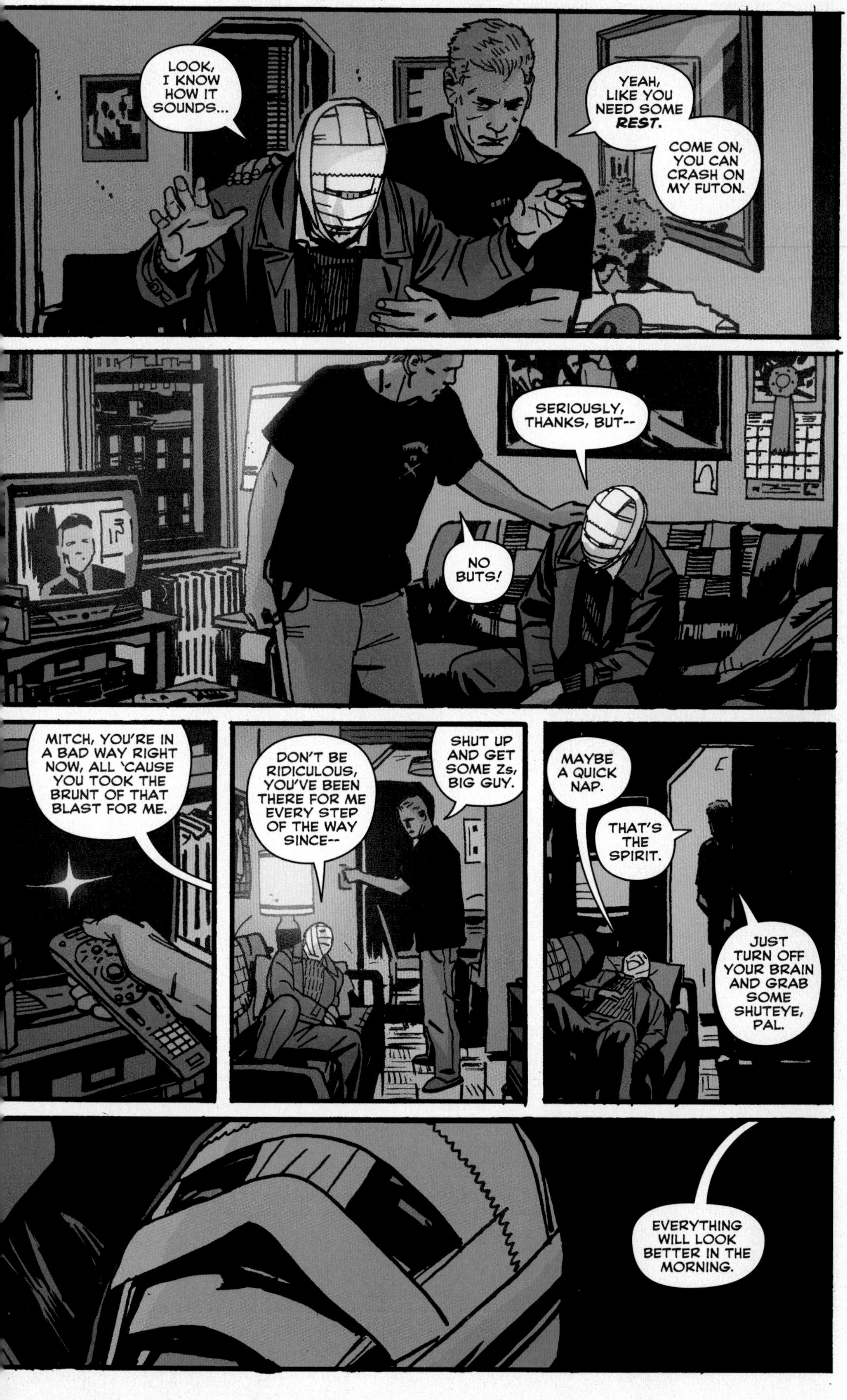
LOOK, I KNOW HOW IT SOUNDS...
YEAH, LIKE YOU NEED SOME **REST**.
COME ON, YOU CAN CRASH ON MY FUTON.
SERIOUSLY, THANKS, BUT--
NO BUTS!
MITCH, YOU'RE IN A BAD WAY RIGHT NOW, ALL 'CAUSE YOU TOOK THE BRUNT OF THAT BLAST FOR ME.
DON'T BE RIDICULOUS, YOU'VE BEEN THERE FOR ME EVERY STEP OF THE WAY SINCE--
SHUT UP AND GET SOME Zs, BIG GUY.
MAYBE A QUICK NAP.
THAT'S THE SPIRIT.
JUST TURN OFF YOUR BRAIN AND GRAB SOME SHUTEYE, PAL.
EVERYTHING WILL LOOK BETTER IN THE MORNING.

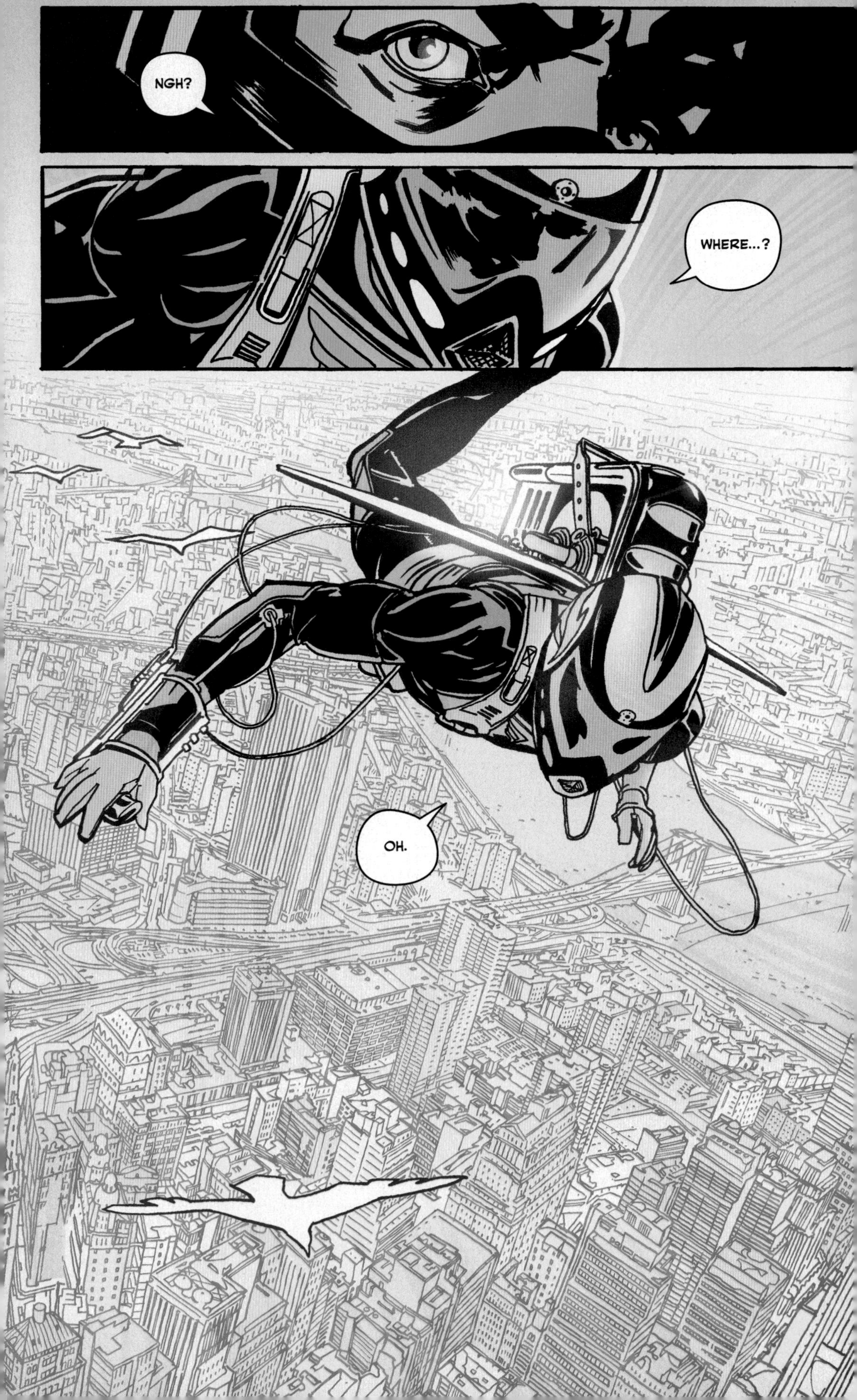
NGH?
WHERE...?
OH.

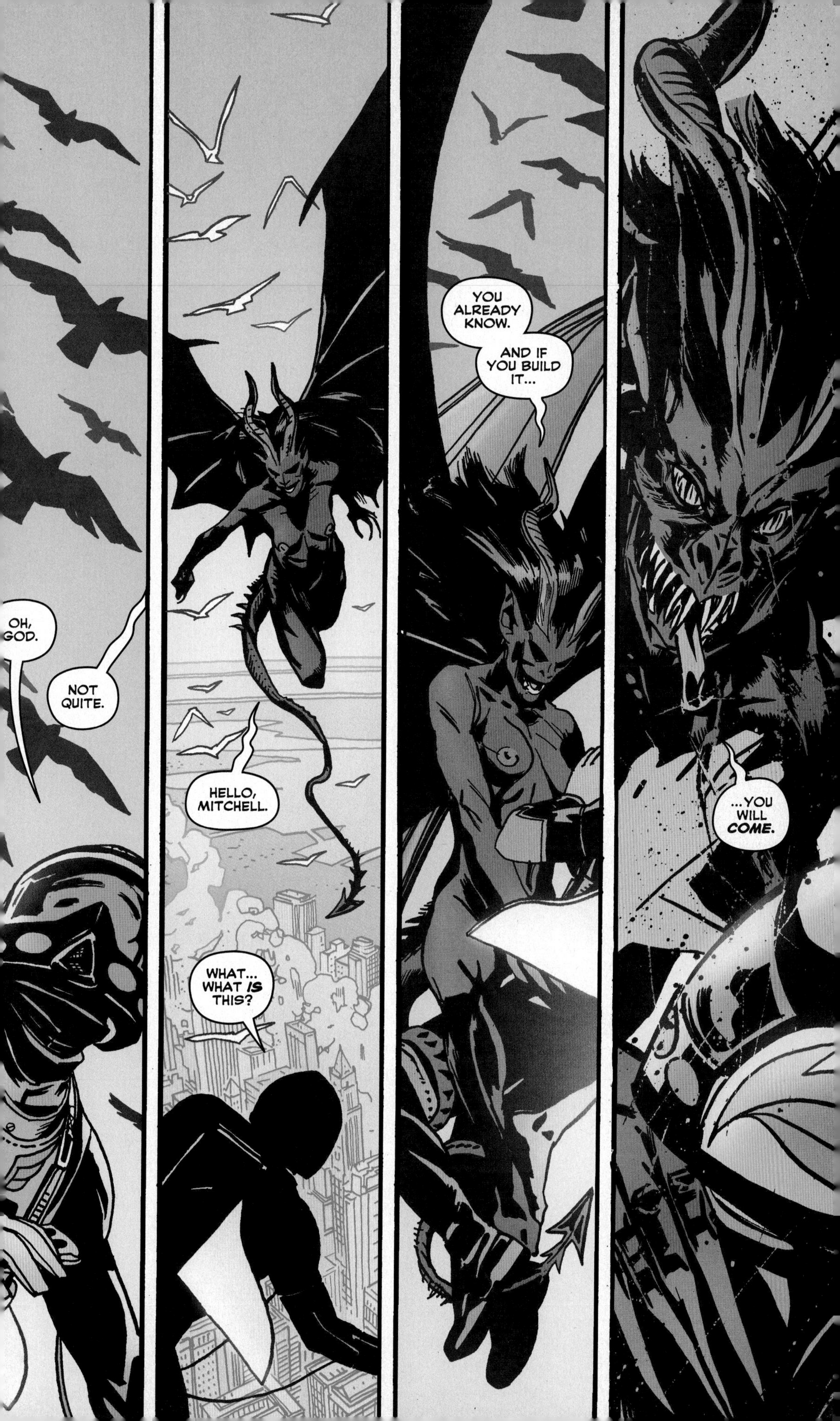
OH, GOD.
NOT QUITE.
HELLO, MITCHELL.
WHAT... WHAT *IS* THIS?
YOU ALREADY KNOW.
AND IF YOU BUILD IT...
...YOU WILL *COME.*

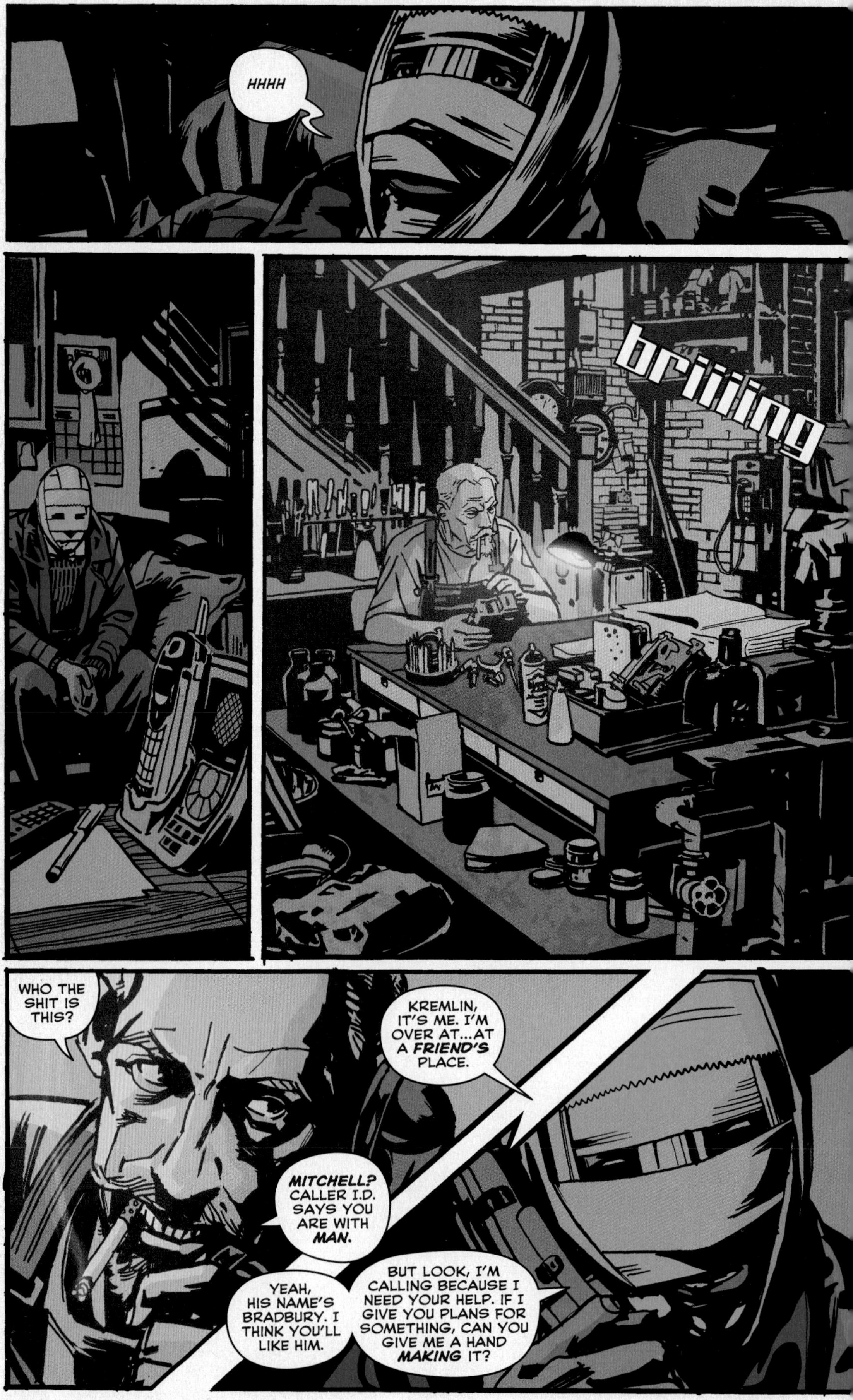
HHHH
briiing
WHO THE SHIT IS THIS?
KREMLIN, IT'S ME. I'M OVER AT...AT A FRIEND'S PLACE.
MITCHELL? CALLER I.D. SAYS YOU ARE WITH MAN.
YEAH, HIS NAME'S BRADBURY. I THINK YOU'LL LIKE HIM.
BUT LOOK, I'M CALLING BECAUSE I NEED YOUR HELP. IF I GIVE YOU PLANS FOR SOMETHING, CAN YOU GIVE ME A HAND MAKING IT?

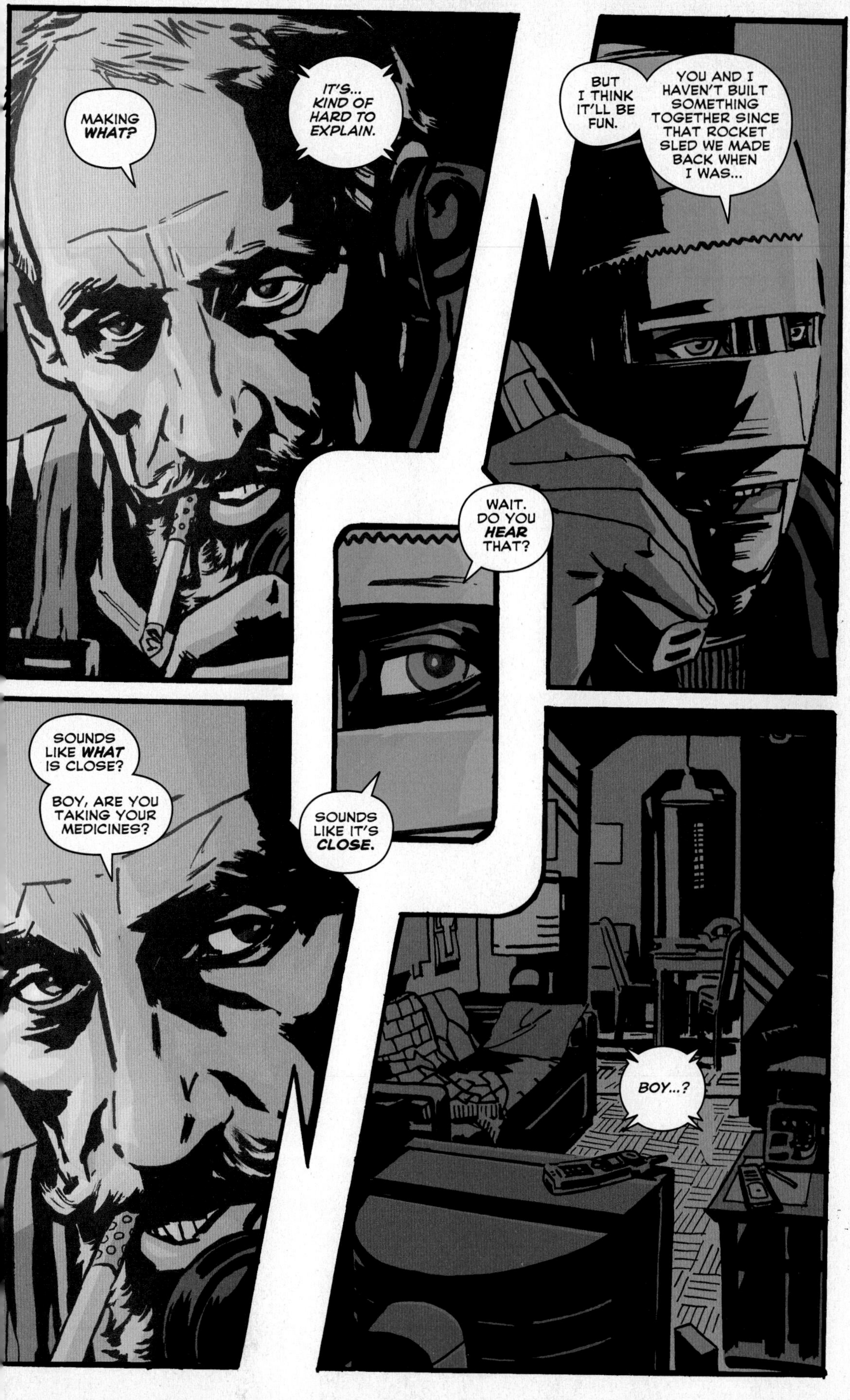
MAKING *WHAT?*
IT'S... KIND OF HARD TO EXPLAIN.
BUT I THINK IT'LL BE FUN.
YOU AND I HAVEN'T BUILT SOMETHING TOGETHER SINCE THAT ROCKET SLED WE MADE BACK WHEN I WAS...
WAIT. DO YOU *HEAR* THAT?
SOUNDS LIKE IT'S *CLOSE.*
SOUNDS LIKE *WHAT* IS CLOSE?
BOY, ARE YOU TAKING YOUR MEDICINES?
BOY...?

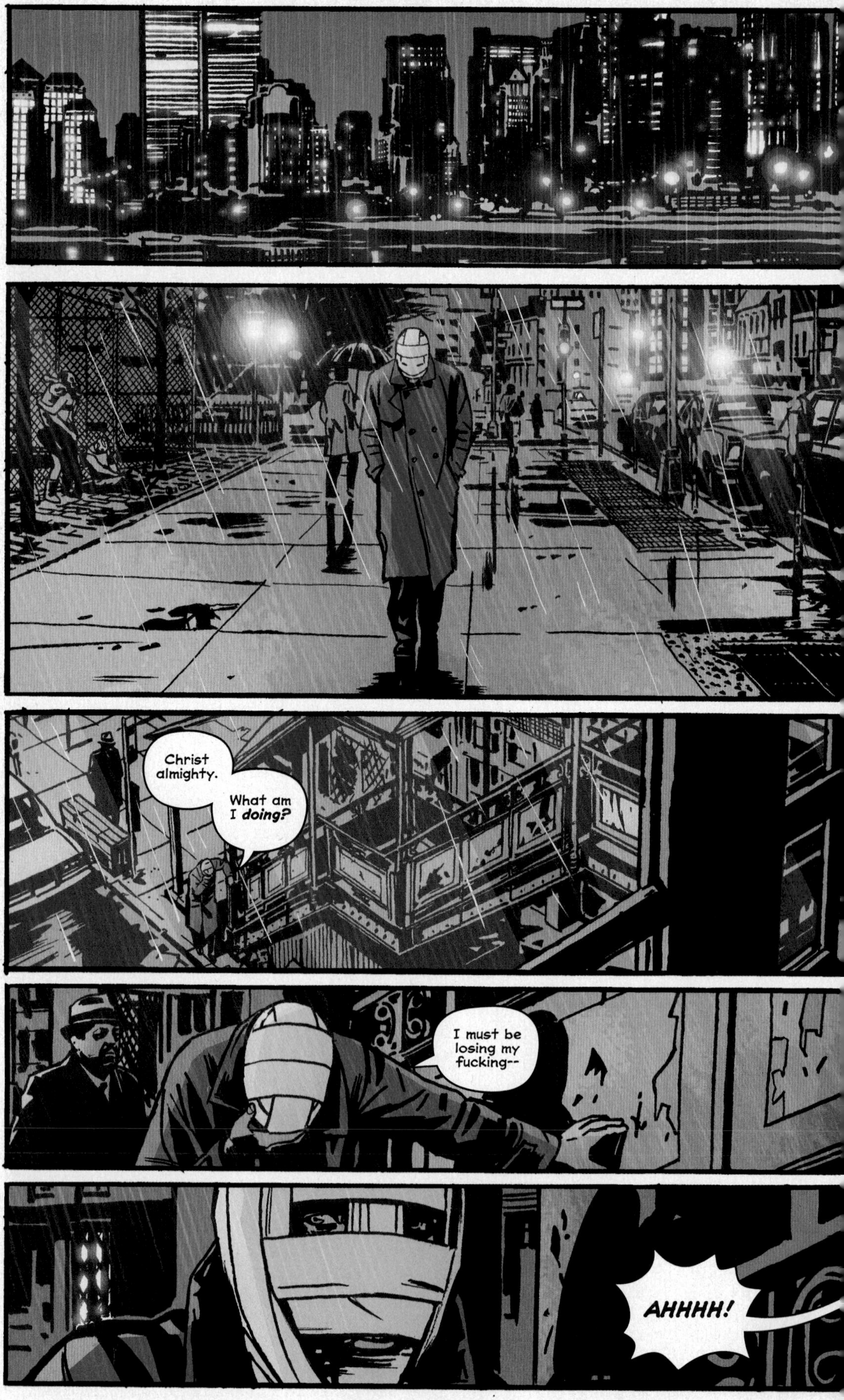
Christ almighty.
What am I *doing?*
I must be losing my fucking--
AHHHH!

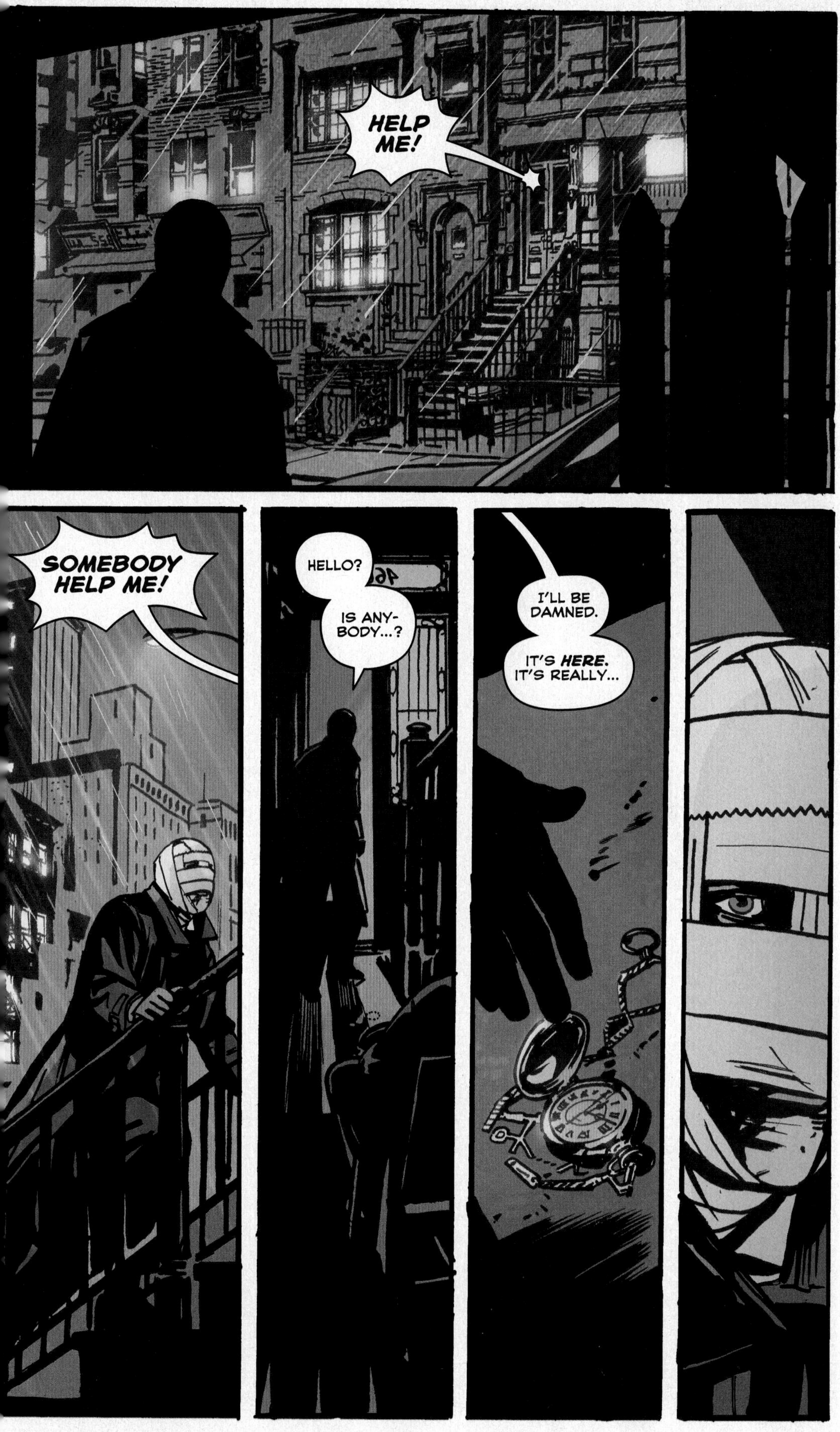
HELP ME!
SOMEBODY HELP ME!
HELLO?
IS ANY-BODY...?
I'LL BE DAMNED.
IT'S **HERE.** IT'S REALLY...

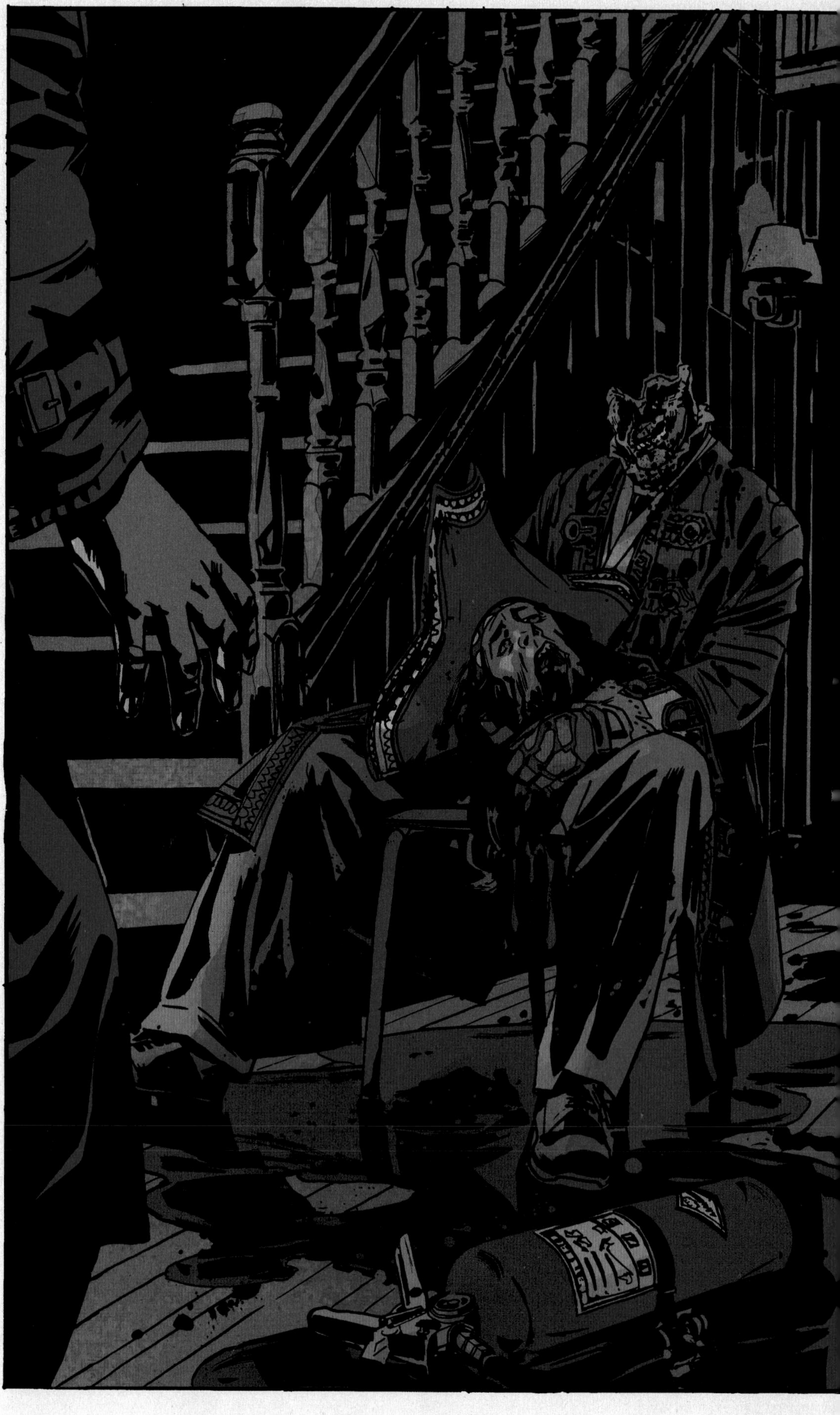

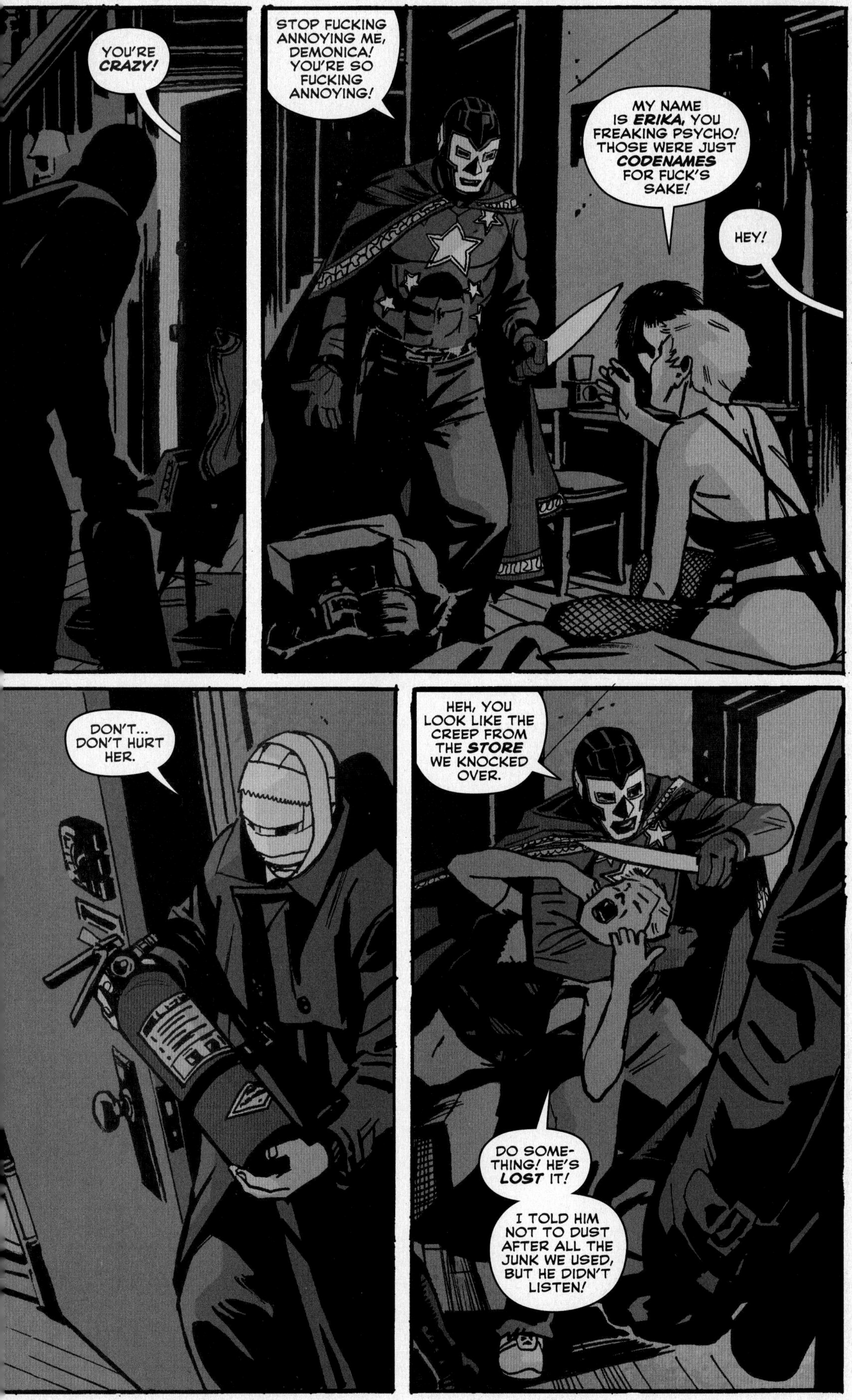
YOU'RE *CRAZY!*
STOP FUCKING ANNOYING ME, DEMONICA! YOU'RE SO FUCKING ANNOYING!
MY NAME IS **ERIKA,** YOU FREAKING PSYCHO! THOSE WERE JUST **CODENAMES** FOR FUCK'S SAKE!
HEY!
DON'T... DON'T HURT HER.
HEH, YOU LOOK LIKE THE CREEP FROM THE *STORE* WE KNOCKED OVER.
DO SOME-THING! HE'S *LOST* IT!
I TOLD HIM NOT TO DUST AFTER ALL THE JUNK WE USED, BUT HE DIDN'T LISTEN!

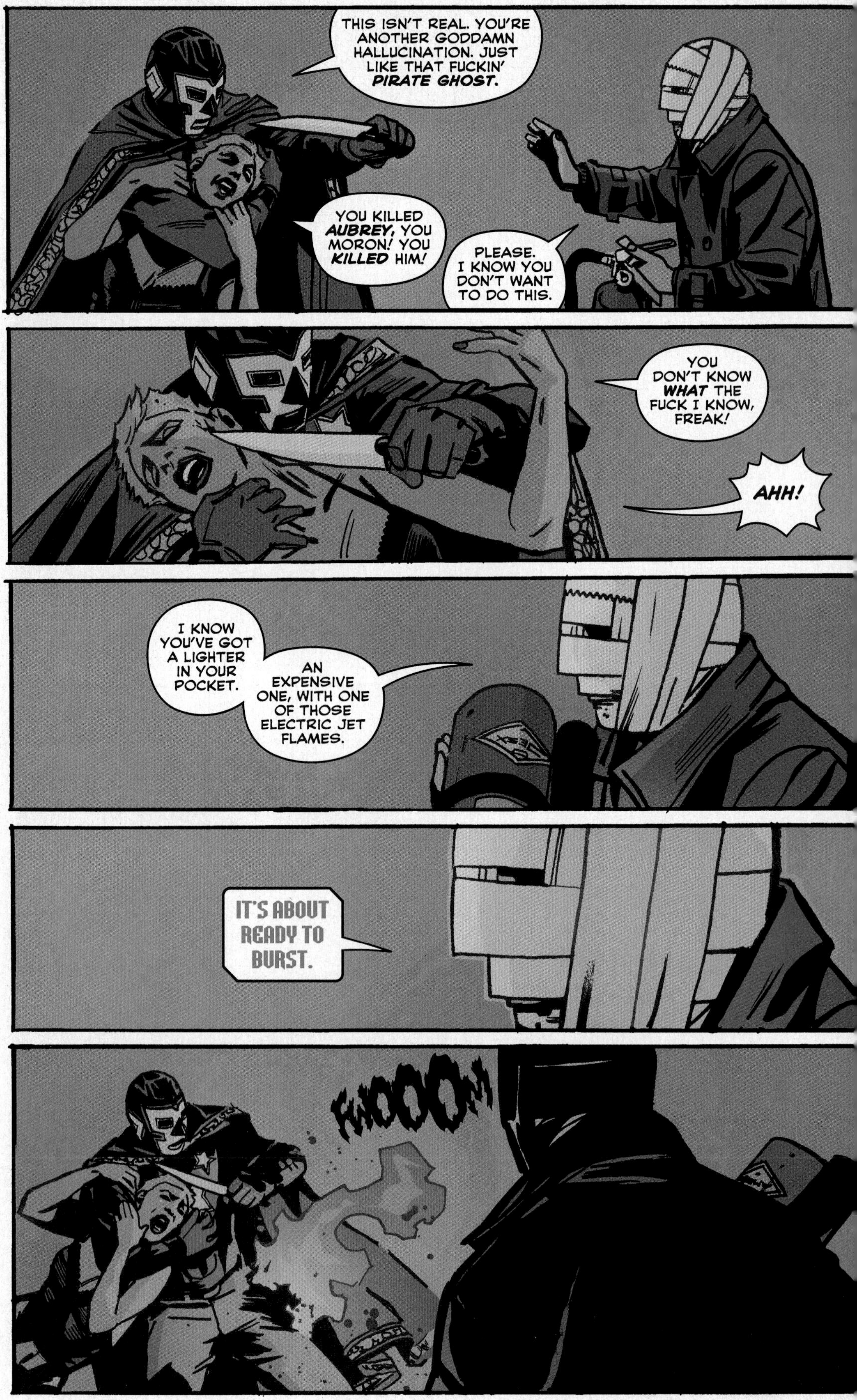
THIS ISN'T REAL. YOU'RE ANOTHER GODDAMN HALLUCINATION. JUST LIKE THAT FUCKIN' ***PIRATE GHOST***.
YOU KILLED ***AUBREY***, YOU MORON! YOU ***KILLED*** HIM!
PLEASE. I KNOW YOU DON'T WANT TO DO THIS.
YOU DON'T KNOW ***WHAT*** THE FUCK I KNOW, FREAK!
AHH!
I KNOW YOU'VE GOT A LIGHTER IN YOUR POCKET.
AN EXPENSIVE ONE, WITH ONE OF THOSE ELECTRIC JET FLAMES.
IT'S ABOUT READY TO BURST.
FWOOOM

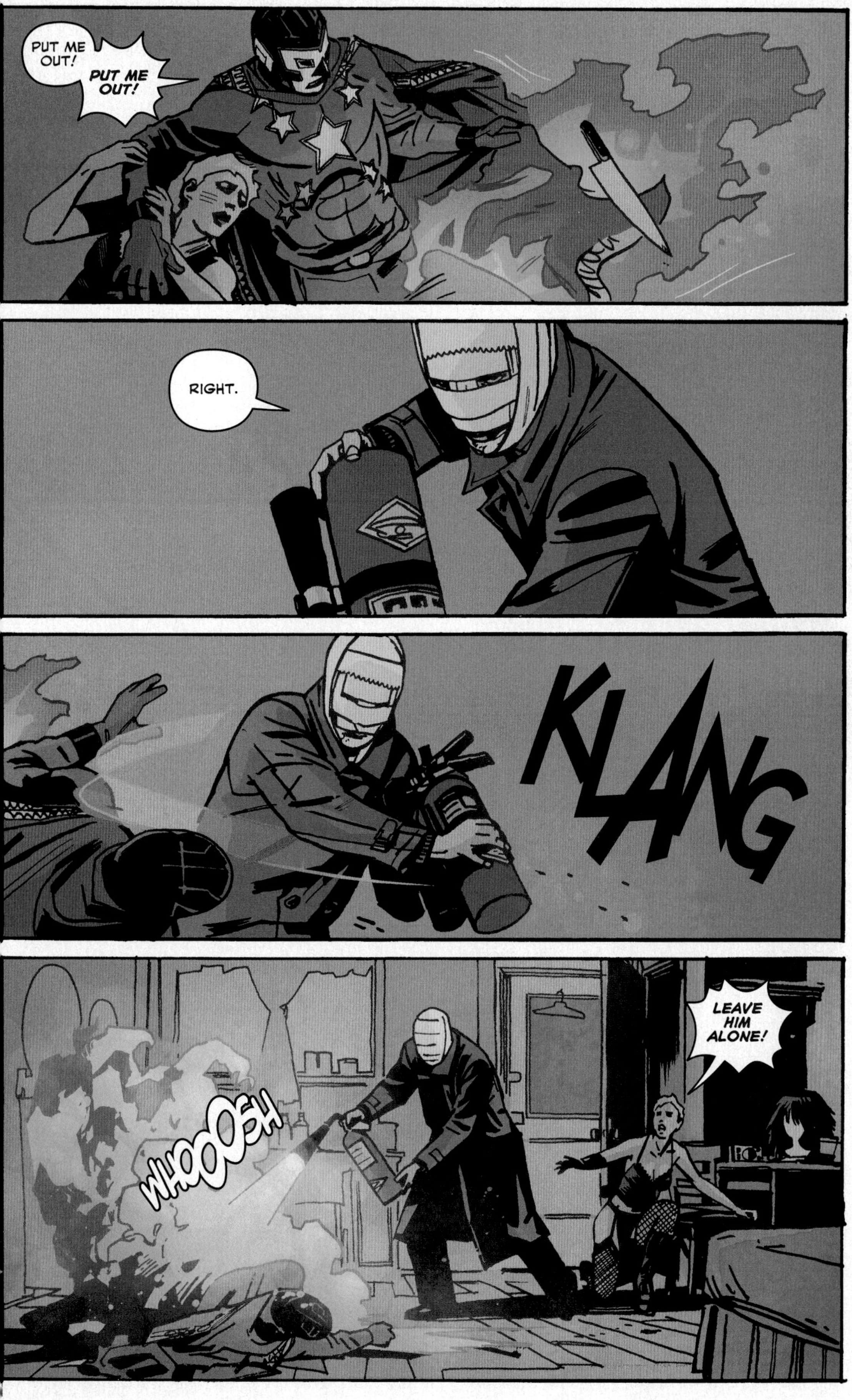
PUT ME OUT!
PUT ME OUT!
RIGHT.
KLANG
WHOOOSH
LEAVE HIM ALONE!

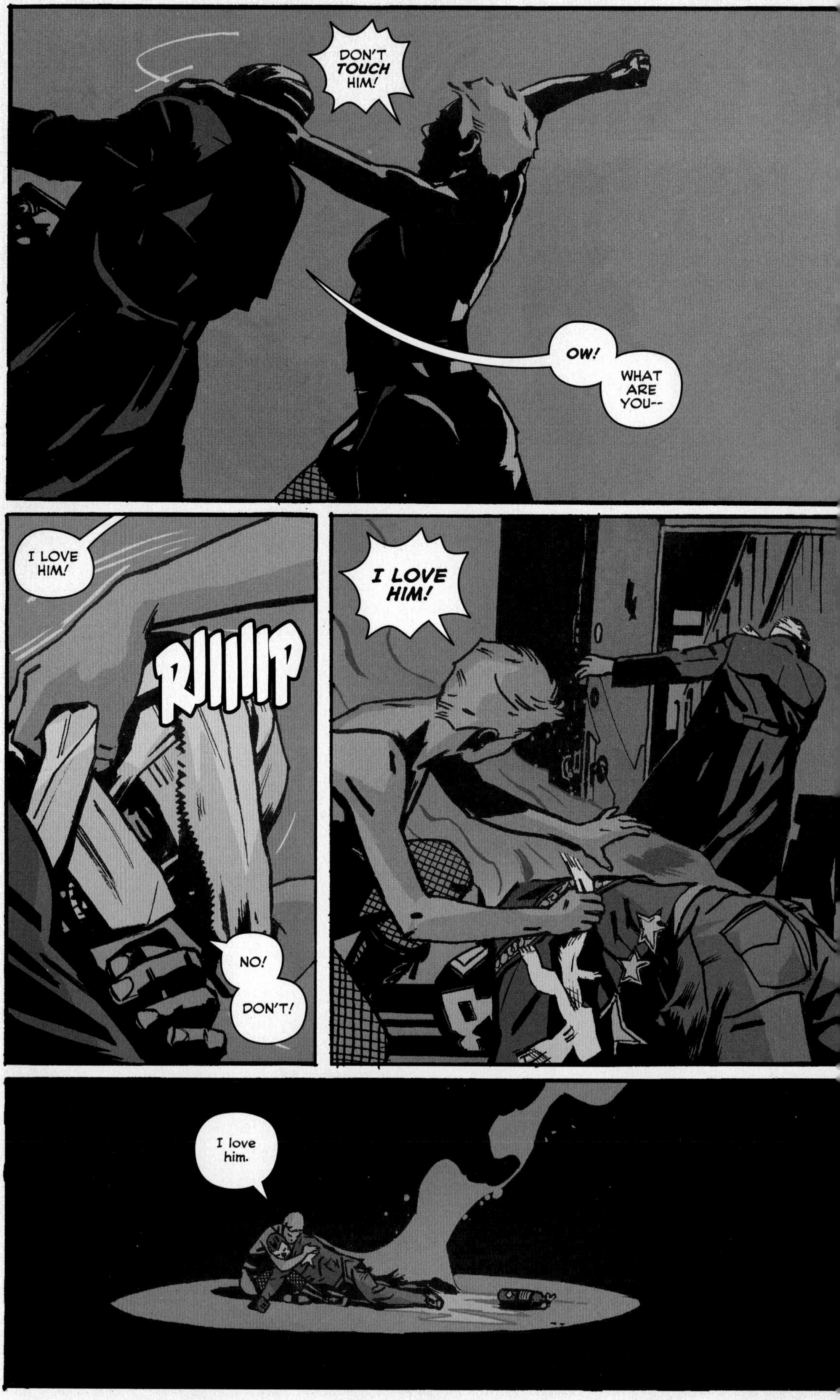
DON'T *TOUCH* HIM!
OW!
WHAT ARE YOU--
I LOVE HIM!
RIIIIP
NO!
DON'T!
I LOVE HIM!
I love him.

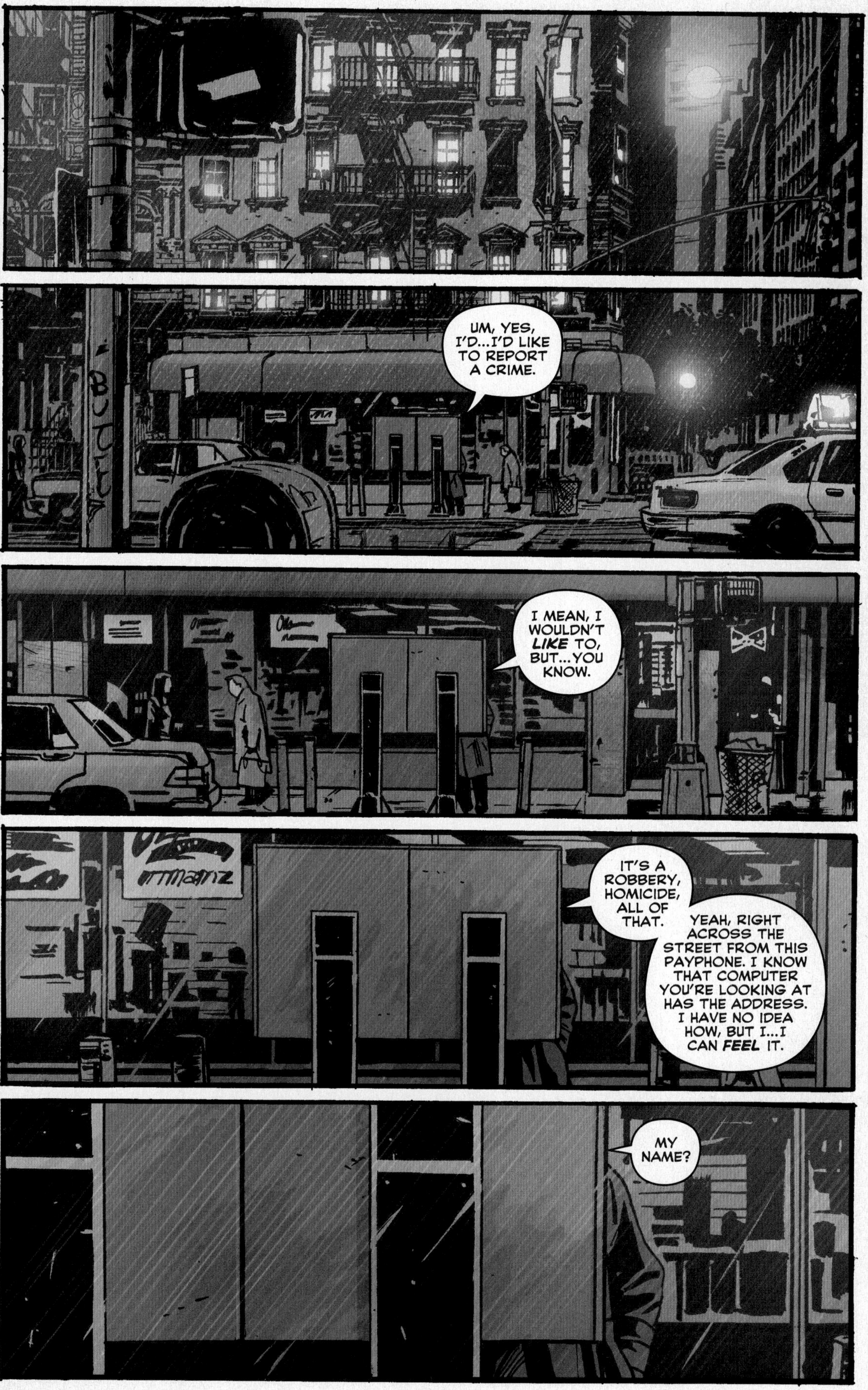
UM, YES, I'D...I'D LIKE TO REPORT A CRIME.
I MEAN, I WOULDN'T *LIKE* TO, BUT...YOU KNOW.
IT'S A ROBBERY, HOMICIDE, ALL OF THAT.
YEAH, RIGHT ACROSS THE STREET FROM THIS PAYPHONE. I KNOW THAT COMPUTER YOU'RE LOOKING AT HAS THE ADDRESS. I HAVE NO IDEA HOW, BUT I...I CAN *FEEL* IT.
MY NAME?

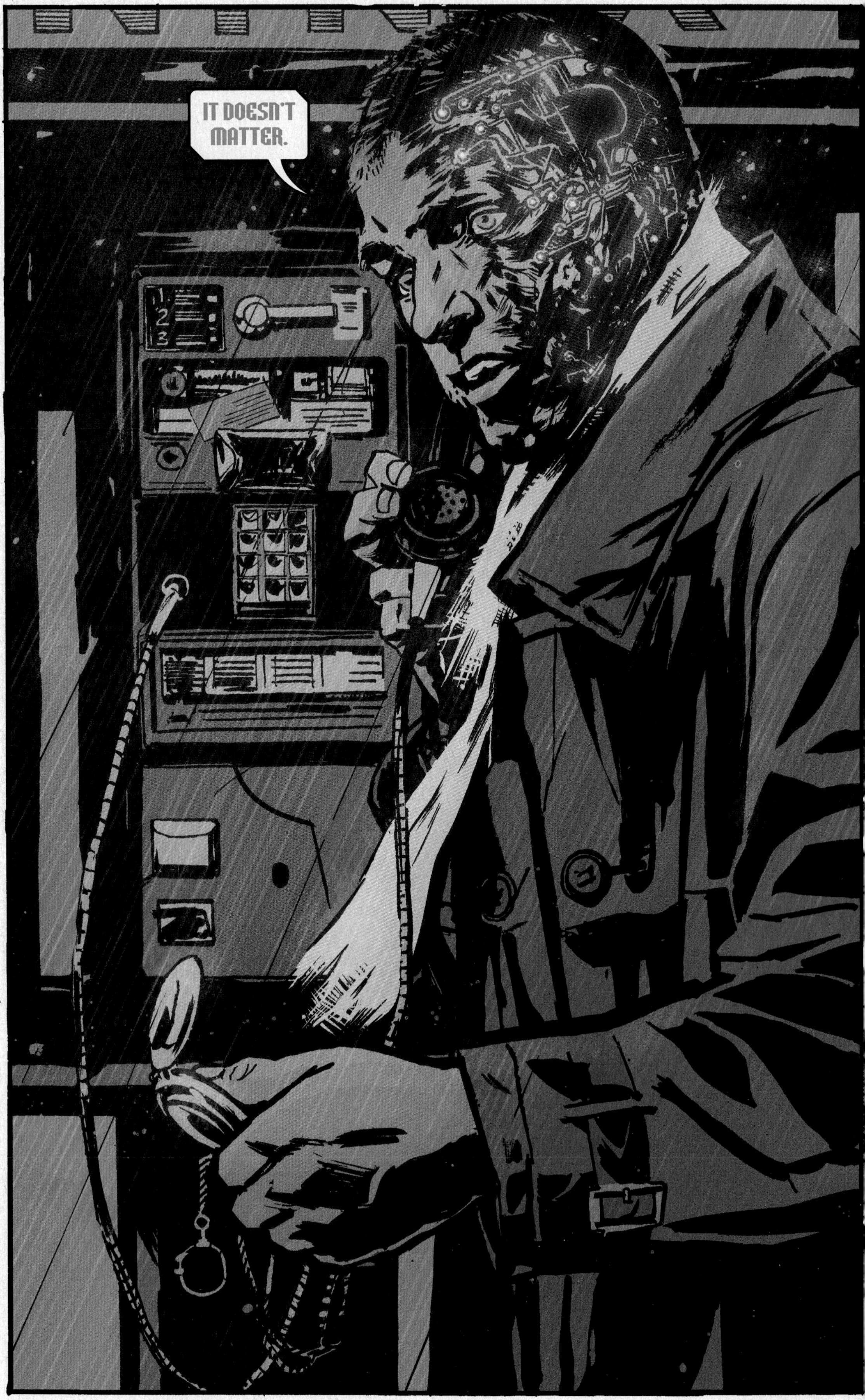
IT DOESN'T MATTER.

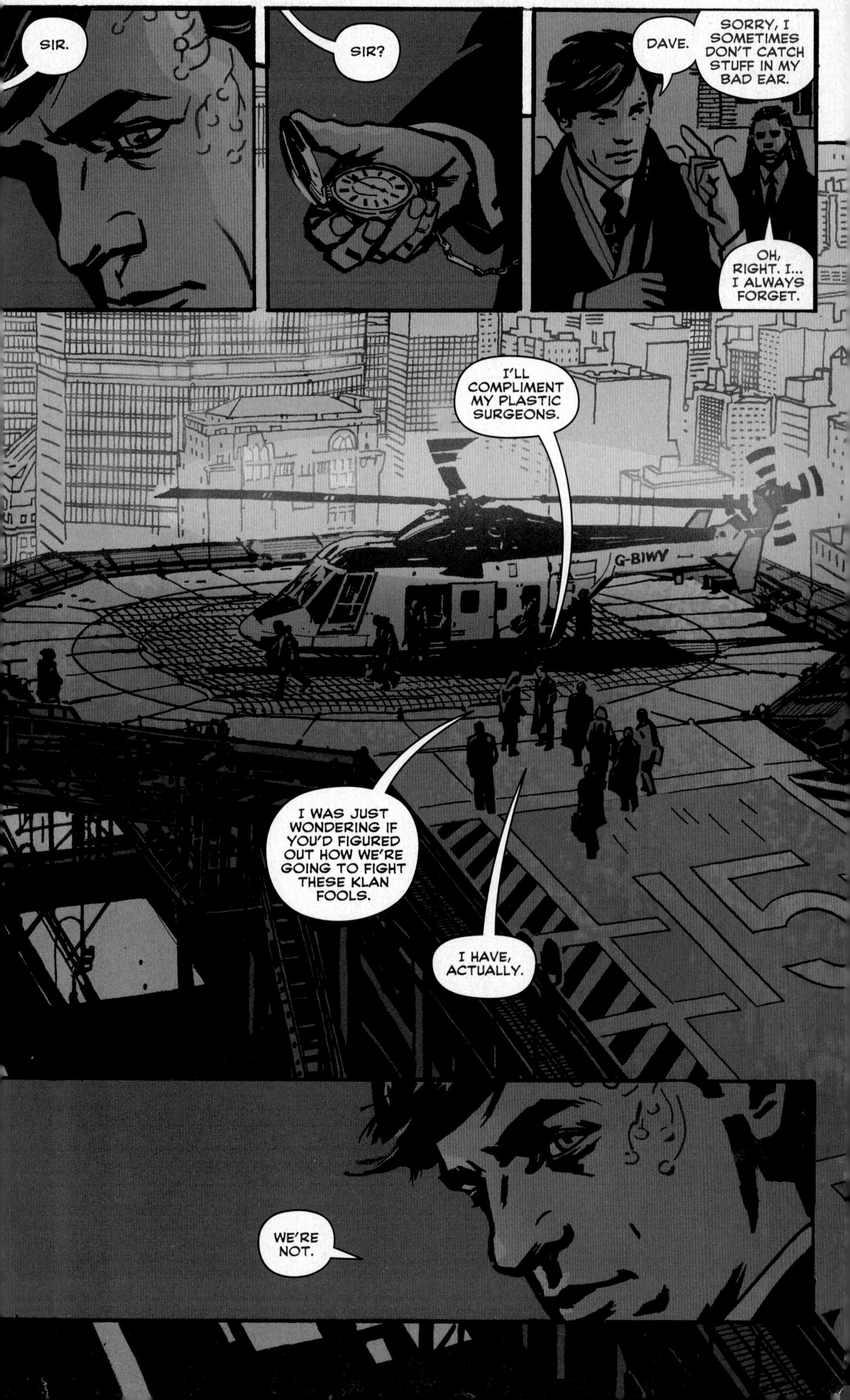
SIR.
SIR?
DAVE.
SORRY, I SOMETIMES DON'T CATCH STUFF IN MY BAD EAR.
OH, RIGHT. I... I ALWAYS FORGET.
I'LL COMPLIMENT MY PLASTIC SURGEONS.
G-BIWY
I WAS JUST WONDERING IF YOU'D FIGURED OUT HOW WE'RE GOING TO FIGHT THESE KLAN FOOLS.
I HAVE, ACTUALLY.
WE'RE NOT.

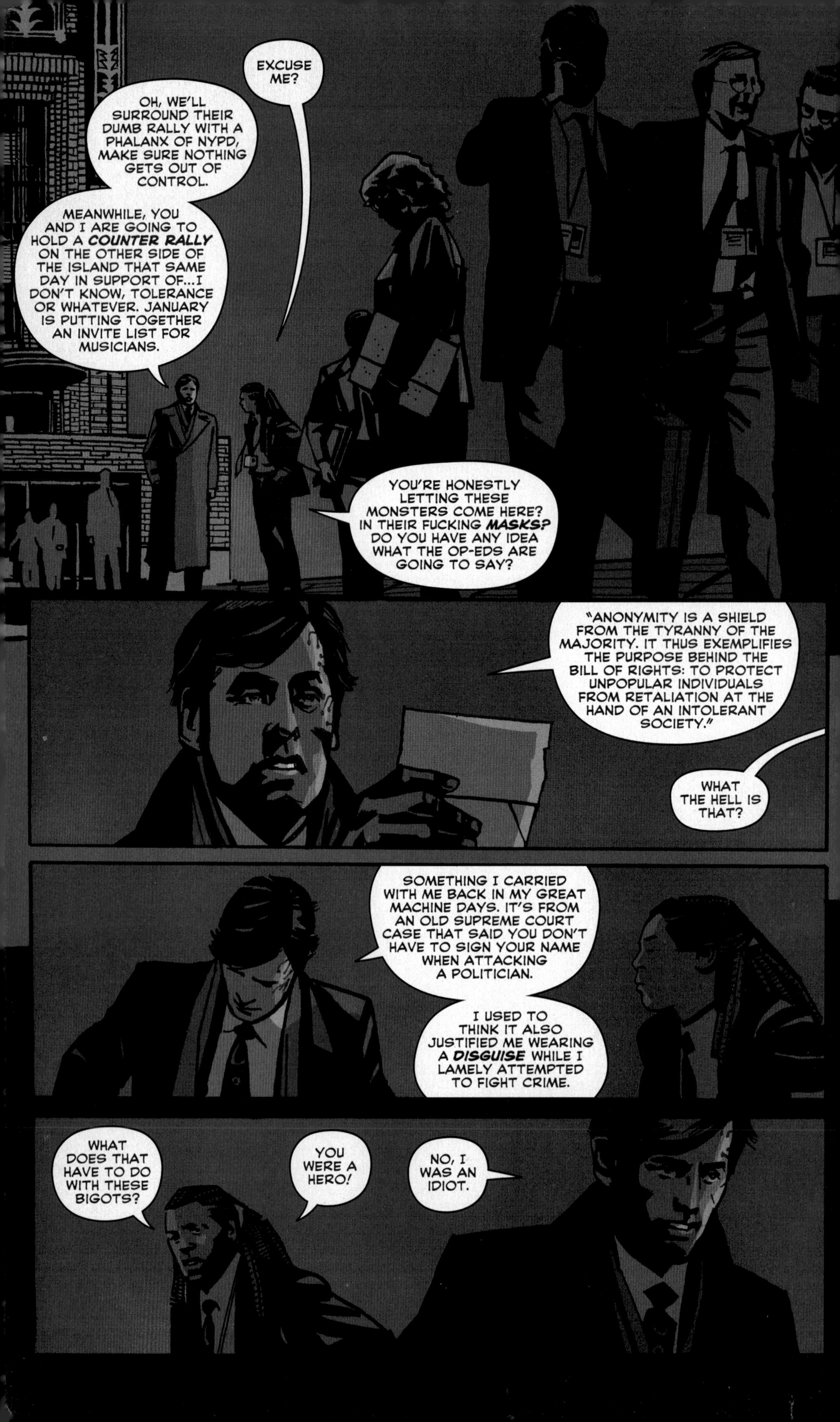
EXCUSE ME?
OH, WE'LL SURROUND THEIR DUMB RALLY WITH A PHALANX OF NYPD, MAKE SURE NOTHING GETS OUT OF CONTROL.
MEANWHILE, YOU AND I ARE GOING TO HOLD A COUNTER RALLY ON THE OTHER SIDE OF THE ISLAND THAT SAME DAY IN SUPPORT OF...I DON'T KNOW, TOLERANCE OR WHATEVER. JANUARY IS PUTTING TOGETHER AN INVITE LIST FOR MUSICIANS.
YOU'RE HONESTLY LETTING THESE MONSTERS COME HERE? IN THEIR FUCKING MASKS? DO YOU HAVE ANY IDEA WHAT THE OP-EDS ARE GOING TO SAY?
"ANONYMITY IS A SHIELD FROM THE TYRANNY OF THE MAJORITY. IT THUS EXEMPLIFIES THE PURPOSE BEHIND THE BILL OF RIGHTS: TO PROTECT UNPOPULAR INDIVIDUALS FROM RETALIATION AT THE HAND OF AN INTOLERANT SOCIETY."
WHAT THE HELL IS THAT?
SOMETHING I CARRIED WITH ME BACK IN MY GREAT MACHINE DAYS. IT'S FROM AN OLD SUPREME COURT CASE THAT SAID YOU DON'T HAVE TO SIGN YOUR NAME WHEN ATTACKING A POLITICIAN.
I USED TO THINK IT ALSO JUSTIFIED ME WEARING A DISGUISE WHILE I LAMELY ATTEMPTED TO FIGHT CRIME.
WHAT DOES THAT HAVE TO DO WITH THESE BIGOTS?
YOU WERE A HERO!
NO, I WAS AN IDIOT.

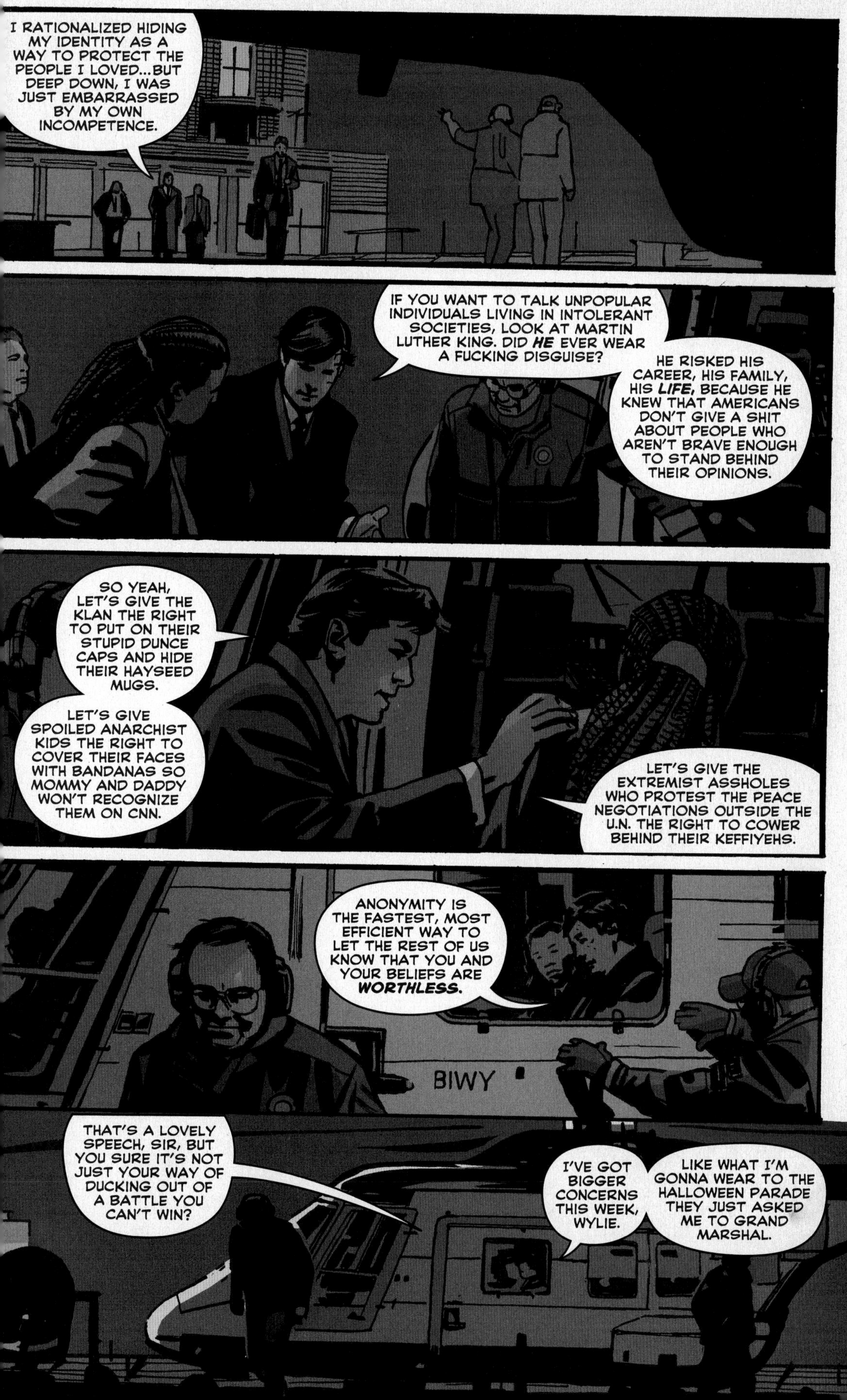
I RATIONALIZED HIDING MY IDENTITY AS A WAY TO PROTECT THE PEOPLE I LOVED...BUT DEEP DOWN, I WAS JUST EMBARRASSED BY MY OWN INCOMPETENCE.
IF YOU WANT TO TALK UNPOPULAR INDIVIDUALS LIVING IN INTOLERANT SOCIETIES, LOOK AT MARTIN LUTHER KING. DID *HE* EVER WEAR A FUCKING DISGUISE?
HE RISKED HIS CAREER, HIS FAMILY, HIS *LIFE,* BECAUSE HE KNEW THAT AMERICANS DON'T GIVE A SHIT ABOUT PEOPLE WHO AREN'T BRAVE ENOUGH TO STAND BEHIND THEIR OPINIONS.
SO YEAH, LET'S GIVE THE KLAN THE RIGHT TO PUT ON THEIR STUPID DUNCE CAPS AND HIDE THEIR HAYSEED MUGS.
LET'S GIVE SPOILED ANARCHIST KIDS THE RIGHT TO COVER THEIR FACES WITH BANDANAS SO MOMMY AND DADDY WON'T RECOGNIZE THEM ON CNN.
LET'S GIVE THE EXTREMIST ASSHOLES WHO PROTEST THE PEACE NEGOTIATIONS OUTSIDE THE U.N. THE RIGHT TO COWER BEHIND THEIR KEFFIYEHS.
ANONYMITY IS THE FASTEST, MOST EFFICIENT WAY TO LET THE REST OF US KNOW THAT YOU AND YOUR BELIEFS ARE ***WORTHLESS.***
BIWY
THAT'S A LOVELY SPEECH, SIR, BUT YOU SURE IT'S NOT JUST YOUR WAY OF DUCKING OUT OF A BATTLE YOU CAN'T WIN?
I'VE GOT BIGGER CONCERNS THIS WEEK, WYLIE.
LIKE WHAT I'M GONNA WEAR TO THE HALLOWEEN PARADE THEY JUST ASKED ME TO GRAND MARSHAL.

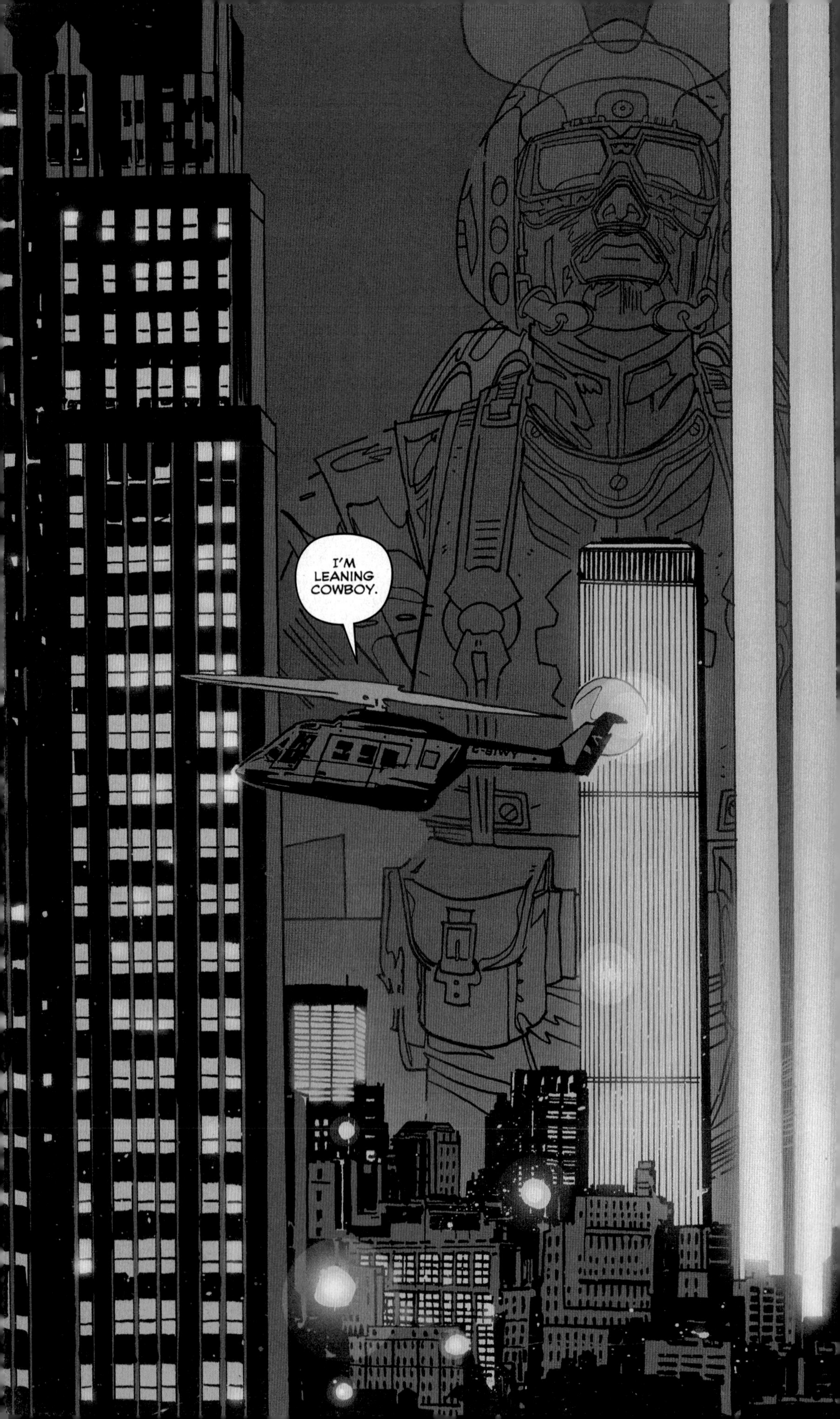
I'M LEANING COWBOY.

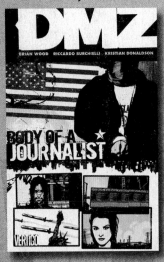

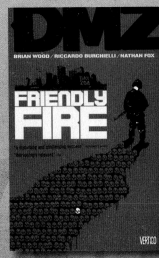